The Virtual University

The Virtual University

An action paradigm and process for workplace learning

Richard Teare, David Davies and Eric Sandelands

Cassell

Wellington House
125 Strand
London WC2R OBB

370 Lexington Avenue
New York
NY 10017-6550

First published in 1998

British Library Cataloguing-in-Publication Data
A catalogue record for this book is available from the British Library.

ISBN   0-304-70327-3 (hardback)
              0-304-70324-9 (paperback)

Typeset by MCB University Press, Bradford, West Yorkshire
Printed and bound in Great Britain by Redwood Books, Trowbridge, Wiltshire

The Virtual University

An action paradigm and process for workplace learning

Workplace
Learning
Series

By
Richard Teare , David Davies and Eric Sandelands

CONTENTS

CONTENTS
continued

About the authors...

David Davies is Deputy Principal of Westhill University College, Birmingham and Director: Prior Learning, Our University for Industry – hospitality worldwide. David has spent much of his career working in continuing education and among other roles, he has been a teacher-trainer at Reading University, a staff tutor at the Open University, Deputy Director of the Welsh Joint Education Committee and Director of Public Programmes at Cambridge University. Whilst at Cambridge, he was jointly responsible for a major national project on the accreditation of adult learning and several work-based learning initiatives. More recently he has developed corporate programmes with Fina Petroleum and BAA Plc and "credit mapping" with the UK operation of the German firm Boehringer Ingelheim.

Eric Sandelands is a specialist in Internet-resourced learning and Director: Publishing, Our University for Industry – hospitality worldwide. He is a Director of Internet Research & Development Centre, Head of Courseware at International Management Centres, and Development Vice-President at the Canadian School of Management. He is Chairman of specialist publisher VUP International which publishes the *Virtual University Journal, Continuing Professional Development* and the *WHATT Journal,* among others. Previously he was Director: Transformational Publishing Unit at MCB University Press, before becoming Chief Executive Officer of its database publishing division, ANBAR Electronic Intelligence.

Richard Teare is Granada Professor at Oxford Brookes University & Director, Our University for Industry – hospitality worldwide. He is also Revans Professor and Academic Chair, International Management Centres and Chairman of the National Society for Quality through Teamwork, UK. He has held professorial roles at three UK universities and worked for national and international hotel companies. Richard is the founding Editor of the *International Journal of Contemporary Hospitality Management* and since 1994, he has directed the HCIMA's *Worldwide Hospitality and Tourism Trends* project with research centres in the UK, Portugal, North America and Australia. He is a consultant editor for Cassell Plc., and his publications include 18 books and more than 80 articles and book chapters.

The Virtual University

4

Section 1: Beyond the boundary: from closed to open systems of knowledge

David Davies

Keywords Ability, Competences, Competitive advantage, Learning, Organizational change, Workplace learning

This account aims to introduce contrasting perspectives on teaching and learning methods, and to detail the growth of new forms and vocabularies of access to learning. As we move towards the new millennium, the development of national, yet diversified, credit frameworks and systems will provide an essential underpinning for the organizational culture that will be needed to sustain the wellbeing and growth of the educational system. These new systems are already being incorporated into the practice of "virtual" education. Lifelong learning has widespread support across the social and political spectrum and its importance can hardly be over-stated as we seek to maintain competitiveness in a changing world. Increasing knowledge and understanding to serve both the needs of the economy and of individuals to play a major role in democratic life has become an agenda of necessity as well as desire. An open society requires open systems of knowledge. A prognosis for the future is submitted where the significance of part-time modular and open flexible learning is evaluated in terms of a curriculum rooted in useful knowledge and competences, acquired at different sites of learning, including the workplace. It is argued that modular structures, using the potential offered by credit accumulation and transfer to different institutions with different missions, can transcend and transform the learning opportunities for students in a mass system of higher education which is rapidly becoming part of a global market economy and society. Continuous lifelong learning involving its key features of open access, recognition of learning wherever it takes place and the growth of new learning networks and partnerships, is at the conceptual heart of the development of the virtual university.

Section 2: A prospectus for organizational learning in the workplace

Supporting managerial learning in the workplace

Richard Teare

Keywords Action learning, Coaching, Competences, Learning, Management studies, Mentoring

Suggests that more and more organizations are attempting to establish a culture of learning that values the knowledge that employees have derived from learning how to perform effectively in the workplace. Reviews recent contributions to the literature on aspects of managerial learning and addresses the question "How do managers learn best in the workplace?" Draws from articles published between 1994-1996 in eight journals: *Executive Development; Journal of Management Development; Journal of Organizational Change Management; Leadership & Organization Development Journal; Management Development Review; Team Performance Management; The Journal of Workplace Learning; The Learning Organization.* Focuses on four themes: managerial learning and work; coaching, mentoring and team development; competences, managerial learning and the curriculum; work-based action learning. Concludes with a summary of the implications for managerial learning.

Enabling organizational learning

Richard Teare

Keywords Leadership, Organizational change, Organizational learning

It is clear from studies of organizations and a considerable body of anecdotal evidence that organizational life is strongly influenced by organizational leaders. In particular, the vision, style of leadership and motivation that enables them to "make things happen" and inspire others to follow their direction. Reviews recent contributions to the literature on aspects of organizational learning and considers how organizational processes might encompass effective learning support for individuals and groups of learners. Draws from articles published between 1994-1996 in seven journals: *Executive Development;*

Journal of Organizational Change Management; Journal of Management Development; Leadership & Organization Development Journal; Management Development Review; The Journal of Workplace Learning; The Learning Organization. Concentrates on three areas: organizational vision; leadership and motivation; organizational change and performance. Concludes with a summary of the implications for organizational learning.

Building and sustaining a learning organization

Richard Teare and Richard Dealtry

Keywords Action learning, Airports, Learning organizations, Management learning, Organizational learning

Considers how to create a learning environment and the implications for learning organizations. Draws on an Internet conference with managers from airport owner and operator BAA plc to debate four themes: modelling the learning process in organizations; organizational readiness; teamworking and learning and networked learning. Relates these to an agenda for organizational learning and renewal.

Relating strategy, structure and performance

Richard Teare, Jorge Costa and Gavin Eccles

Keywords Hospitality industry, Management learning, Organizational development, Performance, Strategic management, Tourism

Considers the inter-linking business relationships between aspects of strategy formulation, implementation and performance as they relate to the hospitality industry. The "relating strategy" theme is developed and elaborated by reviewing approaches to strategy and external analysis, structure and performance. Includes case examples from Forte Hotels, Granada Group plc., Hilton International, Holiday Inn Worldwide and Hyatt International Corporation.

Assessing information needs and external change

Richard Teare and John T. Bowen

Keywords Environmental scanning, Hospitality industry, Industry, Organizational learning, Organizational politics

The managerial activity of learning about events and trends in the organization's environment is known as environmental scanning. This process differs from industry or competitor analysis in two main respects: it is broad in scope and future-directed. Assesses the extent to which information needs are currently met by scanning activities and profiles the "top 30" hospitality industry issues as reflected by UK-based and North American hospitality management journals. Concludes with a priority ranking of the "top 30" issues assigned by UK hotel general managers and summary comments from this group on the implications for organizational learning.

Interpreting and responding to customer needs

Richard Teare

Keywords Consumer behaviour, Consumer marketing, Customer service, Hospitality industry, Service delivery systems, Service quality

Relates aspects of consumer behaviour and in particular the decision process to the procedures and processes for delivery and assuring customer service. The main themes are: understanding customers; designing and delivering services and assuring total quality services.

Developing a curriculum for organizational learning

Richard Teare

Keywords Action learning, Curriculum, Learning organizations, Management learning, Organizational learning, Workplace learning

Addresses the agenda for learning, development and research by presenting an organizational framework for action learning, supported by internet-based resources and tutored sessions in the workplace. Outlines a themed approach, developed in response to corporate needs and aspirations, which is derived from a generic curriculum and augmented to address industry issues and corporate specialisms.

Implementing virtual support for workplace learning

Richard Teare

Keywords Action learning, Electronic publishing, Internet, Learning organizations, Management learning, Workplace learning

Reviews the prospects and potential for meeting industry-specific learning and development needs with particular reference to a "University for Industry" initiative for hospitality and tourism. Its design and implementation draws on a global industry forum and its infrastructure provides: an access point for workplace learning programmes; a resource for addressing project and personal updating needs; a reference point for training and internal corporate communications and a means of interacting with "communities of interest" (such as industry-education linkages).

Section 3: Where the architects meet the building contractors...

Re-engineering knowledge statistics

Gordon Wills and Mathew Wills

Keywords BPR, Knowledge workers, Logistics

Describes the key elements of total logistics systems and their cycle times for requisite service levels at least cost. Shows how these constructs originally emerged from military necessity but have more recently been driven for commercial and manufacturing advantage. Analyses the traditional logistics cycle in academic and professional publishing and then demonstrates how the application of a total logistics system approach with the emerging capabilities of electronics totally transforms the performance of the system, reducing cycle time by 75 per cent. Significantly re-engineers the five key elements of logistics systems – facilities, unitization, communications, inventory and transportation – and rewrites the cost/benefit equation of service levels. Explores the opportunities for backward and forward integration by traditional librarians and

publishers respectively in the re-engineered total system.

Creating virtual support for lifelong learning

Eric Sandelands and Mathew Wills

Keywords Electronic publishing, Learning, Technology

Individuals worldwide are seeking to remain relevant and effective through learning which, if not actually continuous, is an integral part of their working life. Organizations are increasingly recognizing the need to compete on the basis of collective learning and the ability to apply this learning in practice. Technology is increasingly an enabler in this ongoing learning process. Pioneering institutions are developing architectures that support individual and organizational learning. World-class development programmes are being delivered using the "virtual university" model. So too is support for lifelong learning. Issues being addressed include: creating, maintaining and distributing courseware; ensuring access to current and archival literature; programme supervision and the development of a community of learning. Further benefits for scholars of electronic publishing are being realized, but much potential remains untapped.

A learning organization's syllabus

John Peters

Keywords Action learning, Learning organizations, Management development

Aims to address the question "What does a learning organization learn about?" Proposes a syllabus approach which covers six key areas; learning about one's job in the organization; learning about alignment of culture, values and strategy; learning about the likely future; learning about the organization's supply chains; learning how to challenge existing norms and ways of thinking; and developing an organizational memory. Discusses action learning as a developmental methodology which can address most of these syllabus areas. Concludes each section with prescriptive recommendations for practitioners.

Creating an online library to support a virtual learning community

Eric Sandelands

Keywords Action learning, Management development, Virtual reality

Describes how an independent business school, International Management Centres (IMC), has created a virtual library in partnership with database publisher Anbar Electronic Intelligence. Outlines the action learning methodology used by IMC in delivering management development programmes, and the virtual business school model being developed and used. Examines the relationship between the partner organizations, highlighting the benefits each gains from the collaboration. Analyses the benefits being experienced by IMC faculty and students from the virtual library investment to-date, anticipated benefits, and future investment in online information resources.

ISO 9000 as a global educational accreditation structure

John Peters and Gordon Wills

Keywords Education, ISO 9000, Quality assurance, Universities

Argues a market-orientation for the ISO 9000 quality assurance standards. Discusses the experiences of the International Management Centres (IMC) in seeking and gaining certification to ISO 9002. Argues that policing educational process delivery – the keeping of promises – would be a more useful activity for governmental policy-makers than the policing of educational content – the nature of the promise. Summarises in brief the clauses of ISO 9002 as they apply to IMC. Concludes with recommendations to educational institution administrators and policy-makers.

Introduction

The Virtual University – tomorrow's learning organization?
A virtual university must be a real university offering learning opportunities otherwise denied. It must be, above all, a network for life long learning which meets the new learning needs of a new century. Most industrialized modern societies are now embarked on providing mass higher education and increasingly this is provided through a market system. Education has become a positional "good" or commodity which people seek to invest in for personal gain. It is also a social "good" and a means of ensuring equality of opportunity and routes to a better life. One of the ways higher education will seek to be effective on a global basis will be through the efficient use of new communications technology. This technology will be part of the virtual university, which in turn will contribute, it can be argued, to greater economic and social opportunity.

The opening section of this book raises issues and questions about the meaning of the virtual university and about the educational challenges which face teachers and learners. It is concerned with the educational practices which will be needed to make the virtual university work, in addition to the technical means of communication which appear to drive developments in this field. Sections two and three deal with the application of the technological basis of the new learning at the heart of the virtual university and the emergence of a dynamic curriculum, capable of meeting and defining the learning needs of a new century and new generations of learners. Significant developments in serving these needs are described and evaluated and "live" examples are put to the test where learning is examined in the context of new connections and a dynamic curriculum which goes beyond the existing body of knowledge. The virtual university, it is certain, will be a university for industry (and a means of formalizing the learning organization concept) as the workplace continues to develop as a key site of learning for the twenty-first century.

The competitive environment
Universities today compete within and beyond national boundaries for students, for funding, for research and for recognition within the wider society. Financial support from industry has become ever more central to the diverse world of higher education and as industry and commerce has become more and more global in its operations, so have universities. Higher Education has become internationalized as students travel to learn and as providers "export" themselves through distance methods of delivery and new communication techniques such as the Internet, satellite broadcasting, video-conferencing and a whole gamut of "cyberspace" innovations and "virtual" technology. The ever expanding field of telematics is constantly seeking new combinations and variants of these technologies.

The technological changes are paralleled, however, by changes in demand from learners. Students no longer are satisfied with first phase education. Their needs are now increasingly seen to be continuous, throughout a working life and embracing personal growth at all stages of an individual's life. Education is seen by vast numbers of people as a means of empowering their lives and futures. Within the workplace, at least in the advanced market-led societies, knowledge workers are at a premium. The economic futures of those without knowledge skills, qualifications and access to the new learning opportunities is bleak. The future will belong to those who can acquire and apply knowledge and skills which the global markets for labour demand. Knowledge workers or what has been called "symbolic analysts" will require regular updating of their knowledge, skills and competences.

A variety of methods and technologies will be required to satisfy this demand-led market. Curriculum design and planning will play a more significant part in supporting student and employer choice. Modular schemes and credit systems will be extended and deepened to provide genuine choice at the various ages and stages of a lifetime of learning. A more *open system* of teaching which allows students' experience and new knowledge acquired in a variety of learning communities, including vitally that of the workplace, will be needed. The virtual university will be required to expand flexibility and innovative learning and teaching. Teaching and learning methods will need to be re-fashioned *in the mainstream* through the use of a myriad techniques, including distance tuition, modularity, credit accumulation and transfer (CATS), work-based learning, expanded qualification frameworks, and through the recognition and accreditation of prior experiential learning (APEL). The adoption of what have been the marginal concerns of educators will be central to the virtual university.

Structure of the book
Section 1 of this volume: *Beyond the boundary: from closed to open systems of knowledge* introduces information, analysis and debate on these issues. At the heart of this enterprise is the concern to match the needs of students to a new set of possibilities for learning and personal achievement. We believe that this claim is compatible with the needs of industry and with the view that life, not merely income tests the effectiveness of education.

The explication contained in the opening four chapters attempts to capture developments beyond a mere descriptive account of change and innovation. Whilst introducing contrasting and competing accounts of teaching and learning methods and detailing the growth of new forms and vocabularies of access to learning, it is contended that, as we move towards the new millennium, the development of national, yet diversified, credit frameworks and systems will provide an essential underpinning for the organizational culture that will be needed to sustain the wellbeing and growth of the educational system. These new systems are already being incorporated into the practice of "virtual" education and are part of the reality of the virtual university.

Chapter 1 considers the concept and realities of Lifelong learning – a notion that has widespread support across the social and political spectrum and its importance can hardly be over-stated as we seek to maintain competitiveness in a changing world. Increasing knowledge and understanding to serve both the needs of the economy and of individuals to play a major role in democratic life has become an agenda of necessity as well as desire. An open society requires open systems of knowledge.

In chapters 2 and 3, a prognosis for the future is submitted where the significance of part-time modular and open flexible learning is evaluated in terms of a curriculum rooted in "really useful knowledge" and competences, acquired at different sites of learning, including the workplace. It is argued that modular structures, using the potential offered by credit accumulation and transfer to different institutions with different missions, can transcend and transform the learning opportunities for students in a mass system of higher education which is rapidly becoming part of a global market economy and society. Chapter 4 contends that continuous lifelong learning involving its key features of open access, recognition of learning wherever it takes place and the growth of new learning networks and partnerships, is at the conceptual heart of the development of the virtual university.

Section 2 of the book: *A prospectus for organizational learning in the workplace* draws on prior published work and an explication of recent literature to examine aspects of managerial learning and organizational learning. It also considers the challenges for those seeking to design and implement "learning organization" structures and the particular implications for the world"s fastest growing service industry – hospitality and tourism.

The first part of Section 2 examines individual and team learning in organizations and seeks to identify the key questions for managers who are seeking to derive competitive advantage through opportunities for learning and organizational development. Chapter 5 focuses on four themes: managerial learning and work; coaching, mentoring and team development; competences, managerial learning and the curriculum and work-based action learning. Chaper 6 concentrates on three areas; organizational vision; leadership and motivation; organizational change and performance. These concepts are "tested" in Chapter 7 that draws on an Internet conference with managers from airport owner and operator BAA plc. The aim was to identify ways of creating a supportive learning environment and to relate this to an agenda for organizational learning and renewal.

The second part of Section 2 contained in five chapters, aims to "ground" organizational learning by relating it to a rapidly growing service industry. It seeks answers to two key questions: What are the issues and priorities for organizational learning in hospitality and tourism? (chapters 8, 9, 10) and how might "virtual learning" provide industry specific support? (chapters 11 and 12). Chapter 8 considers the inter-linking business relationships between aspects of strategy formulation, implementation and performance and chapter 9 examines the managerial activity of learning about events and trends in the organization's environment by profiling the "top 30" hospitality industry issues as reflected by UK-based and North American hospitality management journals. If managers have discerned the main business issues, then how should they interpret and respond to their customers? Chapter 10 attempts to close the loop on managerial learning by relating industry issues and imperatives to customers and customer-led processes for delivering and assuring customer service. The final two chapters in this section examine how the agenda for learning and development might be addressed in the workplace with reference to a dynamic industry curriculum and a university for industry initiative.

Section 3: entitled *Where the architects meet the building contractors* seeks to draw together the thinking and intellectual energy of those who are designing virtual university models and the contributions of those who are implementing them - the building contractors in our action paradigm.

Chapter 13 adopts a total systems approach to knowledge creation and dissemination in scholarly publishing. It seeks to map out the system as it has evolved over a number of years, then set out a vision of the logistics process in the electronic publishing era. The transformation of the process is stunning, and the threat to existing players unable to adapt, is there for all to see. This revolution provides the infrastructure on which the virtual university can thrive. The vision moves towards the practical architecture for a virtual university business school in chapter 14. Having created a "wish list" of what a 21st century learning institution should offer, it is quite startling to realize just how many of these wishes can be put into action today.

Having created the information and communications infrastructure, what should be the syllabus if we are to support learning organization environments? Chapter 15 identifies six key syllabus areas: learning about your job in the organization, and how to do it better; learning how to create alignment in the organization; learning about the future; learning about the operating environment; learning how to challenge the existing paradigms and developing the organizational memory. Chapter 16 takes us back on the technology trail – but not technology for technology's sake. The key message to emerge is one of partnering and joint-ventures to create world-class libraries in the electronic age. Finally, chapter 17 argues that virtual universities should not be constrained by national boundaries. We don't need to look beyond today to discover that they are not! However, this presents enormous challenges for those who seek to ensure high standards in education. Existing control models simply become obsolete. Such globalization is recognized in most areas of commerce, with basic rules being set by the World Trade Organization. But what of education? According to Peters and Wills, ISO 9000 is ideally placed to provide a global quality assurance and accreditation structure for education providers. It is also argued that it is a much more customer-focused approach than our existing provider dominated mechanisms.

Developing models, implementing change, reflecting, and modifying actions lies at the very heart of action learning-based methodology. It has also been our route map for this journey towards creating a virtual university model capable of supporting our workplace learning objectives. It has been a map that was sketched in initially, detail added while the journey was in progress, then re-drawn once the destination appeared to be in sight. That has been part of the challenge, and a lot of the fun! We hope that this is communicated within these pages.

How will workplace learning evolve in the information age?
The development of the "corporate university" is currently under way with examples from the USA and Great Britain of large companies seeking accreditation for in-company learning. British Aerospace, Motorola, Unipart and BAA plc are examples of very serious attempts to develop industry-located knowledge. Almost all campus-based universities and Colleges of Higher Education in the UK have extensive collaborative links with industry. Education plays a key role in attracting massive inward industrial investment throughout the UK. It is clear therefore that HE institutions are looking for new and innovative ways of devising and delivering provision whilst meeting the challenge of declining public resources. Collaborative work, joint provision, networking of resources and the discovery and application of learner support systems, such as that offered by credit systems and open systems of learning, are all essential ingredients of a new learning relationship between higher education and industry.

The virtual university represents the most advanced form so far of this emergent network of learning. The three sections of this book illustrate the three distinct, yet related developments:

- The importance of continuous, lifelong learning and its key features of open paradigms, learning performance, accreditation and progression for students.

- The significance of an industry-wide model of action learning, supported by an internet learning environment.

- The rapid development of new communications technologies and radical on-line learning resources available through interactive courseware and publishing.

The rapid development of new communications technologies is revolutionizing the delivery of learning experiences. As lifelong learning is increasingly becoming recognized as the route to personal effectiveness and, within learning organization mechanisms, to organizational effectiveness, emerging virtual university models look set to be key to their delivery. Access to global domains of knowledge is now a reality and the Internet brings the generators, brokers and users of knowledge closer together than ever before. The Internet provides the means of interacting with "communities of interest" wherever they exist via "virtual conferencing" and of accessing, searching and using learning resources linked to sophisticated databases of articles, current awareness and archive material. This capability offers the means of enabling a new wave of on-line business learning and providing "real time" links between the knowledge stakeholders – authors, editors, publishers, readers, learners, tutors, industry sponsors and educationalists. These initiatives accord with the Government's much talked of proposals for a "University for Industry" – promoting lifelong and career-long learning as the best means of personal development in the information age and for assuring the competitiveness of UK Plc in the global marketplace.

We should like to thank the respective managing editor and production teams at MCB University Press who assisted us in compiling this volume and in particular Chris Ball and her colleagues. Our thanks to Cassell and especially Ruth McCurry and David Barker for encouraging us to draw together the various strands of our work over the past few years. We should also like to acknowledge the people who have co-authored contributions to this book. They are: John T. Bowen, Jorge Costa, Richard Dealtry, Gavin Eccles, John Peters, Gordon and Mathew Wills. Finally, we should like to thank our family support team. They are: Anna, Benjamin, Chloe, Claire, Emer, Luke, Matthew and Rachel.

Richard Teare, David Davies, Eric Sandelands

SECTION 1

Beyond the boundary: from closed to open systems of knowledge

David Davies

Chapter 1

Towards a learning society

David Davies

Deputy Principal, Westhill University College, Birmingham, UK

Is there a shared vision for learning and continuous education as we move into a new century? In seeking an answer, we are forced to engage with some crucial social issues which affect our individual lives and experiences but whose causes often lie in the wider social and economic movements of the day. It is clear that we are moving towards a "learning society". This term can denote a range of issues and concerns, including the following which are the context of the development described in this volume:

- mass higher education (HE) in developed societies is already with us and universal HE in twenty-first century will be the norm;

- knowledge workers have emerged as crucial players in economic performance and wellbeing;

- the "graduate job" is disappearing, and nearly all worthwhile jobs will soon demand high level skills and qualifications;

- lifelong learning is about investment in personal learning and growth, and this is compatible with corporate investment and growth;

- older divisions such as the academic versus the vocational are dissolving as are distinctions between further and higher education institutions;

- local and global divisions are dissolving in many instances – a common culture of knowledge with shared aspirations is emerging;

- part-time and work-related learning opportunities are moving from the periphery to the centre of concern for many individuals and their employers, and for the providers of education.

We might call these factors the providential side of the equation for a learning society, but there are also threats to the vision of continuous improvement and growth of opportunity. We are moving towards a more fragmented society, where a series of major threats to stability and prosperity can be identified, including:

- de-industrialisation – which has had a massive and uneven impact globally;

- economic crises and permanent unemployment – which is apparently a semi-permanent reality requiring continuous management;

This article first appeared in the *Journal of Workplace Learning,* Vol. 10 No. 4, 1997, pp. 175-182.

- inner-city dereliction and the decay of some traditional urban centres;
- law and order breakdown or its containment at great social cost;
- race and ethnicity as a source of division, tension and in some cases, armed conflict.

We might envisage a breakdown of traditional continuity; what Giddens (1990) calls a "disembedding" of personal life from social life and roles and the emergence of a world of "multiple authorities" where traditional commonalties and structures break down. Whichever perspective we adopt, it is increasingly clear that learning is becoming ever more central to the growth and health of modern economies and social systems. Continuous or lifelong learning, it will be argued, joins the personal needs experienced by each one of us with the imperatives of the labour market and makes nonsense of the old divisions which separated life, learning and work in to compartmentalised spheres and phrases of existence. Conditions of change are demanding a more holistic response from learners, from teachers and from providers of the whole range of educational services and opportunities in those societies which have adopted mass further and higher education.

Key issues
A central question to be addressed is – what kind of knowledge and learning are emerging from innovatory sites at which education is delivered? The focus of the answer is how across time and geographical space, personal learning, previously strongly connected with personal development, is now beginning to articulate with wider, professional learning, especially that related to the workplace.

A fundamental theme within this focus concerns change in what Bruffee (1995) has called the construction of the authority of knowledge. What counts as learning and knowing can be seen as contested terrain and is subject to challenge over time. This theme has become significant in relation to key developments in open learning and "action learning" applied to non-traditional and emergent sites of learning which have in recent times come to include the workplace.

Fundamentally, two contrasting viewpoints can be outlined with respect to how we think about knowledge. First, cognitive and foundational understandings of knowledge assume both the objectivity and externality of knowledge. External reality and objective facts exist and are complemented by a second cognitive entity that we commonly call the subjective self or the inner world. An alternative understanding relies on the assumption that knowledge has no absolute foundations, internal or external. People construct knowledge out of the paradigms (see Kuhn, 1970) or languages available to them whether they are spoken languages or symbolic languages such as algebra or computer languages or paralinguistic forms such as music and dance. Knowledge is seen as neither absolute nor universal; it is local, historically changing and has to be re-constructed time after time on the basis of lived, individual and social experience. Knowledge is understood therefore to be constructed and the "wheel of knowledge", as it were, has to be re-invented by every generation wishing to use it.

The implications for learning and teaching are significant. For example, if we assume education or learning is "given" to people, teachers help students to assimilate and absorb knowledge. Students perform to arrive at pre-determined answers which are validated by the disciplinary paradigm or knowledge community to which the teacher belongs. On the other hand, if we assume teachers help students to construct or re-construct knowledge, there are no pre-determined answers. Learners, therefore, can begin to break the dependency on received wisdom and a received curriculum. This has profound implications for how we conceive lifelong learning. It must now be re-connected with experience and the curriculum must reflect the "real time" and "real place" and "real problems" and needs of learners. Students must be trusted to perform in ways not determined ahead of time by teachers. Their knowledge must not be disconnected from experience. It is the argument of this part of the study that such experience can be characterised as moving historically from closed to open systems and from a monopoly of knowledge (held by the academic disciplines and their practitioners) to a shared and collaborative system of knowledge production. Perhaps surprisingly for traditional classroom based teachers the world of work and management development has provided some key elements of a new paradigm – that of action learning based on the work of Revans (1971, 1982, 1984) and his followers (see Wills, 1993, 1997) where insightful questions plus requisite individual and relevant learning for an enterprise or corporate body are brought together.

Adult learning opportunities have historically been focused on content-laden, closed and "objectivist" views of what counts as learning, and have later come to be focused more on the processes of learning, on multiple levels of experience, on open systems of access and on the recognition of learning achievement whenever and wherever it occurs. The sub themes through which this study evolves are descriptively framed and embrace a number of initiatives and perspectives, ranging from teacher views of pedagogy to the growth of "access" courses with their emphasis on adult experience as the fulcrum on which learning turns (Evans, 1984; Parry 1986). The growth in diversity within British higher education is considered in the context of growth in innovatory practices and the emergence of credit and credit accumulation systems. Modular schemes and qualifications frameworks are explicated in terms of their impact on the wider learning culture and growth of mass higher education.

Starting points
A range of innovations has been evolving since the 1980s and includes:

- the growth of learner centred knowledge and action learning;
- the development of open systems of accreditation and the movement from "closed" to "open" knowledge systems;

- the growing significance of adult learning (andragogy) as opposed to child-focused learning (pedagogy) and teaching methods;
- the development of a national credit framework;
- the growth of credit accumulation and transfer (CATS) within higher education;
- modular courses and the unitisation of the curriculum;
- growth of independent learning opportunities and recognition of prior learning and experience;
- accreditation of previous learning and of experiential learning, known as APEL;
- a focus on learning outcomes (learners) rather than on inputs (teachers);
- recognition of work and work experience as a key source of learning;
- the growth of continuous learning available to all;
- an increasing recognition of the need for lifetime learning opportunities and of their social and economic benefits;
- the explosion of new computer-based communications technologies which are capable of revolutionising teaching and learning practices.

These diverse, yet related, aspects of the education system have had an impact on the wider world of management development, as has the converse, where industry-based innovation has radicalised, in some cases, what further and higher education institutions do.

Perspectives on teaching and learning

Our list of starting points suggests a plethora of fruitful themes which are contributing to the shaping of the university. However, to grasp how lifelong learning is beginning to be a reality for a mass population of learners who will be prepared for the new and ever evolving communications technologies, we need to briefly explore how open learning and open systems of knowledge are merging. It is these open systems and the kind of knowledge they sponsor which are at the heart of the transformation of teaching and learning.

For lifelong education, debates covering the validity and nature of knowledge and how it is to be transmitted have had profound implications on the curriculum. This has been especially the case where formal, classroom-based, didactic methods have been challenged by self-managed, action learning paradigms (see Mumford, 1996; Wills, 1993).

The characteristics of one of these conceptions of teaching have been variously described as "student centred", "progressive", or as "open" pedagogy. The term "pedagogy" refers to the principles and methods of teaching – the ways in which a teacher carries out the task of presenting new knowledge and experience and generally manages the learning environment. Progressive and "open" styles of pedagogy might be seen as peculiarly characteristic of adult teaching and learning which claims a distinctiveness of its own (see Squires, 1987).

Historically and contemporarily there is a continuing tension between views which have asserted the primacy of didactic teaching, with its emphasis on the transmission of socially desirable and approved knowledge required for the order and control necessary to preserve social life or culture and that concerned with personal growth and development.

The argument to be developed here is that we have two different views of classroom relationships, which are based in turn on two very different conceptions of the nature of teaching/learning. Disputes on this issue are not new. The philosophical and practical elements of "progressive" teaching methods can be traced back to the work of Dewey, for instance, in the early decades of this century (see Skillbeck, 1970). "Progressivism" represents in fact an expression of the liberal ideology of schooling which has become deeply embedded in the principles of educational theory. The first approach is consistent with the view of education as necessary for establishing social control, and the successful induction of the young into the industrial-political system. The second accords with the liberal-democratic ideal which emphasises the potential of education for personal development.

Paradigms for teaching and learning: the closed and the open
Two contrasting perspectives or paradigms can be derived and used to inform debate on this issue. The traditional paradigm has fundamentally an objectivist orientation which focuses on the products of learning. The second paradigm is much more orientated to the subjectivity of the student and focuses on the processes of learning. In their organisational forms they are sometimes described as "closed" and "open" types of pedagogy. These concepts refer not simply to the classroom structure in which learning takes place, but also to the boundaries between subjects and areas of teaching responsibility. In other words, they have contrasting perspectives as to what constitutes the "proper" basis for the curriculum and for what counts as knowledge.

Underlying each of the paradigms are different psychological assumptions, different conceptions of curricular knowledge and different vocabularies and beliefs about the status of the student in the interaction of the classroom. They contain different conceptions of teaching and learning. They also offer very different possibilities for learner identity.

The closed or conventional paradigm
Within this paradigm, ability is viewed as the result of a number of prior "factors" in the genetic make-up and personality of individuals. What these are is not really known, but their effects it was thought could be "scientifically" measured through intelligence (IQ, intelligence quotient) tests which provide an "objective" measure of ability. An IQ is not necessarily static it is generally conceded and it may vary over a limited range.

Under the premises of this paradigm, achievement is defined in terms of mastery of specific bodies of knowledge which are mapped out to coincide with particular stages of the learning career. It is the task of the teacher to arrange and present these bodies of knowledge to his/her students. The focus of interest of the teaching tends to be in the products of learning – not in the process. Learning is thought to be most effective when a teacher-expert who knows the subject matter structures and imparts it to those who do not. The higher status of the teacher is maintained during interaction by a teacher's taken-for-granted definition of what shall count as "worthwhile knowledge" and the right to exclude what is not.

The classroom interaction which embodies the principles of this paradigm reflects an "objective" view of both knowledge and the student. The teacher imparts knowledge to recipient learners. Learning is collective in the sense that a nominal pace, sequence and structure for the subject content of a lesson are imposed on all the students in the group together.

The open paradigm

In opposition there has emerged a different paradigm, one version of which is rooted in the social sciences and takes as its central concern the power of the mind to organise experience and meaning. This paradigm emphasises an active rather than a static notion of the mind. The processes of thought are not taken to be reducible simply to the possession of "intelligence", nor to the performance of standardised routines characteristic of, for example, IQ tests. They are, instead, seen to be part of a highly complex personal system of interpretations, intentions and recollections. This paradigm upholds a view that cognition is a growth process and that the mind is capable of unlimited development.

We could describe this as the phenomenological or humanistic paradigm. Deriving from a philosophical tradition which is different in a number of respects from those of the positivistic tradition (see Allen, 1975; Mead, 1962), it has become established in several areas of social scientific enquiry. In educational psychology, its major representatives have been Jean Piaget (1932, 1973), Jerome Bruner (1962, 1968) and George Kelly (1955) each of whom has been involved in exploring theoretically and empirically the constructive processes of the mind. The work of Malcolm Knowles (1970, 1981, 1983) applied a similar perspective to the theme of adult learning and teaching or what became known as andragogy.

The main focus of this paradigm is on the processes of knowing and the learner's organisation of meaning into larger schemes of knowledge and experience. This kind of enquiry has led to a view of learning in which the structuring of knowledge and the processes by which it is acquired are seen to be fundamental to the development of understanding. For the teacher, the essential problem is to understand the logic of the learner's processes of knowing – to understand how the learner interprets and accommodates new knowledge. The relationship between the structures of meaning which the learner habitually uses and the structures which are presented by the teacher is critical.

A central part of the argument is that because all knowledge is external to the self, its meaning has to be reconstructed in terms of the life-world and the existence of the individual approaching it. In other words, it needs an "internal dimension".

As an aspect of her "phenomenological" viewpoint Maxine Green (1971) suggests that any act or process of learning involves three distinct states of consciousness – disclosure, reconstruction and generation. The act of "disclosure" is the bringing of self to the object to be learned; "reconstruction" is the process of interpretation whereby the newly-acquired knowledge becomes incorporated with existing knowledge; "generation" refers to the creative potential which arises in the fusion of the two.

Implications of an open and learner-centred perspective

The learning and teaching interaction which follows from an acceptance of a broadly conceived "phenomenological" paradigm is likely to allow the learner more control over structuring the learning process and experience than is the case with the alternative "closed" paradigm. The teacher is more of a guide than an instructor. Expertise is seen to reside in the ability to stimulate learning rather than communicating the body of knowledge. Thus, the individual is given or takes increased responsibility for his/her own learning.

The prevalence of the "closed" pedagogy in many educational institutions is particularly owing to the reification of subject specialities, as well as departmental separation based on subject expertise. This can lead in the context of higher education to the magnification and inflation of the content of specialist subjects. By pursuing individual interests, however, the learner is very likely to move into areas of knowledge which do not fit conveniently into existing curriculum subjects and specialities. This perspective leads us to consider the significance of choice and of the "thinking student" in the development of teaching and learning strategies. The development of open systems and lifelong learning appears to sponsor the growth of an open and "liberal" approach to what can be learned, with the students' choice playing an ever more significant role.

In the open pedagogy paradigm, the teacher's status as the provider of knowledge is significantly reduced. Control by the teacher is potentially weakened and the learner gains much more control of the pace of learning. The paradox is, however, of the existence of a liberal pedagogy in a wider hierarchical social structure and educational system which may contradict most of the principles of open access to learning.

Applying the "open" paradigm

The belief that alternative methods of teaching and learning were particularly appropriate to adult learners has found expression in several different yet related contexts. The work of Malcolm Knowles (1981, 1983) and Carl Rogers

(1974), focused on adult learners' own projects for learning; Reg Revans (1993) explored action learning and stimulated the foundation of a global school of business-orientated "open learning"; the British Open University gave impetus and organisational form to mass "open" higher education; and the concept of independent learning (see Spencer and Wynne, 1990) connected with the notion of "access" emerged. This wide process, embracing many streams of change, involved essentially a de-constructed curriculum which questioned the authority of traditional knowledge and asserted that knowledge was something to be constructed interdependently, between learners and teachers. Above all, these developments chart the recognition of the fact that there is now in existence what Teare (1998) refers to as the "dynamic curriculum". This curriculum embraces the open paradigm; its pedagogy is similarly open to student experience and it insists that knowledge is crafted from learning experiences, wherever and life figures ever more centrally in accessing and applying lifelong learning.

Lifelong learning and adult experience
Having briefly reviewed open and closed learning styles, we would argue that an alternative and radical view of adult learning associated with the concept of "andragogy", is required to take forward our thinking on educational change and innovation. There are of course a great number of theories claiming to explore and analyse the nature and processes of adult learning. Gagne (1965) and Wilson (1980) have evaluated those theorists who seek to ascribe learning processes to biological factors and mechanical "conditioning". Others such as Bruner have concentrated on the manner in which learners organise their conceptual , cognitive and perceptive experiences and there are other schools of thought which focus on personality and social pressures as critical to learning. In addressing a specifically adult context of learning it may be valid to suggest that all of the above viewpoints are valid as orientations giving different emphases rather than yielding distant categories of learning. This study views adult learning as a process whereby groups and individuals are able to assess the realities they experience and change their behaviour or experience or perceptions as a result. Adult learning is, therefore, concerned with a question of social and individual change.

Following Knowles' work we can identify four major assumptions which distinguish adult learning from childhood learning:

(1) Adults have strong needs to be self-directing. As we get older the self concept moves from dependency on others to self-direction and autonomy.

(2) Maturity brings experience which is a resource for learning.

(3) As life proceeds readiness to learn becomes associated with a person's social role. We, therefore, internalise learning needs in response to our need to know – not because we are told to learn.

(4) As a person grows older and matures problem or project-centred learning takes over from subject-centred learning.

If it is assumed that there is a distinctive pattern of adult learning over the life span of an individual then there are implications for how that learning should be organised. The following principles are, therefore, required to be embodied within the social learning process for adults and they will shape the conditions under which lifelong learning can flourish:

- adult learners are less dependent on teachers as they get older. They are more self-reliant and develop self-learning competency, they can decide on their own direction for learning and become more autonomous;

- individual differences need to be acknowledged. Different individuals will always have a range of abilities in a learning group, which can be both a benefit and a problem in a learning situation;

- whenever new knowledge is acquired it has to be adapted to and assimilated with existing knowledge. The recognition of existing knowledge and experience in all its potential variety represents a challenge to teachers and learners;

- learners in later stages of life require rewards and recognition for their achievements. These may vary, but where previous failure has been encountered, individuals may need to have positive reinforcement;

- active learning and practice and participation should characterise adult learning. Time for learning at later life stages may be at a premium and the sequencing and organisation of learning periods need to be highly relevant to the learner;

- students who have experienced previous failure or simply indifference to learning may require sensitive and appropriate guidance. The significance of personal experience cannot be ignored, but it may provide challenges to the assimilation of new knowledge;

- adult learners display a greater range and stability of cognitive structure and experience which in turn makes them more likely to adopt idiosyncratic approaches to learning. Getting adults to focus on learning techniques is important and these must be meaningful if they are to be effective aids to learning and motivation.

The concept of knowledge embodied in adult and lifelong learning insists that thinking and understanding develop as people interact, consciously and critically in their social context. It insists that there is no fixed or final stage of development and that the teacher-learner relationship is changed within an andragogical approach to learning. There are thus hugely significant implications for continuing learning and higher education when we consider that knowledge quickly becomes out-dated and that the context in which it applies rapidly changes. Where there is continuous change, there must also be continuous learning and the learning society which is emerging will enjoin us to actively and consciously lead these developments, as subjects in the process, rather than as objects in a process beyond and outside our understanding and control. If the learning society is to deliver its promise in full, it must surely do so through an open and innovative set of values and practices which are of concrete use and value to learners. What follows attempts to chart the changes which are shaping what can be learned, what is needed in a learning society and how it is being delivered. The themes concern learning and work, the emergence of a learning framework and the need for lifelong learning competency.

References
Please refer to Chapter 4.

Chapter 2

Learning and work: an index of innovation and APEL

David Davies

Deputy Principal, Westhill University College, Birmingham, UK

The important and far reaching factors which have brought about change in the learning opportunities for adults within higher education are dealt with in this section. Under that rubric, three specific sub-themes of change are explored as a contextual underpinning of what is turning out to be a general re-assessment of the position, role and function of adult learners within universities. First, this involves understanding the exponential growth of lifelong learning, secondly, charting the vocationalisation of learning opportunities and thirdly increasing our understanding of the changing nature of work in relation to education. Following on from this, innovative practice in continuing education is mapped as an aid to our understanding of the whole picture and one element, concerned with the recognition of experience and accreditation (APEL) as a key component of learning, is considered and a short case study is presented.

Adult learners in higher education

The requirements of provision by higher education institutions in the UK have been the subject of much speculation as we move towards a new millennium (Dearing, 1997). What is not in doubt, however, is the fact that participation by adults in all types of higher education has risen and has been matched by a rise in attainments and in the legitimate expectations of mature adult students for both qualifications and quality of provision (Davies, 1995). A key objective has been an improved social result, by which is meant an increase in the range and quality of students successfully entering institutions from all sections of the community, but in particular from targeted groups such as mature students, women, ethnic minorities and employees needing re-training in the context of change in the organisation and availability of work.

The higher education system is now able to offer a variety of contexts from which adults can potentially benefit. Educational variety through an increased diversity of academic programmes is available by subject, award, mode of study and location. Broader learning programmes based on generic skills as well as academic subject knowledge are available, as are a variety of staged awards achieved by students demonstrating effective performance rather than by length of the period of study. Continuing education offers opportunities for

This article first appeared in the *Journal of Workplace Learning,* Vol. 10 No. 4, 1998, pp. 183-194.

flexible and accessible study, more and more linked to accredited courses. Educational mobility and exchange are now realities offering transfer between levels of achievement and across the learning experiences of differing sectors of provision and institutions and even across national boundaries (see Robertson, 1994).

This means a radical change for many higher education institutions which must re-shape and re-conceptualise even their conventional courses. This chapter attempts to chart some of the processes and demands involved in these changes, especially in respect of modular and credit-based academic courses within the adult and continuing education tradition, which are often delivered off-campus.

Higher education is expanding fast. The number of students in the UK rose by almost two thirds in this decade, and by the year 2000 there will be well over 100 university level institutions catering for over 1.5 million undergraduate students. The proportion of 18 year olds entering higher education will rise beyond one in three, yet the overall majority of higher education students (including part-timers) will be over 25 years of age. The important question is how the current system, founded on rationed supply and selective entry, can be adapted to meet the growing demands of students and society alike, while preserving what is good about existing provision. Unless there are significant reforms – embracing among other issues those of course and qualifications, student funding, research and staffing and the provision of continuing education – there can be no successful transition to a mass system, let alone to a universal system of higher education towards which the most advanced industrial societies appear to be moving.

The response of British universities has been varied. Chris Duke (1992) noted some universities' development towards becoming lifelong learning centres. On the other hand, it can hardly be denied that much that is new and innovative flourishes on the margins of an institution's activity rather than at its corporate centre. Duke also noted that in the education system at large, the de facto mainstreaming of adult education is an acknowledged reality. His argument is, essentially, that the contours of a new paradigm can be seen which connect what might appear to be disparate areas. These include the university's role as a centre of recurrent learning and teaching, its role within a regional community, the variable pacing of study and range of flexibility in course provision it offers to its students. The "leitmotiv" of these developments is access, by which is meant the widening of participation via "access" schemes, the development of credit accumulation and transfer (CATS), the modularisation of courses enabling greater student choice, and the onset of new technologically-based learning systems such as that offered by the internet. All of this has occurred in the context of new inter-institutional consortia and franchising of higher education courses to the vocationally oriented further education sector. Both the rise in attainments and the legitimate expectations of mature adult students have been matched by a growth in the number of students requiring qualifications and/or other formal recognition of their learning achievements. Many such students, in the world of continuing education, are almost exclusively off-campus in terms of their physical or geographical location, studying in local neighbourhood centres and have, up to very recently, been viewed as a marginal cohort of university students.

Vocationalisation

Can there be any doubt that the awareness of need for greater social and economic advancement through educational opportunity has been a major factor in forcing through educational change? Following the American experience in the 1960s and 1970s, higher education in Britain in the 1990s has come to be regarded as a fundamental entitlement for a mass client group rather than as a select privilege for a few. As in the American case (see House, 1991), however, we cannot be certain that the promises of achievement and success can be met and the hopes of minorities and disadvantaged groups fully realised. Whether an expanded HE sector can be realistically viewed as a significant part of the solution to the seemingly intractable problems of the economy and the UK's competitive viability is debatable, and the jury is still out!

The changes we are now experiencing in higher education exemplify the assertion that general and liberal education is no longer at the centre of our higher education system. Rather, academic specialisation and technical training hold the centre stage. This is of course no new development and the correspondences with an earlier epoch were noted by House (1991, pp. 8-9) when he observed "The full development of nineteenth century industrialisation is symbolised as much by the appearance of the modern departmentalised research university as it is by the smoke-belching industrial plant with its ever greater division of labour and specialisation". The agenda for change has been set in relation to the increasing value placed on science, technology and the growth of specialist expertise in education and in work. These concerns have been at the centre of curriculum-led change since the 1980s and can be understood as indirectly related to the same socio-economic forces which produced specialisation and vocationalisation in higher and further education. The process is of course part of a larger and longer-term shift of profound character in our social life documented by Perkins (1990) in his work on the rise of "professional society" and by many commentators who have documented the inexorable growth of science and technology as part of modern social life (see Castells, 1996).

In relation to the question of how we understand educational change, the growth of a mass entry high education sector stretching across post-compulsory institutions is an expansion based on increasing vocationalism and specialisation. As such, it is one that challenges previous conceptions of the university's role. It does this by incorporating a broad range of learners at several levels of previous education and, thereby, brings into question the idea of binary divisions between providers; one that has already been seriously eroded by government policy (Robertson, 1993).

This new provision is for people well beyond the traditional age and qualifications categories. This is a response which corresponds to the changing nature of employment, leisure and social patterns which are themselves contingent on the evolving division of labour and our understanding of the nature of work and its availability (Finegold et al., 1992; Gleeson, 1990, 1993).

The arena of work and education is of course a contentious one. We most frequently mean paid work when referring to work but if we were to use the term to encompass the more general notion of productive life it would be possible, arguably, to view work as "a potentially progressive principle for curricula" (Spours and Young, 1988). The argument here is that the tendency to "vocationalise" the curriculum and favour traditional subject specialities in schools and colleges had led to a narrowing of the academic curriculum and a stress on vocational training. This is an education and training emphasising standards, discipline, attitudes and dispositions compatible with employers' views of the proper characteristics workers and employees should possess. This vocationalisation of learning opportunity has become part of new divisions of certification and at the higher levels of attainment has undermined the liberal approach to higher education which favoured general and humanistic approaches or those associated with an "open" pedagogy. Our understanding of the developing needs of employers and employees may, therefore, be enhanced if we can incorporate into this discourse a real sense of the changes occurring in the relationship of work and education.

The intention here is to signal some key aspects of this process. There is little doubt that fundamental changes in western societies' labour markets are taking place and that these have great significance for education. We are now in a "post-Fordist" (see Piore and Sabel, 1984) and modernising society where the mass production techniques of the Ford Motor Company used to manufacture cars in the 1920s and 1930s are declining owing to technological developments. Manufacturing industry is playing a declining role, service sector industries are growing, old skills barriers in the workforce are breaking down and new divisions between "core" and "peripheral" workers are being created. New forms of work and integration of productive processes are being created by the growth of the global economy (see Giddens, 1990; Sherman, 1995).

These changes demand new responses from educators; a flexible relationship between work and education is called for which is more creative and less divisive than the vocationalist perspective prevalent in the 1980s and 1990s. The imperatives of modernisation imply the coming together of education for personal growth and education for work, since it is work which connects us with so many aspects of market-oriented, consumer driven society with its emphasis on personal satisfactions and life chances.

Academic and specialist subjects as we know them cannot, therefore, be the exclusive basis for future routes to higher education since they no longer correspond to the needs of the wider reality, including the economic ones. People must, therefore, prepare themselves for a life of change and less for specific occupations and jobs. Vocation must come to denote the acquisition of more than technical skill and knowledge; individuals must also acquire critical thinking skills and knowledge to enable them to survive the inevitable changes in technical production which can simply obliterate functional occupational skills acquired in the past.

The end of work as we know it?

The nature of work as we know it is undergoing profound change. Work is no longer simply about the nature of occupations, the labour market and employment, but rather it is about how individuals transform themselves and their environments both practically and intellectually through creative and fulfilling activity. Work is increasingly about how "knowledge" comes to be defined as "useful" and education itself is viewed as a form of work which can lead to self-realisation and self-fulfilment at an individual and existential level.

For developed industrial societies the movement from labour intensive production and resources to capital intensive, high technology has profound implications for employment and the organisation and distribution of work. Job loss, de-skilling of individuals and whole groups of people, the emergence of temporary work on a permanent basis and the emergence of career loss and executive unemployment all signal the need for a different approach to education in respect of work and career in modern society (Sherman, 1995).

With regard to the academic curriculum work can no longer be seen as something that happens at a later stage in life. Increasingly the higher education curriculum is embracing the world of work. The meaning of work is shifting under the new circumstances which demand learning renewal throughout a working life. Such learning is increasingly, focused on work and is "action learning" in that it involves "real time" and "real place" problem solving. Work as an educational principle (Wittmann, 1989) is being increasingly recognised so that knowledge and practice are being brought together to form a new curriculum. Knowledge is being constructed by learners in ever more open systems, rather than being assimilated through existing subjects and modes of delivery in conventional educational settings.

Work is increasingly the site where pre-formulated and "textbook knowledge" is being transformed into new knowledge and where new paradigms for knowing and learning are emerging. Perhaps this is not so surprising if we see new knowledge as part of a task and problem-solving environment, where an individual's own existential project may need to be developed. Work is the site where the learner must be a primary actor, acting on the conditions and opportunities which shape experience and personal opportunity. This perspective is "constructivist" and places the management of self learning competence at the centre of development. It is, of course, concomitant with the open learning paradigm and systems outlined in chapter one.

In practical terms this means that companies have now set great value on corporate learning. Increasingly they are declaring themselves to be learning organisations which actively seek to identify the high level competencies which success in the competitive economic environment requires. Work-based learning (WBL) is now seen as a means of capturing corporate learning and its recognition by the academy is increasingly demanded. The learning organisation generates knowledge of its own practice as well as its own product. Such knowledge requires academic and professional recognition which is the point of contact and interface between the world of corporate learning and that of higher education. It is where the credit given for learning achievement crosses the boundary between work and education.

Work viewed as part of a "progressive" curriculum has already been mentioned and it must be stressed in relation to the theme of change and diversity in HE that work is no longer viewed by many just as paid employment. Work is about future employment in the labour market but it is also about work as leisure, work in the home, gift work, voluntary work, and self-employment. Work in these senses implies a new way of looking at the curriculum which includes all these aspects as the basis for the development of knowledge, understanding, skills and qualifications. This theme has been a vital underpinning of course and curricular development for adult, continuing and higher education in the phase of expansion and change in the 1990s.

The nature and organisation of work is a key structural feature of our social system which distributes educational access unevenly and unequally. However, in seeking to understand change at the levels we have touched on, we need to admit the partial significance of many phenomena. There are, for example, financial and policy exigencies determined by government. These have been issued with increasing frequency in the UK and have contributed to the changes sketched out earlier in the argument which referred to the significance of "higher education in the learning society", the title of the monumental report on the National Committee of Inquiry into Higher Education known as the Dearing Report (1997). The growth of a culture of "leisure" has also been of some importance, especially for those able to retire early enough and with sufficient income to buy into the leisure markets. There have also been financial gains available for colleges and universities for expansion and these have been central to the organisational and management issues around productivity and output. Above and beyond all of this, however, is the need for greater expertise and professionalism in an era of partial economic de-construction/ re-construction and its attendant threat, both real and imagined, of mass unemployment.

This is the overall context in which the skill-based and knowledge-based functions of lifelong education and post-school provision have been expanding. The response to the demands of new technology and the need of masses of individuals to adapt to the changing nature of work and the ever evolving division of labour help us account for the uptake of opportunities in both the liberal learning tradition and the vocational education sector. This is an agenda for change shared by the "vocational" further and higher education providers.

Our understanding of what is happening may lead us to be critical of the professionalisation and specialisation of academic life and to wish to re-assert the values of the older academy and of the validity of separate and unequal provision. Or, alternatively, this issue may force us to define new and emergent values which allow us a culture of inclusion for the world of higher education on a basis other than specialisation and expanded vocationalism. The populations and individuals who now participate in this learning culture have emerged into the stream of higher and further provision in the UK in recent years, and there is now mass participation – but participation in what and to what eventual end? These are questions which signal a new and emergent discourse on change and innovation. This explication takes the view that in seeking to innovate, diverse providers can contribute to a totality of common experience which is greater than the sum of the parts.

Can we categorise educational innovation?

It may be thought that by definition to innovate is to break out of constraining boundaries and uniformities and our purpose in asking this question is not to suggest a questionable unity for an essential diversity of practices and beliefs. Rather it is to seek common experience in the light of the need to innovate and initiate change. It is this shared focus of activity, and not divergent institutional structures, which is to be explained.

The last decade has seen an explosion of innovative teaching and learning systems which have been at the heart of post-school education (see Davies, 1997). In one sense the development of access and accessibility to further, adult and higher education has been co-terminous with the increased openness, flexibility and responsiveness to a wide variety of student learning needs; needs which were poorly served and largely invisible in previous eras.

A touchstone for identifying the different levels at which innovation and change occur is that of flexibility available to students. It is how innovative systems meet the specific need of individuals, i.e. their flexibility, which yields information otherwise locked into multi-layered institutions. It is inconceivable, for example, that the flexible needs of individuals will be met without innovation in management, financial, personnel, quality and curricular systems and practices.

The flexibility available to students can be separated into two fundamental categories (Spencer and Wynne, 1990). The first is that of open access arrangements which have been targeted at students for whom conventional qualifications for entry to higher education have been thought to be appropriate. Leaving aside the exponential growth of the biggest single provider of access, the Open University, there has been a huge expansion of "access" courses within the last five years with much provision being made by the British further education (FE) sector and conventional "old" and "new" university continuing education departments. The second category concerns schemes which allow the students to choose the pace of study and to negotiate significant parts of the curriculum for themselves. This last aspect should not be confused with existing correspondence systems which provide courses designed to meet the requirements of an external validating agency or examining body. Neither should it be confused with "modular" or "unit-based" courses which allow choice of module but allow the student no choice of content or input over learning objectives. These latter systems may be called "phantom" open systems and are in reality not commensurate with our definition of the open paradigm and its possibilities.

There is an increasing demand for learning situations which give students genuine flexibility and whose organisational procedures facilitate its growth. Spencer and Wynne have devised a learner flexibility profile which records the nature and extent of student choice. The dimensions they select include the aims and content of learning, methods of assessment, modes of attendance and the pace of learning. A scale of flexibility can be devised to rank and articulate activity within each of these categories. Clearly a flexible and innovative provider will need to judge itself in terms of the curricular levels over which it operates – whether at course, module, degree or other level and at the administrative and organisational levels. The flexibility experienced by an individual student derives from the interaction between learners and teachers within the conditions imposed by, or deriving from, the complex institutional arrangements of a college or providing institution. Both academic and resource controls are involved here in supporting or denying flexibility to individuals. Innovation cannot, therefore, be limited to a single aspect of institutional life; it has to go beyond the existing boundaries and be part of the open paradigm of learning and teaching.

The index of innovation (see Table I) is an attempt to bring into a diagrammatic configuration the major dimensions already mentioned around the key category of student autonomy.

What characterises the types of learner under review here is not just the fact that they are adults. Almost all educational institutions dealing with post-school provision handle adults, including the church, the armed forces, libraries, voluntary associations and a myriad other organisations. Neither can we easily define this client group in terms of what is taught or the level at which it is taught.

The distinctive and perhaps unique character of the learners under discussion here is the credence given to student-centred learning. In this view, learning is centred not only around allowing students some control over curricula and teaching methods but in what Squires calls the "profound" sense that the whole activity of education turns on the student, rather than on the organisation of the curriculum or on the formal certification of learning (Squires, 1987). This approach yields some possible components of individual and collective experience which can contribute to the indicators of flexibility and innovation. The components are, according to Squire's classification – adult learning, adult thinking, adulthood itself and adult development. The first of these is concerned with how teaching and learning occurs with adults and is distinctive. The second is concerned with the kind of "dialectical" and transformative thinking adults are capable of, while the third and fourth categories are focused on adulthood itself, its roles and life experiences.

From adult centred provision	Curriculum content	Assessment methods	Learning	Resources	From openness to access
Recognition of individual experience	Fixed curriculum and subjects	Traditional end of course examination	Formal class-based-didactic	Teacher/subject	Campus-based
Recognition of group experience	Narrow choice of options	Continuous course assessment	Plus informal classes	Centrally allocated	Home-based
Accreditation of prior learning (APL)	Wide choice of options	*Ad hoc* testing of individual objectives	Seminars, tutorials	Interactive resources available on demand	Information technologies
Accreditation of prior experiential learning (AP(E)L)	Content negotiated by students	Self-assessment Group assessment	Projects and problem solving	Resource centres – libraries	Multimedia
Recognition of potential	Modularity and inter-disciplinarity	Accreditation and credit accumulation and transfer schemes (CATS)	Open-ended learning	Student-based	Ongoing student support
Modular system to reflect life experience	Individually negotiated programmed (experience)	Criteria: contents, skills, personal growth	Learning outcomes demonstrated	Community resources	Output-related audit
Social-collective experience	Deconstruction of the formal curriculum	Personal learning statement and professional skills	Academic professional and vocational learning	Partnership	Work-based learning
Social transformations	New curricula and new knowledge		Action learning/self-managed learning	Learning organisations and the illusory classroom	Virtual learning
Towards					Towards

Table I.
An index of innovation

The implications of this are that the curriculum for lifelong learning and the learning society is more diverse than anything that precedes it in the formal system of schooling and in further and higher education. This diversity supersedes the limitations of what is taught as the formal curriculum, since everything from archaeology to zoology is included as is personal, professional and vocational learning. The form and content of continuing, lifelong education is more diverse than any single sector of education can offer and it tests to the limit some conventional distinctions between life and learning. Experience and experiential learning are central, therefore, to what is perceived to be the learning outcomes and processes to be fostered. There is no possibility of role closure, where individuals can be excluded from learning by virtue of their previous experience, or lack of it.

To return to the theme of innovation across the diversity of higher and further education; there is undoubtedly a transformation under way, building on the growth of flexible learning opportunities and the movement for greater access to education. It is possible to discern new and emergent categories of educational experience and aspiration, though it is a far from complete process.

The charting of themes for innovation within an "index" is a simplified and schematic device, which cannot do justice to a complex reality. Nevertheless, it may be possible to derive benefits from its use by bringing a range of potential characteristics of innovation into juxtaposition and thereby creating a repository of ideas and concepts to act as a resource for practice. This process may enable the role of principal agents involved in innovation to be underpinned by a classification and rating of the extent and pace of change. This in turn should facilitate the application of the model as an audit mechanism, as a "theoretical" framework for innovation and as a practical tool for development. An index of innovation is not a completed product, but rather an aid to thinking through common issues facing those who wish to innovate in the field of continuous learning. One of the emergent categories of innovation contained within the index of innovation refers to the recognition and accreditation of prior learning and learning experience, known most commonly as APEL. The following explanation and mini case study is a guide to the issues that arise when the APEL method is used to help expand and transform learning opportunities.

APEL (accreditation of prior experiential learning)

APEL is part of the open system committed to the creation of learning opportunities and the expansion of those opportunities. It is of course about the recognition and accreditation of learning achievements, whether encapsulated in formal and certificated learning or, as is increasingly the case, captured through learning experiences. The recognition of anther's experience and the placing of a value on it, is at the centre of much of our learning and teaching, and it is frequently problematical (see Brown and Knight, 1994).

The contexts within which APEL has developed include a daunting array of themes which have impacted on educational provision and management development. APEL as the focus of many of these themes could be seen as a fulcrum on which learning opportunities for vast numbers of people have turned. It is at the least a point of condensation where debates, theories of learning, models of achievement and the lived experience and reflective capabilities of individuals and groups actually come together to produce a tangible result (a credit or qualification for the individual).

APEL is more than a method or set of practices for granting credit towards a qualification (though it certainly involves that aspect of educational work). APEL is primarily a creative and critical process which for those who adopt its principles and practices leads to a critical re-assessment of existing learning. APEL has significance for the following contexts which are determining the learning outcomes of many learners in the fields of education and work-related learning:

- the concept of lifelong learning into the twenty-first century;
- the coming pre-eminence of the "learning organisation";
- the continuous re-construction of "the curriculum";
- the raising of the status of "credit" within higher education;
- the recognition of new categories of learning achievement.

The accreditation of prior experiential learning: a description
The credit awarded within higher education on the basis of prior learning may take the form of entry into a programme of study, advanced standing within a programme of study, or credit towards an award. Decisions about the type and amount of credit may be based on certificates the learner has gained which demonstrate that learning has been assessed, or may take into account learning from experience which is considered worthy of credit.

Credit is awarded for learning which can be demonstrated, but not for the experience itself! Increasing numbers of higher education institutions are prepared to accept learning from experience, as well as learning which has already been certificated, as a valid indication of achievement.

Learners wishing to take advantage of APEL may do so on the basis of many forms of learning:

- certificated learning from other UK educational institutions;
- experiential learning acquired in paid work;
- experiential learning acquired in unpaid or voluntary work;
- uncertificated learning from self-directed study;
- certificated learning from abroad;
- certificated work-based learning.

The Higher Education Quality Council's *Guidelines on the Quality Assurance of Credit-Based Learning* (1994) states: "provided applicants have fulfilled some of the progression and assessment requirements of the programme of study by means other than attendance on the planned programme and will be able by completing the remaining requirements to fulfil the objectives of the programme and attain the standard required for the award, they may be admitted as a student to any appropriate point in the programme."

Higher Education has become involved in the accreditation of individual programmes which include elements of experience-based learning, which had not previously led to an award. A further extension of this has been the assessment (for credit) of an individual's learning against learning outcomes which have been negotiated by that individual in collaboration with the assessing institution (see Ecclestone, 1994; Employment Department, 1993)

APEL has the potential to widen access, increase flexibility in the curriculum, and enable a positive value to be placed on off-campus learning. It can also serve as a vehicle for learners to integrate theory with practice, and for promoting reflective practice through the identification of learning from experience, and the application of this learning in changed practice. The benefits that result may include the following:

- recognition of learning from experience, and the process of reflection required to construct an APEL claim, often leads to an increased level of confidence;

- preparing a claim for APEL helps to develop independent study skills;

- reflection on experiential learning enhances the theory/practice link, leading to an increased understanding of the two-way flow both from academic learning to practice, and vice versa.

What does APEL involve?
APL claims may involve the presentation of evidence of learning from prior certificated learning, prior experiential learning, or a combination of both. Table II illustrates the process of making an APEL claim (see also Simosko, 1991).

In this context, the APEL process may be divided into three main strands:

- transfer of credit already awarded (direct transfer between similar programmes);

- re-allocation of previously awarded credit ("general" to "specific" credit);

- assessment of learning which has not previously been given a credit value.

Transfer of credit may be possible where a learner has evidence of having undertaken a programme of learning which is directly relevant to the proposed award, and which has already been credit rated within a scheme recognised by the receiving institution.

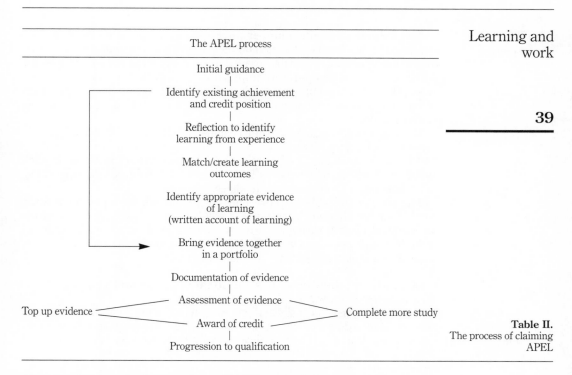

The APEL process

Initial guidance

Identify existing achievement
and credit position

Reflection to identify
learning from experience

Match/create learning
outcomes

Identify appropriate evidence
of learning
(written account of learning)

Bring evidence together
in a portfolio

Documentation of evidence

Assessment of evidence

Top up evidence   Complete more study

Award of credit

Progression to qualification

Table II.
The process of claiming
APEL

The accreditation of prior learning – APEL in operation
Reflection on experience. The learning that is identified through reflection will need to be stated in such a way that it can be assessed. In most cases the processes of reflection and the preparation of an APEL claim are supported by an adviser. Many institutions also offer short courses which help potential APEL candidates to engage in this process of reflection, and ensure that the outcomes are appropriate for academic assessment. Such courses often carry credit in their own right, and so have the potential to increase the amount of credit which can be awarded prior to enrolment on a specific programme.

Increasingly, higher education institutions writing their courses or units in terms of learning outcomes (see Otter, 1992). Where the individual's learning does not directly match existing unit outcomes, or where these do not exist, the outcomes that describe the learning needs to be clearly described and capable not only of being assessed, but also of being ascribed a volume and level of credit.

Increasingly, there is evidence of attempts to reach agreement on level descriptors both within individual institutions and across consortia (see SEEC, 1996a, 1996b). These are based on a range of criteria, including cognitive skills, personal skills, contextual features, degree of learner autonomy etc. As these descriptors become more widely agreed, the reliability of the assessment of APEL claims should increase.

The volume of credit (number of credit points) awarded is generally computed within higher education on the basis of learning outcomes achieved by the learner. This is usually arrived at by comparing the learning in the APEL claim to a comparable taught unit within the institution. Where appropriate, APEL enables learners to design and present individual packages of learning for assessment, not only to match their learning against existing modules or courses.

Many programmes are now being designed in such a way that learners may negotiate their own pathway to an award. This may involve the extensive use of APEL, work-based learning, distance learning and taught modules. In such areas, APEL claims tend to be set in the context of the aims of the programme as a whole rather than individual modules.

The scheme in Table III represents a critical path for a person seeking recognition for previous learning. It is followed by a short APEL case study involving a University provider, two large international business organisations and IMC a business school which has developed the ability to devise and deliver innovative learning programmes in the workplace.

Case study in miniature – international management centres
A basis for credit – the IMC/University connection
This section outlines the tasks and processes which needed to be identified and negotiated in order to deliver APEL in the contexts of programmes of work-based action learning. The actual case involved the University of Surrey and

The APEL process	
Guidance for entry	Information is disseminated to potential claimants on what can be achieved through APEL. Guidance personnel or mentors are identified as able to help.
Individual profiled	Candidates are helped to assemble or write a profile or record of existing and previous achievements with help from a mentor. The evidence of what will be required is identified in order to support a claim for credit.
Evidence building	Candidates collect evidence of learning and start to build a portfolio – workshops can help do this on a collective basis. An internal verifier and an assessor will be identified.
Assessment	The internal verifier reviews the portfolio of evidence and the assessor sets an assessment plan and tasks for the student, to ensure standards and quantity of evidence are met. An APEL module may be undertaken by the candidate which will support the assessment procedure and yield further credit.
Credit awarded	When the assessment process is completed the verifier can recommend credit be awarded. The relevant awarding body will produce external verification and award the credit.
Progression	Candidates review the outcome of their APEL experience and devise plans for further learning. Where possible, integration of personal learning and professional development takes place.

Table III.
A critical path for
seeking recognition for
prior learning

two international corporations as clients of an IMC/University partnership. However, the principles and processes are applicable and adaptable to a plethora of partnerships and what is described represents a usable template.

Credit transfer agreements were required between IMC and the University covering the following IMC programmes:

- IMC – Certificate of Management Studies (CMS)
- IMC – Diploma of Management Studies (DMS)
- MBA

The Memorandum of Association between the University and IMC set out the purposes for which both partners were working together. This joint venture took advantage of IMC's leadership in internet resourcing and delivery of programmes of workplace action learning and research. The approved joint programmes at the postgraduate level (MBA, DMS and CMS) were, however, "paralleled" by the preceding IMC programmes under exactly the same academic titles and covering the same core modules and skills units. The core content, learning outcomes and academic credit achievements were exactly similar for both the University of Surrey IMC joint programmes and those of the pre-joint venture IMC programmes. It was necessary to establish the specific credit rating appropriate for these awards against those of the joint Surrey IMC programmes in order that appropriately registered associates (called students at the University) could transfer their learning credits into a University concurrent award.

The task
Credit rating of professional work-based learning implies structured activity leading to outcomes which can be assessed at HE level. There must be a degree of consensus about the work of such learning in terms of credit values and this require formal recognition within a learning partnership.

Of mutual concern within the IMC/University partnership was the belief that the knowledge base of professional achievements and learning can be fully recognised within the context of academic credit for conventional university awards. "Capability" and the ability to create "new knowledge" in addition to an emphasis on competence or propositional knowledge required recognition of learning achieved off the University campus.

The process
- To specify the principles by which a Joint Academic Board could seek and award HE credit within the approved Surrey IMC awards.
- To describe models of articulation between IMC awards and University academic awards.
- To map the elements of congruity and continuity between IMC and University qualifications in terms of credit requirements, achievements and learning outcomes.

- To develop future guidelines for the accreditation of professional and any form of structured/off-campus learning within the joint venture.
- To secure agreement on the nature of general and specific credit for appropriate awards/off-campus learning.
- To extend access to joint programmes and progression using professional experience and awards.

Procedures for identifying and awarding credit for IMC programmes
Both the University and IMC agreed to:

- Identify what had been learned and its level.
- Identify how learning had been assessed.
- Identify how quality and consistency of learning and assessment had been maintained and controlled.

The evidence to be considered covered:

- Learning outcomes/achievements specified for the programme which fosters academic and intellectual development.
- Specification of learning styles and methods.
- Programme and course content; syllabuses.
- The siting and location of the programme.
- The links to other programmes,

Assessment issues to be explored included:

- The level of the credit awarded within the University's framework, using level descriptors embracing Master's level programmes.
- The range and type of assessment methods used.
- Criteria against which performance has been judged.
- Arrangements for external and/or internal moderation.
- Attempts to include broader educational and academic achievement.

Quality assurance arrangements were agreed for:

- Programme management and quality control procedures (agreed within the joint venture).
- Appropriate admissions procedures and guidance (agreed within the joint venture).
- Resources available to deliver and administer the programme.

Moving the IMC model forward
The formal recognition of appropriate previous learning and its accreditation through a University's APEL procedures normally allows knowledge to be quantified and expressed in terms of credit exemption (or for advanced

standing) towards an award. The IMC joint venture wished to take advantage of procedures whereby candidates from established admission routes are admitted with advanced standing to an appropriate award. It was the case that for bachelor's APEL, the existing University of Surrey Combined Studies Honours degree (BA/BSc) provided a suitable model against which individual claims could be made. For the MBA and linked programmes of DMS and CMS, advanced standing for individuals who had completed the parallel IMC CMS was required. This credit quantity equalled 40 credit points at M level and thus constituted an approximately higher level entry point to the degree of MBA. The rationale for this was that the prior learning is certificated through IMC programmes was of a comparable nature, level and volume to the parts of the programme for which advanced standing/ exemption was sought.

A University's quality assurance procedures in APEL matters are considered to be paramount and are embodied in its regulations. Such procedures cover the various stages of APEL including counselling, assessment and verification as well as the issues of procedural continuity and record keeping. Most APEL processes adopted by University "departments" involve the construction of evidence and assessment methods through portfolios. In the case of APL assessment for IMC programmes the nature and extent of contact between the two partners suggested that an "accelerated track" model for the senior managers on the joint programmes be implemented. The currency of the learning and the closeness of the match between the designated IMC and Surrey IMC programmes suggested that the specific credit requested for IMC awards would serve as a sound basis for subsequent study at a higher level, certificated by the University.

Transfer of credit
Responding to Surrey IMC needs with respect to higher level achievements by senior managers required appropriate methods for recognising APEL. It was the case that the curriculum being followed and the courseware being used within the IMC CMS programme was identical to those of the Surrey/ IMC MBA.

The APEL/Registration Group of the Surrey IMC agreed to recommend that provided Associates on IMC's CMS programme gained a minimum mark of 40 per cent on each assignment and a weighted average of 50 per cent or more, they should proceed with APEL credits to the Surrey/IMC MBA programme and be eligible to study for the balance of 80 credits towards the MBA.

The "accelerated track" APEL model for senior managers
The defining characteristics of the group:

- Senior managers in corporate institutions and companies involved in action learning sets.
- Substantial managerial experience.

- Prepared for admission with credit for management studies and personal achievement.
- Holders of existing qualifications (e.g. in particular CMS).
- Prior qualifications at postgraduate level but not necessarily in management.
- Aware of APL and APEL processes.

Objectives of the accelerated programme
To provide a programme which would:

- Enable senior managers to evidence learning against the credits of the University's Postgraduate Certificate/CMS, the Postgraduate Diploma/ DMS in Management, and the MBA.
- Produce streamlined portfolios over a short time scale.
- Include the use of oral evidence of learning across a number of related learning outcomes, rather than mapping onto the learning outcomes of each individual module.
- Involve peer group and tutor support within in open learning approach.
- Be a learning process in its own right.
- Be time and cost effective for students and staff.

Assessment summary
The assessment required took the form of an extended CV and a cognitive map of abilities and achievements, plus the "standard" assessment of the portfolio as a whole which includes documentary evidence relating to the learning outcomes of the CMS modules completed within the IMC programmes, leading to the CMS.

A recommendation from the academic staff responsible for registering Surrey IMC students forwarded to the Joint Academic Board and appropriate Examination Board for confirmation of the credit to be awarded was to be required.

Towards the end of the process a workbook of APEL procedures was produced which detailed each stage of an APEL claim and facilitated the mapping of learning achievements against higher level academic qualifications and their component credit ratings.

The benefits of APEL
In summary, we can argue the case that:

- APEL is progressive and is part of the open paradigm for lifelong learning; it fosters open access and opportunity for all potential and actual learners.

- APEL is a "keystone" to the recognition of learning and it acts as the cement between experience, learning and qualifications.
- APEL is radical – it sponsors new and fresh methods of learning and assessment.
- APEL has "commensurability"; it can relate to work-based learning and to academic credit.
- APEL facilitates the "re-engagement" with the democratic possibilities of learning outside the institutional boundaries.
- APEL is de-constructivist in terms of institutions – but "compositional" in supporting learners to build up credit based on need and choice.

If lifelong learning is the future, then APEL is a building block, or rather the material along with credit systems which glues together the learning achievements of students.

Consideration must now be given to the gaining and transference of learning opportunities which have been consolidated and extended through the use of innovative credit schemes in continuing learning. A "learning framework" is proposed which draws on the index of innovation and charts the key features of the new learning opportunities which will make a vital contribution to the virtual university.

References
Please refer to Chapter 4.

Chapter 3
The learning framework

David Davies

Deputy Principal, Westhill University College, Birmingham, UK

Impact of modularisation

The key theme of this section is the story of an expanded and diverse population of learners which has accompanied a re-conceptualisation of educational achievement and opportunity in British society. This development turns on a core of important themes, some of which have been introduced in earlier chapters. Learning has been viewed as problematic and experience has been placed more centrally in debates concerning learning for a lifetime; open and closed learning systems (pedagogies) and their relationship to access provision have been addressed and an index of innovation has been outlined involving systems of academic credit (CATS), and the recognition of work and the workplace as a site of lifelong learning has been raised as an issue for exploration. These developments need to be grasped within a learning context or framework of modular courses and programmes. The curricular and organisational innovations that flow from and are part of this learning framework are the subject of this chapter.

The principles of modularity

The basic principle on which modular courses are based is that the curriculum is divided into discrete units or modules which are normally independently assessed. Each unit or module is, therefore, a measured part of an extended learning experience leading to the attainment of a specified qualification, for which a designated number and possibly sequence of units or modules is required. Such requirements may be totally or partially prescribed and be partly or non-negotiable for the student. The group of required modules is usually known as a course or pathway or a programme of study. Each programme of study is located within a hierarchy of awards or qualifications, e.g. certificate, diploma, undergraduate or postgraduate degree and within an award (e.g. undergraduate degree), each unit or module is assigned to a level within a hierarchy of levels (see HEQC, 1995; Theodossin, 1986).

Modularity, as a "principle" which now guides and shapes the majority of degree courses at undergraduate level in the UK, challenges a number of taken for granted structures and professional practices as well as the more generic professional ideologies underpinning them. Examples include the heightened importance of assessment in curriculum design, which now drives teaching and

This article first appeared in the *Journal of Workplace Learning*, Vol. 10 No. 4, 1998, pp. 195-205.

learning. Modularity demands an enhanced level of understanding as to how specified learning outcomes and achievements are aggregated into whole learning experiences which lead to awards and qualifications. It has been argued that flexible modular programmes need to ensure coherence and progression while permitting choice and in turn this requires sophisticated curriculum design and mapping skills, and an effective infrastructure for academic guidance (HEQC, 1995). Modularity is important because it involves a more complex conceptual understanding of the meaning of academic achievement, not least because it requires its adherents to embrace a range and balance of purposes within and beyond higher education. In particular it embraces new conceptions of accreditation which involve recognition of dual outcomes related to academic and vocational learning, it involves recognition of generic key skills and abilities which may have no fixed, pre-ordained curriculum content but which are issue and problem centred and it has positive implications for how achievement is recorded and used by thinking and choosing students who are helping construct their own curriculum as active learners.

Modularisation has radically changed the way higher level education is provided, the way learning opportunities are created and designed and the way learning is assessed. According to the HEQC a large majority of UK higher educational institutions have adopted modular frameworks with a further significant percentage adopting a unitised framework. Across the HE sector in the UK, however, institutions and individuals are at different points on the learning curve. As we enter the new millennium HE as a whole is participating in a step change process which is affecting all aspects of academic, administrative and managerial practice: a situation which is likely to result in conditions which are more responsive to new initiatives and new ways of doing things.

Although there are still many tensions around the introduction of modular frameworks it is clear that institutions see a curriculum framework as a device to enable them to achieve their diverse educational missions. It is therefore to be expected that a range of approaches which have been adopted or designed will evolve to meet this primary purpose. A number of specific aspects of modularisation which are improving the conditions for these initiatives deserve consideration.

First, we are seeing the development of new skills in the design of module or unit-based curricula. Over the period in which modularisation is introduced within an institution we see an evolutionary process in which courses are initially divided up into smaller courses. This is followed by a more radical reappraisal of the pedagogic and epistemological consequences of this change and the shift to constructive rather than deconstructive processes in curriculum design. The process of going modular forces academics to radically reappraise all aspects of their professional practice. In the light of this fundamental change the higher education community is more open to considering the merits of competency-based programmes than it was prior to modularisation.

Second, modularisation is encouraging a much greater focus on assessment in the planning and design stage of modules and programmes (see Atkins *et al.*, 1993; Brown *et al.*, 1994). It is encouraging curriculum designers to be more explicit in the specification of educational purpose, learning objectives and intended learning outcomes at module level and encouraging a closer and more explicit alignment of criteria for the assessment of levels of performance against stated learning objectives. These are the basic design principles which underpin modular courses, though arguably they have been adopted within competence-based learning programmes to a greater extent than within traditional, subject-based awards.

Third, there is a movement within modular frameworks towards the adoption of a learning outcomes-based approach (see Otter, 1992). Notwithstanding the difficulty of interpreting what this actually means in practice, a large percentage of modular higher educational institutions (HEIs) are moving in this direction. The four major UK credit consortia SEEC, HECIW, SCOTCAT and NUCCAT (see InCCA, 1997) are a driving force in this area at a national level. Clearly, familiarity with the language and practice of preparing learning outcomes and using them as the basis for assessment and performance criteria is another essential pre-condition for the development of competence-based degree programmes, around which, for example, most workplace learning has developed.

Fourth, a range of new, educationally exciting and innovative approaches to learning and student assessment has been fostered within flexible modular frameworks, many of which have direct application to the approach being advocated, for example, through the index of innovation (see chapter 2). For example:

- the general move towards a more student-centred approach to learning and increasing emphasis on the autonomy of the learner;
- the greater prominence of independent study based on learner negotiated agreements and the development of skills, guidance and assurance systems to support such personal autonomy;
- the use of new learning materials to support independent study often provided through new communication technologies
- development of active learning projects, and the use of reflective logs and portfolios to support this approach;
- growth in work- and community-based learning schemes including increased opportunity for work-experience, work-placement and programmes which are predominantly based within work or community environments;
- increased emphasis on developing transferable skills across the curriculum;
- the assessment of learner capability;

- a shift in the nature of the assessment model which underlies the modular curriculum.

All these features have prepared the ground for workplace learning and for the recognition of competency-based degrees – which are an organisational corollary of innovative lifelong learning and commensurate with the open paradigm for learning described earlier.

Working within regulated frameworks

The introduction of modular frameworks has led to another important change namely a move from programme- to scheme-based regulatory frameworks to guide, support and regulate academic practice across disciplinary areas. The experience of the various credit consortia in the UK (InCCA, 1997) suggests that there are several important elements covering: curriculum structure; credit-levels-awards; assessment and the management of quality and standards.

Such structures are a necessity in complex, flexible curricular environments where academic practice needs to be guided and controlled across the whole scheme. The idea of a "framework for credit" (see FEU, 1992, 1994; Robertson, 1994) is central to modular developments since it links academic practice and the methodologies and tools used in teaching and learning. The framework shapes both what we do and how it is done. Familiarity with working in such structured environments is another important pre-condition for designing degrees and other academic awards around the elements of the innovatory system described and analysed in chapters 1 and 2.

We will now consider two aspects of the frameworks which are particularly relevant to the new type of degrees and other academic awards, namely the credit and academic frameworks of levels which crucial components of modular provision.

Credit

Credit is the currency of the academic system. A credit is a medium of exchange and is used to give a value to an amount of learning. This amount of learning is frequently expressed as an "outcome" and can vary in size and complexity. Credits are awarded on the successful achievement of a set of clearly defined "learning outcomes", regardless of the actual time involved or the mode of learning. A credit value can be established by agreeing the notional amount of time, including all teacher contact time and independent student learning, needed on average for a learner to achieve the defined outcomes. Once the credit value of a learning outcome(s) is ascertained, the mode of learning or actual amount of time spent studying is not relevant to the number of credits awarded. Credits are achieved at different levels ranging from basic education to postgraduate degrees. Most first degrees in the UK now involve 360 credits achieved over 2 or 3 levels in the "HE CATS" system. (There are a number of credit systems in operation in the UK – see FEU, 1992.)

Credit has been used as a powerful tool for opening up access to learning opportunities by some providers. This is increasingly the challenge facing all providers of higher education. The central proposition turns here on the need for a unified post-16 credit system containing accepted and agreed definitions of outcomes, units and credits and which can lead to a "credit framework" encapsulating the following rationale:

- to increase the participation and achievement of post-16 learners;
- to improve access to learning opportunities and enhance possibilities for progression in education and training;
- to provide for greater choice and give learners a greater say in what, when and how they learn;
- to encourage learners to undertake broader learning programmes whether they are in employment, preparing for employment, preparing for HE or developing basic skills;
- to facilitate the development of a core of knowledge and skills;
- to develop new study combinations which are more relevant to a culture of innovation and which render obsolete division and terminology such as academic/vocational, practical/theoretical, creative/technical, Arts/Humanities/Science;
- to allow specialised and customised education and training.

The relevance of credit systems for learners in the universities
It could be suggested that we should see credit as a "tool" for measuring the quantity and level of educational attainment (FEU, 1994). Since we seek to acknowledge all appropriate learning wherever and whenever it takes place, we are really only looking for a currency to measure and support mobility and progression in various learning environments so as to overcome barriers. Credit is thus about opening up opportunities. This message is the key one for students who may not fully perceive the advantages of credit when they begin their studies.

However, educational innovators have argued that credit can provide a significant number of advantages (see Robertson, 1994). Credit, for example, permits students to study their own choice of subjects and course in order to build up qualifications over a timescale chosen by themselves. This is particularly important for adults engaged in lifelong learning, permitting students to add to their portfolio of credit and qualifications at a rate suited to their individual circumstances at different times of their lives and careers. In addition students can gain recognition for previous work and learning undertaken earlier in life. Credit gained is never lost and ideally there can be no defined timescales in which the student must complete a particular qualification or lose the learning already achieved. Credit also facilitates and encourages progression from level to level and permits transfer between institutions thus widening student choice. A coherent credit framework would permit recognition of such learning which has not been formally recognised in the past.

The benefits to be won for individuals through open choice and the existence of progression routes in continuing education can only be maximised by contact with other institutions and agencies. The Training and Enterprise Councils (TECs), for example, are key mediators between the world of work, employers and their needs. In addition, to link effectively with regional structures, the universities are increasingly reliant on guidance services which are a significant part of the TECs remit. The point of "condensation", where HE credit accumulation systems and credit offered at lower levels in the academic hierarchy come together, may well be used as part of a comprehensive post-school guidance service which can advise on access to all education and training opportunities in a region. It is now clear that the guidance needs of adult learners will increasingly help shape the profile of adult learners (see Davies and Nedderman, 1997).

Mapping and planning the wider curriculum for adult learners where community providers and further and higher education sectors share a common range of adult education opportunities, will become both more desired and more problematic. A national credit and qualification framework confers obvious advantages and these now present an agenda for those in the universities with responsibilities for course development and curriculum management.

The schema in Table III (Chapter 2) was designed to inform both students and tutors about the different credit systems available and to aid an evaluation of the systems in relation to lifelong learners. It allows for comparison between two systems – that of the further education sector (see FEU, 1994) and that of the higher education sector in the UK.

Credit frameworks
The development of a credit-framework is an important enabling and regulating device to facilitate learner mobility between the providers of HE, into and out of HE and between the academic and vocational domains.

According to the HEQC (1995b) over 80 per cent of the HEIs have established a credit framework and most of the institutions which have not formally established such a framework have established a mechanism for the credit-rating of learning when a student wishes to transfer to another institution. Over 90 per cent of the institutions that have developed a credit framework have based their framework on the old Council for National Academic Awards (CNAA) credit scheme which requires 360 credits for a three year degree (i.e. 120 credits per level). All Scottish institutions have adopted the SCOTCAT scheme which is also based on the 120 credits per level or 480 credits for the Scottish four year honours degree.

The later 1990s saw the adoption of "compositional" credit frameworks (see Robertson, 1994) by institutions within two credit consortia in Wales (HECIW) and the South of England (SEEC) and the establishment of a third credit consortia NUCCAT in the North of England which is working to the same principles as those established by SEEC/HECIW. These frameworks are still based on 360 credits for a degree but the basis for construction is the ten hour credit, although there are variations in the way institutional credit frameworks operate.

The development and use of credit accumulation and transfer schemes has led to a sharper focus on the matter of judging levels of intellectual development and attainment in programmes of study or experiential and work-based learning. It has also required institutions to make decisions about "comparability" and relative values of prior experience and past attainment for entry and progression.

Thus, we have gone from a situation where a few institutions have developed local CATs schemes to a situation in which most institutions have established and use a credit framework across all, or most of their provision. Disregarding the inconsistencies between institutional frameworks the main difficulty to be resolved is the articulation of academic and vocational frameworks so that achievement in one framework can be recognised within the other (Table I).

An open credit system	HE CATS credit accumulation and transfer scheme
Open to all users potentially at post-16	Is a credit system, closed to all except HE providers of CATS courses
Is a framework, not a credit system, open to all awarding bodies	360 credits = first degree (Degree = 1200 hours of student learning).
1 credit = 30 notional hours of learning (made up of both taught hours and home study).	Credits count towards a degree (or part of a degree e.g. certificate).
Credit is a notion of value, not dependent on any single award of qualification	Credits are suitable for student wishing to gain a degree or a sub-component of a degree such as a certificate.
Credits can count towards a number of awards	Represents a fairly narrow (higher) range of achievements at post-16.
Flexible, particularly suitable for short courses	A unit or "module" is defined as part of a degree and is therefore pre-determined by the degree structure.
A Unit is defined in terms of what is achieved/learned by students in a given amount of time.	Credits within a qualification are likely to be at the same level.
Allows for achievement of units embracing credit at different levels	Used mainly by the higher education sector.
Used mainly by the further education sector and open college networks.	

Table I.
Schema for credit

The learning outcomes model

A central strategy for the development of credit is the adoption of a "learning outcomes" model, specifying what each student is expected to know, understand or do as a result of the course of study. Outcomes are "quantified" within the national CATS scheme using widely accepted HE credit tariff volumes and notional study time as a working basis. This process is not yet an exact science by any means and practitioners continue to share the national uncertainty about credit values and volumes.

In order to facilitate the process of accreditation, the tutors in HE are now typically asked to provide a detailed syllabus indicating the aims and objectives of the course, the proposed learning outcomes for students, the teaching approach the tutor intends to take and the suggested methods of assessment. This syllabus is often used to negotiate the detailed learning outcomes of the course and the assessment activities with students at the start of the course.

The common element in all the courses is naturally the process of learning. It is the specification of learning outcomes which is the key to accreditation across the range of courses and subjects offered. A learning outcome may be defined as something that a person would be expected to know or to understand or be able to do as the result of a specific learning experience. Once this is defined it is possible to assess the learning that has taken place. Learning outcomes are written in both general and specific terms and may focus on three areas:

(1) Knowledge and understanding of academic content of the course.

(2) Skills – often implicit rather than explicit, for example problem-solving, communication and inter-personal skills.

(3) Personal development – this is often an intangible but keenly felt outcome, for example, enhanced self-awareness, personal confidence and learner autonomy.

The aim of adopting this system is to encourage students to reflect both on what they know and what they can do as a result of their course. It also provides a method of assessing explicit achievements across the full range of subjects and disciplines and is a means of ensuring comparability of standards. The trend towards the identification of learning outcomes shifts the focus of performance to the learner, who must be able to demonstrate the achievement of criteria which attest to successful learning and away from the teacher's ability to provide the inputs to the process. Such a process is naturally contentious and forces professional educators to evaluate the impact of teaching on learning outcomes in higher education (see Entwistle, 1992).

Guidance

The moves toward accreditation, the development of modular courses and the creation of an operational credit accumulation and transfer scheme all contribute to a greater awareness of the need for guidance and better information for students. The advice given is, however, often largely dependant on the goodwill and understanding of the tutor and is likely to vary in quality.

Staff development, not only for teaching and assessment but also for student guidance is considered vital for all concerned with the delivery of programmes to ensure a collective understanding of the experience and expectation of the non-traditional learner. It was also clear that there also needs to be a central referral point to which students and tutors can turn, during the life of a course, for advice and information (see Davies and Nedderman, 1997).

Levels of achievement in academic and vocational learning

The concept of academic level has acquired a new significance in the movement to more flexible credit-based modular systems. However, this trend has not been unproblematic. The British education system is not based on an explicit and rational framework of levels that systematically defines the progressive characteristics of learning and attainment. Rather it is based on a series of qualification frameworks whose relationship to level has not been unambiguously defined (see SEEC, 1996a, 1996b). In the absence of a universal levels framework, notions of level are for the most part equated with the phases of the education system. This situation makes it very difficult to articulate levels across awards frameworks, for example, those concerned with either "academic" or "vocational" learning, and this is one barrier to the development of dual accreditation of programmes in different awards frameworks.

Higher education has always distinguished two fundamental levels in its taught programmes: the undergraduate (bachelor degree level) and postgraduate (Master's degree level). This apparently simple structure is however confused by a range of factors including:

*   postgraduate diplomas/certificates level;
*   the distinction between ordinary and honours bachelor degrees;
*   undergraduate Master's awards;
*   Master's level programmes containing elements of undergraduate level programmes;
*   the HND level;
*   the plethora of level sub-structures within the degree level.

The five level NVQ/SVQ/GNVQ vocational awards framework contains two levels which are relevant to HE but the way these articulate with HE levels has been the subject of much debate. To quote from the recent SEEC project report. "Academic degrees and NVQs awarded for occupational competence may have learning outcomes in common but they are essentially designed and awarded to serve two different purposes. NCVQ, therefore, perceive the VQ and academic frameworks as distinct but complementary. Furthermore NCVQ does not accept the notion of direct linear equivalencies between VQ and HE levels" (SEEC, 1996b). After much consideration SEEC recommended that the sector should work towards a broad alignment of NVQ 4 with undergraduate level and NVQ 5 with the postgraduate Master's level.

The development of flexible modular- or unit-based curricula, credit-based learning, and the accreditation of learning acquired outside the HE environment (either by prior study or within a programme) is resulting in a re-conceptualisation of level in some institutions, from one which defines progression in terms of years of full-time (equivalent) study, to one in which progression is defined in terms of the changing characteristics of learning and attainment expected at different stages in a programme.

The elements of academic level descriptors (SEEC, 1996b) which follow at Tables II and III illustrate this:

These descriptors themselves provide a conceptual bridge between notions of academic and generic skills and incorporate the important dimension of context within which skills are demonstrated. The framework can be extended into professional and vocational areas enabling educational practitioners in each of these domains to appreciate the similarities and differences in concept and design between the various domains.

Levels	Characteristics of context	Responsibility	Ethic understanding
M	Complex, unpredictable and normally specialised contexts demanding innovative work which may involve exploring the current limits of knowledge.	Autonomy within bounds of professional practice. High level of responsibility for self, possibly others	Awareness of ethical dilemmas likely to arise in research and professional practice. An ability to formulate solutions in dialogue with peers,clients, mentors and others
3	Complex and unpredictable contexts demanding selection and application from a wide range of innovative or standard techniques	Autonomy in planning and managing resources and processes within broad guidelines.	Awareness of personal responsibility and professional codes of conduct. Ability to incorporate a critical ethical dimension into a major piece of work.
2	Simple but unpredictable or complex but predictable contexts demanding application of a wide range of techniques.	Management of processes within broad guidelines for defined activities.	Awareness of the wider social and environmental implications of area(s) of study. Ability to debate issues in relation to more general ethical perspectives.
1	Defined contexts demanding use of a specified range of standard techniques.	Work is directed, with limited autonomy, within defined guidelines.	Awareness of ethical issues in current area(s) of study. Ability to discuss these in relation to personal beliefs and values.

Table II.
Operational contexts

Table III.
Cognitive descriptors

Levels	Knowledge and understanding	Analysis	Synthesis/creativity	Evaluation
M	Has great depth of knowledge in a complex and specialised area and/or across specialised or applied areas. She/he may be working at the current limited of theoretical and/or research understanding.	Can deal with complexity, lacunae and/or contradictions in the knowledge base and make confident selection of tools for the job.	Can autonomously synthesise information/ideas and create responses to problems that expand or redefine existing knowledge and/or to develop new approaches in new situations.	Can independently evaluate/argue alternative approaches and accurately assess/report on own/others' work with justification.
3	Has a comprehensive/detailed knowledge of (a) major discipline(s) with areas of specialisation in depth and an awareness of the provisional nature of the state of knowledge.	Can analyse new and/or abstract data and situations without guidance, using and wide range of techniques appropriate to the subject.	With minimum guidance, can transform abstract data and concepts towards a given purpose and can design novel solutions.	Can critically review evidence supporting conclusions/recommendations including its reliability, validity and significance and can investigate contradictory information/identify reasons for contradictions.
2	Has a detailed knowledge of (a) major discipline(s) and an awareness of a variety of ideas/contexts/frameworks which may be applied to this.	Can analyse a range of information within minimum guidance, can apply major theories of discipline and can compare alternative methods/techniques for obtaining data.	Can reformat a range of ideas/information towards a given purpose.	Can evaluate the reliability of data using defined techniques and/or tutor guidance.
1	Has a given factual and/or conceptual knowledge base with emphasis on the nature of the field of study and appropriate terminology.	Can analyse with guidance using given classifications/principles.	Can collect/collate and categorise ideas and information in a predictable and standard format	

The levels issue is crucial in establishing parity between awards frameworks. Probably because academic standards are internalised within an institution, in higher education, relatively little attention has been given to this matter. Although there is debate about the details of such descriptors the process of their construction is in itself important in developing a better understanding of the nature of the learning and assessment process.

To summarise, the conditions are now such that it is more likely that the equivalencies between academic awards and vocational qualifications based on work experience and learning in the workplace can be identified. The key reasons for this are related to:

- almost universal development of module and unit-based curricula and the increasing use of learning outcomes;

- almost universal development of credit frameworks and the experience gained in operating such frameworks;

- the move to more regulated environments in order to support flexible curricula arrangements;

- better understanding of the meanings of level in HE including the development and introduction of levels descriptors;

- the considerable developmental work undertaken by the credit consortia in establishing guidelines for the use of credit level descriptors exploring the relationship between academic and vocational awards frameworks;

- the products of various development projects which provide a tool box for mapping across frameworks.

Table IV helps to explain the diversity of programmes in a hypothetical modular university in partnership with other providers, employers and the wider community. Table IV shows how portfolios of modules developed and owned by schools and colleges at post-16 levels can be assembled in different ways within a common regulatory framework to produce programmes of very different character which lead to a variety of academic awards.

The diagram shows the most common types of curriculum linkages between higher education – further education providers and higher education and employers and higher education and the community. The mechanisms for awarding academic credit for learning accomplished in work or community-based environments, against negotiated learning contracts or agreements, have already been developed by a number of universities (Davies, 1995). However, although the HE awards which are made are academic awards, the new framework offers the potential for the dual accreditation of such programmes within both academic and vocational awards frameworks and for constructing new types of programme based partly on academic and partly on vocational credit. Dual accreditation can be identified as one of the key elements of an open system which emanates from the existence of a learning and qualifications framework.

Level	Qualifications (academic)			Qualifications (vocational)
HE Postgrad	M Credit, M Phil, PG Cert/PG Dip/MA/MSc	Research and practitioner doctorate		Vocationally related postgraduate qualifications
HE/CATS 3	Honours First Degree, B Phil		NVQ 5	Vocationally related degrees PGCE
HE/CATS 2	Diploma in Higher Education		NVQ 4	HND/HNC Professional qualifications
HE/CATS 1	Certificate in Higher Education		NVQ 4	HND/HNC
FE/OCN 3	GCE, A/AS Level	Modern apprenticeship as employment	NVQ 3	GNVQ Advanced Technician Access to HE courses (AVA)
FE/OCN 2	GCSE (A-C)	National Curriculum Youth Training and employment	NVQ 2	GNVQ Intermediate Broad-based craftsmen
FE/OCN 1	GCSE (D-G)	National Curriculum	NVQ 1	GNVQ Foundation Craft Certificates skilled
Adult Basic Entry			Entry level awards	Semi-skilled

Table IV.
Post 16 awards and
qualifications

There are three areas where there is likely to be a demand for such dual accreditation:

(1) area of the accreditation of generic core skills within the HE curriculum;

(2) growing area of partnership or client-negotiated programmes where a university designs and delivers, in partnership with an employer, a customised programme. Learning can involve mixtures of institution-based teaching; in-company research; work-based learning; distance learning and intensive residential study;

(3) area relates to the many individuals who, for personal or professional reasons, would like to participate in a structured and accredited higher level learning process but for whom a complete award-bearing programme would be inappropriate.

Competence and skills
The growth of an increasingly open pedagogy and the emergence of learning frameworks has created a demand for a new curriculum whose focus is less on the traditional academic subjects and more on the individual's achievements.

An increasingly significant development focus for higher education now is on the theme of personal competence and skills. We can identify three main categories which can be subsumed within the notion of competence-based achievement:

- generic or core competence: which includes personal attributes and characteristics and personal transferable skills (also known as core, generic, or common skills);

- occupational competence: ability to perform to recognised standards in the relevant occupational field defined in terms of job-specific outcomes;

- professional competence: performance and capability (see Eraut, 1994).

It might also be worth considering the notion of academic competence as a subset of professional competence in so far as it illuminates the extent to which higher education develops such competencies and skills in its practitioners. The accreditation of academic and vocational learning is a major issue on the agenda of higher education in the second half of the 1990s (see Lloyd-Langton and Portwood, 1994) and even within the liberal tradition of education, it is evident that many students make their study choices for reasons of vocational relevance, as well as personal development.

It is fair to say that some academics have been antagonistic to the idea that the vocational qualifications and occupational standards model would have any general application within higher education. There are four significant developments which are perhaps improving the conditions that will enable educational practitioners to view the idea of assessment models and standards which are based on competency, and the expanding "learning workplace" more favourably.

First, in an attempt to meet one of the primary criticisms of both the academic and professional communities vocational qualifications are now giving greater recognition to the importance of the underpinning knowledge required to demonstrate competency. The definition of competence given in the Beaumont Report (1996) "the ability to apply knowledge, understanding and skills in performing to the standards required in employment. This includes solving problems and meeting changing demands", indicates clearly this important philosophical and conceptual shift.

Second, a development project undertaken by Cheetham and Chivers (1996) has shown how a more holistic model of professional competence might be developed by marrying the "learning outcomes" approach to competence with the notion of the "reflective practitioner". Notions of the latter are expected of, and embedded in many academic cultures and thus there is likely to be an important element of shared language, understanding and empathy in any frameworks which express competence in such terms. This is a model which the academic community might well consider beyond the fields of education psychology and management development where it is embedded (see Schon, 1983; Wills, 1993).

Third, higher education has itself responded to varying degrees to the increasing expectations of society that a degree will equip learners with certain generic attributes, qualities and skills variously described as core skills, personal transferable skills, employment-related and enterprise skills. This has led to increased opportunities for the development of such skills in higher

education and to new strategies for assessment and recording achievement
(Otter, 1997).

The extent to which the development of such generic skills is made explicit
and the relative value placed on such skills in the assessment process is often
not, however, explicit. This is particularly difficult to achieve in flexible
modular schemes with many routes and pathways. This is necessitating the
development of mapping tools to show where such skills are taught, practised
and assessed.

The increased focus on providing opportunities for the development of
generic skills, the development of personal profiling and the emphasis on
learners to reflect on and identify their specific needs are particularly noticeable
in institutions which have embraced the higher education for capability
movement. Of course competence is not the same as capability, but it is allied to
it. In vocational frameworks competence refers to the ability to perform the task
to predefined standards relating to work environments. Capability is a broader
concept, involving personal development and intellectual ability, but the
evaluation of capability involves an evaluation of what people can do against
explicit objectives and outcomes.

The systematic process of developing generic skills across the curriculum in
a flexible modular framework requires commitment to a whole institution
policy which in turn must be aligned to the educational objectives of the
institution. Such policies in themselves constitute an important bridge between
the academic and vocational domains and the institutions which develop them
are most likely to be comfortable with the concept of working across these
domains.

One of the potential benefits of dual accreditation of academic and vocational
learning will be to make the educational orientation more explicit by
identifying the extent to which generic skills and vocational skills and
competencies are being developed. This will be helpful to those teaching and
assessing the programme and will provide additional information to learners
and employers.

A strength of the framework for dual accreditation of generic skills is that it
recognises that the HE curriculum can provide for such skills in a variety of
ways. Some institutions, particularly at level 1, have introduced specific
modules for this purpose. Others, have produced a range of self-study/self-
assessment packs which support the development of core skills. However, the
vast majority of programmes aim to develop such skills across the whole
curriculum. In order to achieve dual accreditation in this model it would need to
be combined with profiling for individual students, combined with evidence
gathering and personal reflection strategies for example through personal logs,
and portfolios of evidence of achievement.

This section has tried to show how the conditions within which the open
paradigm for learning and lifelong learning itself might have improved
dramatically during recent years through the widespread development of:

- curriculum frameworks which are more responsive and flexible and which facilitate the design of a wide range of different types of programme;

- frameworks and policies which enable the accreditation of learning in both academic and non-academic environments and which facilitate learner mobility;

- a growing awareness and appreciation of the range and inter-relationships of academic-generic-vocational-professional skills and competencies;

- awareness and application of outcomes-based approaches in the design and assessment of the curriculum;

- the development of methodologies and tools for mapping skills across the curriculum and the recording of achievement through profiling techniques.

These changes have been accompanied by cultural and attitudinal shifts as new educational values and expectations have developed; as innovators explore uncharted territories, and as new vocationally-orientated subjects have been incorporated into the academic domain.

The learning framework: conclusions
The demand for and acceptability of credit
Broadening student constituencies in continuing education and lifelong learning have created a need for a more adaptive and responsive credit system. It is clear that a large proportion of the students attending University courses nationally can benefit from accredited continuing education (CE) provision (Davies, 1995). But understanding of, and attitudes towards, credit can vary considerably. Many older, often already highly-educated, students accept accreditation reluctantly as an integral part of higher education courses whilst others actively seek credit as a means to a recognised qualification for personal and career development.

Outcomes and assessment
The fullest range of achievement for learners can be recognised through a learning outcomes approach to credit, and by the adoption of clear criteria for student assessment. User-friendly assessment can be integrated into the learning process and at the same time meet appropriate standards criteria.

Academic and vocational credit within continuing education and employment
There is no single site of learning, neither is learning restricted to a particular age or stage in life. Higher education providers are adapting to the need to offer credit for appropriate learning wherever it takes place; at home, at work or at college. Accreditation for the full range of lifelong learning is possible, desirable and can be mapped onto certificated study programmes.

Quality and standards
The award of credit is the start of a cycle of quality assurance which includes external moderation yet allows tutors and learners a high degree of autonomy.

Implications for approaches to teaching, learning and assessment
Tutors are integral to the process of course design and delivery. All models and styles of teaching need to build in elements of assessment as part of the process of learning and tutors must be recognised as key players in the process. However, students also need to be actively involved in the learning process if credit is to be an intrinsic part of their achievement.

Local, regional and national networks
Collaborative networking of education provision with many organisations and agencies is vital to gain progression and transfer opportunities for students. The rules by which credit can be accumulated and transferred towards an award must be clear in order to facilitate coherent patterns of study for students and to safeguard academic standards.

Cultural and institutional change
Credit culture challenges older traditions of exclusion within higher education and requires the democratic engagement and support of the student body, the teachers, the employers and those communities which are the new and emerging sites of learning.

The need for guidance
The need for guidance arrangements must be recognised if adult learners are to benefit from credit and use it for the purposes of access and progression.

APEL
Prior learning and previous experience must be recognised as a legitimate source of credit within the conventional qualifications hierarchy at all levels.

The learner's world
The purposes of education are not negated by credit and the impact on learning made by the learning framework but they do require to be restated. Credit is about measuring achievement in learning and is an increasingly significant part of student progression and opportunity as the era of lifelong learning unfolds.

References
Please refer to Chapter 4.

Chapter 4

Lifelong learning competency in the twenty-first century – a prospectus

David Davies

Deputy Principal, Westhill University College, Birmingham, UK

Continuous change – the need for lifelong learning

Continuous learning is becoming a key issue for persons, for organisations, for nations, and for whole continents. The group of "G7" industrial countries has declared lifelong learning to be a main strategy in the fight against unemployment and there can be little doubt that the more learning an individual can acquire and demonstrate, the greater the chances are for achievement and success in economic life. In the UK lifelong learning has become a major policy objective of successive governments (DfEE, 1996; Fryer Report, 1997).

There are large international companies which estimate that their future profits will be generated with half of their current number of employees, and who will be expected to have twice the level of competence and provide three times the added value compared with the employees of today. More and more employees belong to that group who are outside the core business of the company. They either have to sell their skills and competences on an open market or learn and acquire new and marketable skills. In either case individuals need to renew, upgrade and update competences and skills demanded in the labour market. This need translates into a new emerging lifelong market for basic, further, and continuing education and training on a lifelong basis. As lifetime employment vanishes each individual needs to take on the responsibility for his or her own competence development and education. The best job security is a knowledge base which allows an individual to learn quickly the requirements of a new job. Flexibility and adaptability are key skills for economic security.

What is lifelong learning?

Lifelong learning is simply a predisposition at the individual level to acquire the habit of continuous curiosity. However, it has fundamental significance also at both social and economic levels:

- lifelong learning develops a person's competence throughout his/her lifetime. Competence includes knowledge, skills, capabilities, experience, contacts and networking, attitudes and values;

This article first appeared in the *Journal of Workplace Learning*, Vol. 10 No. 4, 1998, pp. 206-213.

- lifelong learning includes all learning that takes place in different areas of life. It includes formal and informal education and training. Lifelong learning is not only about formal educational achievement;

- lifelong learning is a continuous development process which can be said to belong to an individual. Lifelong learning is not a one-off event, nor a short course;

- lifelong learning provides an individual with the ability to live in a continuously changing world and to cope with a changing society and working life.

Individual competence and lifelong learning

Individual competence involves not merely the gaining of factual knowledge and acquisition of skills. It is also experience gained in all areas of life. Experience provides us with a framework into which we can integrate all new forms of knowledge. Modern communication technologies are constantly transforming the economic infrastructures through which capital, labour and the productive processes on which wealth generation and employment depend. These processes are ever more globally organised as is the circulation of finance and investment capital. Castells (1996) argues that we must conceptualise modern society as a complex network of communication capable of enormous and radical transformations. In modern networking society interpersonal and communal links and associations are an important part of competence. At the level of individual action, values and attitudes determine how willing and motivated a person is to learn and adapt to new situations. Many employers, for example, consider that attitude is the most important criterion when recruiting individuals – is the person capable of adapting to the future requirements and to the vision of the organisation?

Lifelong learning develops all elements of human competence and is, therefore, authentically part of a progressive vision of modern life. Figure 1 outlines the elements involved in lifelong learning.

Challenges for universities

The role of conventional universities has in many respects remained unchanged for centuries. Education has been seen as a foundational phase in a person's life. At the year 2000 and beyond, however, the need for a vastly expanded education system, the diverse expectations placed on learning achievements and the revolution in the methods of learning provide universities and other educational institutions with new roles, new potential and new challenges.

In today's rapidly-changing economic environment and in a de-stabilised society where the certainties of tradition are breaking down, the traditional role of universities as providers of knowledge is greatly challenged. Individuals, trained in specific fields, must cope with business demands that require them to continuously renew their knowledge and competence. Lifelong learners thus become potential customers for universities throughout their lives. Universities for their part are no longer willing or able to be confined to their campuses. The world of learning has, through the use of new communication technologies, and the adoption of open pedagogies and learning frameworks, become truly global.

Adults as students

As the higher education system expands globally (see Dalichov, 1997; Duke, 1992; House, 1991), it is increasingly clear that universities are serving mature adult students, many of whom are working while studying, in very large numbers and that this phenomenon has significant implications for how teaching and learning is organised.

Adult students have already gained experience that helps them to quickly learn new things; they are motivated to learn if they can implement the learning at work. Adult students are often specialists themselves who do not need to be taught. They do not need education, as such! Instead, they need tutoring, guiding, counselling, and access to tools for learning. The open paradigm is, for most adult learners, the most appropriate means of fostering and recognising their learning.

When we consider what students achieve, competence acquired through learning is viewed by most adults as a personal asset in which individuals are

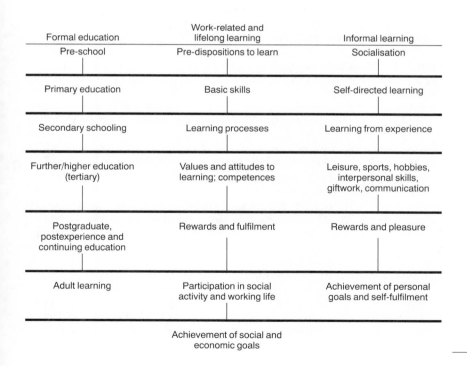

Figure 1.
Elements of lifelong learning

willing to invest. However, it is important that the individual's investment in education be recognised and accepted in the modern international job market. Credits, diplomas, and degrees serve as both signs of personal assets, as well as concrete milestones for lifelong learning. However, since credits for learning achievement are the general prerogative of individual universities within national boundaries, international, transferable credit schemes are needed in order to serve the global needs. Internationally recognised credit allows lifelong learners to transport their knowledge and skills from region to region and country to country – an absolute necessity in the international and increasingly global market place (see Castells, 1996; Dalichov, 1997).

Partnership with working life
The need for increasing employee competence is growing rapidly and the professionalisation of work at all levels is gaining ground. Businesses are now looking for new approaches to competence development and human resource development that will share the development responsibilities and commitment (see Teare *et al.*, 1997). They are seeking partnership with professional providers of education and training; alliances with those organisations whose core activity is competence and capability development of the individuals who comprise their core workforce. The future for lifelong learning is likely to be based on interactive partnerships between the worlds of management and work-based learning and that of open and virtual university networks and frameworks which are described in this volume.

New roles in networks
On a global basis industry is restructuring in networks with members of different sizes and types. The competitiveness of a network requires that all members meet the same competence requirements. An industry network needs a partner who can take care of the competence development needs of the network and the provision of learning opportunities for all network members. These tasks could well be organised and developed by universities which conceivably have a new role in industry networks as the developers and co-ordinators of network-based competences and as the providers of network-based competence opportunities. In a "network society" such as that posed by Manuel Castells, universities must begin to re-define their role and functions. If the challenge is great, so is the scope for development as higher education becomes ever more universal and ever more central to the idea of a learning society.

Lifelong learning infrastructure
Lifelong learning requires an infrastructure containing providers and distributors of education, training and learning; common principles and policies; accreditation systems; degrees and diplomas; methods of transferring learning into credits and a usable framework for credit accumulation and transfer.

Universities, it can be plausibly asserted, should provide an international lifelong learning infrastructure which makes it possible to continue studies in another country without detriment to the credit for learning achievement already acquired. The infrastructure should also provide for Europe-wide (or even global) recognition of personal and professional competences. In practice, a good infrastructure implies that universities agree on basic rules for recognition and credits, and the principles of credit transfer. They also need to agree to co-operate in providing competence development and learning for both individuals and organisations.

The infrastructure for lifelong learning needs to form a common framework with common principles and policies for providing learning opportunities, assessing learning outcomes, accrediting learning achievements and transferring credit. The principles should include the following:

- study and learning modules which recognise various levels and amounts of achievement;
- flexible combinations of modules;
- individual study/learning plans;
- recognition of individual learning styles;
- many providers and many modes of learning;
- common principles for assessing and accrediting learning achievement;
- transfer and accumulation of credits;
- industry-university co-operation networks;
- recognition of prior learning and experience (APEL).

Towards open systems
Educational institutions have long been very much closed systems. Earlier chapters have documented the emergence of open paradigms for learning and teaching which take universities beyond the single dimension of a campus-based institution. Being part of multi-dimensional networks means that universities and educational institutions may interact in different ways and in various directions. Being innovative and proactive means that they should be sensitive to changes and new demands. Understanding that they are parts of various processes highlights the importance of their relationships with many external partners. As a result of all this, they cannot be closed systems; instead they have to be open systems which have interactive relationships with many partners (Wheatley, 1994). Learning can thus take place anywhere and everywhere and cannot be forever constrained by traditional boundaries which are of dubious relevance to modern needs. Universities and other promoters of learning must become open systems, living organisms which are in a dynamic relationship with other organisms in society and are there where learning is taking place. This may not of course be inside the walls of the campus!

From teaching to learning organisations

The university itself should have an organisational structure which allows continuous development of its students' core competencies. The core modules which define competence could be combined according to each student's needs and be complemented by a customised cluster of competences for each client or client group. Departments could build up flexible curricula and recommended paths for degrees and diplomas from the modules provided by academic pools for different customer groups. This concept of the university insists that a learner-centred approach should be taken which structures the organisation into processes based on client/learner needs. This is the practical expression of the open paradigm for learning.

Universities are becoming genuine learning organisations and providers of a wide variety of opportunities for lifelong learning. The learning organisation analyses future competence needs and communicates them to students. It provides learning opportunities in the areas of its own core competencies and access to other areas through its development networks. The learning organisation gives lifelong learners a support network. For example, study counsellors help learners to make their personal learning and development plans with individual learning objectives. This may involve acquiring certificated awards such as certificates and diplomas as part of a degree or a pathway of studies recognised by the university or other educational institutions. Tutors help learners to access the best sources of learning and to acquire a combination of study modules and experience learning situations that meet both quantitative and qualitative learning targets. Universities can also assist employers to provide employees with mentoring and can help company managers and team leaders to become corporate leaders of learning. These features figure largely in the vision of the virtual university described in later chapters, yet in aspiring to this we must remember to remain committed to the variety and diversity of learning required by an open system. In relation to the question of learning competences it may be the case that a new set of core competences will emerge as the university itself begins to view itself as a learning rather than a teaching organisation.

New skills and competences

To meet the challenges outlined in these four chapters it has been argued that new tasks and new ways of operating require new skills on the part of teachers and learners. It is no longer enough to be an expert in a subject discipline and thus students must be multi-skilled as well as possessing a range of core skills and competences. A university's expertise must now cover not only subject knowledge but a spectrum of key abilities which a competent graduate has mastered as part of the degree programme.

Table I lists the new abilities requiring individuals, to go beyond subject expertise. Such abilities could be the basis of an "abilities curriculum", as suggested by Otter (1997) and also assist in the recognition of core skills required at higher education levels of achievement.

Continuous competency and competitive advantage

There can be no conclusions to the "prospectus" outlined in these opening chapters. The only certainty, as the truism puts it, is that there can be no certainties and that change will occur continuously, if unevenly and in unsuspected ways. It is worth noting, however, that there are certain key features apparent which are shaping the emerging systems of learning. There is, as we have seen, a "learning framework" in existence and some key values, practices and paradigmatic activities are already in place. Teachers are already convinced that they must be facilitators of learning rather than transmitters of pre-digested subject knowledge. Knowledge construction between learner-teacher and the learning environment is accepted as a desired objective as is the methodology of active reflection rather than passive evaluation of learning experience. There is a growing acceptance of the concept of open learning systems which seek to offer learning opportunities at all ages and stages of life. Continuous learning is the focus of discourse rather than the language of

Problem solving, managing tasks	Focusing on achieving key objectives
	Using analytical and conceptual thinking
	Search information and apply techniques
	Making decisions
Team work	Using logical and rational argument to persuade others
	Sharing information to achieve goals
	Understanding the needs of others and building positive relationships
Creativity and imagination	Able to provide new solutions and choices
	Able to seek alternative solutions
Communication skills	Oral and written skills
	Ability to express oneself verbally
	Listening skills – counselling skills
Self-awareness	Taking responsibility for one's own learning
	Dealing with pressures and emotions
	Knowing one's own mental models
	Able to adapt mental models to changed circumstances
	Setting realistic targets for oneself and others
	Being aware of changes, curiosity
Managing	Retrieving, analysing and synthesising data information and information
	Using information technology
Systems thinking	Understanding the whole picture of the meaning of how things are related
	Application of knowledge to practical tasks
Learning skills	Learning to learn
	Understanding one's own learning style
	Understanding learning processes
Personal mastery	Personal vision and values
	Strong sense of reality
	Understanding the value of competency
	Able to move from competence to "capability"

Table I.
Core competencies for
lifelong learning

phases and stages. Learning experience is sought as opposed to immersion in a sequence of taught lessons.

If there is a learning society currently being borne in the interstices of the old forms of schooling and education, then it is being manifested in the new systems of learning and communication dealt with in this study. However, a virtual reality, if it is to be "real", must build upon the competencies and skills outlined above, and there are new competencies required to meet these new needs. Individuals will be required to excel in abstract and creative thinking, in experimentation and in collaborative and enterprising learning. Their knowledge will be "constructed" as they progress through the phases of formal and informal learning. Work will undoubtedly play a major part in the shaping of each individual's learning agenda and each individual will be called on to develop and integrate their own learning skills over a lifetime of meaningful work and learning activity. The university system will play its part as a progressive and open system as described in these chapters and its emergence within a "virtual" reality is imminent.

However, as individual institutions respond to the emerging need for new competencies and lifelong learning opportunities, there will be a need to spell out how the education system can help us adapt, survive and succeed in an increasingly globalising economic environment. Higher education is increasingly important to economic competitiveness and to social cohesion and the benefits of both, it can be argued, are co-terminous.

Competitive economic advantage flows from:

- Open and recurrent access to education and training for all who can benefit.
- The highest levels of educational achievement for the greatest number who are able to benefit.
- Systems for vocational, technical and specialised training.
- High, explicit and rising standards.
- Investment of finance and social capital.
- Mobility of trained and specialist personnel.
- Creativity and the freedom to innovate.
- Respected and high quality HE outside Universities.
- An opportunity culture and widened participation.
- Many citizens moving into Science and Technology.
- Academic learning to include vocational education and training.
- Partnership in provision of lifelong learning.
- Close connection between education and employment.

- Companies investing heavily in ongoing training and personal growth for individuals.
- Individual and social worth and value recognised in diverse ways.

At the level of the learning organisation we shall need to spell out the core competencies and abilities of lifelong learning that we shall sponsor within the new and open learning organisations. Universities, whether virtual or conventional, will need to demonstrate and deliver this agenda for competitive market success and individual achievement. The question of lifelong learning is thus central to the future of not only universities but to the core economic and social agendas which sustain our way of life.

Abbreviations
"Access" preparatory courses leading to higher education for mature adult students

AP(E)L	Accreditation of prior experiential learning
APL	Accreditation of prior learning
CAT(S)	Credit accumulation and transfer (systems)
CNAA	Council for National Academic Awards (now defunct)
DFEE	Department for Education and Employment – (Government)
FE	Further Education (sector)
FEU	Further Education Unit (of the DES)
GCE	General Certificate of Education ("A" level)
GCSE	General Certificate of Secondary Education
GNVQ	General National Vocational Qualification(s)
HE	Higher Education (sector)
HECIW	Higher Education Consortium for Credit in Wales
HEFC(E)	Higher Education Funding Council (England)
HEI(s)	Higher Education Institutions
HEQC	Higher Education Quality Council
IMC	International Management Centres – Buckingham
IPPR	Institute for Public Policy Research
InCCA	Inter-Consortium Credit Agreement
IQ	Intelligence quotient
Key skills	Applied skills which underpin effective performance in work and life, e.g. communication, numeracy, problem solving.
Lifelong learning and lifetime learning	The means by which people have ongoing opportunities to develop their talents
NCVQ	National Council for Vocational Qualifications (now QCA, Qualifications, Curriculum Agency)
NUCCAT	Northern Universities Consortium for Credit Accumulation and Transfer
NVQ(s)	National Vocational Qualification(s)
PPD	Personal and Professional Development (programme)

SEEC	South East England Consortium for Credit Accumulation and Transfer
SVQs	Scottish Vocational Qualification(s) (equivalent to NVQs)
SCOTCAT	Scottish Credit Accumulation and Transfer
TEC	Training and Enterprise Council(s)
OCN	Open College Network(s)
UCE	University continuing education
VQ	Vocational Qualifications
WEA	Worker's Education Association
WBL	Work-based learning

References

Allen, V.L. (1975), *Social Analysis,* Longman, Harlow, Essex.

Atkins, J., Beattie, W.B. and Dockrell (1993), *Assessment Issues in Higher Education*, Department of Employment.

Beaumont, G. (1996), *Review of 100 NVQs and SVQs*, DfEE – Report, London.

Brown, S. and Knight, P. (1994), *Assessment in Higher Education,* Kogan Page, London.

Brown, S., Rust, C. and Gibbs, G. (1994), *Strategies for Diversifying Assessment in Higher Education*, Centre for Staff Development, Oxford.

Bruffee, K.A. (1995), *Collaborative Learning: Higher Education, Interdependence and the Authority of Knowledge,* Johns Hopkins University Press, Baltimore, MI.

Bruner, J.S. (1962), *On Knowing,* Harvard University Press, Cambridge, MA.

Bruner, J.S. (1968), *Toward a Theory of Instruction*, W.W. Norton, New York, NY.

Castells, M. (1996), *The Rise of the Network Society*, Blackwell, Oxford.

Cheetham, G. and Chivers, G. (1996), "Towards a holistic model of professional competence", *Journal of European Industrial Training,* Vol. 20 No. 5, pp. 20-30.

Dalichov, F. (1997), "A comparative study of academic credit systems in an international context", *Journal of Studies in International Education*, Autumn, pp. 21-32.

Davies, D. (1995), *Credit Where It's Due,* Employment Department, University of Cambridge.

Davies, D. (1997), "From the further education margins to the higher education centre?, Innovation in continuing education", *Education and Training,* Vol. 39 No. 1.

Davies, D. and Nedderman, V. (1997), "Information and on-course guidance to continuing education students", *Managing Guidance in Higher Education,* HEQC, London, pp. 46-55.

Dearing, Sir R. (1997), *Summary Report – Higher Education in the Learning Society*, National Committee of Inquiry into Higher Education, NCIHE, Crown Copyright, July.

DFEE (1996), *Lifelong Learning: A Policy Framework,* HMSO, DfEE, London.

Duke, C. (1992), *The Learning University – Towards a New Paradigm,* Open University Press, Buckingham.

Ecclestone, K. (1994), *Understanding Assessment: A Guide for Teachers and Managers in Post-Compulsory Education,* NIACE.

Employment Department, (1993), *Assessment Issues in Higher Education.*

Entwistle, N. (1992), *The Impact of Teaching on Learning Outcomes in Higher Education*, CVCP, London.

Eraut, M. (1994), *Developing Professional Knowledge and Competence*, Falmer Press, London.

Evans, N. (1984), *Access to Higher Education: Non-standard Entry to CNAA First Degree and DipHE Courses*, CNAA Development Services Publication, CNAA, London.

FEU (Further Education Unit) (1992), *A Basis for Credit?*, FEU, London.

FEU (Further Education Unit) (1994), *Towards a Credit Framework,* FEU project Report, University of Cambridge.

Finegold, D. *et al.* (1992), *Higher Education – Expansion and Reform,* IPRR, London.

Fryer Report (1997), *Learning for the 21st Century, National Advisory Group for Continuing Education and Lifelong Learning,* DfEE, November, London.

Gagne, R.M. (1965), *The Conditions of Learning,* Holt, Rheinhart and Winston, New York, NY.

Giddens, A. (1990), *The Consequences of Modernity,* Polity Press, Cambridge.

Gleeson, D. (1990), *The Paradox of Training: Making Progress out of Crisis,* Open University Press, Milton Keynes.

Gleeson, D. (1993) (unpublished), *Legislating for Change: Missed Opportunities in the Further and Higher Education Act,* Keele University.

Green, M. (1971), "Curriculum and consciousness", *Teachers College Record,* Vol. 73 No. 2, December.

HEQC (1994), *Guidelines on the Quality Assurance of Credit-Based Learning,* HEQC, London.

HEQC (1995), *Towards a Better Understanding of the Meaning of Academic Standards in Modular Design,* HEQC, September, London.

Hillman, J. (1996), *A University for Industry: Creating a National Learning Network,* IPPR, London.

House, D.H.B. (1991), *Continuing Liberal Education,* National University Continuing Education Association, New York, NY.

InCCA (1997) (Inter-Consortium Credit Agreement), (SEEC and Anglia Polytechnic University) involving SEEC, HECIW and NUCCAT.

Kelly, G. (1955), *The Psychology of Personal Constructs,* Volumes 1 and 2, W.W. Norton & Co., New York, NY.

Knowles, M.S. (1970), *The Modern Practice of Adult Education,* Associated Press, New York, NY.

Knowles, M.S. (1981), *The Adult Learner: A Neglected Species,* 2nd ed., Gulf, Houston, TX.

Knowles, M.S. (1983), "An andragogical theory of adult learning", *Learning about Learning: Selected Readings,* Open University Press, Milton Keynes.

Kuhn, T.S. (1970), *The Structure of Scientific Revolutions,* University of Chicago Press, Chicago, IL.

Lloyd-Langton, M. and Portwood, D. (1994), "Dual accreditation of work based learning: the relation of NVQs and academic credit", *Journal of Higher and Further Education,* Vol. 18 No. 2, Summer.

Meade, G.H. (1962), *Mind, Self and Society,* University of Chicago Press, Chicago, IL.

Mumford, A. (1996), "Creating a learning environment", *Journal of Professional Human Resource Management,* 4 July, pp. 26-30.

Otter, S. (Ed.) (1992), *Learning Outcomes in Higher Education,* Unit for the Development of Adult Continuing Education (UDACE), Leicester.

Otter, S. (1997), *An Abilities Curriculum,* Department for Education and Employment.

Parry, G. (1986), "From patronage to partnership", *Journal of Access Studies,* Vol. 1 No. 1, April, pp. 43-53.

Perkins, H. (1990), *The Rise of Professional Society: England since 1880,* Routledge, London.

Piaget, J. (1932), *The Moral Judgement of the Child,* RKP, London.

Piaget, J. (1973), *The Child's Conception of the World,* Paladin, London.

Piore, M. and Sabel, C.F. (1984), *The Second Industrial Divide: Possibilities for Property,* Basic Books, New York, NY.

Revans, R.W. (1971), *Developing Effective Managers,* Longman and Praeger.

Revans, R.W. (1982), *The Origins and Growth of Action Learning,* Chartwell Bratt.

Revans, R.W. (1983), *The ABC of Action Learning*, Chartwell Bratt.

Revans, R.W. (1984), *The Sequence of Managerial Achievement,* MCB University Press, Bradford.

Robertson, D. (1993), *Higher Education – Expansion and Reform*, Institute for Public Policy Research, London.

Robertson, D. (1994), *Choosing to Change: Extending Access, Choice and Mobility*, HEQC, London.

Rogers, C. (1974), *On Becoming a Person,* Constable, London.

Schon, D.A. (1983), *The Reflective Practitioner: How Professionals Think in Action*, Basic Books, New York, NY.

SEEC (1996a), *Credit Guidelines, Models and Protocols*, May.

SEEC (1996b), *Guidelines for Credit and Consortium General Credit Rating*, SEEC/DfEE.

Sherman, B. (1995), *Licensed to Work,* Cassell, London.

Simosko, S. (1991), *APL – A Practical Guide for Professionals.*

Skillbeck, M., (1970), *John Dewey*, Collier- Macmillan, London.

Spencer, D. and Wynne, R. (1990), *Embedding Learner Autonomy in Further Education in Wales,* WJEC, Cardiff.

Spours, K. and Young, M. (1988), *Beyond Vocationalism: A New Perspective on the Relationship between Work and Education,* University of London Institute of Education, London.

Squires, G. (1987), *The Curriculum beyond School,* Hodder & Stoughton, London.

Teare, R. (1998), *Developing a Curriculum for Organisational Learning,* MCB University Press, Bradford.

Teare, R., Ingram, H., Scheuing, E. and Armistead, C. (1997), "Organisational teamworking frameworks: evidence from UK and US-based firms", *International Journal of Service Industry Management,* Vol. 8 No. 5.

Theodossin, E. (1986), *The Modular Market*, FESC, Bristol.

Wheatley, M. (1994), *Leadership and the New Science, Learning and Organisation from an Orderly Universe,* Berrett-Koehler Publishers, San Francisco, CA.

Wills, G. (1993), *Your Enterprise School of Management,* MCB University Press, Bradford.

Wills, G. (1997), *Engendering Democratic Action,* MCB University Press, Bradford.

Wilson, J.P. (1980), "Individual learning in groups", in Boyd, R.D. *et al.* (Eds), *Redefining the Discipline of Adult Education,* Jossey-Bass, San Francisco, CA.

Wittman, L.C. (1989), *Working Class Education: Towards a Relevant Relationship between Work and Education,* University of London Institute of Education, October.

SECTION 2

A prospectus for organizational learning in the workplace

Richard Teare

Chapter 5
Supporting managerial learning in the workplace
Richard Teare

*Granada Professor, Oxford Brookes University, and Academic Chair,
International Management Centres*

Introduction
Evidence suggests that more and more organizations are attempting to establish a culture of learning that values the knowledge that employees have derived from learning how to perform effectively in the workplace. However, an organizational initiative to "learn more and do better" is unlikely to flourish if it is imposed and the contention here is that it is necessary to begin by encouraging and motivating individuals to learn and to take the initiative in identifying their own learning needs. This article reviews recent contributions to the literature on aspects of managerial learning and addresses the question "how do managers learn best in the workplace?" The review is drawn from articles published between 1994-1996 in eight journals: *Executive Development; Journal of Management Development; Journal of Organizational Change Management; Leadership & Organization Development Journal; Management Development Review; Team Performance Management; The Journal of Workplace Learning; The Learning Organization.* The review focuses on four themes: managerial learning and work; coaching, mentoring and team development; competences, managerial learning and the curriculum; work-based action learning and concludes with a summary of the implications for managerial learning.

Theme 1: managerial learning and work
The relationships between managerial learning and work are wide-ranging and Table I identifies a number of sub-themes that reflect this. The variables include: how managerial work is defined and how individual work preferences influence work styles, managers' use of their time and interpersonal communications; identifying and realizing the potential for development and the means of achieving it through formal and informal learning goals.

Shenhar and Renier (1996) see the main task of management as "getting results through the work of others for the benefit of the client". They depict a parallel process of questioning and applying skills and knowledge, drawn from four sub-domains – technical, human, operational and strategic. The key tasks stem from the "what" and "how" of managing:

This article first appeared in *International Journal of Contemporary Hospitality Management,* Vol. 9 No. 7, 1997, pp. 304-314.

Authors	Focus	Sub-theme
Shenhar and Renier (1996)	Applies a modular approach to defining managerial work and roles so that managers can assess the complexities of their own jobs and related development needs	Defining managerial work
Margerison and McCann (1996b)	Outlines the eight main types of work in organizations (advising, innovating, promoting, developing, organizing, producing, inspecting, maintaining) and advocates self-profiling or work preferences so as to understand and work effectively with others	Preferences and managerial work
Oshagbemi (1995)	Discusses the nature and the reality of managerial work and how managers spend their time	Managers' use of their time
Margerison and McCann (1996a)	Profiles five key communication skills – enquiring, diagnosing, summarizing, proposing and directing. Relates these skills to either a problem-centred or solution-centred focus and describes a self-assessment resource for use in personal and team development	Communication skills and managerial work
Dixon (1995a, 1995b)	Summarizes a study undertaken in 46 privatized firms concerned with middle managers and their attitudes towards the culture change they had experienced during the privatization process	Middle management potential and development
Megginson (1994)	Considers the challenges posed by helping managers to learn when they are reluctant to take responsibility for the direction of their own development or seem unable to learn from their own experiences	Planned and emergent managerial learning
Mumford (1994)	Investigates how managers learn from experience with reference to a study of 21 directors in 15 UK organizations and proposes four managerial approaches (intuitive, incidental, retrospective and prospective)	Learning from experience
Barclay (1996)	Emphasizes the value of real world experience in learning about management – especially interpersonal skills development, learning about one's organization and industry and learning how to manage personal development and self-understanding	Learning from experience with learning logs

Table I.
Managerial learning and
work

- What is management? – spans aspects of science and art; encompasses people, technology and money; relates to the systemized use of resources, processes, situations and relations; involves taking responsibility for achieving results, for people and for organizational activity.
- How to manage? – requires information gathering, decision taking and action; uses and develops interpersonal skills, involves planning, organizing, staffing, leading and controlling.

Commenting on the patterns and interactions associated with managerial work, Oshagbemi (1995) observes that:

> …not only are managerial functions varied, but also the locations where these are performed, the people managers interact with and the duration of managerial activities. In addition, managers experience different forms of fleeting contacts and interruptions during the course of their working day. This is a feature that may hinder their creative work, if care is not taken (p. 32).

His findings suggest that improvements in the use of managerial time can be obtained by focusing attention on: the management of meetings; the management of paper and desk work activities; delegation and supervision and the management of fleeting contacts and interruptions.

McKenna (1994) reviews the changes that are affecting managerial work – he sees increasing discontinuity, uncertainty, ambiguity and complexity – and believes that traditional approaches to management development are not sufficiently flexible to cope with these conditions. Instead, he proposes a forum for "generative learning" so that managers can challenge assumptions and paradigms; enable participants to challenge themselves and achieve "higher order" learning that enlightens rather than merely refreshes. Personal learning needs are central to the forum concept so that "value added" initiatives are generated from the reality of the middle manager's own world. In order to capture own world realities, McKenna advocates the use of a "complexity map" (Figure 1). The complexity map seeks to portray a personalized view of reality for each participant attending the forum and a snapshot of how their learning needs are woven into it and might be deduced from it. In particular, the map helps to identify some of the personal paradigms and assumptions that need to be challenged in order to "stretch" the participant. In so doing, the map provides a basis for action by depicting the reality-based "real plays" that confront participants, together with the patterns and interrelationships on which they need to act in order to leverage personal development and business improvement gains from the complexities that surround them. This form of cognitive mapping offers a dynamic and personalized means of enabling managers to assess their current capabilities and learning needs. Set in the context of a generative learning forum, it provides a diagnostic tool for self-managed learning and development.

Dixon (1995a, 1995b) relates a study of privatized firms to the culture change needed to "release" the potential of middle managers working in newly privatized organizations. She outlines her findings with reference to the views of managers on the need to: invest in education and training; create, translate and share the "new" strategic vision; establish constructive channels for communicating with senior managers; develop incentives and rewards; and break with tradition by encouraging middle managers to initiate and lead. Dixon observes that: "The overwhelming demand from middle managers was for the organization to invest in education for all levels of employee. There was an implication that the organization needed to be creative in the type of training and education provided as the 'traditional' approaches were no longer appropriate…" (Dixon, 1995b, p. 11).

Mumford (1994) examines the proposition that managers learn in hindsight by reviewing the experiences they have had and, less frequently, learn by identifying in advance how to use opportunities for learning as a means of self-development. He uses evidence from a study conducted over a three-month period by personal interview, with 21 directors from 15 UK organizations to characterize four approaches to learning. The purpose of the interviews was to discuss the respondents' experiences at work and what they had learned from them so as to explore how they might use alternative ways of analyzing experiences and ultimately enhance their capacity to learn at work. The four approaches defined by Mumford are:

- *The intuitive approach* – learning from experience, but not through a conscious process. Learning or developmental issues are rarely, if ever, mentioned, as this approach sees managing and good business practices as synonymous with learning.

- *The incidental approach* – learning by chance from activities that prompt the individual to reflect and review. Typically, this includes unusual occurrences and planned activities with unanticipated or undesirable outcomes.

- *The retrospective approach* – learning from experience by reviewing what happened and reaching conclusions about it. Prompted mainly by mishaps or mistakes, but those who use this approach are more inclined to draw lessons from unexpected variances.

- *The prospective approach* – includes retrospective components and an element of planning to learn before an event takes place. Here, future events are seen not merely as things to be successfully completed but as opportunities to learn. Mumford adds: "Individuals using this approach

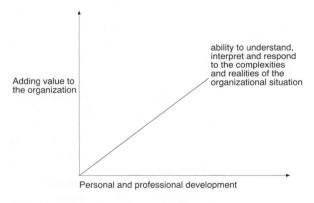

Figure 1.
Interrelationships between personal and organizational development

Source: adapted from McKenna (1994, p. 9)

are expectant learners with their antennae constantly tuned in to the possibility of learning from a whole variety of experiences" (p. 6).

Theme 2: coaching, mentoring and team development

The learner support provided for managers – whether it be individual coaching and mentoring or work group related, plays an integral role in workplace learning. Table II lists a set of sub-themes that spans: the role of coaching in developing managers (including the application of sports coaching techniques to team-building in business); mentoring and other forms of organizational support; learning and team development; work group dynamics; and learning and cross-functional team development.

Phillips (1996) examines the possibilities for using coaching as a management tool and considers its part in the management process. He identifies a number of applications and outlines the roles and responsibilities of both the coach and those being coached. He sees flexibility as the key with the coach acting as an enabler. Bloch (1995) relates "soft" skills development in the workplace to enabling employees to achieve their potential and she uses evidence from a study to emphasize the perceived value of internal coaching to organizations:

> Individuals who are given ownership of their own development and career management are usually more highly motivated than those whose paths are mapped out for them. *Yet the survey found that only around one-third of the companies surveyed encouraged individuals to take responsibility for their own development.* Over half said the development of future top managers should be the joint responsibility of the individual, his or her line manager, and the company. However, what actually happens in practice is sometimes very different. As one respondent remarked: "Responsibility for development is meant to be tripartite, but we spend out lives trying to get the line manager involved" (pp. 20-21).

Forret *et al.* (1996) review the issues involved in the development and implementation of in-company mentoring programmes, with reference to interviews with managers in five organizations who had established their own programmes. Scandura *et al.* (1996) address the question: "Why do mentors engage in mentoring?" and discuss the role of leadership in the development of leader-supported mentoring processes. They offer an array of insights on the process of mentoring and the range of relationships that need managing if the programme is to yield benefits for mentors, mentees and the organization as a whole. Clawson (1996) presents mentoring as a valuable form of social development and raises questions about how mentoring might be shaped by the era of electronic communications. He views mentoring as a vital support mechanism in the information age and poses a number of questions for mentors to address in the information age:

- How will people find their protégé or mentor counterparts in the new era? Will they continue to work through face-to-face meetings or will there be forums set up on the Internet like the personal ad columns in newspapers?

Authors	Focus	Sub-theme
Bloch (1995)	Reports that 14 respondents (from a survey of 39 firms) cited internal coaching as a key method used to develop managers: more than 25 per cent of the sample were used using external consultants as mentors	The role of coaching in developing managers
McNutt and Wright (1995)	Observes numerous parallels between sport and business and suggest that the methods used by successful sports coaches might be used to improve employee performance	Applies sports coaching techniques to team-building in business
Veale and Wachtel (1996)	Describes Coca-Cola Foods' coaching and mentoring programmes and relates mentoring to human resource development strategy	An integrated approach to coaching and mentoring
Forret, Turban and Dougherty (1996)	Provides a "how to" overview on the steps involved in setting up a mentoring programme and outlines the benefits of such a programme for the organization and for the mentees and mentors	A practical guide to mentoring
Booth (1996)	Contrasts mentoring with typical employee/manager relationships and considers the advantages and disadvantages and how gender influences the mentoring process with reference to a case study of two supervisory mentoring relationships	Mentoring and other forms of organizational relations
Beeby and Simpson (1995)	Describes a non-prescriptive means of assisting managers to recognize and work on change issues. The approach uses a cognitive mapping technique to draw on the experiences of managers and to define causal problems and appropriate responses	Cognitive mapping and learner development
Strachan (1996)	Reviews the organizational literature and identifies the role of teamworking in building a learning organization	Learning and team development
Kur (1996)	Depicts patterns of team behaviour using a series of temperaments. Reflects the dynamic qualities of groups of individuals working separately and interacting together to achieve agreed tasks	Work group dynamics and learning
Proehl (1996)	Reviews the effectiveness of cross-functional teams in tackling broad scale organizational problems. Identifies some of the difficulties in sustaining cross-functional team effort and considers the implications for team development	Cross-functional team development

Table II.
Coaching, mentoring and
team development

- How long will these relationships last? (With e-mail providing worldwide support, there is no proximity reason for breaking them off when the mentee is promoted or transferred.)
- How can companies take advantage of the new technologies and the new insights about mentoring to foster and encourage healthy, working developmental relationships among their employees?

- How will cross-cultural mentoring work out? Will there be early examples to encourage and guide subsequent generations?

Theme 3: competences, managerial learning and the curriculum
The extent to which workplace learning can be formalized and even measured in relation to specific outcomes is considered here. Table III depicts an array of sub-themes relating to: the attainment of core competences and their relationship to individual performance; open and distance learning in management; self-managed learning; relating management development to current and future needs; university and community learning networks; the future orientation of MBA programmes and relating course design to organizational learning.

Lane and Robinson (1995) report on a study undertaken on behalf of the Management Charter Initiative (MCI). The study sought to determine the main areas of decision taking and action which are of strategic importance to organizations and need to be implemented effectively (Figure 2).

These are:

- *Understanding and influencing the environment.* Identifying and evaluating opportunities and threats or obstacles for the organization in relation to its internal and external environments.
- *Setting the strategy and gaining commitment.* Contributions to developing and communicating the mission, objectives, goals, values and policies of the organization and its units.
- *Planning, implementing and monitoring.* Developing and implementing programmes, projects and operating plans for the organization.
- *Evaluating and improving performance.* Reviewing and evaluating objectives and policies and their implementation.

Pierce *et al.*'s (1995) follow-up survey confirms the significance of these core competence areas and they report a high level of agreement and acceptance among senior managers from a wide range of organizations.

Loan-Clarke (1996) reviews aspects of the debate about the merits of implementing MCI standards and questions whether a national standards-based approach can, in fact, deliver improved managerial performance. The most fundamental criticism concerns the claim regarding the relevance of the management standards to all organizations. Loan-Clarke argues that it is not possible for the standards to have specific contextual relevance so as to reflect organizational culture and industry sector requirements. He believes that it may be more appropriate for the MCI to emphasize the exchange value national standards, rather than its specific value to individual employers. A CBI review of NVQs in 1994 recommended that a core set of competences, with choices from a range of options, may be the best way of tailoring competence-based development to specific individual and organizational needs. Yet, the emphasis of management NVQs still places greater value on being assessed for a qualification than the process of learning and development.

Authors	Focus	Sub-theme
Lane and Robinson (1995)	Reviews aspects of the management charter initiative (MCI) and its aim of establishing standards of good practice for managers in the UK	Competences for managers
Ashton (1996)	Reports on how Holiday Inn Worldwide has implemented competency-based human resource strategies which provide a direct link between individual performance and business objectives	Core competences and individual performance
Davies (1996)	Surveys the literature on open and distance learning (includes flexible, self-paced and resource-based learning) and identifies a gap that might be partially filled by a more comprehensive model of open learning in management development	Open and distance learning in management
King (1996)	Describes IKEA's self-managed learning programme which is being used to support its expansion plans and to strengthen its competitive position	Self-managed learning
Kilcourse (1995)	Decries the rapid proliferation of business schools and asserts that dynamic, continuous change poses new challenges for managers, requiring a different form of management development	Relating management development to current needs and future needs
Critten (1996)	Makes a case for a new kind of partnership between universities and their local communities within which organizational as well as individual learning can be recognized, developed and accredited	University and community learning networks
Carnall (1995)	Examines the changes which are likely to occur in MBA programmes during the coming decade. Predicts that the "third generation" MBA will place more emphasis on the learning process than its curriculum and content	The future orientation of MBA programmes
Zuber-Skerritt (1995)	Explores ideas and issues related to management education and development for the new learning organization and presents an example of a course design for experienced managers which is work-based	Relating course design to organizational learning

Table III.
Competences,
managerial learning and
the curriculum

Ashton (1996) explains how a series of core competences were identified and defined by Holiday Inn Worldwide (HIW). High and low performers were selected by management for behavioural event interviews with external consultants and this activity yielded details of career highlights, job challenges and difficulties. After this, high performance role models were constructed around nine core competences viewed by HIW as effective predictors of job performance, relative to key organizational criteria.

The competence areas are:

- *Customer service orientation*. Understanding and acting on the needs of others to serve them better.

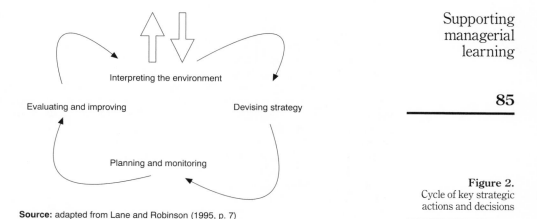

Interpreting the environment

Evaluating and improving

Devising strategy

Planning and monitoring

Source: adapted from Lane and Robinson (1995, p. 7)

Figure 2.
Cycle of key strategic
actions and decisions

- *Flexibility*. The ability to adapt and work effectively in varied groups and situations.
- *Commitment to organizational values*. Acting consistently, in accordance with corporate values and standards.
- *Achievement orientation*. A desire to improve performance, related to challenging objectives and standards of excellence.
- *Initiative and proactivity*. Self-motivation, persistence and reaching beyond the job description for potential outcomes.
- *Organizational influence*. Influencing others effectively.
- *Creative problem solving*. Identifying patterns in problem situations that are not obviously related and achieving solutions.
- *Enablement*. Inspiring acceptance of added responsibilities and accountabilities.
- *Developing others*. To enhance talent or performance.

The competence model is viewed as an integral approach, spanning selection, training and development and performance management. During selection, applicants are assessed on two business unit criteria – position requirements stated in the form of knowledge, skills and abilities (KSAs). These are the basic qualifications for a given job, together with the core competences and applicants must meet the minimum threshold in both areas before a job offer is made. In relation to performance management, specific KSAs are agreed between managers, supervisors and operatives at the beginning of each year, with appraisals twice annually at mid-year (optional) and at year-end (compulsory). Managers are expected to seek inputs from an employee's peers,

customers or, if applicable, subordinates so as to ensure that the review is as
rounded and accurate as possible. The review process is meant to be open,
discursive and encompass aspects of negotiation and task clarification.

Hilgert (1996) reasons that for a working executive, the decision to pursue an
advanced academic degree is a major choice that involves a significant
commitment of time and effort as well as an array of implications for family,
social and professional commitments. Hilgert investigates the reasons why
executives take this decision and identifies differences by age group. For
respondents in their 30s, the meaning of pursuing advanced study centres on
issues of increased self-confidence and growth, authority and status. For the
late 40s respondent, education goals tend to reflect a considered view of "what
next" in life and a reaffirmation of self; these considerations also affect
respondents embarking on a course of study in their 50s, with the added
incentive of a planned career change and/or preparation for a post-retirement
career. Almost all the study respondents said that support and encouragement
from workplace colleagues was important to them and in the majority of cases,
represented a significant source of positive meaning for educational activities.

Hilgert (1995) poses a series of questions relating to the outcomes of an
executive MBA programme: Does the significant investment of time, self and
economic resources result in a substantial broadening of perspectives? Have the
graduates moved towards a more global, integrative view of their
organizations? Are the graduates more flexible and better equipped to deal with
change? And how are these outcomes reflected through the various aspects of
self? His study uses survey and interview techniques and his data reveal a
number of "life changing" developmental outcomes. The data showed that the
educational experience impacted on the personal self, the career self and the self
in significant relationships. More specifically, the study revealed that
developmental changes had occurred in that there appeared to be evidence of
increasingly complex thinking processes and cognitive structures, changes in
world view, perceptions of self, and approaches to problem solving. Baruch and
Leeming (1996) present the results of a study concerned with the design of a
business school MBA curriculum. They explain how the views of its past
students were sought. Graduates saw adaptability and flexibility as key
considerations in building a programme that could cater for both generalization
and specialization and provide the appropriate learning skills to equip future
graduates with the competences seen as desirable in business.

Kilcourse (1995) observes that the scale and pace of change that managers in
most industries must now respond to is both unprecedented and discontinuous
in nature. The responsive organization is now leaner and flatter than ever
before and Kilcourse believes that: "...teams in tomorrow's commercial
maelstrom will need 'hands on' help in turning 'here and now' problems into
learning opportunities. In short, they will need the kind of help at present
available from only a handful of business schools". Bolton (1996) sees the
problem as but one form of criticism levelled at existing business school
curricula and describes an initiative to re-position an MBA programme in

collaboration with human resource professionals so as to produce a more innovative, international, practical and reflective study experience. A further example of collaborative programme development comes from Blackburn and Fryer (1996) who describe a management development course that encompasses work-based learning, mentoring and accreditation of prior learning.

Lorange (1996) advances the proposition that business schools should be learning organizations with the faculty member as the learner and contributing to various modes of organizational learning. Osborne (1995) makes a similar set of points and, using the analogy of expensive trains heading off the rails, asserts that business schools must learn to do what they teach – i.e. become learning organizations – if they are to stay relevant in a rapidly changing world. Zuber-Skerritt (1995) profiles an approach that she views as highly relevant to personal and organizational learning. She describes an executive MBA course by action learning which is work-integrated, learner-centred, problem-focused, interdisciplinary in nature and founded on adult learning principles. It aims to facilitate organizational learning and development as well as the personal and professional development of senior managers, who are able to upgrade their knowledge and skills and exchange their work experience and ideas with fellow executives in small groups.

Theme 4: work-based action learning

Work-based action learning seeks to relate the curriculum to learner needs and aspirations and to the organizational setting. In so doing, it is seen to be relevant and to deliver benefits for individuals (managerial learning) and for the sponsor (organizational learning). The sub-themes in Table IV relate to articles that address the steps involved in: using action learning in the learning organization; relating action research to managerial development; action learning and its impact on corporate culture; using action learning and research skills in the workplace; contributions from the learning set in action learning and measuring return on investment from management education.

Cusins (1996) defines action learning as a "dynamic syndrome" or flowing together of four primary activities, each of which enhances the others. These are experiential learning, which is problem-oriented and with problem solving it is augmented by the acquisition of additional relevant knowledge and the support of a co-learner group. O'Neill (1996) believes that a willingness to "learn how to learn" and the ability to learn from experience are among the best ways of coping with continuous change. She views action learning as an effective means of helping individuals to acquire new learning skills and the learning adviser plays an instrumental role in this process. In contrast to the traditional business curriculum, a "dynamic" syllabus for work-based action learning seeks to address specific, relevant questions for the organization and its members, rather than following a prescribed, "static" list of topics. A dynamic curriculum guides individuals to draw from the body of knowledge and an array of other sources (such as company literature and other contextualized information).

Dilworth (1996) sees a need to interrelate academic and workplace domains and argues that by addressing either domain in relative exclusion from the other risks creating a workplace context where learners are able to grasp real-world problems but lack the underlying academic knowledge to solve them.

Limerick *et al.* (1994) consider the characteristics of an action learning organization in terms of its bias for reflection-in-action, formation of learning alliances, development of external networks, multiple reward systems, the creation of meaningful information, individual empowerment, leadership and vision. They conclude that the knowledge-generating organization that engages in these kinds of activities is more likely to be able to survive in turbulent market conditions.

McNulty and Canty (1995) foresee that tomorrow's managers will have be: "...simultaneously and consecutively specialists and generalists, team players and self-reliant, able to think for themselves as a business of one and plan accordingly". They believe that to succeed, managers will have to commit themselves to a lifelong learning career, at the heart of which will be: "...knowing oneself and knowing what one has to offer in the 'de-jobbed'

Authors	Focus	Sub-theme
Harrison (1996)	Critically examines the concepts of action learning (AL) and the learning organization and concludes that AL offers the potential to develop strategic awareness and thinking even in turbulent environmental conditions	Using action learning in the learning organizations
Chan (1994)	Relates an action learner's experience of action research and discusses how AL and action research deliver a balance of knowledge and action, academic rigour and managerial relevance	Relating action research to managerial development
Reeves (1996)	Compares two companies' use of action learning, one primarily for individual staff development, and a second where action learning's questioning, problem-solving ethos had pervaded corporate life	Action learning and its impact on corporate culture
Howell (1994)	Presents a case study of the International Management Centres (IMC) and shows that its graduate managers can operationalize AL and action research to bring about organizational, professional and personal development as well as productivity improvements	Using action learning and research skills in the workplace
Mumford (1996)	Identifies a gap in the current literature on action learning re: drawing contributions from set members as distinct from facilitators. Offers a method that might be used to overcome this bias	Contributions from the learning set in action action learning
Wills and Oliver (1996)	Report on a four-year impact analysis of action learning MBA programmes. The findings reveal an array of benefits for employing investment from organizations and show that individual managers gained a variety of "soft" benefits	Measuring return on investment from management education

Table IV.
Work-based action
learning

marketplace". This new emphasis demands different kinds of development programmes: those which emphasize learning not teaching, action not theory and business results not classroom results.

Wills and Oliver (1996) describe how action learning's focus on company-specific issues makes it easier to review the "hard" return on investment for the enterprise. They conclude that training and development managers can and should measure the "value added" by evaluating the organizational and financial impact of their own organization's investment in management education. In so doing, they feel that a "budgetarily supportive culture" is more likely to emerge. This approach would also help to highlight the range of "softer" personal benefits derived by individual participants. These include: changed behaviours, growth in confidence and learning from fellow members of the small action learning group or set. Peters and Smith (1996) also consider ways of achieving the best return on a learning investment. They suggest that the organization should identify its self-motivated, high-potential managers and sponsor them to explore the learning agenda for tomorrow's leaders and change agents. Key issues are likely to include: getting things done within the organization's cultural and political norms; taking risks within a psychologically safe environment; learning how to act with others, how to act alone and how to self-develop; comprehending and shaping the present and future strategic agenda for the organization. Peters and Smith argue that the best way to address this kind of company-specific agenda is by formalizing a work-based or action learning programme of study:

Success in an organization depends on far more than acquiring technical knowledge and management concepts. It comes from an understanding of and a feel for factors such as organizational politics and culture, the art of influencing others, the ability to delegate, the skills of timing, presentation and selling ideas, not just having them. These are the qualities we expect from organizational leaders, and without them, and without a developmental approach to gaining such qualities, the emergence of effective leaders will continue to be a hit-and-miss affair (p. 8).

Implications for managerial learning
In designing and implementing a programme for managerial learning in the workplace it is helpful to consider the following points:

(1) How are the participants roles defined (scope, tasks, responsibilities, relationships), how do they currently enact their roles (gather information, take decisions and action, contribute to key activities such as planning, organizing, staffing, leading and controlling) and what improvements would participants like to achieve for themselves, their work group and the wider organization?

(2) What are the external variables affecting managerial work (e.g. related to sources of discontinuity, uncertainty, ambiguity, complexity) and

how might the programme enable parallel, ongoing learning to occur so that managerial skills and knowledge keep pace?

(3) How can the programme encourage participants to enhance their capacity to learn from work by using a variety of ways of analyzing experiences (e.g. intuitive, incidental, retrospective, prospective approaches) so that learning becomes self-sustaining?

(4) What forms of learner support should be used (e.g. coaching, mentoring, team development) so as to help people to learn, widen and strengthen organizational participation and embed a culture of learning?

(5) Who will coach and mentor and what are the resource and development implications?

(6) What are the core and specialist levels of competence, how will these by built-in to the programme and measured for attainment? How will these considerations affect the form(s) of learning and the methods of delivery?

(7) How will the efforts of participants be recognized – formally (e.g. accredited learning and the completion of an academic award), informally (e.g. support, encouragement, study time) and professionally (e.g. enhanced career prospects)?

(8) How will programme outcomes "add value" for participants and the organization as a whole? How can the programme encourage others to take responsibility for recognizing and responding to their own development needs?

(9) How can the benefits of workplace learning be readily identified and "sold" to participants, their superiors and subordinates? How can the reactions of sceptics and opponents be anticipated and effectively dealt with?

(10) How might "return on investment" (time, resources, individual and organizational effort) be measured and monitored?

References

Ashton, C. (1996) "How competencies boost performance", *Management Development Review,* Vol. 9 No. 3, pp. 14-19.

Barclay, J. (1996) "Learning from experience with learning logs", *Journal of Management Development,* Vol. 15 No. 6, pp. 28-43.

Baruch, Y. and Leeming. A. (1996), "Programming the MBA programme – the quest for curriculum", *Journal of Management Development,* Vol. 15 No. 7, pp. 27-36.

Beeby, M. and Simpson, P. (1995), "Developing strategic processes for change in top management teams", *Executive Development,* Vol. 8 No. 1, pp. 20-2.

Blackburn, P. and Fryer, B. (1996), "An innovative partnership in management development", *Management Development Review,* Vol. 9 No. 3, pp. 22-5.

Bloch, S. (1995), "Coaching tomorrow's top managers", *Executive Development*, Vol. 8 No. 5, pp. 20-2.

Bolton, A. (1996), "Joint architecture by HR specialists and business schools", *Management Development Review,* Vol. 9 No. 1, pp. 22-4.

Booth, R. (1996), "Mentor or manager: what is the difference? A case study in supervisory mentoring", *Leadership & Organization Development Journal,* Vol. 17 No. 3, pp. 31-6.

Carnall, C. (1995), "The third-generation MBA: global reach and 'local' service", *The Learning Organization*, Vol. 2 No. 2, pp. 18-27.

Chan, K. C. (1994), "Learning for total quality an action learning approach", *The Learning Organization,* Vol. 1 No. 1, pp. 17-22.

Clawson, J.G. (1996), "Mentoring in the information age", *Leadership & Organization Development Journal,* Vol. 17 No. 3, pp. 6-15.

Critten, P. (1996), "A learning community in the making – Middlesex University's new MA in personal and organizational development", *The Learning Organization*, Vol. 3 No. 5, pp. 14-17.

Cusins, P. (1996), "Action learning revisited", *The Journal of Workplace Learning,* Vol. 8 No. 6, pp. 19-26.

Davis, H.J. (1996), "A review of open and distance learning within management development", *Journal of Management Development,* Vol. 15 No. 4, pp. 20-34.

Dilworth, R. L. (1996), "Action learning: bridging academic and workplace domains", *The Journal of Workplace Learning*, Vol. 8 No. 6, pp. 45-53.

Dixon, P. (1995a), "Releasing middle management potential: Part 1", *Executive Development,* Vol. 8 No. 5, pp. 23-5.

Dixon, P. (1995b), "Releasing middle management potential: Part 2", *Executive Development,* Vol. 8 No. 7, pp. 11-13.

Forret, M.L., Turban, D.B. and Dougherty, T.W. (1996), "Issues facing organizations when implementing formal mentoring programmes", *Leadership & Organization Development Journal,* Vol. 17 No. 3, pp. 27-30.

Harrison, R. (1996), "Action learning: route or barrier to the learning organization?", *The Journal of Workplace Learning*, Vol. 8 No. 6, pp. 27-38.

Hilgert, A. D. (1995), "Developmental outcomes of an executive MBA programme", *Journal of Management Development,* Vol. 14 No. 10, pp. 64-76.

Hilgert, A. D. (1996), "The working executive: the developmental role of executive degree programmes", *Journal of Management Development,* Vol. 15 No. 7, pp. 47-61.

Howell, F. (1994), "Action learning and action research in management education and development: a case study", *The Learning Organization,* Vol. 1 No. 2, pp. 15-22.

Kilcourse, T. (1995), "The business of business schools", *The Learning Organization*, Vol. 2 No. 2, pp. 32-5.

King, S. (1996), "European cases of self-managed learning", *Management Development Review,* Vol. 9 No. 2, pp. 8-10.

Kur, E. (1996), "The faces model of high performing team development", *Leadership & Organization Development Journal,* Vol. 17 No. 1, pp. 32-41.

Lane, G. and Robinson, A. (1995), "The development of standards of competence for senior management", *Executive Development,* Vol. 8 No. 6, pp. 4-8.

Limerick, D., Passfield, R. and Cunnington, B. (1994), "Transformational change: towards an action learning organization", *The Learning Organization*, Vol. 1 No. 2, pp. 29-40.

Loan-Clarke, J. (1996), "The management charter initiative – a critique of management standards/NVQs", *Journal of Management Development,* Vol. 15 No. 6, pp. 4-17.

Lorange, P. (1996), "A business school as a learning organization", *The Learning Organization,* Vol. 3 No. 5, pp. 5-13.

McKenna, J.F., Cotton, C.C. and Van Auken, S. (1995), "Business school emphasis on teaching, research and service to industry: does where you sit determine where you stand?", *Journal of Organizational Change Management*, Vol. 8 No. 2, pp. 3-16.

McKenna, S. D. (1994), "Leveraging complexity: the middle manager's dilemma", *The Learning Organization*, Vol. 1 No. 2, pp. 6-14.

McNulty, N.G. and Canty, G.R. (1995), "Proof of the pudding", *Journal of Management Development*, Vol. 14 No. 1, pp. 53-66.

McNutt, R. and Wright, P.C. (1995), "Coaching your employees: applying sports analogies to business", *Executive Development*, Vol. 8 No. 1, pp. 27-32.

Margerison, C. and McCann, D. (1996a), "Five skills to improve performance", *Team Performance Management*, Vol. 2 No. 1, pp. 14-16.

Margerison, C. and McCann, D. (1996b), "Men and women at work", *Team Performance Management*, Vol. 2 No. 1, pp. 22-4.

Megginson, D. (1994), "Planned and emergent learning: a framework and a method", *Executive Development*, Vol. 7 No. 6, pp. 29-32.

Mumford, A. (1994), "Four approaches to learning from experience", *The Learning Organization*, Vol. 1 No. 1, pp. 4-10.

Mumford, A. (1996), "Effective learners in action learning sets", *The Journal of Workplace Learning*, Vol. 8 No. 6, pp. 3-10.

O'Neill, J. (1996), "A study of the role of learning advisers in action learning", *The Journal of Workplace Learning*, Vol. 8 No. 6, 1996, pp. 39-44.

Osborne, R.L. and Cowen, S.S. (1995), "Business schools must become learning organizations – or else", *The Learning Organization*, Vol. 2 No. 2, pp. 28-31.

Oshagbemi, T. (1995), "Management development and managers' use of their time", *Journal of Management Development*, Vol. 14 No. 8, pp. 19-34.

Peters, J. and Smith, P. (1996), "Developing high potential staff: an action learning approach", *The Journal of Workplace Learning*, Vol. 8 No. 3, pp. 6-11.

Phillips, R. (1996), "Coaching for higher performance", *The Journal of Workplace Learning*, Vol. 8 No. 4, pp. 29-32.

Pierce, C., Hannon P. and Wilson, L. (1995), "The standards of competence for senior management: field test results", *Executive Development*, Vol. 8 No. 6, pp. 9-12.

Proehl, R.A. (1996), "Enhancing the effectiveness of cross-functional teams", *Leadership & Organization Development Journal*, Vol. 17 No. 5, pp. 3-10.

Reeves, T. (1996), "Rogue learning on the company reservation", *The Learning Organization*, Vol. 3 No. 2, pp. 20-9.

Scandura, T.A., Tejeda, M.J., Werther, W.B. and Lankau, M.J. (1996), "Perspectives on mentoring", *Leadership & Organization Development Journal*, Vol. 17 No. 3, pp. 50-6.

Shenhar, A.J. and Renier, J. (1996), "How to define management: a modular approach", *Management Development Review*, Vol. 9 No. 1, pp. 25-31.

Strachan, P.A. (1996), "Managing transformational change: the learning organization and teamworking", *Team Performance Management*, Vol. 2 No. 2, pp. 32-40.

Veale, D.J. and Wachtel, J.M. (1996), "Mentoring and coaching as part of a human resource development strategy: an example at Coca-Cola foods", *Leadership & Organization Development Journal*, Vol. 17 No. 3, pp. 16-20.

Wills, G. and Oliver, C. (1996), "Measuring the ROI from management action learning", *Management Development Review*, Vol. 9 No. 1, pp. 17-21.

Zuber-Skerritt, O. (1995), "Developing a learning organization through management education by action learning", *The Learning Organization*, Vol. 2 No. 2, pp. 36-46.

Chapter 6
Enabling organizational learning

Richard Teare

*Granada Professor, Oxford Brookes University, and Academic Chair,
International Management Centres*

Introduction

It is clear from studies of organizations and a considerable body of anecdotal evidence that organizational life is strongly influenced by organizational leaders. In particular, the vision, style of leadership and motivation that enables them to "make things happen" and inspire others to follow their direction. In seeking to release the potential that exists inside the organization in order that it might perform well and respond to change, the contention here is that individuals need to learn and develop at least as quickly as the pace of external change. If this is to be achieved, the structures, processes and procedures adopted by organizations must encourage and support personal growth rather than impeding or even discouraging it. In essence, organizations "learn" from individuals and groups or teams as they share insights and experiences and in so doing, capture "new" knowledge and understanding. This article reviews recent contributions to the literature on aspects of organizational learning and considers how organizational processes might encompass effective learning support for individuals and groups of learners. The review is drawn from articles published between 1994-1996 in seven journals: *Executive Development; Journal of Organizational Change Management; Journal of Management Development; Leadership & Organization Development Journal; Management Development Review; The Journal of Workplace Learning; The Learning Organization.* The review concentrates on three areas: Organizational vision; Leadership and motivation; Organizational change and performance and concludes with a summary of the implications for organizational learning.

Theme 1: Organizational vision

Allen (1995) sees "vision" as the starting-point, the anchor and the means of communicating a sense of organizational direction to its members. In practical terms, he suggests that a vision statement can provide an organizational road map to guide its future development – provided that it is: coherent enough to create a recognizable picture of the future; powerful enough to generate commitment to performance and that it emphasizes what realistically can be and clarifies what should be. Among other sources, he bases his interpretation on the Old Testament view that without a vision the people will perish

This article first appeared in *International Journal of Contemporary Hospitality Management*, Vol. 9 No. 7, 1997, pp. 315-324.

(Proverbs 29:18 and Hosea 4:14). Richardson and Thompson (1995) describe some of the characteristics of modern business environments and relate these to a vision of the strategic competences that organizations are likely to need in the future. These are summarized in Table I.

Richardson and Thompson observe that organizations will need to rethink their vision if they are to equip themselves with the competences needed to succeed in the future, not least because of the preoccupation with financial performance indicators and related information systems in the past. For instance, to remain competitive, the organization must accept the need for challenge and change and the right of others to have their say. Similarly, customer responsiveness is more likely to be achieved by empowered staff and

Trend	Response	Implications
Towards larger operating arenas	Organizations will need to draw on and assimilate information from a wider range of external sources	Competence in environmental surveillance; empowered personnel productive strategic alliances and learning communities
Towards more, and more diverse, influences	Skill in developing "helicopter vision" to facilitate a strategic overview and planning for the organization's future development	Competence in strategic analysis; enabling fast, effective communications; contingency planning, crisis avoidance and management
Towards greater speed of change	The ability to reflect the dynamics of external change internally so that strategy, communications and decision making keep pace	Competence in listening to the issues raised by stakeholders; envisaging successful futures; adapting the organizational vision; changing course if necessary
Towards greater external power and threat	Organizational readiness to respond to the laws of chaos and catastrophe theory: a change in one part of a system can ricochet through the whole system, often in a seemingly random and unpredictable way	The ability to: respond and adapt to the aspirations of powerful stake-holders; change direction to meet new demands as they arise; monitor for new market phenomena; devise political strategies and negotiate expertly
Towards greater competitiveness	Acceptance that free market policies attract more competitors providing more choice for customers. Realization that competitiveness may mean new processes, products and services and/ or reduced costs of production	Willingness to: improve competitive, innovative, product quality and and customer responsive competences; make effective choices about when to leave marketplaces, about which new ones to enter
Towards resource depletion and life-threatening pollution	Willingness to re-consider beliefs about what organizations should be and what they should do to protect ecosystems	Plan to be "greener" more environmentally responsive, productive in resource usage, collaborative and socially responsible

Table I.
Business trends: envisaging strategic responses

Source: Adapted from Richardson and Thompson (1995, pp. 17-19)

goals and performance measures that reflect the "new" competences that the organization is seeking to develop.

Table II highlights some of the issues that influence the concept and application of organizational vision. These include the need for regular updating and review (with reference to current and future planning and organizational direction); the need to consider the interrelationships between organizational complexity, information, organizational structure and learning

Authors	Focus	Sub-theme
Allen (1995)	Presents a visioning action plan that represents all organizational stakeholders. The model promotes participative agreement throughout the visioning process. Observes that organizational members should agree with the vision and put it into daily practice.	Defining organizational vision
Richardson and Thompson (1995)	Assess a number of related trends occurring in business environments and considers the implications for developing requisite strategic competences in organizations	Relating future impacts to organizational competence
Benbow (1995)	Reports on a study of how organizational leaders view their development, responsibilities and succession, together with their vision on social issues	Implementing and updating organizational vision
Bell and Tunnicliff (1996)	Examines how companies plan ahead and argues that current strategic planning and re-engineering approaches alone will not enable them to compete in the future. Promotes an inclusive stakeholder approach to pooling knowledge and resources	Future planning and organizational direction
Gault and Jaccaci (1996)	Suggests how periodicity can be used with complexity theory to enable businesses to understand their position in the periodic cycle of gather, repeat, share and transform	Interrelating complexity, information, organizational structure and learning
Smith and Saint-Onge (1996)	Contends that in dealing with change, the mindsets of the organization's managers are the most critical factor. Suggests that the best way to deal with mindsets is to prevent them from hardening by promoting a culture of active learning	Establishing an evolutionary organization
Theobald (1996)	The pace of change and divergent views about "what next" suggests no "safe" future. Those who advance the maximum growth model assume ecological adaptability (among other variables) and are likely to place decision-makers under greater stress because of this	Future scenarios for organizational development
McDermott and Chan (1996)	Argues that corporate commitment to stakeholders is not an option but a necessity for companies aiming to build competitive advantage. Asserts that customer loyalty is obtained through trust and this must be won by paying equal attention to all stakeholders	Towards "flexible, intelligent relationship management strategy"

Table II.
Organizational vision

and the evolutionary role of organizational vision (encompassing future scenarios for organizational development).

Benbow (1995) observes that business leaders do recognize the seriousness of the external threats from increased global competition and greater regulatory and/or political intervention. Coupled with this they are also aware of the need to broaden their future social agenda and foresee that their responsibility is likely to be broader and more complex. Paradoxically, chief executives tend to look inwards for advice and the majority seem to rely on colleagues as the most valued source of ideas and inspiration rather than seeking views from customers or consultants. This is apparently because they are sceptical about the value of external experts, preferring to rely on coaching by those in post and on personal experience. In contrast, Bell and Tunnicliff (1996) describe the activities of a "future search" conference where a sizeable number of stakeholders are brought together to explore the past, agree the present and draw up action steps for the future. They see this as a forum for learning where stakeholders can identify common problems and explore higher order solutions.

Gault and Jaccaci (1996) note that successful businesses are, of necessity, using their complex environments to become planned cultures of learning and creativity. Here, "successful" companies are the ones that understand the connection between learning on the one hand and creativity and profitability on the other.

Smith and Saint-Onge (1996) outline an approach to influencing management thinking that encourages managers to think and act responsively, thereby promoting the concept of an "evolutionary organization" (EVO). They contend that the wellspring of real learning lies within the organization itself and that it can be released by channelling aspirations, imagination and experimentation. To achieve EVO status, they say it is necessary to create an organizational climate that accords with a particular ideal or vision – that learning is integral to the roles of all employees. In changing the rules and emphasizing the learning imperative, all employees are forced to change their habits of thinking and learning without necessarily knowing that this is happening. To acquire new insights and learn from them, frequent interaction among members of the organization must occur. In so doing, people understand more and begin to depend on one another to a greater extent. Further, the EVO structures the organization so that employees are forced to solve their own problems and so expertise is enhanced and reinvested. "Experts" learn to become even more expert as they take incrementally bigger risks and, when they succeed, they acquire the kind of knowledge that increases the likelihood of future success. In this way, Smith and Saint-Onge believe that around 75 per cent of the organization's members will become active learners (They estimate that around 15 per cent of managers in any given organization are likely to be active, continuous learners, that 60 per cent possess the potential to learn if they are convinced of the need to do so and that the remaining 25 per cent are unlikely to respond.) Senior management's main role in an EVO is to provide leadership, look outwards, create a business vision and strategy, and build the organization's intellectual capital.

McDermott and Chan (1996) observe the passing of an organizational era – one which is characterized by the shift from the command-and-control type to the information-based type. The new form of structure involves a fundamental re-shaping of managerial responsibilities, of communication and information flows, and of interpersonal relationships. Chan (1994) emphasizes the importance of relationships built on "sincerity, trust and integrity" (see Figure 1). The principle and values of "flexible intelligent relationship management strategy" (FIRMS) is seen as a means by which the chain of relationships linking customers, workers, suppliers, distributors and even competitors might be managed. Action learning is presented as the guiding philosophy of FIRMS for achieving world-class performance. Ultimately learning is related to action, for without activity, the authors assert, there is no feedback.

Theme 2: Leadership and motivation

The role of organizational leadership is a multifaceted one that draws on an array of professional skills and personal qualities. Table III reflects this and provides an indicative list of articles relating to topics such as: the role of the

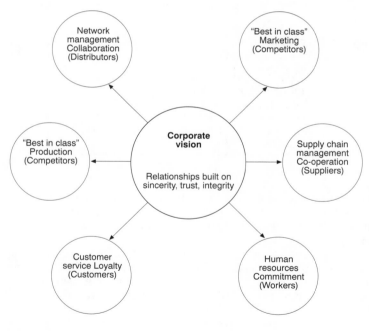

Source: adapted from Chan (1994, p. 20)

Figure 1.
Relating corporate
vision to core business
activities

Authors	Focus	Sub-theme
Kenton (1995)	Considers the company director's role and questions conventional thinking about the myopic pre-occupation with short-term cost cutting and rationalization. Asserts that directors should possess a strong sense of purpose and a vision for the long term	The role of the company director
Tait (1996)	Reports on in-depth interviews with 18 business leaders, focusing on the qualities and skills they felt to be essential for success in directing and guiding a large organization	The attributes of organizational leadership
Richardson (1995a)	Relates the job of learning organization leader to prescriptions for implementing classically administered productivity improvement and an alternative approach to facilitating self-organizing learning networks	Leadership contexts and roles for learning
Richardson (1995b)	Examines the dangers of "self-enacted reality" strategic drift and the need for planning and control systems that reflect the harsh realities of the marketplace	The politically aware leader
Kur and Bunning (1996)	Describes a three-track process for executive leadership development intended to develop a cadre of strategic business leaders for the next decade	Executive leadership development
Brooks (1996)	Explores the role of leadership in initiating and sustaining a major process of change. Finds that leadership change requires leaders to think culturally and to be guided by a cognitive model of change while focusing on the politics of acceptance	Leadership of a cultural change process
Carr (1996)	Questions whether individuals, using psychoanalytic insights, can learn from their experience of leadership. Believes that leaders can develop insights in an experiential manner and concludes that most develop them by listening, hearing and responding	Learning from leadership
Carling (1995)	Argues that leadership is the main factor in enhancing human performance and is the all-important key to unlocking the latent potential of individuals, both in business and in sport	Harnessing individual and team potential

Table III.
Leadership and
motivation

company director; the attributes of organizational leadership; leadership
contexts and roles for learning; political awareness; executive leadership
development; the leadership of a cultural change process and learning from
leadership.

Tait (1996) identifies the self-reported attributes of effective leadership from
a sample of 18 business leaders. The interviewees formed two sub-groups –
those in their mid-50s or older with reputations among their peers and the
public as outstanding managers/leaders ($n = 9$) and a second group of younger
chief executives who had been five years or less in the role. Reflecting on the
group's responses, Tait believes that the qualities of effective leaders will
remain largely unchanged in the future.

The "recipe" for effective leadership encompasses: clarity of vision (derived from the ability to reduce a complex reality to the critical essentials); credible communication and interpersonal skills (to sell the vision and inspire people to action); sincerity, generosity and self-mastery (to inspire trust and withstand the loneliness of leadership) and high levels of motivation and physical energy (to achieve the extraordinary). Tait adds:

> These qualities, combined with a self-critical, open, flexible and lifelong learning approach that draws on a track record of broad functional experience, early successful line management experience, international experience (increasingly) and the lessons to be learned from managing in diversity and adversity in fast-changing conditions, will continue to be what it takes to reach the top in the new millennium (p. 31).

Taylor and Taylor (1996) note that leaders are largely responsible for setting the tone for an organization and this is reflected in how they approach given tasks, how company guidelines are interpreted and how employees are treated. The sum total of senior executive behaviour and beliefs ultimately becomes the organization's "philosophy" on how it conducts its business. If organizational members are to interpret the action of senior managers, it is helpful to understand the organizational priorities that drive their actions. Knippen and Green (1996) provide a stepwise approach for discerning the motivations of organizational superiors and suggest ways in which these might be explored. They also observe that the priorities that influence motives and behaviours frequently change in relation to circumstances, events and other factors.

Richardson (1995a) explores the spectrum of learning-related leadership tasks, ranging from classically administered ("hard") to facilitated self-organized, learning networks ("soft") approaches. He concludes that the learning organization of the future will be a place in which networks of learning communities thrive, despite the influence of "maverick" groupings of employees. To maintain these networks, the organizational leader must deploy "harder" planned approaches and "softer" political, social and cultural approaches at the same time. The network of learning communities within the organization is the knowledge resource of the enterprise, vested in its workforce and their individual and collective expertise. McCrimmon (1995) considers the prospects for what he calls "knowledge workers" in organizations, linked to the trend towards knowledge-intensive businesses. He argues that the development of new products and services will depend increasingly on leadership from knowledge workers who are at the leading edge of their technical field. This development, he feels, threatens the traditional role of the "generalist" manager who holds a formal leadership role in the organizational hierarchy. He believes that the solution is to elevate the status of the knowledge workers and reward them accordingly so that they might exert informal influence through their singular performance or innovation-led contribution without burdening them with too much unnecessary managerial and administrative work. If those with leadership potential in knowledge-based projects and generalist roles are to perform well, they must receive appropriate development. Klagge (1996) presents a generalized process for defining, discovering and developing personal leadership in organizations. He advocates the use of 360° performance evaluations to detect leadership qualities and suggests that employees with the potential to assume leadership roles need to be encouraged by a combination of recognition, rewards and training.

Theme 3: Organizational change and performance

The literature relating to organizational change and performance seems to converge wherever organizational imperatives for change are considered. Typically this means that organizations change because they have to remain competitive and perform well and consistently over time, not from choice. Table IV considers some of the implications of this for human resources (adapting to the needs of flexible working); for making structural adjustments (e.g. relationships between information flow and organizational performance, integrating intelligence systems and learning) and for decision making (organizational self-reflection; using decision rules to guide organizational decision making). The methods used to measure performance are in themselves an indicator of how far and how quickly an organization has been able to adapt to change and there are many strategic issues and options to consider. These include: the prospects for using "learning partnerships" to leverage improved organizational performance; promoting diversity as a means of enhancing organizational performance and using "soft systems" to relate strategic change to career and management development planning.

Coping with change in the workplace

Old (1995) argues that what she calls "whole system" organizational change occurs on three levels: transactional (observable ongoing work); systemic (strategy, structure, culture, rewards, technology, information) and "deep" structure (underlying patterns). Old reasons that a well integrated change methodology is needed if organizations are to respond well to change and embed new thinking and a change orientation in the organization's "deeper" systems and interactions. Field (1996) observes that many workplace changes are occurring because of developments in technology and especially the convergence of computer and telecommunication technologies:

> In the age of the virtual office, global networking and cyberspace meeting rooms, IT is increasingly defining workforce systems and the control of management information. The medium is, in a sense, becoming the management message where E-mail, desk-top conferencing and workgroup software are tomorrow's everyday management tools (p. 7).

Field argues that the pervasive influence of "instant" communications in the workplace presents a significant opportunity for human resource managers. He believes that they should be shaping an organizational response by building and managing "in-house" expertise in this sphere of change management. As and when human resource departments grasp this opportunity they will play a key role in determining the success (or failure) of the organization's ability to come to terms with new working practices. Macadam (1996) offers some

Authors	Focus	Sub-theme
Field (1996)	States that flexible working methods have become an enduring feature of the modern employment market and estimates that by the year 2000 one quarter of the UK working population will be involved in flexible working	Adapting to the needs of flexible working
Kock, McQueen and Baker (1996)	Discusses the relationships between knowledge, information and data and relates these to the concept of knowledge organizations which rely on knowledge workers and intense information flow	Information flow and organizational performance
Venugopal and Baets (1995)	Examines the capabilities of information technology as a support function for organizational learning and presents a framework for integrating intelligent systems with "real time" learning events	Integrating intelligence systems and learning
Keating, Robinson and Clemson (1996)	Describes a process for facilitating organizational self-reflection and advocates the use of action research to design, enact and observe aspects of organizational performance	Organizational self-reflection
Lyles (1994)	Shows that firms develop decision rules that help future decision-makers to distinguish between similar and dissimilar situations. Findings from a study also reveal attempts to maintain flexibility and to encourage innovative responses to "new" events	Using decision rules to guide organizational decision making
Lorange (1996)	Describes a managerial approach for creating or strengthening organizational learning through partnership with external partners	Learning partnerships and organizational performance
Harung and Harung (1995)	Suggests that to benefit from "unity in diversity" it is necessary to encourage empowerment, decentralization and self-management and then seek to integrate differences of view, guided by the organizational vision and a shared set of values	Diversity as a means of enhancing organizational performance
Bolton and Gold (1995)	Explains how the Nationwide Building Society used soft systems methodology to analyze career aspirations and map them against personal development needs and organizational development and performance criteria	Career and management development using soft systems approach
Stone (1996)	Reviews the literature that points to a "revolution" in business performance measurement and the greater use of "soft" employee-related measures. Study findings reveal that fewer companies than predicted are using or developing alternative performance measures	Performance measurement

Table IV.
Organizational change
and performance

guidance on how to overcome the barriers associated with organizational change. In particular, he suggests ways in which negative attitudes such as resentment, depression, distrust, stress, disloyalty and lack of productivity – often manifest in staff who are about to experience a major change – might be channelled in a more productive way.

Lacey (1995) reviews the role of internal consultants in organizational change and development and compares the role with that traditionally played by external consultants. She finds that internal consultants frequently have to cope with problems associated with role confusion, compartmentalization, marginality, unclear career paths, lack of continuity, varying client expectations and departmental jealousies. She adds that internal consultants would be able to perform more effectively if these pressures were clearly identified and better understood.

Learning from experience
Lyles (1994) observes that organizations do learn from their experiences and can remember incidents from the past that may influence future actions. This assumes that they consciously seek to develop the necessary skills to discriminate effectively between actions that have been successful and the appropriateness of deploying a "tried and tested" course of action in "new" circumstances. Kransdorff (1996) notes that while most organizations use post-project reviews, internal audits and/or oral post-mortems to learn from their own experiences, the problem with these techniques is that they rely on retrospection, which makes them susceptible to partial and selective memory recall by managers who, after the event are unlikely to be neutral or objective. Kransdorff offers a prescription for tackling the uncertainties of memory recall and defensive reasoning and helping managers to use the benefits of hindsight more effectively. Learning from experience and organizational "self-reflection" can in themselves generate opportunities for organizational learning as depicted in Figure 2.

Gustavsson and Harung (1994) argue that the level of collective consciousness determines the quality of life and the level of performance of an organization. They suggest that organizational learning is mainly restricted to the "surface areas" of awareness: action, senses, active thinking, but at deeper levels of consciousness (such as feeling and intuition), much less progress has occurred. They propose a concept of learning that aims to facilitate a greater awareness of the capacity for organizational development. Their study findings reveal that it is possible to achieve the transformation of both individual and collective consciousness by using Eastern style meditation techniques to heighten awareness of the capacity for continued growth. Srikantia and Pasmore (1996) also consider the concept of awareness, focusing on the roles of conviction and self doubt in organizational learning processes. They explore how these negative feelings and emotions impede the individuals' development and how they might be overcome so that learning processes might enable individuals to contribute more effectively to the corporate effort.

Organizational learning and performance
Fulmer (1995) describes MIT's Center for Organizational Learning and its four main areas of activity: learning laboratory projects related to generic management issues; team-related "dialogue" projects; a CEO leadership project

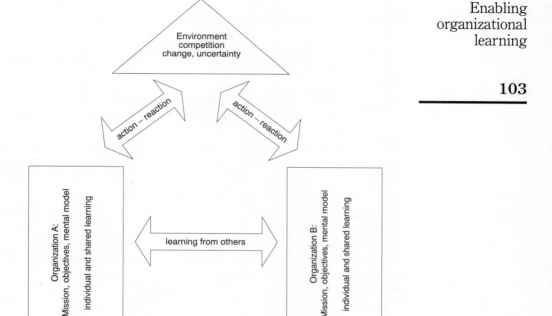

Source: adapted from Venugopal and Baets (1995, p. 24)

Figure 2.
Opportunities for
organizational learning

and a learning organization curriculum project. Roth and Senge (1996) say that more collaboration between researchers and practitioners is needed to establish "best practice" models of organizational learning. To do this, they suggest that more needs to be done to establish consensus about the research territory, research methods and goals, and how meaningful field projects can be designed and conducted. McDougall and Beattie (1996) report on a two-year project designed to evaluate the processes and outcomes of learning groups and suggest that lessons learned from this project can be applied to help to maximize learning and performance in groups in a wide range of organizational contexts.

Mirvis (1996) and Ford and Ogilvie (1996) present a broad review of theory and research about organizations and show how alternative schools of thought explain the different outcomes from routine and creative action in organizations. Mirvis contends that knowing "how" and "why" these different outcomes are achieved makes it easier to help people to "unlearn" old habits and develop new behaviours. Mirvis also considers the extent to which holistic thinking and work arrangements can be used to promote organizational learning and how measures to enhance collective consciousness might enable people to learn how to learn.

Lorange (1996) suggests that a learning partnership between an organization and one or more external catalysts should be founded on four propositions:

P1: organizational learning depends on complementary factors: the discovery of new knowledge and the ability to adapt to the subsequent changes required.

P2: organization learning takes place in two complementary places: inside the organization (a closed system) and outside (an open system) in a joint effort with other corporations – in a benchmarking mode.

P3: organizational learning is a deliberate process.

P4: external catalysts can play a critical, positive role in the organizational learning process.

Lorange proposes a number of partnership activities, each with performance-related benefits for the host organizations. These include: joint discovery and research projects; workshop and benchmarking activities; in-company tailored partnership programmes and organizational network activity assessments. The potential benefits to be derived from intra and inter-organizational learning are shown in Figure 3.

Lewis (1996a, 1996b) argues that, while total quality management had separate origins from the "culture" movement, the two fields have, in effect, converged as the desire to achieve "excellence" and "quality improvement" imply either "change" or "working with the prevailing culture of the organization". In order to investigate the range of business performance

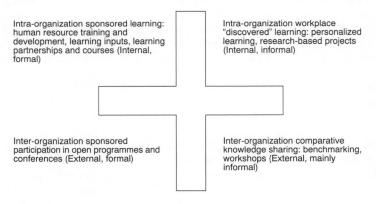

Figure 3.
Dimensions of
organizational learning

Source: adapted from Lorange (1996, p. 14)

measures used by UK companies, Stone (1996) conducted a survey of the Times Top 500 companies. The study sought to probe the issues relating to the use of so called "soft" employee-related performance measures, such as employee satisfaction, morale and commitment. The results, derived from 45 companies, indicated that few of the companies reporting were using or even developing innovative "soft" measures as a counterbalance to "harder" financially-related measures. The findings suggest that the "balanced scorecard" approach is impeded by lack of company evidence that "soft" performance measures yield similar benefits to financially-led ones.

Implications for organizational learning

To enable organizational learning to occur as effectively as possible, as an outcome of both formal programmed learning and informal self-reflection, it is helpful to consider the following points:

(1) How can the organization equip itself to detect and respond appropriately to market trends? What processes and procedures are needed to isolate any given pattern of external events, devise suitable responses and ensure that the implications for re-aligning resources and competences are addressed? How should the organization assimilate the "new" knowledge that it acquires from this continuous cycle of adjustment and re-alignment?

(2) Should the organization make a deliberate attempt to interrelate complex internal and external environments to planned organizational cultures for learning and creativity? If so, how might the concept of an "evolutionary organization" (EVO) be launched? What are the organization's ideals or vision for an EVO? How can organizational members be encouraged to think and act responsively and without unnecessary constraint so that natural curiosity drives workplace learning?

(3) What kind of organizational structure is appropriate now and in the future? To what extent could and should the organization move towards facilitated self-organized learning networks so that budgets, resources, targets and goals for learning are "released" to groups of employees, each "managing" enterprise activities? How will the differing roles of "knowledge workers" and generalists be reconciled if this approach is adopted?

(4) How should the organization adjust its information flows so as to take advantage of real time communications (virtual office, global networking via internet and intranet) for transacting its business? How could communications technologies be used to create a searchable knowledge network within the organizations to support the learning effort?

(5) What action is needed to ensure that learning from experience is "captured" and that opportunities for organizational learning from self-reflection (individual and shared learning) and from studying other organizations are acted upon?

(6) How might learning partnerships with external catalysts be used to organize joint discovery and research projects, workshop and benchmarking activities, in-company tailored partnership programmes and organizational network activity assessments?
(7) What performance measures does the organization currently use most often and why?
(8) Should "soft" employee-related performance measures (e.g. commitment, employee satisfaction, self-development, morale) be given more emphasis? How might the full range of organizational performance measures be related to improvements arising from the organizational learning effort?

References

Allen, R. (1995), "On a clear day you can have a vision: a visioning model for everyone", *Leadership & Organization Development Journal,* Vol. 16 No. 4, pp. 39-44.

Bell, M. and Tunnicliff, G. (1996), "Future search for stakeholders", *Management Development Review,* Vol. 9 No. 1, pp. 13-16.

Benbow, N. (1995), "Preparing for tomorrow", *Executive Development,* Vol. 8 No. 7, pp. 29-30.

Bolton, R. and Gold, J. (1995), "Career management at Nationwide Building Society using a soft systems approach", *Executive Development,* Vol. 8 No. 4, pp. 22-5.

Brooks, I. (1996), "Leadership of a cultural change process", *Leadership & Organization Development Journal,* Vol. 17 No. 5, pp. 31-7.

Carling, W. (1995), "Winning through leadership", *The Journal of Workplace Learning,* Vol 7 No. 4, pp. 27-30.

Carr, W. (1996), "Learning for leadership", *Leadership & Organization Development Journal,* Vol. 17 No. 6, pp. 46-52.

Chan, K.C. (1994), "Learning for total quality an action learning approach", *The Learning Organization,* Vol. 1 No. 1, pp. 17-22.

Field, R. (1996), "The flexible workforce: redefining the role of HR", *Management Development Review,* Vol. 9 No. 1, pp. 5-7.

Ford, C.M. and Ogilvie, D.T. (1996), "The role of action in organizational learning and change", *Journal of Organizational Change Management,* Vol. 9 No. 1, pp. 54-62.

Fulmer, R.M. (1995), "Building organizations that learn: the MIT Center for organizational learning", *Journal of Management Development,* Vol. 14 No. 5, pp. 9-14.

Gault, S.B. and Jaccaci, A.T. (1996), "Complexity meets periodicity", *The Learning Organization,* Vol. 3 No. 2, pp. 33-9.

Gustavsson, B. and Harung, H.S. (1994), "Organizational learning based on transforming collective consciousness", *The Learning Organization,* Vol. 1 No. 1, pp. 33-40.

Harung, H.S. and Harung, L.M. (1995), "Enhancing organizational performance by strengthening diversity and unity", *The Learning Organization,* Vol. 2 No. 3, pp. 9-21.

Keating, C., Robinson, T. and Clemson, B. (1996), "Reflective inquiry: a method for organizational learning", *The Learning Organization,* Vol. 3 No. 4, pp. 35-43.

Kenton, B. (1995), "What is a director's role?", *Executive Development,* Vol. 8 No. 2, pp. 16-18.

Klagge, J. (1996), "Defining, discovering and developing personal leadership in organizations", *Leadership & Organization Development Journal,* Vol. 17 No. 5, pp. 38-45.

Knippen, J.T. and Green, T.B. (1996), "What motivates your boss?", *The Journal of Workplace Learning,* Vol. 8 No. 3, pp. 15-18.

Kock, N.F., McQueen, R.J. and Baker, M. (1996), "Learning and process improvement in knowledge organizations: a critical analysis of four contemporary myths", *The Learning Organization,* Vol. 3 No. 1, pp. 31-41.

Kransdorff, A. (1996), "Using the benefits of hindsight – the role of post-project analysis", *The Learning Organization*, Vol. 3 No. 1, pp. 11-15.

Kur, E. and Bunning, R. (1996), "A three-track process for executive leadership development", *Leadership & Organization Development Journal*, Vol. 17 No. 4, pp. 4-12.

Lacey, M.Y. (1995), "Internal consulting: perspectives on the process of planned change", *Journal of Organizational Change Management*, Vol. 8 No. 3, pp. 75-84.

Lewis, D. (1996a), "The organizational culture saga – from OD to TQM: a critical review of the literature. Part 1 – concepts and early trends", *Leadership & Organization Development Journal*, Vol. 17 No. 1, pp. 12-9.

Lewis, D. (1996b), "The organizational culture saga – from OD to TQM: a critical review of the literature. Part 2 – applications", *Leadership & Organization Development Journal*, Vol. 17 No. 2, pp. 9-16.

Lorange, P. (1996), "Developing learning partnerships", *The Learning Organization*, Vol. 3 No. 2, pp. 11-19.

Lyles, M.A. (1994), "An analysis of discrimination skills as a process of organizational learning", *The Learning Organization*, Vol. 1 No. 1, pp. 23-32.

Macadam, C. (1996), "Addressing the barriers of managing change", *Management Development Review*, Vol. 9 No. 3, pp. 38-40.

McCrimmon, M. (1995), "Bottom-up leadership", *Executive Development*, Vol. 8 No. 5, pp. 6-12.

McDermott, M.C. and Chan, K. C. (1996), "Flexible intelligent relationship management: the business success paradigm in a stakeholder society", *The Learning Organization*, Vol. 3 No. 3, pp. 5-17.

McDougall, M. and Beattie, R.S. (1996), "Learning from learning groups", *The Journal of Workplace Learning*, Vol. 8 No. 3, pp. 26-30.

Mirvis, P.H. (1996), "Historical foundations or organization learning", *Journal of Organizational Change Management*, Vol. 9 No. 1, pp. 13-31.

Old, D.R. (1995), "Consulting for real transformation, sustainability, and organic form", *Journal of Organizational Change Management*, Vol. 8 No. 3, pp. 6-17.

Richardson, B. (1995a), "Learning contexts and roles for the learning organization leader", *The Learning Organization*, Vol. 2 No. 1, pp. 15-33.

Richardson, B. (1995b), "The politically aware leader: understanding the need to match paradigms and planning systems to powerful, turbulent fields, environments", *Leadership & Organization Development Journal*, Vol. 16 No. 2, pp. 27-35.

Richardson, B. and Thompson, J. (1995), "Strategy evaluation in powerful environments: a multi-competence approach", *Leadership & Organization Development Journal*, Vol. 16 No. 4, pp. 17-25.

Roth, G.L. and Senge, P.M. (1996), "From theory to practice: research territory, processes and structure at an organizational learning centre", *Journal of Organizational Change Management*, Vol. 9 No. 1, pp. 92-106.

Smith, A.C. and Saint-Onge, H. (1996), "The evolutionary organization: avoiding a Titanic fate", *The Learning Organization*, Vol. 3 No. 4, pp. 4-21.

Srikantia, P. and Pasmore, W. (1996), "Conviction and doubt in organizational learning", *Journal of Organizational Change Management*, Vol. 9 No. 1, pp. 42-53.

Stone, C.L. (1996), "Analysing business performance: counting the 'soft' issues", *Leadership & Organization Development Journal*, Vol. 17 No. 4, pp. 21-8.

Tait, R. (1996), "The attributes of leadership", *Leadership & Organization Development Journal*, Vol. 17 No. 1, pp. 27-31.

Taylor, R. and Taylor, C. (1996), "Trouble at the top: assessing the upper-level executive", *The Journal of Workplace Learning*, Vol. 8 No. 7, pp. 13-15.

Theobald, R. (1996), "The inevitably surprising future", *The Learning Organization*, Vol. 3 No. 2, pp. 30-2.

Venugopal, V. and Baets, W. (1995), "Intelligent support systems for organizational learning", *The Learning Organization*, Vol. 2 No. 3, pp. 22-34.

Chapter 7
Building and sustaining a learning organization

Richard Teare

*Granada Professor, Oxford Brookes University, and Academic Chair,
International Management Centres, and*

Richard Dealtry

Director, DSA Business Consultants, Harborne, UK

Introduction
This article considers how to create a learning environment and the implications for learning organizations. The literature reveals that many organizations are experimenting with "new" approaches to learning, coupled with current and future business goals (see Table I). The chapter draws on the views and experiences of members of two organizations undertaking workplace learning programmes at postgraduate level. The debate about aspects of in-company learning took place at an Internet conference entitled "The Learning Organization – Concepts and Realities" and the observations of managers and other contributors are reported here. Key themes are summarized and related to an agenda for organizational learning and renewal.

Creating a learning environment
Mumford (1996) observes that the concept of a learning organization is the subject of wide-ranging debate. He detects great interest by human resource professionals who recognize the value of organizational learning and a tendency towards cynicism by line managers who need to be convinced that it offers a recipe for actioning desirable objectives. In response, Mumford examines the nature of a learning organization and suggests how to achieve it by "Creating an environment where the behaviours and practices involved in continuous development are actively encouraged" (p. 27). Mumford sees the main benefits of creating a learning environment as:

- ensuring the long-term success of the organization;
- making incremental improvements a reality;
- ensuring that successes and best practices are transferred and emulated;
- increasing creativity, innovation and adaptability;
- attracting people who want to succeed and learn and retaining them;

This article first appeared in *The Learning Organization,* Vol. 5 No. 1, 1998, pp. 47-60.

Authors	Focus	Sub-theme
Mumford (1996)	Considers the concept of the learning organization and outlines an approach to creating a meaningful learning environment, beginning with a self-diagnosis of managerial behaviours and practices	Managerial roles in creating a learning environment
DeFilippo (1996)	Describes elements of the learning organization model developed by Pratt & Witney as the company embraced cellular manufacturing. Reveals how productive units have changed their culture from strict hierarchical control to higher employee involvement	Integrated support for cell-oriented business units
Harung (1996)	Examines evidence of relating to the link between mature corporate culture and high levels of collective performance. Observes that a key feature of advanced organizations is the ability to satisfy all stakeholders simultaneously. Uses a case example to explore this	Relating learning to stakeholder needs and expectations
Wright and Belcourt (1996)	Illustrates the role of on-the-job training (OJT) in operationalizing learning organization concepts. Argues that practical training provides a tangible sign of action that appeals to line managers and helps to put theory into practice	Relating training to broader-based organizational learning
Coulson-Thomas (1996)	Examines the impact of business performance re-engineering (BPR) in a sample of European-based firms. Findings suggest that BPR efforts yield short-term benefits but tend to neglect longer-term learning and efforts to source and sustain competitive advantage	Balancing short- and long-term perspectives on organizational developmnent
Heraty and Morley (1995)	Explores how to conduct research in organizations and emphasizes the importance of ensuring that the research design appropriately reflects the values and experiences of organizational members	Relating action research to the learning organization
Borzsony and Hunter (1996)	Outlines a five-year learning-through-partnership programme established in a university. Explains the background to partnership and learning organizations, the action research framework and the practical processes and techniques used to turn the idea into reality	Learning partnerships
White (1994)	Calls for a deeper exploration of the changes in thinking and behaviour necessary to create a learning organization. Explores the shift from information to knowledge and the potential this affords for creative learning development in organizations	Creativity and the learning culture

Table I.
Creating a learning
environment

- ensuring that people are equipped to meet the current and future needs of the organization.

The first step in diagnosing the interactions that occur in the "learning environment" is to examine the active roles of managers and the related

behaviours. Beyond this, Honey and Mumford define four roles that managers
should adopt so that opportunities for learning can be prioritized:

(1) *Role model* – demonstrate (behaviour and actions) personal enthusiasm
for learning and development.

(2) *Provider* – be a conscious and generous provider of learning and
development opportunities for others and an active supporter and
encourager whenever opportunities are taken up.

(3) *System builder* – build learning into the system so that it is integrated
with normal work processes and embedded in the conscious agenda.

(4) *Champion* – the importance of learning for other parts and the
organization as a whole.

DeFilippo (1996) traces the current interest in the learning organization to the
work of Senge and his widely read book *The Fifth Discipline* (1990). Senge
contends that the only long-term sustainable source of competitive advantage in
an organization is for it to learn faster than its competitors and if it is to achieve
this, it needs to be more effective than the sum of its parts. Senge offers a
framework for learning founded on five key areas or disciplines:

(1) *Systems thinking* – understanding the whole rather than just the
fractional parts of organizational thinking and behaviour.

(2) *Personal mastery* – a readiness to continually renew personal learning
and to relate this to organizational work.

(3) *Shared vision* – related to conviction, commitment and clarity of intent
that generates a need for learning and the collective will to learn.

(4) *Mental models* – that assist managers to challenge their own
assumptions and views of the "current reality".

(5) *Team learning* – to encourage work groups to engage in dialogue.

Harung (1996) describes a series of steps that he portrays as a transition from
task-based to value-based organizational development. Task-based
organizations are characterized by command and control hierarchies where a
comparatively small number of senior managers make decisions and develop
policies. In these "power-driven" organizations he suggests that employees are
most likely to be promoted if they perform in a prescribed way. Beyond this,
process-based organizations require a more open, participative framework and
as they mature, they may become more value-based as they strive to satisfy a
wider group of stakeholders. Harung highlights the organizational changes that
occur during the transition from task-based to value-based development (see
Table II).

The learning organization – concepts and realities
The literature tells us that many organizations are experimenting with "new"
approaches to learning and coupling these with process improvement among

Task-based organizational behaviour	Value-based organizational behaviour
Top down initiative and command	Empowerment, dispersed initiative, self management
Managers and employees	Self-sufficient knowledge workers and co-leaders
Few effective managers	Many effective members
Emphasis on hierarchy (vertical)	Emphasis on network (horizontal)
Rigid organizational structures	Self-organized, fluid and sometimes spontaneous groups
Many and elaborate rules	Shared vision, few and simple rules
Sharp division of labour	Overlapping and multidimensional work
Clear-cut organizational edges	Customer and supplier participation
Slow mass production	Rapid adaptation to customer needs
Managers control and solve problems	Leaders symbolize unity and exemplify maturity
Win-lose assumption and opposition	Win-win assumption and mutual support
Divergent individual and organizational needs	Meet individual and organizational needs concurrently
Range of anti-social even anti-organizational behaviour	Co-existence of freedom and ethical behaviour
Outer organizational promotion	Inner personal growth
Individuals and the organization compete against others	Individuals and the organization compete against self
Conventional path following	Post-conventional path following
Achievement is goal related as are rewards	Achievement is process and goal related as are rewards
Limited avenues for self-fulfilment	Focus on actualization of self and others

Source: Adapted from Harung, 1996, p. 24

Table II.
Towards a learning
organization: transitional
steps and characteristics

many other initiatives (see Table III). The challenge is often to "do more with less" and to "be smarter and act smarter" in responding to the complexities of change. Perhaps this is best summarized by the statement attributed to Revans: "… an organization's capacity to learn must exceed the rate of change imposed on it". The Internet conference "The Learning Organization – Concepts and Realities" sought to explore aspects of organizational learning and to relate them to our understanding of the meaning and relevance of the "learning organization" as a corporate entity and its relationship to two organizations in particular, BAA plc and Fina plc. Participants were managers undertaking action learning programmes at postgraduate certificate, diploma and MBA levels respectively and four articles, together with a summary overview and discussion points for each, were used as a conference discussion resource (see Appendix).

What is a learning organization?
In broad terms, a learning organization can be viewed as a social system whose members have learned conscious, communal processes for continually:

- generating, retaining and leveraging individual and collective learning to improve the performance of the organizational system in ways important to all stakeholders; and
- monitoring and improving performance (Drew and Smith, 1995).

Authors	Focus	Sub-theme
Buckler (1996)	Examines the process by which individuals in organizations learn, and develops a model to facilitate continuous improvement and innovation in business processes. The model is designed to be applied and used by managers	Modelling the learning process in organizations
Drew and Smith (1995)	Argues that radical change is more likely to succeed if attention is first paid to organizational readiness. Offers a framework for radical "change auditing" and "change proofing" the firm to increase its capacity to withstand and exploit unexpected and rapid change	Organizational readiness
Teare et al. (1997)	Presents case studies from 14 UK and US-based manufacturing and service firms. Provides an array of evidence that work-based teams are making a significant contribution to organizational learning	Teamworking and learning
Richardson (1995)	Examines the challenges for leaders of modern, networked learning organizations as they: strive to innovate and respond to marketplace conditions, develop through the medium of strategic alliances and explore ways of "getting more for less"	Networked learning
Peters (1996)	Considers the question: "What does a learning organization learn about?" and proposes a syllabus approach in six areas with steps for implementing it. Discusses action learning as a developmental methodology and offers recommendations for practitioners	A learning organization's syllabus
Hitt (1995)	Addresses the question "What does a learning organization look like and how does it differ from the more traditional organization?" Offers a systems view defined as "an organization that is striving for excellence through continual organizational renewal"	Organizational renewal

Table III.
The learning organization:
concepts and realities

In 1996, BAA's management committee reviewed and endorsed a strategy for training and development which would help the company to address its key challenges. This was not intended to be a once only effort but the start of a continuous assessment process focusing on efficiency and effectiveness in learning. Tony Ryan, BAA's director, Training and Management Development explains:

In BAA we have come to realize that every one of our business strategies will require continuous upgrading and this will impact on the competences and skills of our people. Investments in technology, capital equipment and process changes are substantial but these inputs cannot realize the goals of growing the business and staying ahead of the competition without a matching investment in people. The company's mission statement aims to enable all our employees to develop their potential and to make a direct contribution to the company's success. Our Chief Executive, Sir John Egan, has repeatedly stated that we will do everything possible to avoid job losses and protect continuity of employment. These goals can only be achieved if the company takes positive steps to encourage and support learning and this means that every employee should accept the need to adopt the habits of lifelong learning and see new skill demands as opportunities not threats.

To encourage learning, BAA focuses on meeting customer needs, sharing "best practice" and by managing the accumulation of knowledge which supports the organization's core competences, identifying "new" learning opportunities. Further, the organization is geared to "benchmark" against world-class business performance and align its organizational processes and management practices so that improvements in all areas can be implemented without impediment. BAA's interest in the concepts and realities of the learning organization stems from this and its own belief that the capacity and willingness to learn will be in competitive terms, the most critical success factor in the twenty-first century.

Theme 1: modelling the learning process in organizations
Buckler (1996) reviews the importance of: focus (to plot a course for the learning effort) the environment (which facilitates learning) and the techniques (which enable learning to be efficient) and the relative contributions made by "taught" and "discovery" methods of learning. He depicts a journey (ignorance, awareness, understanding, commitment, enactment, reflection) and reviews: the role of leadership in creating a learning environment; questioning; developing a shared vision and ownership; enabling and removing barriers. After this, he presents and discusses: the learning support system (systematic, led, team and individual learning support, experimentation, learning resource information support); learning needs diagnosis; progress reviews and the company policy deployment process.

Buckler observes that learning effectiveness is dependent on the environment for learning and the efforts of organizational leaders and managers in creating, sustaining and encouraging the appropriate conditions for learning to occur. Mark Johnston believes that "… the quest for knowledge by individuals is the main driving force …" and that the individual's personal journey can be channelled via team learning and ultimately organizational learning with the aid of facilitators and mentor support. He adds that the team leader should be a "disseminator of opportunity" and thereafter the learner should be encouraged to disseminate to the wider team by sharing newly acquired insights and knowledge. Johnston views this as the most difficult but ultimately the most rewarding aspect of teamworking. Chris Drabble relates Buckler's views on the learning environment to BAA's own vision for learning. He observes that BAA's efforts to become a learning organization are making a tangible difference to the culture of the company.

The "new" culture, facilitated by various empowerment tools is inevitably permeating the various parts of the company at a variable pace. Drabble believes that the pace of change is related to the depth of understanding and the varying degrees of acceptance in the minds and behaviours of the company's managers. To address the issue, he suggests that a core strand of BAA's internal communications strategy might focus on explaining and reiterating the advantages of creating and sustaining a learning environment and its implications for ongoing business improvement. The scale of the challenge implicit in becoming a learning organization also raises the question as to whether BAA should be attempting to embed the new culture in all areas of activity simultaneously or whether an incremental style of change guided by the corporate vision might allow more rapid progress.

While most see the creation of a learning environment as the means of supporting the learning organization, especially in its early stages, Mike Speed warns that the environment itself is all too often a limiting factor as "... the people who 'fit in' will be those whose cognitive style aligns itself with the organization's values and beliefs". Speed sees large traditional-style organizations which aim for consistency, efficiency and stability as relatively conformance-driven employers. Here, the characteristics of an individual with a preference for a "taught" learning style correlates closely with the qualities that are espoused in such organizations. The relatively "static" nature of their processes, procedures, structure, culture and behaviours serves to reinforce compliance and conformance to the unwritten norms that permeate organizational life. So, if a problem presents itself, individual managers and the organization as a whole will attempt to deal with it by applying its normative patterns and doing things better by adapting what they already do. Grant Thompson makes some similar points – he feels that conditioned responses (normative behaviour in "static" organizations) stifle empowerment and creativity. In contrast, Speed thinks that organizations with a more "dynamic" style and a preference for discovery and innovation are more likely to see organizational norms as part of the problem. If so, it is probable that individuals will be encouraged to find a better way of doing things:

> It is an age old argument of whether to do things better or to do better things. With either extreme of style, an organization and its members will limit its own responses when confronting non-routine problems.

Speed uses this argument to advance the cause of teamworking with the aim of "unfreezing" the organizational mindset and avoiding decision making that is skewed to either extreme. At the heart of the matter is the self-reinforcing nature of organizations which so often fail to take account of the spectrum of cognitive styles. The problem can be traced to recruitment and selection which still tends to favour people who will "fit" the job and company as a whole. Those who interview and select are so often themselves steeped in a system that expects and rewards certain behaviour. It is partly for this reason that internal recruiters are trusted to make the "right" decision. In summing-up, Speed observes that in time and with appropriate support and possibly incentives, people can learn new behaviours, but of vital importance is the recruitment and selection process. If the learning organization is to take shape, Speed believes that this is a key conduit for new thinking and should be used to broaden the organization's resource of cognitive styles rather than maintaining a comparatively narrow status quo.

Buckler contrasts the relative merits of "taught" and "discovery" methods of learning but according to Erwin Rausch, the sequence and interplay between the two is equally important. Rausch describes a diagram that he has found helpful in shaping his own approach to learning. He offers this as a foundation for organizational learning as well as a guide for the individual learner concerned with absorbing and integrating "new" learning with what is already familiar:

> The diagram is a vertical, pyramidal spiral which starts at the bottom with "acquisition of new knowledge" then turns up to "demonstration of the new knowledge". On the third level is "personal application of the new knowledge" and on the fourth level of the spiral is "feedback". Thereafter the spiral repeats the same levels in ever smaller form, dramatizing the smaller amount that has to be learned before full knowledge and skill competence has been reached. Starting from this simplistic diagram, I have come to the conclusion that some "teaching" at the very beginning is necessary before "discovery", which is a combination of demonstration and personal application, can find fertile ground.

Rausch, an educationist with professional and publishing interests in learning, prefers taught elements in the form of sharply focused questions or guidelines based on a sound framework or model of the subject area. He adds: "… when learners explore how the guidelines apply in a specific situation or even a hypothetical scenario, there is a direction to 'discover' and far more learning can take place than if the 'discovery' lacks conceptual foundation and guidance."

Peter Rebbeck identifies with Buckler's schema of taught vs discovery models and feels that by taking a broad view, it is possible to derive benefits from both. Reflecting on a recent BAA project, Rebbeck provides a good illustration of mutual dependency:

> BAA has been focused on improving the efficiency of its construction programme. We have been benchmarking the industry worldwide in order to identify where current best practice lies. Those involved have been using the "discovery" model to undertake the project. Following the initial phase, a series of handbooks and guidelines were produced which mainly use the "taught" model so that our project staff can acquire "new" knowledge. The advantage here has been to "level the playing field" in a consistent and speedy manner. The next challenge is to build on current best practice and deliver world class performance by encouraging pioneering projects which break new ground in process and technology terms. Arising from this, BAA has to learn to cope better with the challenges and opportunities of experimentation.

Rebbeck sees much scope for improvement ahead and several current challenges arising from the combined taught-discovery approach but first, the stages of what Buckler calls "commitment" and "enactment" have to be achieved – this is not so much to do with the "it's not my job" syndrome but the "whys" of learning. Second, construction professionals are by tradition and expectation, wedded to the taught model. The discover model is alien to them and yet if they are to acquire new knowledge they need to adopt this approach to build on their existing base of expertise.

Elaine Saunders provides an interesting example of learning by discovery during a fire drill when participants are normally expected to conform to a taught pattern of behaviour:

> The best fire practice I have ever been involved in at BAA occurred shortly after I joined the company and, for reasons unrelated to the fire drill, two exits were blocked ... it took valuable time before people "woke up" and thought about what they were actually doing and found an alternative exit. People seemed to learn far more from this exercise than they had from many other "conforming" taught methods.

Saunders makes the point that especially in situations like this, creative thinking to address the unexpected has a small but key role to play in addition to conforming with best practice ground rules on the steps that should be followed in the event of a fire. Commenting from Australia, Elyssebeth Leigh, an educationist, observes that the fire drill example reflects both a problem and an opportunity for learning in learning organizations. Leigh describes this as a tension between taught skills and discovered knowledge:

> ... the problem/learning opportunity as I encounter it in university classes – is the stress that emerges when adults are first encouraged to question habitual behaviours. In a recent class – part way through a semester-long simulation – this erupted into sustained debate about the "radical" nature of the learning process being encountered ... I used the metaphor of the Israelites' "golden calf" which was made when Moses "abandoned them" for three days and they were desperate for some sense of "certainty" in the midst of the fearsome uncertainty of an alien and vast "desert". While understandable – I suggested – as a sign of human fears, the "calf" (a short-term sign of security and "normality") ensured they wandered for 40 years in that same desert. Another student then suggested that the timespan ensured all those involved (at an adult level) were dead and those who arrived in the promised land were ready for the new life and structures and values required. The metaphor seems to have worked, at least as a means of causing those fixated on "tangibles" to re-consider their own needs in this context.

Leigh says that she is careful to avoid criticism and tries to open-up dialogue between the two ends of the learning spectrum. She adds that these ideas may have wider relevance with the tension between the two ends of the spectrum requiring a continuing exercise of "moving towards balance".

Responding to Elyssebeth Leigh's "fire drill" observations, Grant Colligan, a member of BAA's Fire Service, says that he has used the taught model throughout his career but in fact, the discovery model is widely used. However, Colligan believes that the interplay between the two methods has yet to be adequately developed in the workplace and that BAA's strategy for learning will encourage this. Rounding-up the discussion, Laurence Matthews observes that the fire drill illustration "... points up the difference between actually learning something and learning what you were supposed to, which was presumably the agenda in the minds of the organisers of the drill". Matthews also comments on Leigh's point about the "tangibles" of learning. "There are obvious psychological needs for the individual, but it also seems to be a factor in marshalling external approval for the effort – e.g. proving the worth of learning to the budget holder ..."

Theme 2: organizational readiness

Drew and Smith (1995) interpret focus, will and capability as: the organization's knowledge and awareness of potential change, its willingness to address such change and its abilities to exploit and withstand change. They review the contribution of benchmarking (learning); action learning; organizational climate (development); commitment to supporting continuous learning and creativity. To conclude, they present a change audit approach for diagnosing needs re: organizational learning and developing initiatives to enhance organizational capacity for change. The approach is illustrated by referring to IKEA's response to opportunities for growth in international markets.

David Towler responds to Drew and Smith's article with an array of points that he feels have been omitted or should be approached in a different way. First, he notes that managers generally have a full workload and that it is unrealistic to seek to overlay a "change audit" and expect managers to perform as normal. Peter Rebbeck makes this point too and readily sees a connection between managers being too busy to handle the "now" and the "future" at the same time. Second, Towler believes that change is more readily achieved by the individual and, extending outwards, the behaviours of groups of individuals who collectively determine organizational behaviour. To get this far – convincing individuals of the need to change the organization (and not the other way around) and to maintain momentum, Towler asserts that the learning organization must be founded on three fundamental principles – trust, honesty and integrity – mentioned just once in the article. Roy Truett makes a similar point and says that he values honesty, openness and clarity when it comes to explaining the reasons for change.

Towler observes that many organizations try to build a learning environment on top of a culture that is traditional, hierarchical and competitive and then they wonder why their efforts fail. Who, for example, is going to commit themselves to action learning, building a shared vision and team learning if they see their colleagues engaging in "old" culture politics and succeeding, possibly at the learner's expense? A learning environment is also costly in the sense that it must be properly supported if learning is to become part of the individual's working life. Among other things, it means that management systems have to be re-geared to learning outcomes that are seldom easy to predict in conventional terms. How then might the behaviours of individuals be channelled so that a culture of learning is reinforced? Towler believes that competences contribute to a learning organization in two ways. First, as individuals build on their own portfolio, it adds value to the learning process as a whole. Second, competences (as specified by NVQ and MCI among others) provide a clearly defined process standard for doing a given job or series of tasks and this is crucial to achieving high level performance. Drew and Smith fail to make this point, nor do they comment on the role of appraisal systems, particularly 360° appraisal that can be related back to the underlying principles of trust, honesty and integrity. Towler feels that it is feasible to implement a system of empowerment founded on process standards so that freedom to

Building a
learning
organization

117

manage is seen as the outward sign of the learning organization's inner values – a key indicator of a true learning environment.

Drew and Smith propose that organizations should designate a chief change officer (CCO) and in the context of organizational learning, Paul Davies questions whether this role should be part of the remit of the human resources function or a separate, more neutral role. Jon Phillips feels that a CCO should have a wider remit so as to draw on external as well as internal considerations. He proposes a semi-independent "think tank" that is not accountable to any specific function within the company. Further, it would need to be sufficiently liberal minded and radical in outlook to encompass a wide range of perspectives and a rich variety of inputs in terms of the seniority, function and geographical location of its members. Phillips suggests that an MBA action learning set meets these criteria and Davies agrees that the think tank role would accelerate the learning of both the set and the organization.

Turning to change proofing and specifically change audits, Andrew Elliott wonders whether the concept is seen as nothing more than a form of insurance by senior management. Jon Phillips believes that the need for intelligent and thorough environmental scanning has never been more important for companies whose business objectives are threatened by external pressures. He believes that awareness is part of the solution, but willingness to respond is more often the key challenge. A key question is when does a threat become real and enduring rather than merely a further obstacle that must be overcome? This is a particularly appropriate question for the aviation industry as it participates in the current debate about airport expansion. Elaine Saunders identifies a set of strategic-level questions that BAA should seek to answer (relating to the proposed Terminal 5, key customers and the prospect of Government interventions) and feels that a wider set of "group think" ideas might be facilitated by holding an open, internal session via intranet and thereafter, ideas might be filtered, sorted and actioned as appropriate. Grant Colligan agrees and feels that there is scope for a different form of contingency planning by deriving inputs from the active learners that BAA is sponsoring. This accords with the notion of a learning organization that is striving for excellence through continual renewal.

Theme 3: teamworking and learning

Teare *et al.* (1997) consider the rising importance of the "process paradigm" as a means of improving service and responsiveness and an "ingredients of change" programme (management commitment; education; measurement; recognition; regeneration) promoted by the National Society for Quality through Teamworking. The authors provide case illustrations and outcomes that reflect the activities of teams formed to address and solve problems or to identify improvement opportunities which have been identified and given to the team. They are single project teams that usually disband on completion of the given task; outcomes from self-directed team projects and cases of organizational commitment to total people involvement with quality and employee activities as key elements.

Elaine Saunders relates the article to BAA's own team initiatives and wonders whether teamworking has been over-emphasized, to the point where people feel compelled to work as part of a group even when the work they are doing might be better carried out independently. Despite this, Gary Smith sees a divide opening up between those who manage or supervise others (and are encouraged to attend teambuilding courses) and the supervised workforce as a whole who do not generally attend courses about teamworking. He feels that there should be a team dynamics course that is open to all so that the benefits of teamworking are more widely understood and the inputs that individuals can make are better stated. Siew Kam Soon reinforces this point by relating the variety of inputs to the efficiency of the group effort. Here, different learning styles and preferences encourage individuals to learn from each other and play to the various strengths in any given group.

Elaine Saunders relates team outcomes to the need for wider recognition and observes that BAA's appraisal systems do not appear to take account of the individuals' contribution to cross-disciplinary team effort. She suggests that a "learning log" approach might be adopted so that the project leader can write comments in the individual learning logs of team members. As members move from project to project, they accumulate entries in their personal learning log that enable individuals to reflect on their own learning and on what they have been able to contribute to the team and second, his or her line manager can take account of this in one-to-one appraisal meetings. The learning log "profile" might also provide a helpful indicator of the comparative maturity of teams throughout the organization. If individuals were required to make a specific number of contributions, each to different teams each year, the learning log would provide a meaningful basis for assessing overall team effectiveness. Beyond this, "effective" team members might be given more scope in selecting the projects they work on, together with other forms of non-monetary reward. Peter Rebbeck agrees and adds that the way in which teams are chaired should be reviewed so that a clearer understanding of how to "professionalize" the role emerges. He sees the key skill as being expert facilitation in the areas of timekeeping, encouraging involvement, effective resource utilization and optimal team member participation.

Theme 4: networked learning

The learning organization literature emphasizes the importance of "self-organizing, learning communities" in and around organizations. To keep pace, employees need to be encouraged to take more responsibility for creating and managing innovatory projects in contexts of depleted resource bases and from positions as network collaborators rather than administrators. Richardson (1995) sees the notion of "empowerment" as central to the concept of the learning community culture and suggests a number of steps:

(1) develop new top management perspectives on control;

(2) design the use of power;

(3) establish self-organizing teams;

(4) develop multi-cultures;

(5) present challenges and encourage risk-taking;

(6) improve group learning skills;

(7) create resource slack.

Further, he provides an illustrative case study: how a new leader has reforged success through the strategy of "organization as a network of facilitated learning communities". After this, he suggests that informal networks utilize three types of relationship network based on advice, trust and communication needs and considers how to: avoid the pitfalls of the networked organization and understand the new skill requirements for managing in the networked organization. Two short case illustrations are provided: "headhunting the modern middle manager" and "orchestrating change from the middle". The article concludes with a review of the personal development and reward packages needed to maintain managerial commitment and motivation.

Eric Sandelands likens the role of sponsoring networked learning to that of "midwife" to the learning organization. He profiles BAA's aspirations to be a "virtual" learning organization at his Virtual University Press Internet site (http://www.openhouse.org.uk/virtual-university-press/). Elaine Saunders stresses the importance of firmly embedding the new style BAA learning culture as a precursor to becoming a truly empowered learning organization. She sees some parts of the organization changing more quickly than others and this is manifest in a sense of enthusiasm arising from new ideas like "creating successful teams" and "freedom to manage" in the airport terminals. Saunders is also encouraged by the comparatively recent introduction of courses designed to develop senior managers like "sharing the vision" and "growing the business".

There was previously no real provision for on-the-job development apart from technical training and these courses provide a means of promoting in-depth thinking about the business and its long-term development. Roy Truett says that empowerment is still viewed with a degree of suspicion because of the complexities of relating it to the needs, preferences and expectations of individuals throughout the company. He believes that a more visible reward package for all employees would help to overcome the barriers to its full adoption, including an element of performance-related pay with eligibility extended to all. Jennifer Anderson reflects on the means of communicating the principles of empowerment and believes that the information is available but that the message is inconsistent. She believes that the central message of empowerment should be communicated face-to-face either by managers to teams or in a roadshow format. Anderson stresses the importance of presenting a consistent organization-wide message: "… if the information is only readily available to more senior managers then the rest will only receive the picture that top management chooses to present and this, regardless of the 'sharing the vision' and 'growing the business' programmes is still varied in content and quality".

The issues raised in the resource articles and the responses and examples given by participants at the Internet conference suggest that there is considerable scope for crafting and embedding a learning organization model that is meaningful and relevant to those who are actively engaged in the endeavour. A summary of the main recommendations arising from the discussion is given in Table IV.

Towards an agenda for learning and renewal

Peters (1996) proposes a syllabus-driven approach for the aspiring learning organization, inter-linking six areas which can be addressed by designing interventions for individuals, groups and organizational systems. The syllabus areas are:

Themes	Recommendations
Modelling the learning process in organizations	• Use internal communications to explain and encourage personal learning and to promote its application to ongoing business improvement. "Sell the benefits" as often and in as many different ways as possible, throughout the organization • Aim to recruit and retain people with different cognitive styles and skills to avoid "organizational cloning" • Aim to use taught and discovery methods, and where appropriate, a combination of both • Encourage creative thinking and its application to "opportunities for learning"
Organizational readiness	• Seek to enact change through individuals rather than "overlaying" an agenda for organizational change on the workforce as a whole. Use workplace learning founded on core values of trust, honesty and integrity to encourage personal development • Establish one or more independent action research sets to examine future scenarios and implications. Draw the set membership from people with different learning styles, skills and from a variety of organizational functions
Teamworking and learning	• Communicate the benefits of teamworking as widely as possible and link individual inputs to team outputs via the appraisal process. Use a learning log to enable team members to reflect on the effectiveness of their own inputs. Establish targets for team participation (ongoing and different teams) and encourage shared learning
Networked learning	• Seek to embed a culture of learning by devoting time and resources to developing a wider and deeper understanding of the concept of empowerment. Link this to on-the-job training and development, explain and communicate the benefits at all levels of the organization and emphasize the benefits to individuals as well as the organization

Table IV.
The learning
organization: some
recommendations

(1) Learning about the participant's own job in the organization and how to do it better.

(2) Learning how to create alignment between culture and strategy in the organization so that initiatives "fit" the context from inception to implementation.

(3) Learning about the future by exploring the value of techniques for scenario planning and anticipating the likely implications for personal and organizational competency development.

(4) Learning about the operating environment and the supply chain – essentially Peter Senge's "fifth discipline" of systems thinking.

(5) Learning how to challenge existing schools of thinking and avoid myopia so that personal and organizational mindsets are open to change and to new ideas.

(6) Developing an organizational memory for the purpose of capturing, storing and retrieving knowledge and expertise.

The syllabus is for the organization as a whole and its members who should participate according to their personal learning agenda and the organizational imperative. However, the sequence of its implementation is of some significance. Peters suggests that the learner's own job should be the starting point, as improvements here will yield organizational benefits from the outset. After this, the longer-term debates should be established about the future, future competences and how to network learning throughout the organization's supply chain. The framework also provides a basis for monitoring the kind of organizational adjustments needed to maintain creativity and productivity and for routinizing improvements by creating and drawing on a knowledge base that constitutes the organization's bank of knowledge capital. In essence, the learning organization is one that has found a workable and meaningful way of systemizing organizational learning and all its component parts (see Figure 1).

Hitt (1995) emphasizes the purpose of a learning organization in his definition "… an organization that is striving for excellence through continual organization renewal" (p. 17). He adapts the McKinsey 7-S framework to provide a systems view of the learning organization:

- Shared values – excellence and organizational renewal.
- Leadership style – catalyst.
- Team – synergistic so that members learn together and provide a greater value than the sum total of individual contributions.
- Strategy – learning map with scope for discovery and adaptation.
- Structure – dynamic networks.
- Staff – people who want to learn, preferably throughout their careers.
- Skills – generative learning.
- Measurement system – a balanced score card approach using critical success factors to emphasize and measure: excellence, organizational renewal and financial performance.

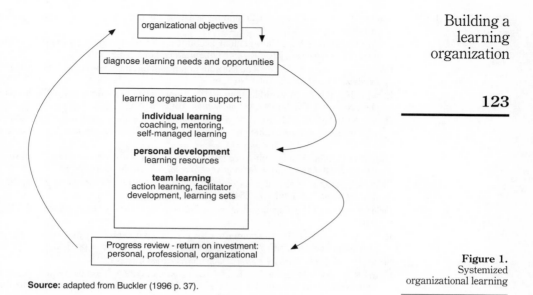

Figure 1.
Systemized
organizational learning

Illustrative critical success factors include:

- excellence (e.g. conformance to specifications, zero rejects, on-time delivery, customer satisfaction);
- organizational renewal (e.g. cross-functional teamworking, the value of learning networks, working with customers, suppliers and other organizations, staff development, investment in research and development, process redesign, continuous improvement); and
- financial performance (e.g. meeting revenue, cost, profit contribution targets).

In summing-up Hitt observes that the learning organization is a new paradigm that reflects a process rather than an end state. He observes:

> Embracing and implementing the paradigm of the learning organization will be no easy task. There will be obstacles. And one of the most challenging obstacles will be to overcome the resistance of those managers who have fully embraced the traditional organizational paradigm – and are successful. Why should they change? There is an important reason why they should change. And that is the quest for excellence. In this quest, managers want to know how to achieve excellence and how to maintain it. The learning organization points the way: excellence through organizational renewal (Hitt, 1995, p. 25).

References

Borzsony, P. and Hunter, K. (1996), "Becoming a learning organization through partnership", *The Learning Organization,* Vol. 3 No. 1, pp. 22-30.

Buckler, B. (1996), "A learning process model to achieve continuous improvement and innovation", *The Learning Organization,* Vol. 3 No. 3, pp. 31-9.

Coulson-Thomas, C.J. (1996), "BPR and the learning organization", *The Learning Organization,* Vol. 3 No. 1, pp. 16-21.

DeFilippo, J.S. (1996), "Management accounting learns to adapt to Pratt & Whitney's manufacturing cells", *The Learning Organization*, Vol. 3 No. 2, pp. 4-10.

Drew, S. and Smith, P. (1995), "The learning organization: 'change proofing' and strategy", *The Learning Organization,* Vol. 2 No. 1, pp. 4-14.

Harung, H.S. (1996), "A world-leading learning organization: a case study of Tomra Systems, Olso, Norway", *The Learning Organization*, Vol. 3 No. 4, pp. 22-34.

Heraty, N. and Morley, M. (1995), "A review of issues in conducting organization-level research with reference to the learning organization", *The Learning Organization,* Vol. 2 No. 4, pp. 27-35.

Hitt, W.D. (1995), "The learning organization: some reflections on organizational renewal", *Leadership & Organization Development Journal*, Vol. 16 No. 8, pp. 17-25.

Mumford, A. (1996), "Creating a learning environment", *Journal of Professional Human Resource Management*, Vol. 4, July, pp. 26-30.

Peters, J. (1996), "A learning organization's syllabus", *The Learning Organization*, Vol. 3 No. 1, pp. 4-10.

Richardson, B. (1995), "How to administer the networked organization: tips from the theory and practice of management", *The Learning Organization*, Vol. 2 No. 4, pp. 4-13.

Senge, P. (1990), *The Fifth Discipline,* Doubleday, Garden City, NY.

Teare, R., Ingram, H., Scheuing, E. and Armistead, C. (1997), "Organizational teamworking frameworks: evidence from UK and US-based firms", *International Journal of Service Industry Management,* Vol. 8 No. 3, pp. 250-63.

"The Learning Organization – Concepts and Realities" (1997), contributions from participants at an Internet conference held in association with BAA plc and Fina plc, Top Management Global Forum at: http://www.mcb/co.uk/topman, 20 April-1 July.

White, M.G. (1994), "Creativity and the learning culture", *The Learning Organization*, Vol. 1 No. 2, pp. 4-5.

Wright, P.C. and Belcourt, M. (1996), "Down in the trenches: learning in a learning organization", *The Journal of Workplace Learning,* Vol. 8 No. 4, pp. 24-8.

Appendix: The Learning Organization – Concepts and Realities (1997)

Internet conference held from 20 April-1 July 1997 at the Top Management Global Forum at: http://www.mcb/co.uk/topman in association with BAA plc and Fina plc

Theme 1: modelling the learning process in organizations

Buckler (1996) examines the processes by which individuals in organizations learn, and develops a learning process model to facilitate continuous improvement and innovation in business processes. The model is designed to be applied and used by managers working in organizations. The article discusses: learning as a process that results in changed behaviour and the "hows" of learning (techniques to help the learning process) (pp. 31-3); the "whys" of learning – creating an environment which provides meaning and the "whats" of learning – enabling a focus on organizational goals (pp. 33-6); a learning process model.

Sub-set discussion points:

(1) As you read the article, highlight or underline significant points and note down own personal reactions: think about your own learning: what works best for me? my team colleagues?

(2) Contrast the taught and discovery models of learning (Table I, p. 32). Discuss the extent to which elements of both models support (or impede) workplace own learning and organizational learning. (Note: consider the interrelationships between focus, environment, technique (Figure 1, p. 32) as they apply to your own learning needs.)

(3) Consider the learning process model (Figure 4, p. 37) in relation to your own personal and organizational setting and needs. How might the model be implemented? What refinements and/or additions are needed? What else needs to be considered?

Theme 2: organizational readiness
Drew and Smith (1995) link organizational learning with strategies for effecting corporate transformation and make the key point that radical change is more likely to succeed if attention is first paid to organizational readiness. They offer a framework for radical "change auditing" and "change proofing" the firm to increase its capacity to withstand and exploit unexpected and rapid change. The article presents: a model for organizational change and learning (pp. 5-7); learning and the three-circle framework (pp. 7-8); a change audit, change proofing and organizational learning (pp. 9-12).

Sub-set discussion points:
(1) As you read the article, highlight or underline significant points and note down own personal reactions: What caught your attention in this article? What good ideas does it contain?
(2) Review the questions in Tables I, II and III (p. 9) and relate them to your own experience and knowledge of organizational readiness. Consider whether aspects of the three elements (focus, will, capability) are in your view, relatively under- or over-developed. Discuss the reasons for this.
(3) Read the "indicators of balance, congruence and harmony" (Table IV, p. 10) what organizational responses might you recommend? (Own team, own department/ section, wider perspective or all of these.)

Theme 3: teamworking and learning
Teare *et al.* (1997) present case study findings from 14 UK and US-based manufacturing and service firms, most with mature teamworking structures. Taken together the findings provide an array of evidence that work-based teams are making a significant contribution to organizational learning, performance improvement and corporate renewal. The article addresses: processes or functions? the role of teamworking; total teamworking; single problem, management promoted projects; continuous improvement, self-directed team projects; frameworks for organizational learning.

Sub-set discussion points: Review the main features and principal outcomes of:
(1) Single problem, management promoted projects.
(2) Continuous improvement, self-directed team projects.
(3) Frameworks for organizational teamworking.

Discuss the extent to which each of the three teamworking structures might be used to promote the benefits of organizational learning (use case examples from the article to support your views.) Summarize your discussion with some specific recommendations.

Theme 4: networked learning
Richardson (1995) examines the challenges for leaders of modern, networked learning organizations as they: strive to innovate and respond to marketplace conditions; develop through the medium of strategic alliances and explore ways of "getting more for less". The article addresses: how to facilitate a learning community culture (pp. 4-7); how to intervene to improve informal networking (pp. 7-13).

Sub-set discussion points:
(1) Review the "seven steps for managers" (How to facilitate a learning community culture, p. 5). Consider the implications for your: own management style; own organization. Conclude with some specific recommendations.
(2) Read: Case study 1 (new organization in a formerly bureaucratic profession) (pp. 5-6). Consider the statement "… innovative organization design goes some way to resolving many of the problematic issues faced by more traditionally managed organizations". What implications do you foresee for your organization? (See p. 6: and consider the relevance of: groupthink; organizational paradigms; power and political issues.)
(3) Read: "How to intervene to improve formal networking" (pp. 7-8). What can we learn from this approach? How can we apply it? What are likely benefits and problems?

Chapter 8

Relating strategy, structure and performance

Richard Teare

Granada Professor, Oxford Brookes University and Academic Chair, International Management Centres,

Jorge Costa

Professor and Vice Chancellor at Fernando Pessoa University, Porto, Portugal, and

Gavin Eccles

Manager at Business Performance, Sunninghill, Ascot, UK

Introduction

The aim of this article is to examine the interlinking business relationships between aspects of strategy formulation, implementation and performance as they relate to the hospitality industry. The "relating strategy" theme is developed and elaborated in relation to three parts: strategy and external analysis; strategy and structure; strategy and performance.

In order to make well-informed strategic decisions a wide array of information about the external environment is needed. To establish this context, the relationships between strategy and external analysis are examined in Part 1, followed by an examination of the concept of environmental scanning and its role in strategic planning. The aim here is to consider the many ways in which external forces and events influence the organization and arising from this, the contention that a systematic review of the external environment is the logical starting point for strategic planning. While as yet, there are few hospitality company examples of the integrated scanning-planning approach advocated here, there is little doubt that the benefits outweigh the costs associated with creating and building a linkage of this kind.

The relationships between the external environment and an organization's strategies and structures are dynamic ones and the extent to which adjustments can be manipulated or managed so as to achieve a desirable form of co-alignment is examined in Part 2. The degree of organizational flexibility and responsiveness to external change depends in part at least, on the features and characteristics of organizational design. A review of prior research reveals that hotel firms in particular have sought to monitor and balance the internal forces that more often than not, conflict with one another. A structure and strategy

This article first appeared in *The Journal of Workplace Learning,* Vol. 10 No. 2, 1998, pp. 58-75.

effectiveness framework is used to depict the main factors thought to affect the co-alignment principle. It is widely assumed that strategic planning produces results in the sense that it assists the organization to perform better. While the planning-performance literature appears inconclusive, there are nonetheless indications that the two concepts are positively related. The aim of Part 3 is to review the planning-performance issues arising from the hostile takeover of Forte plc by Granada Group plc in January, 1996. The analysis provides a basis for highlighting some of the key challenges for hospitality firms and the complexity arising from the contextual setting of organizations, in terms of enhancing the strategic effectiveness of the contribution made by managers.

The concept of strategy
Quinn (1980) defines strategy as a pattern or plan that integrates an organization's major goals, policies and action sequences into a cohesive whole. Webster (1994) calls this the building block of strategic management and notes that a secure foundation (strategy) is needed if the process (strategic management) is to function properly. In this sense strategy provides the link between where the organization is at present and where it would like to be in the future. Mintzberg (1994) portrays strategy as a plan – a direction, a guide or course of action into the future – and as a pattern, that is, consistency in behaviour over time. Most organizations began their strategic planning cycle by updating and revising their business objectives in relation to performance reviews in key areas (such as people, standards and business development), achieved results and development priorities (Storey and Teare, 1991; Teare *et al.,* 1992).

Mintzberg discerns a difference between strategy as a plan and strategy as a pattern, the former being an intended strategy and the latter a realized strategy. Further, he differentiates between intended and realized strategies and observes deliberate strategies, where previous intentions were realized and emergent strategies, where patterns are developed without conscious effort. While plans may go unrealized, patterns may appear without preconception and so the distinction between intended strategies and realized strategies is an important one. In fact, what managers say will be the company's action and what really happens is not always the same thing and in this context, realized strategies assume greater importance than intended ones (Costa and Teare, 1995).

It is worth noting that the characteristics of the strategic process have evolved over time. Aaker (1984) detects an evolutionary pattern of management thinking about strategy, characterized by different points of emphasis. Aaker depicts a series of phases beginning with a budgeting and control phase and thereafter, long-range planning, strategic planning, strategic management and strategic marketing management. These terms have similar meanings and are often used interchangeably. The basic distinctions between these concepts are shown in Table I.

Johnson and Scholes (1993) suggest that strategic management differs from operational management because the issues are less familiar and more complex (see Table II). The main tasks are to:

	Budgeting-control	Long-range planning	Strategic planning	Strategic marketing management
Time period	From 1900s	From 1950s	From 1960s	From mid-1970s
Management emphasis	Control deviations and manage complexity	Anticipate growth and manage complexity	Change strategic thrust and capability	Cope with strategic surprises and fast-developing threats and opportunities
Assumptions	The past repeats	Past trends will continue	New trends and discontinuities are predictable	Planning cycles inadequate to deal with rapid changes
The process	Periodic	Periodic	Periodic	Real time

Table I.
The strategic process:
evolutionary phases

Source: Costa and Teare (1995, p. 69), adapted from Aaker (1984)

Strategic management	Operational management
• Ambiguity, complexity, non-routine	• Routinized
• Organization-wide, fundamental	• Operationally specific
• Significant change, environment or expectations driven	• Small scale change resource driven

Table II.
Differences between
strategic management
and operational
management

Source: Costa and Teare (1995, p. 70), adapted from Johnson and Scholes (1993)

- understand the strategic position of the organization (strategic analysis);
- formulate possible courses of action, evaluate them and select the most appropriate one (strategic choice);
- plan how the chosen strategy should be put into effect and manage the changes required (strategic implementation).

Strategic analysis is primarily concerned with deriving an understanding of the strategic situation which any given organization faces (Johnson and Scholes, 1993) and the tasks involved can be viewed in relation to three sub-areas: external analysis, internal analysis and culture and stakeholder expectations analysis (see Table III).

Part 1: Strategy and external analysis
External analysis
Johnson and Scholes (1993) relate the task of analyzing the external environment to three main sub-areas: auditing environmental influences, structural analysis of the competitive environment and the identification of the organization's competitive position (see Table IV).

Aaker (1984) suggests four sub-areas: customer analysis, competitive analysis, industry analysis and environmental analysis. Even though the main divisions are different the same elements of analysis are contained in both frameworks: customer; competition; industry; and environment (Table V).

External analysis	Internal analysis	Culture/stakeholder expectations
Environmental analysis	Performance analysis	Cultural context of strategy
Customer analysis	Strategy review	Stakeholder analysis
Competitive analysis	Strategic problems	Power
Industry analysis	The internal organization	Organizational purposes
	Cost analysis	Business ethics
	Portfolio analysis	
	Financial resources and constraints	
	Strengths and weaknesses	

Source: Costa and Teare (1995, p. 71), adapted from Aaker (1984) and Johnson and Scholes (1993)

Table III.
Elements of strategic
analysis

Auditing environmental influences	Structural analysis of the competitive environment	Identifying the organization's competitive position
Political/legal	The threat of entry	Competitive analysis
Economic	The power of buyers and suppliers	Strategic group analysis
Socio-cultural	The threat of substitutes	Market segments and market power
Technological	Competitive rivalry	Market share and market growth
		Market attractiveness and business strength

Source: Costa and Teare (1994, p. v), adapted from Johnson and Scholes (1993)

Table IV.
Analysing the external
environment: three
sub-areas

Customer analysis	Competitive analysis	Industry analysis	Environmental analysis
Segments	Identity	Attractiveness	Governmental (or political)
Motivations	Performance	Key success factors	Economic
Unmet needs	Objectives	Size	Cultural (or social)
	Strategies	Structure	Technological
	Culture	Barriers to entry	Demographic
	Cost structure	Cost structure	
	Strengths	Distribution channels	
	Weaknesses	Trends	
		Growth	
		Product life cycle	

Source: Costa and Teare (1994, p. v), adapted from Aaker (1984)

Table V.
Analysing the external
environment: Aaker's
four sub-areas

Analysis of these elements is a vitally important ingredient of strategic planning and decision making as each one offers different insights and inputs to the strategic process. The main purpose of environmental analysis is therefore to detect, monitor and analyse current and potential events and trends that create opportunities or pose threats for the organization (Costa and Teare, 1994).

The elements most frequently associated with environmental analysis are: political, economic, social and technological – often known as "PEST" analysis. There are however, other approaches and sequences of action such as: scanning, monitoring, forecasting and assessment. The stages consist of:

- Scanning the environment to identify signs of current and potential environmental change;
- Monitoring specific environmental patterns and trends;
- Forecasting the future direction of environmental changes; and
- Assessing current and future environmental impacts and implications for the organization.

While the outcomes of this sequence of analysis are of value, the process of engaging in it is no less important. Undertaking the activity in itself promotes commitment, understanding and organizational readiness in terms of anticipating and responding to external events.

Environmental scanning
Research shows that the degree of importance attached to environmental scanning in a company can be inferred by the way scanning activities are integrated into the overall planning process (Fahey and King, 1977). As companies grow in size and complexity their need for formal strategic planning increases accordingly and with it, the need for a systematic approach to environmental scanning (Jain, 1984). It seems likely therefore that the effectiveness of strategic planning is related to the capacity for and willingness to undertake environmental scanning. In this context, the most obvious tasks are gathering data for: medium- to long-term planning, organizational development and design, devising scenarios and meeting agendas and for management education. Jain (1984) argues that scanning improves an organization's ability to respond to change in a variety of ways by:

- helping the organization to detect and capitalize on opportunities at an early stage;
- providing an early signal of impending problems;
- sensitizing an organization to the changing needs and expectations of its customers;
- providing a base level of information about the environment;
- providing intellectual stimulation to strategists in their decision making;
- assisting the organization to improve its public image by showing that it is sensitive to its environment and responsive to it.

If environmental scanning is to be taken seriously it should be:

- integrative (part of the planning and decision-making system of the firm);

- relevant to strategic planning (focus on strategic issues and provide assistance for strategic decision making);
- holistic in approach (so as not to miss any signals).

Costa *et al.* (1997) list some of the main considerations relating to the design of an environmental scanning process:

- The process needs to consider the widest possible range of influences on the organization's main activities.

- The purpose of environmental scanning is not to foretell accurately the future but to plot the issues which are likely to impact on the company so that it is ready to cope with them when they arise – this must be understood by all participants.

- The outcomes of environmental scanning should promote a proactive rather than a reactive stance.

- It is not sufficient for managers to understand the plan that arises from the scanning process, it is important that they understand the thinking that has led to its development.

- The scanning process should focus managerial attention on what lies outside the organization and allow them to create an organization which can adapt to and learn from that environment.

There are two approaches to environmental scanning: the outside-in or macro-approach and the inside-out or micro-approach (Fahey and Narayanan, 1986). The former adopts a broad view of the environment and considers the full range of external issues facing the organization. Its main concerns are longer-term trends, the development of alternative views or scenarios of the future and identifying implications for the industry in which the organization operates as well as implications for the organization itself. The inside-out approach takes a narrower view of the environment. It typically focuses on fewer external issues as the aim is to counter-balance these with internal influences. In this sense, the organization's perspective is "bounded" or constrained by internal. The main differences between the two approaches are listed in Table VI.

Implications
Organizations are in constant interaction with their environment and this gives rise to a phenomenon known as the "environmental-organizational interface". The environment of an organization consists of the outside forces that directly or indirectly influence its goals, structure, size, plans, procedures, operations, input, output and human relations. The importance of understanding the environment is critical, as a firm which examines its environment carefully and frequently tends to achieve a higher than average level of economic performance (Costa and Teare, 1996). In relation to the hospitality industry, Olsen *et al.* (1992) argue that environmental scanning helps managers to foresee favourable and unfavourable influences and initiate strategies that will enable

	Outside-in	Inside-out
Focus and scope	Unconstrained view of the external environment	View of external environment constrained by the organization
Goal	Broad environmental analysis before considering the organizational implications	Environmental analysis related to current organizational needs
Time horizon	Typically 1-5 years, sometimes 5-10 years	Typically 1-3 years
Frequency	Typically periodic review	Typically regular assessment
Strengths	Avoids organizational blind spots; identifies broader array of trends; identifies trends earlier	Efficient, well focused analysis; focuses on implications for organizational action

Table VI.
The outside-in and
inside-out perspectives
on environmental
scanning

Source: Costa *et al.* (1997, p. 10), adapted from Fahey and Narayanan (1986)

their organizations to adapt to the environment. Aaker (1983) provides a practical response to this task in the form of a "strategic information scanning system" (SISS) framework. The SISS consists of six steps: Steps 1 and 2 specify information needs and sources, Steps 3 and 4 identify the participants of the system and assign them to the scanning tasks and Steps 5 and 6 relate to the storage, processing and dissemination of information (see Table VII).

The SISS framework can provide useful strategic information, achieved by focusing on target information needs, allocating effort among those exposed to relevant information and building a system for storing, processing and disseminating information. To develop and implement an environmental scanning process that is relevant to the organization and feasible to implement, it has to be based on an inside-out perspective. This means that participants should be selected from those members of the organization exposed to relevant information. The information itself should be analysed in accordance with the organizational structure, its inferred importance and the storage and dissemination tasks carried out by the participants. By adopting this approach, hospitality organizations could make full use of the available information at low cost.

Part 2: Strategy and structure
Burns and Stalker (1961) view structure as a process in itself – a means of holding together an organization so that it is able to determine its own destiny. Organizations that operate in dynamically changing and uncertain environments tend to need organic/flexible structures and processes while more stable environments lend themselves to more familiar mechanistic bureaucratic

Steps	Tasks
1. Specify information needs	(a) Competitors/potential competitors; (b) market – segments; (c) size, growth; (d) environmental relating to the firm; (e) areas likely to impact on firm; (f) Likelihood of trends/events happening; (g) nature of the response time
2. Specify information sources regularly/	(a) Identify useful/most useful; (b) identify those read occasionally; (c) identify shows/meetings to be seen possibly/certainly; (d) identify which customers/suppliers seen regularly/occasionally; (e) identify which customers/suppliers are casual/close contacts
3. Identify participants process	(a) Those executives/staff directly involved in the planning (b) Those also exposed to useful information sources e.g. field sales
4. Assign scanning tasks	(a) Identify highly useful information sources and assign a small number of those exposed to the source to scan regularly; (b) single information sources can be partitioned and participants assigned to an area of their interest or background; (c) same process for information deemed merely "useful"
5. Storage and processing of system	(a) Storage can be a set of files or computer database information; (b) no ambiguity as to where information is stored or routed; (c) information should be sent to a central point to be filed /processed
6. Dissemination of information	System could vary from (a) a simple file set (b) a summary provided prior to planning process (c) continuously updated computer-based retrieval system

Source: Costa and Teare (1996, p. 18), adapted from Aaker (1983)

Table VII.
Strategic information
scanning system

structures. Eccles *et al.* (1997) list some of the main functions of organizational structure which provide:

- a formal allocation of work rules;
- channels for collaborative working;
- boundaries of authority and lines of communication;
- a means of allocating power and responsibility;
- prescriptive levels of formality and complexity.

The concept of co-alignment
If strategy is about realizing a plan, then in implementing it, a suitable means of structuring resources and activities must be found and maintained. Olsen (1993) uses the term "co-alignment" to describe the "best fit" relationship between strategy and organizational structure. He observes that without co-alignment between structure, strategy and the environment, organizations may experience difficulty in achieving long-term success. The concept of co-alignment is depicted in Figure 1.

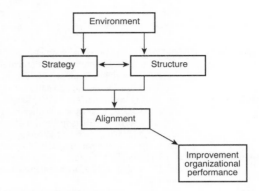

Figure 1.
Aligning organizational
strategy, structure and
environment

Source: Eccles, Teare and Costa (1997, p. 42)

Aligning strategy and structure in hotel firms

In terms of output and employment, the service sector became increasingly dominant in Western economies during the 1980s and is now influencing worldwide economic development. For this reason, much of the strategic thinking and planning of international firms is concerned with managing and marketing services (Teare *et al.*, 1990). In the hospitality industry, rapid expansion in both domestic and international markets began in the 1980s as market growth and competition stimulated product innovation and the application of new methods and technologies to production and service delivery systems, among other initiatives (Teare, 1989; 1991).

Holiday Inn Worldwide. In a study of firms operating in American and European markets during the mid-1970s managers identified a number of factors which were critical to success. Above all was a standardized product which could be packaged, branded and distributed as effectively in export markets as at home (Calver and Teare, 1994). This approach is exemplified by Holiday Inn Worldwide's (HIW) brand extension strategy, used to drive HIW's international expansion programme during the early 1990s (Parker and Teare, 1991; 1992). The original Holiday Inn concept or "core brand" gained international recognition for setting and achieving consistently high standards in product design and service. The brand extension strategy enabled HIW to transfer its high recognition and acceptance levels from its mid-market positioning to both economy and de luxe categories. This enabled HIW to offer three distinctive products, built around the "core brand" concept and each aligned with a specific market segment, at the right price and location.

Hyatt International Corporation. Set in the context of a predicted two billion global business and tourism related travel movements by the year 2000, Hyatt International Corporation (Hyatt) adopts an entrepreneurial approach to strategic planning and development. Equally important is its organizational structure, which is designed to respond to regional needs and opportunities and maintain its global network of hotels and resorts (Chorengel and Teare, 1992).

Hyatt favours an entrepreneurial style of development which draws heavily on one year business plans produced at hotel or unit level. This exercise involves unit managers from all departments in a comprehensive examination of local and regional market trading conditions. The exercise is also designed to integrate with a review of operational factors ranging from "quality" issues such as refurbishment needs to an appraisal of performance targets, in terms of both occupancy levels and financial results on a month by month basis for the year ahead. In producing their plan, unit managers are also required to make assumptions about what is likely to happen in the general business environment and what may happen in the near future. From a corporate perspective, the aim is to identify and assess all of the opportunities that are likely to occur within each region as quickly as possible and to a large extent, the unit level plans facilitate this. Following on, corporate staff look at the plans and the assumptions that have been made on a regional basis in order to see how politics and economics have been interpreted. In South East Asia for instance, the stability and vitality of business in Malaysia, Singapore and Thailand are closely interlinked, so regional assessments are essential. Ultimately, the Chief Executive's role is to go through the assumptions and predictions, noting scenarios which need to be monitored carefully, particularly if it is felt that the impact of uncontrollable factors may be critical. By reviewing the prospects for the year ahead from a global perspective and before unit business plans are fully developed, it is possible to provide the regions and individual units with a strategic overview of key global trends and developments in the Americas, Europe and Asia Pacific. This provides a macro perspective from which regional and unit managers can draw as they prepare their detailed action plans.

The whole approach to data gathering, evaluation and planning is therefore entrepreneurial, involving the regional organizations as much as possible so that managers throughout the global network are encouraged to identify and respond to opportunities via a streamlined planning process, with the centre providing co-ordination and control support. As planning responsibility is shared throughout the global organization, changes in local market conditions can be identified rapidly. When for example, the complex process of change began to gain momentum in Eastern Europe, details of development opportunities began to emerge instinctively from all parts of the global organization. The information came from managers at all levels in the organization who were either witnessing change, or gathering market information from talking to business travellers and others with experiential knowledge of what was actually happening. The sensitivity, involvement and sense of collective responsibility which characterizes Hyatt's entrepreneurial approach to the market thereby provides a rich source of data for planning purposes, enabling the centre to clearly identify and prioritize development possibilities and potential.

A secondary, but nonetheless important factor which facilitates effective relations between the corporate and regional organizations is the high degree of stability which exists within the organization as a whole. In 1992, the four most senior executives of Hyatt had service records ranging from 14 to 21 years and there were many other managers who had been working with Hyatt for ten years or more. This produces a stabilizing influence on the culture of the company, because many of the general managers were food and beverage or other line managers when the senior executive team of the early 1990s were managing hotels. Consequently, the views and personalities of senior managers throughout the company are familiar, which is an advantage during detailed planning discussions, as the managers know and understand how others will be thinking and feeling. This in turn encourages more junior managers to exchange views and to communicate new ideas more freely. To actively encourage the generation of new ideas, a regionally-based planning approach is used and Hyatt's decentralized style supports this, rather than frustrates it. In fact Hyatt has consciously tried to maintain a very informal structure and way of handling information and ideas, by emphasizing personal communication and the two-way flow of ideas. This fosters a sense of commitment through accessibility so that the relationships between Hyatt's corporate and regional organizations might accurately be described as an extended family arrangement.

Although lines of communication are generally relaxed and informal, it is necessary to work at maintaining mutually supportive networks within the overall organization. To maintain a sense of vitality and unity of purpose, managers are encouraged to ask questions whenever they meet guests, other business representatives or travel. In this way the organization is exposed to different kinds of thinking and varied opinions from which it can learn. The process of interaction can be stimulated in a variety of different ways. For example, all of the general managers are invited to attend a conference at approximately 18-month intervals. This is a low key event with varied sporting and social activities, enabling the business agenda to be conducted in an informal and interesting way, during which the managers can interact in a relaxed atmosphere. The approach is to put people together, guide them, pair reserved and extrovert individuals during discussion sessions and the objective of all of this is to enable them to learn from each other. Wherever possible an attempt is made to broaden the agenda so as to stimulate wider discussion of important business issues. The purpose is to stimulate the general managers to continually update their own knowledge about the economics of the business, seek to understand what the customer wants and the market needs and then communicate their analysis to line managers.

The degree of responsiveness within the organization as a whole during the early 1990s was also related to a deliberate attempt by the Chief Executive to shift the emphasis from the centre to the regions. At one time Hyatt was a highly centralized organization, with 20 Vice President positions in the Chicago office. In 1992, Hyatt had five Vice Presidents and a much stronger regional focus. Hyatt's credo – to remain responsive – means that it is vital to observe, to talk to people, to look at the company strengths and weaknesses and if necessary, to be prepared to change any part of the organization that might prevent Hyatt from staying close to its customers.

Olsen (1989) observes that in the late 1980s, hotel firms had to come to terms with the tougher competitive conditions associated with a maturing industry (in particular: more products, more competitors). He predicts that the long-term survivors will direct their strategies to reflect the conditions that exist in this type of environment and in so doing, they will need to consider:

- the evolving nature and characteristics of a maturing marketplace;
- the relevance of strategies for protecting market share in the face of fierce competition;
- the means of decentralizing organizational structures, to allow "real time" decision making at appropriate levels in the overall hierarchy;
- the recruitment and retention of managers who are sufficiently adaptable to be able to interpret and respond to dynamic change;
- how to foster a "strategic approach" to managing the business in all areas and at all levels.

The implications for managing hotel operations are depicted in Figure 2.

Implications
Tse and Olsen (1990) believe that corporate and competitive strategy is converging as more emphasis is placed on the means of competing successfully within a given hospitality industry sector and market segment. The key

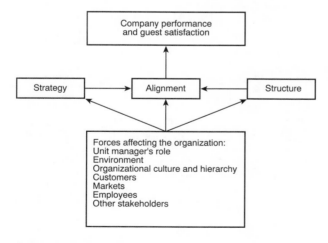

Source: Eccles, *et al.* (1997, p. 60)

Figure 2.
Issues affecting hotel
unit performance

question driving the strategic process is how does the organization develop and sustain competitive advantage? It seems likely that unit managers will be encouraged to take a broader, strategic view of this question as they are well placed to interpret and respond to the localized issues affecting their operation. In essence, this should facilitate a sharper focus on key business issues as well as a more sophisticated response to customer needs. If this is to be achieved, the traditional autocratic style will need to be replaced by a modern team-building approach so that unit managers are encouraged to create a more vibrant business climate. This "new vision" for unit managers and enhanced responsibility for maintaining co-alignment is likely to encompass:

- the continuous improvement of processes and "getting things right – first time";

- a customer focused culture – which emphasizes the importance of listening to customers;

- responsibility for maintaining "open" channels of communication – upwards, downwards and across the organization.

Mintzberg (1989) adds to the list of variables in the context of maintaining alignment between strategy, structure and the marketplace (see also Figure 3):

- flexibility – allowing employees to generate ideas and participate in decision making;

- adaptability – developing an organizational structure that is able to respond as marketplace conditions change;

- empowerment – giving employees the scope to be creative, to generate new ideas and participate in decision making;

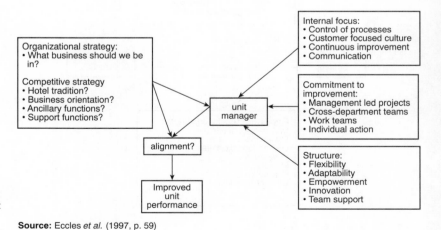

Figure 3.
A strategy, structure, effectiveness framework for appraising hotel unit performance

Source: Eccles *et al.* (1997, p. 59)

- innovation – encouraging employees to try new ideas and "re-invent" processes;

- team support – providing mutual support, encouragement and sharing (learning, improvement, vision).

Part 3: Strategy and performance: a case example

Strategy has been defined as a pattern or plan that integrates an organization's major goals, policies and action sequences into a cohesive whole. This does, however, raise some key questions about the strategy-performance relationship (Teare *et al.*, 1996) such as:

- Who should be involved in strategic decision making and why?

- How flexible does strategy need to be in order to respond to unforeseen opportunities and threats posed by dynamic operating environments?

- How do environmental and strategic choices affect performance?

- Is organizational performance mainly a measure of profit and return on investment or should it seek to ensure a balance between many indicators of success?

- How should firms evaluate their relative strategic success?

The following case study reviews the acquisition of Forte plc. the longest established UK hotel company by Granada plc. The Granada Group, a television and leisure conglomerate launched a £3.3 billion hostile takeover bid for Forte on 22 November 1995, in one of the UK's most expensive takeovers this decade. This marked the end of family control of a hotels group created by Lord Forte in the 1930s. The aim here is to identify the factors underpinning Granada's success and in particular, the implications for relating strategy, structure and performance.

Forte plc
During the 1960s and 1970s, Charles Forte masterminded the transition from a small family run food-service operation to the largest hotel chain in the UK, with assets ranging across many hospitality businesses – from its stake in the Savoy Group to the Little Chef and Happy Eater chains that serve Britain's road network. After a 15 year career with the company, Rocco, Lord Forte's son, was appointed Chief Executive in 1982. It was assumed that he would adopt his father's rather autocratic style of management, when in reality the opposite seems to have happened. This may have been due to a desire to establish his own credentials for the role rather than seeking to emulate his father's past achievements. In essence, he asserted his authority by gradually replacing his father's appointees to the board.

In their place he recruited younger executives with established track records, both in the hotel business as well as general commerce. Second, Sir Rocco sought to build Forte into a multinational company in keeping with its size and significance. He became Chairman of the company in 1992 holding both roles until Forte was subject to the Granada bid when under pressure from the City, he proposed that the Chairmanship should pass to Sir Anthony Tennant.

Prior to the takeover, Forte operated 346 hotels in the UK, representing 24.4 percent of the total roomstock of publicly quoted hotels, making it the largest hotel operator in the UK overall and in the Capital too. The London hotel market is expected to grow by 5 percent annually until the end of the decade and this forecast emphasizes its strategic importance to hotel operators (Eccles *et al.,* 1996).

The following sections review Forte's strategic direction during the period between 1990-1992 from the perspective of the Chief Executive. In particular, Forte's approach to strategic planning and the role of its operating divisions in planning and performance reviews (Forte and Teare, 1990; 1991) and the impact of growth on the company's organizational structure (Forte and Teare, 1992) (see Table VIII).

The Chief Executive's perspective on strategic planning. Strategic planning was not viewed as a static process, it evolved as the size and structure of the company changed. The strategic thrust came from a dialogue between the centre and its operating divisions, who prepared their own strategic plans. The plans then formed the basis of a discussion from which a corporate plan was constructed. Assuming that the various operating divisions were being managed effectively, the expectation was that they would generate their own drive and there were a number of functional specialists at the centre who were responsible for sustaining the debate. Their task was to review market developments and the wide range of information which had to be collected, reduced and disseminated for use at every organizational level in the company. Information gathering was primarily a task for the marketing function and

---

Summary of Rocco Forte's principal objectives and
achievements as Chairman (1992-1995 inclusive)

- A re-organization of the firm to create a sharper and more focused company with shorter lines of communication, a lower cost base and a stronger customer orientation.
- A reduction in Forte's overall debt by disposing of its stake in Kentucky Fried Chicken and Gardner Merchant and reducing its share in Alpha airport catering.
- A re-focusing of Forte's management and financial resources on the core hotel and restaurant activities.
- A strengthened management team – achieved by recruiting a new team of executives with a broad range of skills and international experience.
- The introduction of a long-term incentive plan for senior executives to motivate them to achieve outstanding performance.
- The creation of a management team to focus on sales and marketing development and a greater emphasis on quality and service standards.
- A programme of refurbishment and re-investment in existing assets.

Table VIII.
Forte's strategy and
structure (1992-1995)

Source: Eccles *et al.* (1996)

each major sector of the business had its own marketing team which collected information. The categories included in-company research data, commissioned research undertaken by consultants and publicly available research reports. Information from these sources was summarized and circulated for decision-making purposes. It thereby informed the debate between the Chief Executive and the divisional Managing Directors and critically, the decisions which were taken about future developments. The need to establish priorities was related to the size of the company and the degree of difficulty associated with seeking to develop every sector of the company simultaneously. This meant consolidating some areas of the business in order to finance expansion in others. Decision support was provided by a divisional reporting procedure which constituted a formal mechanism for strategic planning. This was supplemented by informal meetings which took place throughout the organization. In particular, the informal meetings between the Chief Executive and divisional Managing Directors which were thought to provide a flexible and effective way of reviewing strategic issues.

The impact of growth on the organizational structure. A process of decentralization took place so as to devolve more authority and responsibility for decision making. This action helped to create strong divisional teams and to channel the energy and enthusiasm within the company in a productive way. To balance the move towards greater divisional autonomy, management development courses, especially at senior level, were inter-divisional. The advantages were that managers and functional specialists could meet each other, learn about each other's businesses, exchange ideas and benefit from the diversity of experience and knowledge that was available to them. Although Forte had an identifiable corporate culture, there was a difference of approach in each division which related to the Managing Director's particular interests and priorities. The need for a degree of flexibility related to the issue of ownership of ideas and business methods. Managers who were committed to the businesses they ran needed the freedom to make decisions and when they achieved success, to gain the recognition that they deserved.

Forte's strategy for "building on strength" during the 1990s sought among other priorities, to focus on opportunities for international development. The decision to re-define the Group's identity arose from a sustained period of development during the 1980s, during which time the nature of the company had been progressively changing too. In reality, this meant that certain parts of the Group were much bigger than they had been at the beginning of the 1980s and it had become apparent that a stronger and clearer corporate identity was needed. The aim was to find the best fit between Forte's products and market segments and to communicate benefits to customers, which would in turn make the business more efficient to manage, both from the point of view of selling to customers and in terms of the internal operation of the business. It became evident that a corporate re-branding initiative was needed so as to consolidate Forte's achievements by projecting its strengths and capabilities more effectively. Although numerically Forte had the biggest hotel portfolio in the

UK, it had not been optimizing the associated advantages and rival companies operating better focused hotel brands were gaining market share. The key issue was how to brand the distinctive hotel products and at the same time, link then together in an effective way. Among other options, it involved considering whether "Forte" should be used as an endorsement, or as part of a brand name. Ultimately, the reason for linking "Forte" with the brand name, was that it was felt that it would unify the separate and distinctive hotel brand types in the portfolio. The concept was reinforced by the international benefits of using "Forte" which in Latin languages means "strength".

The most significant implication of the new brand structure in operational terms, arose from the discipline of defining the operational standards for all types and levels of business activity within the Group as clearly and precisely as possible. Previously, the degree of tolerance had been wider and so variations in operating standards were inevitable. This undesirable source of variety was removed by defining brand standards for all aspects of product specification and delivery. Accordingly, this made it easier to identify and take action against sub-standard performance, as the organization as a whole was more focused on achieving performance and quality targets in every division of the business. It was thought that this would bring benefits for the customer, who would be able to see the differences which might be achieved in relation to the product specification and the greater consistency of the operating standards. The company as a whole benefiting from the impact of greater consistency in all its communications. There was also a better sense of structure and cohesion arising from the perception that the Group has taken a step forward by emphasizing the importance of the developments that lay ahead.

The role of operating divisions in planning and performance reviews. Assessing the performance of key competitors in the marketplace assists with strategy formulation and clarifies, where appropriate, acquisition priorities. For example, it is possible to identify a business which is not operating at optimum efficiency. This may signify an acquisition opportunity if the evidence suggests that performance could be improved. When the company was smaller, the issue of financing new development was less contentious, but as strategic planning was viewed as a divisional responsibility, more ambitious development plans were emerging. The need to debate options and priorities has therefore become central to the strategic planning process. As a direct consequence of this, corporate aims and objectives were continually monitored to determine where the company should be heading and what the emphasis for the future should be. These considerations determined when and how changes to the product portfolio were made. All of these issues influenced the direction and structure of the company during the early 1990s because it could not sustain growth in every division at the same time and at the same pace. The approach to development in the early 1990s was to keep a wide range of options under consideration for every sector of the business. To maximize growth in the shortest possible time, it was necessary to examine the potential for growth and in so doing, to pose a number of key questions:

- What is the maximum potential of each operation?
- How do we reach the point where we are realizing this potential if we decide to support development?
- How much will the development cost?
- How quickly can we penetrate the market to achieve market leadership?

These are the balances that were set in order to examine development decisions. Once these issues had been dealt with, a corporate plan began to take shape and priorities could be established. This was necessary because without issuing shares, financial resources were finite. There was also a limit to the amount of borrowed money that could be utilized without over-gearing the business.

It was not thought possible to run the business effectively without the aid of key performance indicators and ratios and the management statistics used by Forte were refined as new information technology became available, so that relatively sophisticated measures of business performance might be deployed. Computer-based real time analysis of management information had largely replaced manual methods, so that it was possible to review the contribution made by different customer types in every unit of a division. This level of feedback could support a variety of strategic decisions such as where, when and who to sell to and the most effective way of reaching particular target market segments. Additionally, emphasis was placed on short-term forecasting at an operational level so that costs could be adjusted in relation to expected demand two or three weeks beforehand. This was thought to have been an important initiative because simultaneous adjustments or even retrogressive cost-cutting to offset the effects of an unexpected shortfall in demand are relatively unhelpful options. In so far as operational costs were concerned, Forte considered itself to be more responsive in the short term than many other comparably sized companies. Though in planning capital expenditure a longer-term view was important, as capital decisions would inevitably affect the future direction of the business.

Consistent performance regardless of the trading conditions is the key measure of a well run business, an objective which Forte sought to achieve during the early 1990s. Companies like Sainsbury's and Marks & Spencer performed just as well in terms of profit growth during the recessionary period of the early 1980s as they were during the boom years of the late 1980s and consistent performance was Forte's main goal. Related to this was the perceived need to stimulate a re-alignment of thinking and practice at the operational level, given increased levels of competition and slower rates of growth in demand during the early 1990s. This would require more emphasis on cost control than during the boom years of the 1980s, but also more creative thinking about ways of maintaining a competitive edge.

Granada plc
The recent history of the Granada Group is characterized by rapid growth achieved by means of mergers and acquisitions and the dynamism of its

management team. Granada is UK focused, with a diverse range of activities in three business divisions: rental and computer services; television; and leisure and services. During the past ten years, Granada identified and successfully dealt with an array of internal organizational issues. These are reflected in four phases: financial instability (late 1980s until 1991); business re-structuring (completed in 1991); profit growth which is especially noticeable from 1993 onwards and coupled with this, the pressures of success (Costa *et al.*, 1996).

The financial instability phase. The initial phase of financial instability ran from the latter part of the 1980s to 1991, culminating in a collapse in profit for the period. The key features were:

- A divisional structure that suggests partial lack of central control.

- A rapid increase in the amount spent on investments and acquisitions, which appear to have been either poorly planned or poorly controlled.

- High levels of cash absorbency.

The business re-structuring phase. By 1991, Granada's shareholders and management team had realized that they were facing a crisis. Gearing had reached 97 percent with cash interest cover falling. The Group's management initiated a period of change, led by Gerry Robinson, the new Group Managing Director and Chief Executive, appointed in November 1991. The successful turnaround included a series of disposals and a rights issue (that reduced the Group's year-end gearing to 50 per cent), increased central control and increased cost and margin awareness.

The profit growth phase. Following the re-structuring, Granada entered a profit growth phase. By late 1992 the new management team had been in position long enough to assess the Group's future strategic direction and improve its day-to-day operating efficiencies. During 1993, Granada announced earnings per share growth in excess of 10 per cent and a cash inflow of £127 million. In addition to profit and cash flow improvements, the new team achieved:

- Improved central management control and reporting systems.

- Greater operating margins in most of its divisions.

- A series of well integrated acquisitions that enabled Granada to diversify quickly and effectively.

The pressure of success phase. Winnington-Ingram and Winston (1994) predicted that Granada would become a victim of its own success if the company failed to maintain a balance between cash resources and earnings growth. Granada had become a well managed cash producing company with above (but declining) average earnings growth. Winnington-Ingram and Winston posed two questions:

(1) When Granada had completed its exercise in trimming excess costs from its current activities, which parts of the company would be the major engines of growth?

(2) Granada's growth and expenditure figures indicated increased levels of unallocated cash flow from 1995 onwards, with its balance sheet moving to a net cash position by the end of the 1997 fiscal year. The question was what would Granada do with its surplus cash?

The Granada bid for Forte

On 22 November 1995, Granada launched a hostile bid for Forte plc and in its final offer document, Granada raised the bid offer for Forte from £3.28 billion to £3.8 billion. The bid outcome was announced on 23 January 1996 and Granada won the support of 65 per cent of Forte's shareholders. Until a few days before the vote many investors thought that Forte would win, re-entering the marketplace as a better focused business. In the last few days the pendulum swung, mainly because Granada raised their offer and due to the last minute decision by Mercury Asset Management (MAM) to back Granada's case.

As the largest individual city fund holder in Forte with a 14 per cent stake, MAM concluded that Granada's bid and subsequent plans would yield the best return and prospects for maximising the value of Forte's assets. The two-month battle between Granada and Forte was mainly played around the financial strength, the management skills and the proven track record of Granada ranged against a company that was in the process of consolidating its business but had failed to deliver the best value for money to its shareholders (Teare *et al.*, 1997).

In a document published on 14 December 1995, Granada sought to highlight the differences between the two companies:

- *Value:* Forte has mortgaged the future in order to create an appearance of value now and in doing so, has materially impaired future values. Granada's Increased Offer, on the other hand not only crystallises greater value for you now, but gives you the prospect of significant further enhancement in years to come.

- *Strategy:* Forte's management has decided to dismember the company, selling core businesses with good prospects too cheaply and reducing Forte to just part of its hotels business. Granada would capture the benefits of owning both hotels and restaurants and release their true profit potential.

- *Management:* The track records of the two management teams differ sharply: Granada's management has provided its shareholders with significant returns; Forte's management has presided over a steady erosion of value, has failed its shareholders for too long and has lost credibility.

Granada's claim is based on the certainty of the increased offer and the future promise of greater value based on its track record. It also states that its detailed plan to improve Forte's profits will result in significant earnings. Granada's analysis of its own strategy states that: "...strategy is firmly based on two parallel themes which are at the heart of the Group's success – Focus and

Breadth: Focus on core businesses, to maximize growth in each of those businesses. Breadth across a range of related core businesses, to minimize risk to shareholders from a downturn in any core market".

A successful acquisition meant for Granada the creation of a group with four strong core activities, Leisure and Services, Television, Hotels and Rental. From Granada's perspective, each of these core businesses is substantial in its own right, yet none overwhelms the others; it would have leading market positions in each sector; and the risk from economic downturn is minimized. Seeing the company as a "well balanced group" Granada defines its current strategy as emphasizing focus for growth and balance against risk.

In its final offer document Granada posed a question to Forte's shareholders: "Who can deliver greater value, both now and in the future?" Granada's "offer" was as follows:

If you accept Granada's offer you get:
- The best value now and in the future.
- A balanced Group with four strong businesses offering the opportunity for significant earnings enhancement.
- A management team with a track record of delivering.
- 12.5 per cent Gold Card discount at Forte restaurants and hotels, including Little Chef and Travelodge.

If you reject Granada's offer you get:
- A disposal of good cash generative businesses at a price that hands the upside to the buyer.
- An unbalanced company over-exposed in a sector that is highly capital intensive and vulnerable to a downturn.
- Some £900 million of debt and a significant backlog of capital expenditure.
- A top management that has consistently failed to deliver adequate levels of profit and cash, even before selling cash generative businesses.
- The prospect of a falling in price.

This comparison substantiates the takeover strategy adopted by Granada which proved to be successful as it was in previous takeovers. The two-month battle between Granada and Forte was mainly played around the financial strength, the management skills and the proven track record of Granada, against a company which was in the process of consolidating its business but had failed to deliver the best value for money to its shareholders. It shows that hostile takeover bids are feasible provided that the bidder is prepared to pay enough and the circumstances are appropriate. In the final analysis, the bid succeeded because Fund managers saw Forte as a company that had underperformed for many years and its own bold defence of the bid served to underline its previous complacency. Comments made about Forte by Gerry Robinson and others during the bid were evidently taken seriously by shareholders and as the final vote approached, many senior figures in the industry started to question Forte's managerial approach and in particular its determination to retain its comparatively poor profit generating luxury hotel operations. Forte had also failed to respond convincingly to other criticisms, namely a lack of competitiveness in its international operations and its over dependence on UK markets which generate around 80 per cent of total profits.

The Granada bid for Forte contains many lessons for large multinational businesses. At no time before 22 November 1995 did Forte think that they were about to be involved in a takeover bid. A sense of invulnerability and complacency could have been avoided and as Granada have shown, no public limited company is safe from takeover. A hostile bid implies that investors have to decide to back either existing management or new management. Both parties have to justify their performance, long-term strategy and any proposed changes. The potential acquirer must also explain its strategy and how it will create long-term shareholder value.

In analysing Granada's track record in takeovers and acquisitions it is evident that the senior management team used a blueprint which draws from its strategic capability and prior experience combined with a proven ability to apply tight cost controls. The main procedures supporting this framework are financial reporting, functional reporting and investment appraisal (see Tables IX and X). Granada's experience in making successful acquisitions (such as:

Source	Contributory factors to Forte's unsuccessful defence of the Granada bid
Management	• "Command structure" management style – divisions run from head office by a large team • Centralized and complex management structure and reporting • Insufficient emphasis on cost savings and ineffective mechanisms for identifying excessive costs • Underutilization of assets – energy focused on "trophy hotels" high cost, low profit operations • Insufficient working capital to re-invest in core businesses • Complacency – the need to be aware of and understand external threats (likely predators) and pressures (from stakeholder investors) and be ready and able to respond
Portfolio and markets	• Strong concentration and over-reliance on the UK market • A diverse portfolio of hotels and restaurants, not sufficiently differentiated in the marketplace
External pressures	• Slow to adapt to stakeholder needs and expectations • Ownership over-representation of investors – 80 per cent of Forte plc was owned by pension fund investments, with 14 per cent held by one company, Mercury Asset Management • Low share price and returns, making the company more vulnerable to takeovers than it anticipated

Source: adapted from Teare *et al.* (1997)

Table IX.
Forte plc: post-takeover reflections on strategy, structure and performance

Source	Contributory factors to Forte's unsuccessful defence of the Granada bid	
Financial reporting	A rolling three year strategic review process which is part of a comprehensive planning system, together with an annual budget approved by the board	The results of operating units are reported monthly, compared against individual budgets and forecast figures are reviewed on a month by month basis
Functional reporting	The risks facing the business are assessed on an ongoing basis	A number of key areas, such as treasury and corporate taxation matters are subject to regular review by the board. Other areas, such as detailed insurance risk management and legal matters come under the direct control of the executive team and are continually monitored
Investment appraisal	The Group has a clearly defined framework for controlling capital expenditure (including appropriate authorisation levels) beyond which such expenditure requires the approval of the board	A prescribed format for capital expenditure appraisal places emphasis on the commercial and strategic logic for the investment and due diligence requirements in the case of business acquisitions. As a matter of routine, projects are also subject to post-investment appraisal after an appropriate period

Source: Teare *et al.* (1997, p. 8)

Table X.
Granada's internal
financial control
procedures

Pavilion Services, Direct Vision Rentals, London Weekend Television, Sutcliffe Group) reflect the capabilities of its management team and the operating efficiencies achieved and these acquisitions were in fact earnings enhancing. The combination of strategic ability, excellent cash production and the tight cost control practised by Granada are probably its major strengths.

Granada have stated that they do not intend to focus solely on hotels (24 per cent of the Forte business) but to develop Forte's extensive roadside budget hotel and restaurant businesses. The consolidation and development phase will present an interesting challenge as Granada's management team set about the process of integrating the parts of Forte that it wants to keep, disposing of under-performing assets and re-energizing one the UK's biggest hotel and catering businesses.

Summary
In reviewing the implications arising from the interrelationship between the external environment, strategy, structure and performance, it is possible to identify a number of key issues for learning in hospitality organizations:

Strategy and external analysis
   (1) How might the organization assign environmental scanning tasks so as to detect and interpret the likely impact of external events?

(2) Who should be involved in "inside out" environmental scanning? Who will identify information needs and sources and assign scanning tasks? How will information be stored, processed and disseminated so that it provides timely, well focused and meaningful inputs to organizational learning and updating?

Strategy and structure

(3) How should the organization seek to develop and sustain forms of competitive advantage now and in the future?

(4) Should unit managers adopt an enhanced role in the ongoing task of maintaining alignment between the strategic variables of structure, strategy and environment? What additional contributions could they make to organizational efforts to: improve processes, embed a customer-focused culture and maintain "open" internal communication networks?

(5) How might workplace learning programmes be used to optimize: flexibility (e.g. employee participation in idea generation and decision making); adaptability (e.g. responding quickly to changing market conditions); empowerment (e.g. giving employees the scope to be creative and to experiment); innovation (e.g. allowing employees to "re-invent" processes and procedures) and team support (encouraging, sharing and providing mutual support).

Strategy and performance

(6) To what extent should financial, functional, asset and investment performance influence the organization's strategic direction?

References

Aaker, D. (1983), "Organizing a strategic information scanning system", *California Management Review,* Vol. 25 No. 2, pp. 76-83.

Aaker, D. (1984), *Developing Business Strategies,* John Wiley, New York, NY.

Burns, T. and Stalker, G.M. (1961), *The Management of Innovation,* Tavistock, London.

Calver, S. and Teare, R. (1994), "Hospitality marketing strategies and international development", in Witt, S. and Moutinho, L. (Eds), *Tourism Marketing and Management Handbook,* 2nd ed., Prentice-Hall, pp. 434-41.

Chorengel, B. and Teare, R. (1992), "Developing a responsive global network of Hyatt Hotels & Resorts", in Teare, R. and Olsen, M.D. (Eds), *International Hospitality Management: Corporate Strategy in Practice,* Pitman, London and John Wiley, New York, NY, pp. 339-45.

Costa, J. and Teare R. (1994), "Environmental scanning and the Portuguese hotel sector", *International Journal of Contemporary Hospitality Management,* Vol. 6 No. 5, pp. iv-vii.

Costa, J. and Teare, R. (1995), "The process of environmental scanning as a tool for strategic management", *Revista Portuguesa de Gestao,* special issue on Tourism Marketing and Management, Vol. 4, pp. 67-81.

Costa. J. and Teare, R. (1996), "Environmental scanning: a tool for competitive advantage", in Kotas, R., Teare, R., Logie, J., Jayawardena, C. and Bowen, J.T. (Eds), *The International Hospitality Business,* Cassell, London and New York, NY, pp. 12-20.

Costa, J., Eccles, G., Teare, R. and Knowles, T. (1996), *Granada Group: A Successful Story of Mergers and Acquisitions*, The European Case Clearing House, Cranfield.

Costa, J., Teare, R., Vaughan, R. and Edwards, J. (1997), "A review of the process of environmental scanning in the context of strategy making", in Teare, R., Farber Canziani, B. and Brown, G. (Eds), *Global Directions: New Strategies for Hospitality and Tourism,* Cassell, London and Herndon, VA, pp. 5-38.

Eccles, G., Costa, J. and Teare, R. (1997), "The relationship between organizational structure and strategy", in Teare, R., Farber Canziani, B. and Brown, G. (Eds), *Global Directions: New Strategies for Hospitality and Tourism,* Cassell, London and Herndon, VA, pp. 133-64.

Eccles, G., Costa, J., Teare, R. and Knowles, T. (1996), *Managerial Implications within a Hostile Takeover: A Case of Forte PLC*, The European Case Clearing House, Cranfield.

Fahey, L. and King, W. (1977), "Environmental scanning in corporate scanning", *Business Horizons,* August, pp. 61-71.

Fahey, L. and Narayanan, V. (1986), *Macroenvironmental Analysis for Strategic Management,* West Publishing, St Paul, MN.

Forte, R. and Teare, R. (1990), "Responding to the competitive challenge of the 1990s", *International Journal of Contemporary Hospitality Management,* Vol. 2 No. 3, pp. i-iii.

Forte, R. and Teare, R. (1991), "Strategic planning in action: the Trusthouse Forte approach", in Teare, R. and Boer, A. (Eds), *Strategic Hospitality Management: Theory and Practice for the 1990s,* Cassell, London, pp. 3-8.

Forte, R. and Teare, R. (1992), "Building on strength at Forte PLC: a structure and strategy for the 1990s", in Teare, R. and Olsen, M.D. (Eds), *International Hospitality Management: Corporate Strategy in Practice,* Pitman, London and John Wiley, New York, NY, pp. 163-70.

Jain, S. (1984), "Environmental scanning in US Corporations", *Long Range Planning*, Vol. 17 No. 2, pp. 117-28.

Johnson, G. and Scholes, K. (1993), *Exploring Corporate Strategy: Text and Cases,* 3rd ed., Prentice-Hall, London.

Mintzberg, H. (1989), "The structuring of organizations", in Asch, D. and Bowman, C. (Eds), *Readings in Strategic Management,* Macmillan, London.

Mintzberg, H. (1994), "The fall and rise of strategic planning", *Harvard Business Review,* January-February, pp. 107-14.

Olsen, M.D. (1989), "Issues facing multi-unit hospitality organizations in a maturing market", *International Journal of Contemporary Hospitality Management,* Vol. 1 No. 2, pp. 3-6.

Olsen, M.D. (1993), "Accommodation: international growth strategies of major US hotel companies", *Travel & Tourism Analyst,* Economic Intelligence Unit, Vol. 3, pp. 51-64.

Olsen, M.D., Tse, E. and West, J. (1992), *Strategic Management in the Hospitality Industry,* Van Nostrand, New York, NY.

Parker, A.C. and Teare, R. (1991), "A brand extension strategy for European expansion", *International Journal of Contemporary Hospitality Management,* Vol. 3 No. 2, pp. i-ii.

Parker, A.C. and Teare, R. (1992), "A brand extension strategy for Holiday Inn Worldwide development", in Teare , R. and Olsen, M.D. (Eds), *International Hospitality Management: Corporate Strategy in Practice,* Pitman, London and John Wiley, New York, NY, pp. 110-62.

Quinn, J.B. (1980), *Strategies for Change: Logical Incrementalism*, Irwin, Homewood, IL.

Storey, A. and Teare, R. (1991), "Formulating a strategy for growth in a regional contract catering company", *International Journal of Contemporary Hospitality Management,* Vol. 3 No. 3, pp. i-iii.

Teare, R. (1989), "The hospitality industry in the 1990s: some critical developments", *Marketing Intelligence & Planning – In Action*, Vol. 7 Nos 9/10, pp. 48-9.

Teare, R. (1991), "Developing hotels in Europe: some reflections on progress and prospects", *International Journal of Contemporary Hospitality Management,* Vol. 3 No. 4, pp. 55-9.

Teare, R., Moutinho, L. and Morgan, N. (1990), "Managing and marketing services: emerging themes for the 1990s", in Teare, R. *et al.* (Eds), *Managing and Marketing Services in the 1990s,* Cassell, London, pp. 249-51.

Teare, R., Adams, D., Storey, A. and Boersma, T. (1992), "Creating business synergy: a new passenger services strategy for P & O European Ferries", in Teare, R., Adams, D. and Messenger, S. (Eds), *Managing Projects in Hospitality Organizations,* Cassell, London, pp. 5-32.

Teare, R., Costa, J., Eccles, G. and Ingram, H. (1996), "Strategy and performance: a direct relationship?", *Hospitality Management Research: State of the Art,* Electronic Conference sponsored by the International Journal of Contemporary Hospitality Management and MCB University Press, 10 April-10 September 1996 on: URL: http://www.mcb.co.uk. Main conveners: Peter L. Jones, UK, K. Michael Heywood, Canada/USA, J.S. Perry Hobson, Asia Pacific.

Teare, R., Eccles, G., Costa, G., Ingram, H. and Knowles, T. (1997), "The Granada takeover of Forte: a managerial perspective", *Management Decision,* Vol. 35 No. 1, pp. 5-9.

Tse, E. and Olsen, M.D. (1990), "Business strategy and organizational structure: a case of US restaurant firms", *International Journal of Contemporary Hospitality Management,* Vol. 2 No. 3, pp. 17-23.

Webster, M. (1994), *Strategic Hospitality Management: The Case of Swallow Hotels,* Leeds Metropolitan University, unpublished MPhil Thesis.

Winnington-Ingram, R. and Winston, C. (1994), *Investment Research UK and Europe: UK Hotels and Leisure,* Morgan Stanley & Co. International Ltd, London.

Chapter 9

Assessing information needs and external change

Richard Teare

*Granada Professor, Oxford Brookes University and Academic Chair,
International Management Centres, and*

John T. Bowen

*Director of Graduate Studies and Research, Harrah College of Hotel
Administration, University of Nevada, Las Vegas, USA*

Introduction

The managerial activity of learning about events and trends in the
organization's environment is known as environmental scanning. This process
differs from industry or competitor analysis in two main respects; it is broad in
scope and future-directed. Looking back, the 1980s was a decade of turbulence
for hotel companies. Inflation, terrorism, recession, war, political upheaval,
global airline restructuring and the continued advancement of technology are
but a few of the major events influencing performance. While some of these
affected firms operating in other sectors of the hospitality industry, hotel firm
leaders might reasonably be expected to learn from the past and think ahead so
as to ensure that their companies are better equipped to face similar events as
and when they re-occur. The purpose of this article is to assess the extent to
which information needs are currently met by scanning activities and second,
to profile the "top 30" hospitality industry issues as reflected by the UK-based
and North American hospitality management journals. The chapter concludes
with a priority ranking of the "top 30" issues assigned by UK hotel general
managers and summary comments from this group on the implications for
organizational learning.

Does environmental scanning assist strategic planning?
Most authors agree that the main functions of environmental scanning are: to
learn about events and trends in the external environment; to establish
relationships between them; to make sense of the data and to extract the main
implications for decision making and strategy development. In the hospitality
industry, most hotel chains are aware of the need to relate environmental
information to long-range plans, but so far, the majority seem more concerned
with gathering sufficient information to make short-term decisions. In fact, to

This article first appeared in *International Journal of Contemporary Hospitality Management*,
Vol. 9 No. 7, 1997, pp. 274-284.

derive the main benefits from environmental scanning, the activity should be
linked to the formal planning process. A study of hotel chains in Portugal
(Costa *et al.*, 1996) sought to explore these interrelationships and address three
questions:

(1) How do planning and non-planning chains differ in their approach to
strategy making?

(2) What external factors do planning and non-planning chains regard as
affecting their performance?

(3) What type of scanning process is followed by planning and non-
planning chains?

The findings reveal that the differences between "planners" and "non-planners"
in their approach to strategy making are not significant. Both groups show
concern for the long term but non-planners are generally less proactive in their
efforts to understand the behaviour of competitors. This is especially evident in
relation to anticipating competitor behaviour and developing long-term
competitive advantage. The non-planning approach to strategy making
appears to be more participative than the planning approach, although a
written strategy seems to be easier to communicate both internally and
externally. In terms of decision making, both groups reported their decisions as
being frequent, opportunistic and market oriented. This pattern would suit non-
planners but for organizations with a formal planning approach, their plans
have to be flexible to allow this type of behaviour. Overall, the scanning
methods used by both groups are similar and the sources are the same, with a
predominance of informal sources. The existence of a strategic plan does not
seem to affect the scanning behaviour of firms. These findings suggest that the
hotel firms sampled rely mainly on experience, intuition and informal, personal
information gathering to construct their view of the future.

Is it possible to foresee the future?
Evidence suggests that executives who are able to scan their business
environment will derive benefits for their business from doing so, especially if
they are able to detect threats and opportunities and respond accordingly. Yet,
many choose not to devote much energy to the scanning of their business
environment because they are uncertain about the cause and effect relationships
which exist between environmental events and firm performance. Second,
executives are reluctant to engage in a significant scanning activity if they have
concerns about the quality of the sources of information available to them. A
third concern relates to the difficulty of correctly assigning probabilities to the
likelihood of events actually occurring in the environment and their impact on
the firm. Thus, it is often easier to make decisions about more immediate
threats and opportunities rather than long-term trends. The first comprehensive
survey of chief executive officers (CEOs) of multinational hotel chains
sponsored by the International Hotel Association (IHA) sought to assess the

environmental scanning practices of member hotel firms and to learn how their executives view the uncertainty of the global business environment (Olsen *et al.*, 1994). Additionally, the survey sought to determine the key issues that are driving the strategies of these firms and their view of patterns of change in the industry. Aspects of this study are re-visited in the following section.

Assessing information needs

Accurately perceiving the environment is a difficult task and to assist this effort, a classification of the environment is needed. A general category refers to broad-based arenas such as the economic, political, socio-cultural, technological and ecological domains. The forces and trends in this category represent the most difficulty for scanners when they try to identify threats and opportunities, as they are the most abstract and the timing of their development is more difficult to estimate. The task category (customers, suppliers, competitors, regulators) is usually easier to scan, the timing is more easily understood, and the impact is more predictable. The functional category (finance, human resources, operations, administration, marketing, research and development) narrows the scan to specializations within the firm (see Table I). By scanning these categories of the environment, the executive can then decide on the appropriate sources of information to use, both personal and non-personal.

How do executives scan?
The question most often posed by executives when developing strategic plans is: what are the most significant threats and opportunities we will face in the short and long term? The survey questionnaire with responses from 52 CEOs (or their designates), sought to address the following areas:

- Did respondents view various aspects of the environment of their operating domain as stable or volatile? (See Table II).
- How frequently did they scan various categories of their environment?
- What level of interest did they have in scanning various events and trends occurring in their environment?
- Do they rely more on internal and personal sources than external and impersonal ones?

General environment	Task environment	Functional environment
Political	Customers	Finance
Technological	Suppliers	Human resources
Economic	Competitors	Operations
Socio-cultural	Regulators	Administration
Ecological		Marketing research and development

Table I.
Categories of the
business environment

Source: Olsen *et al.* (1994)

Category	Variables
Suppliers of food, beverage and operating supplies	Prices charged, product quality standards, product/service expectations, introduction of new products
Competitors' actions	Supply of rooms, rates charged, renovation and refurbishment, new services and facilities offered, attempts at differentiating the product
Customers' demand	For your services, for new facilities/services
Financial/capital markets	Interest rates: availability of capital, cost of capital other than debt
Labour markets	Wages and salary rates, availability of employees, union activities
Government regulations	Regarding rates you can charge, regarding room, food and beverage quality, regarding provision of your services, affecting personnel/labour decisions,affecting sales and marketing, affecting accounting/bookkeeping, imposing new tax measures
Technological development	In the application of computers and communication technologies, in the application of expert systems/decision support systems, in reservation systems, in training and development

Table II.
Operating domain
variables used to assess
the relative degree of
stability-volatility

- Who is responsible for scanning activities in their firm?
- What types of decisions depend on the firm's scanning activities?
- What are the most important threats and opportunities for their firms in the next one and five-year periods?

Of the respondent firms, 60 per cent, were multinational in their scope of operations. As many as 85 per cent of these firms had less than 50 hotels each. It is these multinationals (as opposed to firms whose scope was strictly national) which indicated greater interest in scanning current/future conditions of the labour market, new legislation/regulations enacted or considered for enactment, acquisition of existing competitors by firms outside the industry, and current/future cost of real estate. Faced with a greater diversity of environmental conditions in the different countries they operate in, international firms seem to be more conscious of environmental scanning than are firms which are national in scope.

Environmental scanning and performance
The study produced enough evidence to show that better scanning of the environment leads to improved performance. For instance, the study indicates that:

- Firms with higher growth in sales show greater interest in customer-related issues.

- Firms with higher growth in income show greater interest in demographic changes in terms of product/service demands, competitor product/service offerings, and new technological developments with industry applications.

- Firms with high growth in rooms show slightly more interest in customer needs/trends, demographic changes in terms of product/service demands, expansion plans of competitors, competitor pricing strategies, and new technological developments with industry applications.

Overall, there was a stronger short-term focus among respondents, characterized by a relatively consistent view of the key short-term issues. As might be expected, a broader range of opinions and priorities characterize the longer-term view (see Table III). The attention paid to short-term issues appeared to be directed at the high impact concerns of the economy, financing and customer needs and expectations. While it is important to focus on these issues, it is also important for executives to keep track of events that are influencing change in the longer term.

Environment strategy	One year (early 1990s)	Five-year (late 1990s)
Economic	Recession, low inflation	Slow economic recovery, Pacific Rim explanation potential, low hotel real estate values
Political	Instability, shifting government policies, increasing taxation of the industry	Instability, shifting government policies, increasing taxation of the industry, regional trading blocks
Socio-cultural	Diversity and changing profile of customers, security issues	Diversity and changing profile of customers
Technological	Integrating new technology, cost of investment, improved MIS	Integrating new technology, cost of investment, distribution and capacity control
Ecological	Adapting current lodging/tourism products, education of costs and issues	Restrictions on property development
Finance	Availability of long-term financing	Availability of long-term financing, fluctuating cost of capital
Marketing	Pricing strategies, brand positioning	Protecting brand identities
Human resources	Skilled labour shortage	Skilled labour shortage
Operations	Skills upgrading	Better management systems (consistency and reliability)

Table III.
Short-term and long-term threats and opportunities

Source: Olsen *et al.* (1994)

The survey findings revealed a gap in both the provision and use of hospitality and tourism industry databases. The Hotel and Catering International Management Association (HCIMA) had also identified a need to provide an enhanced information service in the form of its Worldwide Hospitality and Tourism Trends (WHATT) CD-ROM product which was established in 1994 (Teare, 1995a). WHATT uses a classification scheme designed to provide an overview of the many types of industry-related information in the public domain (Cullis and Teare, 1996). The product, with its three key information sources, addresses hospitality and tourism research (International Hospitality and Tourism Research Register with four categories: academic, associations, government, industry); industry trends (as reflected by academic journals in the World Trends database) and industry current awareness (contained in the HCIMA's Current Awareness Bulletin). The research teams responsible for maintaining the Research Register and World Trends databases in Europe, North America and Australia respectively, provide an on-going review and assessment of industry changes and this is disseminated by means of an annual publication. The following section profiles the structural changes that are occurring in the hospitality industry in the UK and North America and in response, lists the priorities assigned by a panel of general managers.

Assessing external change
The Annual Review of Hospitality and Tourism Trends, published in the *International Journal of Contemporary Hospitality Management,* draws on several thousand records contained in two of the three WHATT databases (*World Trends, Research Register)* to interpret and comment on the themes portrayed in the literature, by academic research and by the wide range of reports emanating from industry, analysts, consulting firms, trade and professional associations and government organizations. The 1995 and 1996 publications provide a thematic analysis of the articles published in European and North American-based academic journals spanning a seven year period from 1989-1995. The aim here is to present the "top 30" issues emerging from the Annual Review so far, and to assess their implications for hospitality operations in the UK with reference to priority rankings made by a panel of 25 hotel general managers in the UK.

To facilitate the task of identifying key developments in the literature, a "top 15" is derived for each of the European and North American segments of the *World Trends* database, using different focal points (or themes) to avoid repetition. The themes are: business performance improvement; personal and organizational development; service improvement and competitiveness (UK) and marketing, human resource management and organizational issues (North America).

Patterns in management, service improvement and business performance (United Kingdom)
The following issues were identified from an analysis of articles in four UK-based hospitality and service industry journals: *International Journal of*

Contemporary Hospitality Management; International Journal of Hospitality Management; International Journal of Service Industry Management and the Service Industries Journal. Each issue is discussed briefly and some examples are provided. The examples relate to the journals that were analysed – for example, Harris (23), refers to citation (23) in "Hospitality operations: patterns in management, service improvement and business performance" (Teare, 1996). The "top 15" also draws on the 1995 Review (see also Teare, 1995b).

The top 15 issues are clustered into three themes: business performance improvement; personal and organizational development; service improvement and competitiveness, and the relationships are shown in Figure 1.

Business performance improvement
Top five: strategic systems; business performance measures; process and quality improvement; radical business structures and approaches; sustainable business development.

Strategic systems. Computer-based "strategic" systems – capable of delivering organization-wide benefits – embrace a range of initiatives, from external analysis (or environmental scanning) linked to business planning to systems for locational analysis of new units, yield management and facilities management. Information technology provides a feasible way of harnessing full operational capability and Donaghy *et al.* (5) review the application of yield management to profit maximization. The main challenge is to engage the full potential of information technology and Crichton and Edgar (6) foresee that as technology develops further, the concept of managing complexity as opposed to minimizing or adapting to it will be become more important.

Business performance measures. Managers depend on an array of tools to gauge workplace success and it has been argued that a balanced set of measurements is needed. Brander Brown and McDonnell (3) investigate

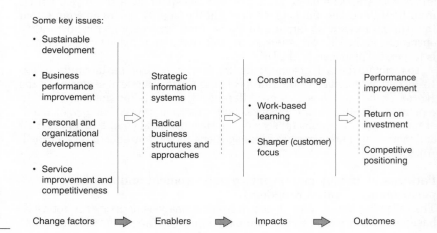

Figure 1.
Patterns in
management, service
improvement and
business performance

whether "the balanced score-card" performance measurement method provides a practical solution. They found that hotel general managers saw benefits in preparing a detailed score-card for each of the areas or departments controlled by senior managers within an individual hotel, providing the score-cards are reviewed and updated regularly. In this way, unit management teams can share the responsibility for achieving goals relating to a set of critical success factors for the unit as a whole.

Process and quality improvement. Yasin and Zimmerer (4) link the application of "benchmarking" to the hotel's ability to achieve its goals in the area of quality improvement. They present a practical framework for this which defines both the operating and service subsystems of the hotel and propose specific methods for quality improvement in each. Congram and Epelman (11) recommend the use of the structured analysis and design technique (SADT) to review service processes and achieve improvements. However, the concept and application of continuous quality improvement (CQI) has yet to make a significant impact on the international hospitality business, but it appears inevitable as organizations seek to establish a dynamic, quality-driven culture of process improvement.

Radical business structures and approaches. The notion of "business excellence" introduced by Peters and Waterman in the early 1980s was derived from a study of successful firms, some of whom were unable to sustain their achievements in the longer term. Caruana *et al.* (1) evaluate the concept of business excellence as it relates to a sample of large UK service firms and Burgess *et al.* (30) examine the "success studies" in the context of multi-unit and multinational hotel groups and internationalization. The pace of change in the competitive arena and need to "re-invent" traditional methods (that impede responsiveness) calls for new ways and methods or organizing business activity.

Sustainable business development. While internal systems and procedures are important, Kim and Olsen (40) note that public concerns and greater external awareness are influencing trends in facilities management and design. Improvements in energy conservation and recycling mean that "green" marketing strategies will be more widely adopted in the future, especially as new design technologies enable hotels and resorts to use natural resources more efficiently (41).

Personal and organizational development
Top five: work-based learning; the adaptive manager; the adaptive organization; the responsive employee; teamworking.

Work-based learning. A number of studies have sought to identify career path competences for hotel managers (see for example, 17 and 18) and while there are core requirements, managerial effectiveness needs to be viewed in relation to a framework for continuous skills and knowledge updating, in keeping with the pace of change that is occurring (19-23). The workplace is increasingly seen as the learning environment of the future and organizations will need to encourage a personal commitment to learning.

The adaptive manager. It is evident that many managers are enjoying successful careers and are well suited to the nature of the work involved but there are signs that managerial roles are becoming more stressful. There are a number of key contributory factors including: the breadth of choice available to consumers in mature markets; the pressure to "do more with fewer people" to preserve or enhance profit margins; and the pace of change in business and commerce as a whole. In response, some organizations are seeking to build on the skills, talents and experience available to them by establishing a "learning organization" culture, climate and approach to business and human resource development.

The adaptive organization. Evidence suggests that hospitality firms are generally bound by traditional working methods and employment policy in comparison with other service industry firms. A more open-minded approach is needed to maximize the potential that exists in the industry's skilled and unskilled workforce. The concept of life-long learning and the mechanisms for supporting this are yet to be firmly established. The impact of new technology, maturing markets and other agents of change mean that managers, supervisors and operatives need to adapt and regularly update their skills and knowledge base. This calls for a closer "learning partnership" between industry and education and more flexible, work-based delivery mechanisms for education and training.

The responsive employee. In general terms, rates of innovation have been held back by traditional methods and practices. This is particularly the case in the human resources field where low pay, low esteem jobs have contributed to high rates of labour turnover. There are, however, signs that different approaches to managing and deploying human resources are being used. Several writers have reported encouraging results from studies of flexible working (45, 46) and Luckock concludes that job roles can be re-shaped in a more flexible way to suit both employees and employers. A more imaginative approach is needed though, and a good deal more could be done to make jobs more interesting, less stressful and less unsocial from the employee's viewpoint.

Teamworking. To compete successfully, organizations need to encourage innovation and a culture of continuous improvement in business processes, quality and service. The key implication here is that managers should seek to create an organizational climate that supports the change agenda and enhances the nature of communications between employees and employees and customers. To promote openness and involvement, traditional styles of management will need to be replaced by a teamworking structure and beyond this, self-managed work teams.

Service improvement and competitiveness
Top five: market sensitivity and competitiveness; service customization; customer orientation; measuring service quality; service excellence.

Market sensitivity and competitiveness. A growing body of evidence suggests that service firms are experimenting with a wide array of approaches and methods designed to narrow the gap between the provider and the consumer of services. Edvardsson (42) argues that it is not sufficient to focus on the encounter with the customer but that organizations should study all the critical incidents in the production chain so as to derive a deeper understanding of how weaknesses affect customer satisfaction with the end product. The alignment between groups of customers which constitute market segments, product specification and consistent service delivery reflects the product differentiation challenge. It seems likely that brands based on customized service packages will be needed in the future so that marketing strategy might emphasize service enhancement as well as socially and ecological responsible leisure and tourism experiences.

Service customization. The concept of mass customization has emerged, in part, from a decade of debate centred on the mass production of inexpensive, commodity-like products or services (the assembly line approach) on the one hand and premium-priced, individually-tailored and highly differentiated offerings on the other. Hart (7) observes that much of the power of mass customization, like total quality management before it, lies in its visionary and strategic implications. Its application should enable companies to produce affordable, high-quality goods and services, but with shorter cycle times and lower costs. The key dimensions of his diagnostic framework for assessing the potential for mass customization are: customer sensitivity, process amenability, competitive environment and organizational readiness. Taylor and Lyon (8) discuss the application of mass customization to food service operations and its likely adoption in a rapidly maturing marketplace.

Customer orientation. A compatible service customization step is for management to create an appropriate form of internal customer orientation and Stauss (9) notes that a deliberate and sustained effort is needed to create a climate that promotes a customer's viewpoint of work activities, processes and non-standardized support services. Customer orientation also implies a readiness to measure and where necessary improve the quality of service and support in keeping with customer expectations.

Measuring service quality. Lee and Hing (10) assess the usefulness and application of the SERVQUAL technique in measuring service quality in the fine dining sector. They demonstrate how easily and inexpensively the technique can be used to identify the strengths and weaknesses of individual restaurants' service dimensions. The interpersonal aspects of service delivery are potentially the most difficult to audit and improve. A useful starting point is to undertake a programme of job analysis for service staff to identify the best fit between tasks, behaviours and personal attributes. Papadopoulou *et al.* (12) identify the dimensions of a higher customer contact with the food and beverage operative's job as perceived by managers, supervisors and operatives and examine within-source and between-source differences in perceptions. Their study confirms the versatility of job analysis as an organizational and diagnostic tool. Among other uses, it depicts the dimensions of a job, the related personal qualities and experience and the training implications. In most cases, it is also helpful to profile ideal combinations of age and experience for different service roles, especially as the industry relies heavily on younger workers (13).

Service excellence. Corporate level concern about service excellence has stimulated interest in employee empowerment. In theory, empowered employees will be more committed to ensuring that service encounters satisfy customers as they have the necessary discretion and autonomy to "delight the customer". Lashley (14) explores the implications of empowering employees and provides a framework for understanding managerial motives in selecting different forms of empowerment and their consequences for achieving improvements in customer service.

Managing change in the US hospitality industry: human resource, marketing and organizational trends (North America)

The following issues were identified from an analysis of articles in four hospitality journals published in North America during the period from 1989-1995 inclusive. Each issue is discussed briefly and some specific research examples from these journals are provided. Citations are related to the journals that were analysed: *The Cornell Hotel and Quarterly Restaurant Administration* (Prabhu, 1996), *Florida International University Hospitality Review* (Bowen, 1996), *Hospitality Research Journal* (Blum, 1996), and *The Journal of Travel and Tourism Marketing* (Hu, 1996).

The top 15 issues are grouped into three themes: marketing, human resource management and organizational issues, and the relationships are shown in Figure 2.

Marketing

Top five: customer retention; internal marketing; segmentation; product design; promotion.

Internal marketing. Internal marketing is marketing aimed internally at the firm's employees. The objective is to ensure that employees are able and willing to deliver quality service. Internal marketing integrates human resource management with marketing and so the review spans these functional areas. Sternberg (Prabhu, 1996, p. 10) for example, reports on the benefits of empowerment to hospitality operations. One of the most important processes associated with internal marketing is the orientation of employees. Kennedy and Berger (Prabhu, 1996, p. 13) recommended ways to increase the effectiveness of orientation programmes. Dienhart and Gregoire (Blum, 1996, p. 11) provide evidence to suggest that a sense of increased job satisfaction and job security may improve an employee's customer focus. Rainero and Chon (Bowen, 1996, p. 4) suggested how marketing principles can be used to attract quality employees. Hotels in a given class offering similar services and superior customer service is one way to differentiate a product and gain competitive advantage and in this endeavour, internal marketing should be viewed as an integral part of the customer service programme.

Customer retention. A 1990 article in the *Harvard Business Review* reports that a 5 per cent increase in customer retention can add 25 to 85 per cent to the bottom line. This article initiated a research frenzy in the customer retention and customer loyalty area. Several studies published in the *Cornell Quarterly* (Prabhu, 1996, pp. 34-35) looked at frequent guest programmes and an ongoing study at the University of Nevada Las Vegas is currently investigating customer loyalty in luxury hotels.

Segmentation. A simple and concise definition of marketing strategy is: "selecting market segments and developing an effective marketing mix for those segments". As firms fine tune their marketing strategies and approaches to segmentation and explore emerging markets, the segmentation issue has become increasingly important to practitioners and, in turn, to academics interested in observing hospitality markets. For instance, the ageing baby boomers generation has been the subject of an array of academic research (see for example, Bowen, 1996, pp. 43-47).

Product design. A number of articles consider the importance of product attributes to the consumer and several studies reveal how managers might fine tune their products to create more value. For instance, Evans and Murman (Bowen, 1996, pp. 48) review the value added attraction of guest room personal hair care products and Kapoor (Bowen, 1996. p. 49) identifies the food attributes that are important to the young adult segment. Other researchers have

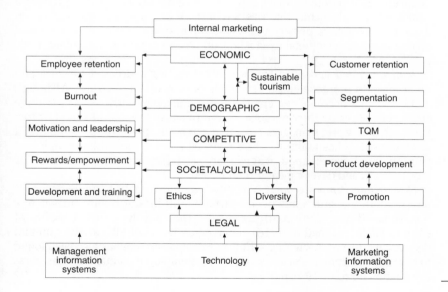

Figure 2.
Environmental
influences on US
academic research

investigated the product attributes that help to create value in a range of different market segments.

Promotion. Promotion is the perennial favourite of marketing researchers. Uysal and Schoenbachler (Hu, 1996, pp. 37, 39) examine the use of advertising in destination marketing. Other study clusters include: the use of marquees as promotional tools, the impact of publicity from restaurant reviews and advertising in the gaming sector.

Human resource management

Top five: employee retention; burnout; motivation and leadership; rewards and empowerment; development and training

Employee retention. Historically, the US hospitality industry has been plagued by labour shortages and triple-digit employee turnover rates. George (Bowen, 1996, p. 6) found employee turnover rates of 150 per cent with an average cost of $2,500 per incident to be common. Turnover, associated costs, and methods of reduction are some of the most frequently addressed topics in the field of hospitality research. The US Bureau of Labor Statistics predicts 165,000 job vacancies annually in the food service industry and the demand for workers will grow by 2 to 3 per cent annually (Bowen, 1996, p. 2). This and other figures have led some researchers to analyse the potential use of non-traditional sources of labour. Older workers, working mothers, and the disabled are a few sources that may help to alleviate the predicted labour shortage.

Burnout. Another cause of turnover, particularly among middle-level managers (Prabhu, 1996, p. 16), is the phenomenon of burnout. The prevalence of burnout is higher in service industries where the job involves a high degree of interaction with clients. The Maslach Burnout Inventory has frequently been used to measure a person's level of burnout in relation to: personal accomplishment, emotional exhaustion, and de-personalization (Prabhu, 1996, p. 15).

Motivation and leadership. One way of attempting to decrease turnover and burnout is to increase employee levels of motivation to work. Although motivation is a personal and emotive issue, outside incentives can encourage employees to renew their personal commitment to the job they hold. If this approach is to work, managers must understand the needs of their employees. A survey of 278 hospitality workers revealed that the three things employees wanted most were: good wages, job security, and opportunities for advancement and development (Prabhu, 1996, p. 11).

Rewards and empowerment. The most obvious form of tangible reward is pay related, but much has been written about intangible incentives too. Sparrowe (Blum, 1996, p. 4) discovered that psychological benefits of empowerment seemed to increase perceived levels of job satisfaction and decrease job turnover intentions. Employee empowerment has also been found to improve operational efficiency and increase employee productivity and guest satisfaction (Prabhu, 1996, p. 10).

Development and training. All the above topics relate to the development and training of employees in the hospitality industry. Employee retention and motivation can be increased through empowerment, which must be accompanied by appropriate training. On the other hand, burnout and turnover may be reduced through employee empowerment and personal development programmes. Although many agree that training is important, few firms seem willing to pay for it. Conrade (Prabhu, 1996, p. 2) found that 77 per cent of the US lodging firms he surveyed spent less than 1 per cent of their payroll expenses on training. If, as previously mentioned, training affects so many other important areas, should not we "pay" more attention to it?

Organizational
Top five: sustainable tourism; ethics/social responsibility; employee diversity; use of technology; information systems.

Ethics/social responsibility. The value of trust is increasing and the growing number of alliances and partnerships in the industry means that firms must rely on and trust each other. Internally, there are signs that firms are paying more attention to ensuring that their employees are treated equitably and ethically (Prabhu, 1996, pp. 17-18). Additionally, more corporations are accepting a degree of social responsibility for community care in locations where they operate their businesses. For instance, Schmidgall (Bowen, 1996, p. 40) reports on the findings of a survey of hotel managers in which he seeks reactions to a number of ethical considerations and scenarios.

Sustainable tourism. Sustainable tourism involves two elements, preserving the environment and preserving the culture. In North America the research in this area has focused mainly on the environment. Ways of reducing solid waste in hotels have gained the attention of several researchers, Jaffe (Bowen, 1996, p. 41) and Shanklin (Blum, 1996, p. 63) and in tourism, Manning and Dougherty (Prabhu, 1996, p. 45) discuss the need to manage capacity of tourist destinations. Other focal points for research include: the development of environmental programmes in hotels, the impact of hospitality businesses in national parks and ecotourism.

Employee diversity. The Asian and Hispanic population in the USA is growing at a faster pace than the population in general. It is also interesting to note that women now hold more senior positions in corporations than ever before and this trend is accelerating. In the near future the white male will become a minority in the workforce and when this occurs the workforce will consist of an array of minority groups. Christenson (Blum, 1996, p. 7) stated that firms must identify how to benefit from a diverse employee group. He claims those that do not will be operating at a disadvantage. Other studies in this area include: the employees of workers with disabilities (Prabhu, 1996, p. 19), economically disadvantaged employees (Bowen, 1996, p. 3) and the use of older workers as a source of labour (Bowen, 1996, pp. 1-2).

Use of technology. The application of technology covers all areas of hospitality operations and there were many articles published during the review period on the use of technology. Chevernak (Blum, 1996. p. 53) discusses the potential uses of fibre optic cable to transmit information both within the hotel and to link the hotel with organizations around the world. A number of articles in the *Journal of Travel and Tourism Marketing* discuss the application of technology to marketing (Hu, 1996, pp. 9, 45-58) and several articles in the *Cornell Quarterly* discuss the application of technology to training (Prabhu, 1996, p. 8-9). See for example, Kasavanva's work on the use of technology in food and beverage operations (Prabhu, 1996, pp. 30-31).

Information systems. The increasing pace of change and employee involvement in information gathering means that most firms are interested in developing better ways to access, capture and process information. These issues are reflected in a number of articles published in *Florida International Review* (Bowen, 1996, pp, 108-111) concerned with information systems. For example, one article by Jenso (Bowen, 1996, p. 111) discusses the outsourcing of information systems.

What are the priorities?
A group of 25 hotel general managers participating in a seminar on market trends and industry issues held during Spring 1997 were asked to record their own responses to the "top 30" issues. After this, participants were asked to rank order their own "top 10" set of priorities from the list of 30 issues. An overall ranking was devised by allocating ten points for a first place ranking, nine points for a second place and so on. The priority ranking is shown in Table IV.

Summary comments
Seminar discussion summary points reflect the participants' own "top 10" priority ranking and reveal a number of implications for organizational learning.

People
The problem of retaining high calibre employees is related to the industry's inability to attract the right people (managers claimed that entrants have unrealistic expectations regarding hours of work and wages). The highest level of turnover occurs if expectations are not met during the first few weeks of employment.

High turnover is also attributed to inadequate training and lack of ongoing development for employees – a need exists for initial management training and continuous, self-directed learning for all. "Investors in People" is seen as a positive step (especially for managing front-line employees) but other areas are viewed as equally important, e.g. leadership training, "adaptive manager" techniques, information management skills and responding effectively to challenging financial targets (among many others). Maximizing "effectiveness" both individually and in team performance is seen as the prime means of delivering better results – financial, customers, employees, systems.

1 Customer retention (91 = 7.4 per cent)
2 Motivation and leadership (88 = 7.2 per cent)
3 Development and training (83 = 6.8 per cent)
4 Employee retention (66 = 5.4 per cent)
5 Radical business structures and approaches (60 = 4.9 per cent) (top 5 – 31.7 per cent)
6 Market sensitivity and competitiveness (58 = 4.7 per cent)
7 Teamwork (57 = 4.6 per cent)
8 Rewards and empowerment (56 = 4.6 per cent)
9 Strategic systems (55 = 4.5 per cent)
10 Process and quality improvement (52 = 4.2 per cent) (top 10 – 54.3 per cent)
11 The adaptive organization (51 = 4.2 per cent)
12 Measuring service quality (50 = 4.1 per cent)
13 Internal marketing (49 = 4.0 per cent)
14 Business performance measures (47 = 3.8 per cent)
15 Work-based learning (46 = 3.7 per cent) (top 15 – 74.1 per cent)
16 Service excellence (45 = 3.7 per cent)
17 The responsive employee (42 = 3.4 per cent)
18 Sustainable business development (39 = 3.2 per cent)
19 The adaptive manager (36 = 2.9 per cent)
20 Information systems (35 = 2.9 per cent)
21 Use of technology (34 = 2.8 per cent)
22 Customer orientation (30 = 2.4 per cent)
23 Service customization (22 = 1.8 per cent)
24 Employee diversity (12 = 1.0 per cent)
25 Promotion (8 = 0.7 per cent)
26 Product design (7 = 0.6 per cent)
27 Burnout (5 = 0.4 per cent)
28 Ethics and social responsibility (3 = 0.2 per cent)
29 Segmentation (1 = 0.1 per cent)
30 Sustainable tourism (0 = 0 per cent)

Note:
Total points = 1,228, scores rounded to nearest decimal place, total 100.2 per cent, $n = 25$

Table IV.
Priority issues for the
UK hotel sector (ranked
by a group of 25 hotel
general managers in
the UK)

Business

Participants are keen to see industry-wide improvements in strategic systems, especially relating to information and yield performance. In turn, this will help to focus more attention on organizational indicators that are harder to monitor and measure but are potentially important measures of success (e.g. effectiveness of communications, morale, "best practice breakthroughs").

Branding and brand awareness coupled with operational consistency and perceptions of quality are seen as key issues now and in the immediate future, especially in relation to the trends towards the "outsourcing" of hotel restaurants.

The top priorities (31 per cent of the total score)

Overall, the discussion groups felt that the most pressing priorities for the UK hotel sector are: customer retention and being customer-focused; motivating employees with a vision of the long term; and personal development so that employees are equipped with the skills necessary to "make things happen". Other key benefits will include improved retention rates among the pool of "good" managers and operatives and this is linked to development initiatives to lead, motivate, inspire, recognize and reward the workforce.

References

Blum, S. C. (1996), "Organizational trend analysis of the hospitality industry: preparing for change", *International Journal of Contemporary Hospitality Management,* Vol. 8 No. 7, pp. 20-32.

Bowen, J.T. (1996), "Managing environmental change: insights from researchers and practitioners", *International Journal of Contemporary Hospitality Management,* Vol. 8 No. 7, pp. 75-90.

Costa, J., Eccles, G. and Teare, R. (1996), "Environmental scanning and strategic planning activities by hospitality managers", in Kaye Chon, K.S. (Ed.), *Advances in Hospitality and Tourism Research,* Omnipress, Wisconsin, pp. 174-88.

Cullis, A. and Teare, R. (1996), "Information technology: its uses in strategic analysis", in Kotas, R., Teare, R., Logie, J., Jayawardena, C. and Bowen, J.T. (Eds), *The International Hospitality Business,* Cassell, London and New York, pp. 77-87.

Hu, C. (1996), "Diverse developments in travel and tourism marketing: a thematic approach", *International Journal of Contemporary Hospitality Management,* Vol. 8 No. 7, pp. 33-43.

Olsen, M.D., Murthy, B. and Teare, R. (1994), "CEO perspectives on scanning the global hotel business environment", *International Journal of Contemporary Hospitality Management,* Vol. 6 No. 4, pp. 3-9.

Prabhu, S. (1996), "Challenges for hospitality and tourism educators: a North American perspective", *International Journal of Contemporary Hospitality Management,* Vol. 8 No. 7, pp. 52-62.

Teare, R. (1995a), "WHATT's available? Hospitality", *Journal of the Hotel and Catering International Management Association,* December 1994/January 1995, No. 147, pp. 20-1.

Teare, R. (1995b), "The international hospitality business: a thematic perspective", *International Journal of Contemporary Hospitality Management,* Vol. 7 No. 7, pp. 55-73.

Teare, R. (1996), "Hospitality operations: patterns in management, service improvement and business performance", *International Journal of Contemporary Hospitality Management,* Vol. 8 No. 7, pp. 63-74.

Chapter 10
Interpreting and responding to customer needs

Richard Teare

*Granada Professor, Oxford Brookes University and Academic Chair,
International Management Centres*

*Granada Professor, Oxford Brookes University and Academic Chair,
International Management Centres*

If managers are to tackle the challenge of meeting the individual needs of customers, it is essential to ensure as far as possible, that their expectations are met. These are fed by the needs, motives and preferences that fuel the decision process. Although the fields of learning, motivation and personality research are broad ranging, it is necessary to appreciate the rich complexity of influences that the consumer feels and thinks about during the various stages of decision making. Collectively, this conscious and subconscious set of influences guides our decision making by providing a meaningful, personal preference structure. Ultimately this tests and confirms (or rejects) the value of received impressions and the acceptability of actual experiences. Beyond this, the organizational implications for designing and delivering services need to be related to what is known and what might be learned about current and prospective customer groups. The aim of this article is to relate aspects of consumer behaviour and in particular the decision process to the procedures and processes for delivery and assuring customer service. The main themes of the article are understanding customers; designing and delivering services; and assuring total quality services.

Understanding customers

The unpredictability of consumer behaviour has much to do with individual differences and the way in which people categorize purchase decisions. In an effort to identify the interrelationships between influences which occur during decision making, researchers often devise frameworks or models which portray relationships and in so doing, enrich our theoretical understanding of consumer decision making. A decision model seeks to represent the often complex array of factors (or variables) which influence consumer decision making. It can be regarded as "..a blueprint which shows the essential elements of a larger system..." (Karmarck, 1983). In essence, the model seeks to simulate or approximate as realistically as possible the complications of consumer preference, choice and purchase behaviour.

This article first appeared in *The Journal of Workplace Learning,* Vol. 10 No. 2, 1998, pp. 76-94.

Making sense of consumer research

The aim here is to review the relevance and usefulness of theory generating approaches to exploring customer reactions and insights in hospitality and tourism settings (Teare, 1990; 1991). The potential value of theory development in marketing is sometimes neglected and more often underestimated. Foxall (1986) attributes this to a reluctance by practitioners and applied researchers to engage in academic speculation or to extend "intuitive" theoretical explanations. However, there is much common ground and theoretical explanations can be considered valuable if they perform one or more of the following functions:

• The means of classifying, organizing and integrating information relevant to the factual world of business.

• A technique of thinking about marketing problems, and a perspective for practical action.

• An analytical tool-kit to be drawn on as appropriate in the solution of marketing problems.

• The possibility to derive, in time, a number of principles, or even laws, of marketing behaviour.

Kelly (1963) states that theory should possess several qualities: "A theory may be considered as a way of binding together a multitude of facts so that one may comprehend them all at once. When the theory enables us to make reasonably precise predictions, one may call it scientific". By unifying facts into theory, an explicit framework is created within which deductions can be made and future events anticipated. The framework should:

• Facilitate the integration of new ideas, and the production of testable hypotheses.

• Provide a better understanding of the phenomena represented by systemizing facts, and facilitate modification in the light of subsequent observations.

The value of a theoretical framework (or model) must also be seen in the context of the problems which arise from attempting to construct and test theory in isolation from existing theory (Teare, 1988). Reviewing developments in consumer research, Arndt (1976) observes: "In spite of the quantitatively impressive literature tonnage, the marketing contributions to consumer behavior seem to be flawed by serious shortcomings…". Several of the criticisms Arndt makes are related to established research paradigms and in particular, the fragmentation arising from the many "…non-cumulative empirical research investigations…". Jacoby (1978) among others, has argued that any given theory only has meaning and significance within the paradigm from which it is derived. The dominant tradition in consumer research is the cognitive school (or paradigm), which assumes that consumers have the capacity to receive and process a wide array of information, especially during pre-purchase search.

Foxall (1986) observes that the success of the cognitive paradigm seems to have held back various alternative forms of theoretical progress. In part, this is because the methodological tradition in marketing tends to reflect a "theory testing" rather than a "theory generating" emphasis. The former approach is well suited to commercial settings which have been extensively researched, but there are many facets of the consumer-producer interface in hospitality and tourism which have yet to be fully explored. In this context, theory generation can provide an effective way of exploring specific issues relating to consumer decision making.

The principles and concepts of theory generation tend to draw more heavily upon qualitative methods, as they offer an appropriate array of techniques for uncovering and exploring relationships. This combination also tends to facilitate a more broadly-based study than conventional theory testing (which focuses on the relationships between two or more specified variables). This provides a richer, more holistic picture with potentially many opportunities for integrating data within an evolving theoretical framework or model for a specific setting or even industry sector. Given the criticisms of general decision models and the difficulties of operationalizing them, these points coincide with the expectations of "good" marketing theory.

The research context

A fundamental concern of marketing is to establish how and why consumers buy a particular product or range of products. This is a challenging issue as there are many conscious and unconscious reasons why people engage in different types of buyer behaviour. Some of the reasons are rational, some emotional while others are specific to a particular segment or group of buyers. To identify patterns of purchase behaviour in given product fields, a continuous programme of research is needed. This should seek to probe unconscious reasons and behaviours using qualitative research methods as well as tracking responses by questionnaire.

Hospitality services and the consumer perspective. The variable and intangible nature of many hospitality and tourism services stems from the way in which they are packaged and delivered to the consumer. Typically, services are consumed at the point of consumption and the consumer participates in the production process by making choices and interacting with service staff. The dynamics of the interaction between the producer and consumer are influenced by the specific needs and expectations of each customer. For instance, hotel customers might reasonably expect to receive an array of benefits from a consumption experience. These include:

- Meeting basic functional (or physiological) needs such as hunger, thirst and sleep.

• Satisfying more complex expressive (or psychological) needs like
enjoying the hotel surroundings, feeling safe, secure and relaxed;
fulfilling lifestyle-related aspirations like using and appreciating
luxurious facilities and selecting from an appealing choice of food and
wine menus.

The key issue here is not simply providing an opportunity for people to fulfil
their individual needs, but exceeding their expectations and thereby ensuring
that the benefits (sources of satisfaction) greatly outweigh potential disbenefits
(sources of dissatisfaction). Case studies of marketing effectiveness (Teare and
Williams, 1989) and service improvement (Teare, 1994d, pp. 81-95) show that
this task is far from easy to achieve and sustain. This is partly due to the
difficulty of assuring the consistency of service delivery but also because
expectations differ from person to person. Figure 1 (Teare, 1994a,
p. 7) emphasizes the need for co-alignment between consumer expectations and
the design and delivery of hospitality/tourism services. The diagram depicts a

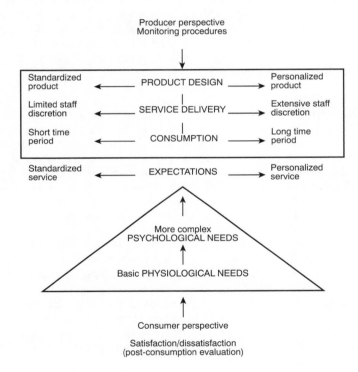

Figure 1.
The interdependency of
hospitality services

Source: Adapted from Teare, R. *et al., Marketing in Hospitality and Tourism:
A Consumer Focus,* Cassell, London, 1994, p. 7

continuum of expectations derived from personal needs and product-related perceptions of the type of consumption experience sought. It suggests that consumers expect to receive a service package which is mainly standardized or personalized, depending on the price and perceived complexity of the consumption experience:

- Standardized service equates with perceptions and/or prior knowledge of consumption over a short time period, with limited staff discretion during service delivery. These characteristics relate to expectations of a standardized product experience such as a fast food restaurant meal with a comparatively low average spend.

- Personalized service equates with perceptions and/or prior knowledge of consumption over a long time period, with extensive staff discretion during service delivery. These characteristics relate to expectations of a personalized product such as staying in a luxury resort hotel, with a comparatively high average spend.

Broad distinctions of this kind are helpful, but service branding requires a more rigorous approach if the intention is to enable the consumer to differentiate between competing brands in his/her own mind.

Towards a framework for interpreting consumer decision making
Relatively low cost, low risk, repeat purchases are sometimes described as "routinized response behaviour". In contrast, infrequent, higher cost purchases are typically characterized by a more complex decision process including a deliberate period of information gathering. This type of buying decision is normally referred to as a "high involvement purchase". This section reviews the range and type of influences which affect consumer decision making, with particular reference to the more complex high involvement decision process.

Modelling hospitality/tourism decision making. General decision models provide a theoretical framework which can lend meaning to observations of consumer behaviour. The practical value of a model increases as the framework is refined by the discovery of unique patterns of behaviour in given product fields. A descriptive model of the consumer decision process for hospitality services is shown in Figure 2 (Teare, 1994a, p. 10). It shares a number of characteristics with Moutinho's vacation tourist model (Teare, 1994b, p. 17). For instance, they both reflect the relatively high investment cost of hospitality/tourism services, given that the return on investment (in the form of benefits derived) is mainly intangible. They also point to the fact that "satisfaction" is derived from many transient impressions and experiences that occur during consumption and these affect the consumer's state of mind at the end of the consumption period. Further, the consumer's psychological state of mind is likely to affect the way in which the consumer approaches subsequent hospitality/tourism purchase decisions and the information sources used to overcome feelings of perceived risk relating to high involvement purchases.

The pre-purchase stage of the decision process. The pre-purchase stage of a complex decision-making process is influenced by a number of variable factors (see Figure 3, (Teare, 1994b, p. 19)). They include: the consumer's preference structure; information search behaviour; prior product experience; the extent of product involvement; the feeling of perceived risk; the extent of role specialization and the role of decision rules in choice.

Preference structure. Individual differences between people – the consumers of products and services – are deeply embedded in the concepts of personality, socialization (impressions from childhood and adolescence) perception and learning. These and other influences form a unique combination which define the consumer's preference structure. In specifying his model of vacation tourist

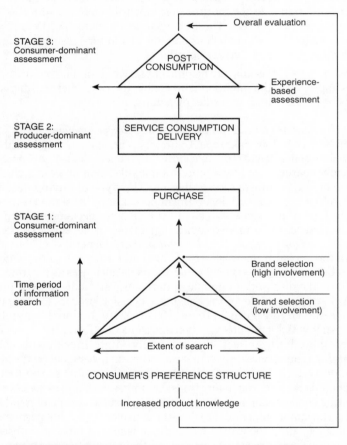

Figure 2.
The consumer decision
process for hospitality
services

Source: Adapted from Teare, R. *et al., Marketing in Hospitality and Tourism: A Consumer Focus,* Cassell, London, 1994, p. 10

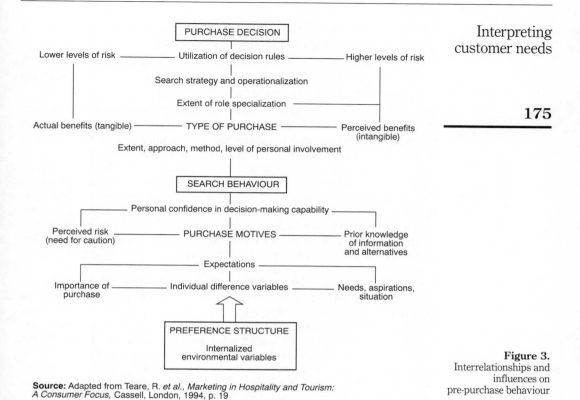

Source: Adapted from Teare, R. *et al., Marketing in Hospitality and Tourism: A Consumer Focus,* Cassell, London, 1994, p. 19

Figure 3.
Interrelationships and
influences on
pre-purchase behaviour

behaviour, Luiz Moutinho draws on three behavioural concepts – motivation, cognition and learning. He portrays a sequence of behavioural events, triggered by purchase motives, which activate cognition (mental processing of information) and learning. In this context, behaviour is defined as a function of intention to act, which is influenced by situational factors that mediate between intended and actual behaviour:

- Cognition refers to the mental processes of knowing, perceiving and judging which enable people to interpret the world around them. An individual's map of reality or cognitive map is therefore a subjective view of the world, based on personal beliefs, values and experiences.

- Learning can be defined as a change in behaviour related to a specific outcome or arising from practice, ranging from its narrower definition as the acquisition of knowledge or skill to less conscious forms of psychologically-based evaluation. For example, consumers "learn" from consumption experiences and, outcomes (satisfaction or dissatisfaction) influence subsequent purchase decision behaviour.

- Motives initiate behaviour and serve to direct it towards actions with specific outcomes. The desired outcomes are often closely related to personal needs and aspirations.

The pre-decision stage of Moutinho's model consists of one field (the preference structure) and three sub-fields which aim to show how information is processed by means of stimulus filtration, attention and learning and the application of choice criteria. In this instance, the consumer's preference structure for a tourist destination is influenced by internalized sources (such as cultural norms and values, family and reference group influences, financial status, social status) and the consumer's own affective judgements. These are derived from and influenced by individual differences arising from the consumer's own personality, lifestyle, perceptions and purchase motives. Here, the consumer's preference structure may also be influenced by travel-specific information like exposure to travel stimuli portraying attributes such as quality, price, distinctiveness, prestige, service and availability.

Chisnall (1994) notes that marketing researchers have spend much time and effort analysing personality traits such as sociability and aggressiveness in the hope of establishing buyer behaviour connections with personality types. Some have also attempted to explain buying habits related to particular products in terms of these characteristics, but the empirical evidence is not very convincing. The nature of the problem is summarized by Kassarjian and Sheffet (1981) in reporting on a wide-ranging review of the relationship between purchase behaviour and personality which they define as consistent responses to the world of stimuli surrounding the individual. They conclude that: "…the correlation or relationship between personality test scores and consumer behaviour variables such as product choice, media exposure, innovation, segmentation, etc., are weak at best and thus of little value in prediction".

It is generally difficult to determine the extent to which all the main preference structure components can be interpreted or even fully understood. Individual differences imply variability between internalized sources of influence and so the task is a challenging one. However, attempts to investigate the likely impact of individual difference variables can yield meaningful information about what and how consumers think about competing brands in a given product field as well as what they expect to derive from a given purchase.

Information search behaviour. The extent of pre-purchase search behaviour is largely determined by consumer preferences and in particular, the availability and accessibility of information and the number of acceptable purchase options. The extent of information search is related to a number of factors including perceived benefits, risk and household roles, brand preferences and differences between alternatives, prior knowledge, experience, time and financial pressures. In essence, search activity increases when the consumer believes that the purchase is important, that there is a need to learn more, or when information is easy to obtain and utilize (Newman, 1977).

Prior product experience. Prior experience is an important variable as "familiarity" with a given product and "expertise" relating to a particular product field influence how confident the consumer is likely to feel about a given purchase and how much external information is needed prior to making an informed choice. Search behaviour generally begins with the recollection of information from memory as the consumer tries to determine whether choice can be based on prior experience. Insufficient information or experience is likely to activate external information search.

Product involvement. Involvement has been defined as "…an unobservable state reflecting the amount of interest, arousal or emotional attachment evoked by the product in a particular individual…" (Bloch, 1981). This variable, perhaps more than others, characterizes a complex purchase where the consumer is actively seeking to synthesize information and resolve feelings of risk and uncertainty. Low involvement purchases are normally characterized by a much higher degree of passive or unconscious information processing, mainly because the risk, symbolic (or sign), status or hedonic value of the product is not sufficiently important to warrant a higher level of personal involvement.

Perceived risk. In the context of decision making, risk is related to uncertainty about the product. The sense of risk is commonly associated with the place and mode of purchase and the financial and psycho-social consequences of product purchase.

Role specialization. Closely related to information search in joint/family decision making, role specialization is commonly linked to the use of specialist skills and considerations like convenience and time allocation. A high proportion of decisions relating to hospitality/tourism services are likely to involve joint/family discussion and/or role specialization and hence, there is a need to consider in detail:

(1) the extent to which prior experience influences family decision-making responsibilities for evaluating the consumption experience, storing information for future use and utilizing the stored information when the need arises and

(2) how families make decisions rather than simply who is involved.

These issues are important because the nature of family relationships and the financial and time constraints faced by the family provide a reasonably self-contained decision-making environment.

Decision rules. As noted earlier, decision-making processes range from simple or routinized to more complex ones. The same principle applies to product choice – when an alternative that has performed well in the past is selected, a simple choice process has been used. Such a process, repeated many times, may become established as an integral part of a behavioural sequence. This acts as a guiding principle or decision rule that can be applied to subsequent choice decisions. More complex choice processes occur when non-compensatory choice principles are invoked. Typically this happens when a weakness in one product attribute is not compensated by the strengths of another. To overcome this, the consumer may begin to rate choice criteria using a mental weighting or subjective probability approach. It is interesting to note that the composition and individual importance of choice criteria are likely to vary at different stages in the decision process. Further, evidence suggests that consumers are able to recall how a non-compensatory choice was made from alternatives but recalling how the choice set of alternatives was formed in the first place is more difficult. A key consideration is likely to be price information which is frequently used as an indicator of product quality, especially if product information is limited.

The purchase decision. Commenting on the relationship between pre-purchase activities and the purchase decision, Olshavsky and Granbois (1979) observe that:

- Many purchases are likely to occur out of necessity, due to deeply rooted preferences, conformity to group norms or imitation of others based on recommendations from personal or non-personal sources.

- Even if the purchase decision is preceded by a choice process, it is typically limited to the evaluation of a few alternatives, little external search, few evaluative criteria and simple evaluation processes.

- A stronger emphasis on the study of situational factors is necessary and to achieve this, observational research methods need to be used more widely so as to reduce a traditional dependence on model-based predictions of consumer behaviour.

The situational context in which decision making occurs equates to a point in time and space and there are five commonly re-occurring situational factors. They are:

(1) physical surroundings;

(2) social surroundings;

(3) antecedent states;

(4) task definition; and

(5) the temporal (or time) perspective of the decision process.

Task definition is defined as "…an intent or requirement to select, shop for, or obtain information about a general or specific purchase…" (Belk, 1975).

Hospitality/tourism services are delivered in a wide variety of situations and physical environments and it is reasonable to assume that a relationship exists between self-confidence in varying situations and the level of satisfaction derived from the consumption experience. Providing a further link is the concept of situational self-image and the notion that the consumer develops a repertoire of self-images which vary as the situation requires. Interpreting this view, the consumer who is selecting a hotel might be expected to seek confirmation that he or she will feel comfortable in a given physical environment and with the services provided. Situational, personal and interpersonal factors which influence the purchase decision are shown in Figure 4 (Teare, 1994b, p. 27).

Consumption and post-consumption stages of the decision process. Satisfaction plays a significant role in mediating between intentions and behaviour. Although consumers are not always able to recall the detail of past evaluations, prior feelings of satisfaction/dissatisfaction do provide a meaningful link between expectations and experience, especially prior to making a re-purchase decision (see Figure 5, Teare, 1994b, p. 28).

Satisfaction equates to the fulfilment of a motivating state or the meeting of an expectation, through the purchase of a product or service. In the context of tourist satisfaction with a destination area it is defined as: "...the result of the interaction between a tourist's experience at the destination area and the expectations he had about that destination area..." (Pizam *et al.*, 1978). In this instance, satisfaction is derived from the evaluation of tourist product components such as accommodation, eating and drinking experiences, destination accessibility, attractions, cost and services. The outcome – satisfaction (or dissatisfaction) is derived from the weighted sum total of comparative assessment ratings, guided by expectations and reference standards. Studies of consumer satisfaction tend to subscribe to one of two alternative explanations:

(1) that satisfaction results from the confirmation of expectations and dissatisfaction from disconfirmation; or

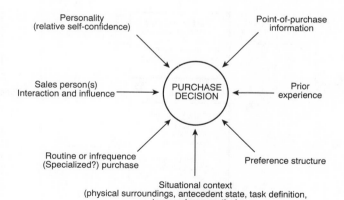

Source: Adapted from Teare, R.*et al., Marketing in Hospitality and Tourism: A Consumer Focus,* Cassell, London, 1994, p. 27

Figure 4.
Factors influencing the
purchase decision

(2) that satisfaction/dissatisfaction is derived from measurements made against experience-based norms.

Confirmation/disconfirmation of expectations. Prior to brand purchase and use, the consumer formulates expectations about brand performance in a given situation. After using the brand, the consumer compares perceived actual performance with expected performance. Confirmation of expectations and a

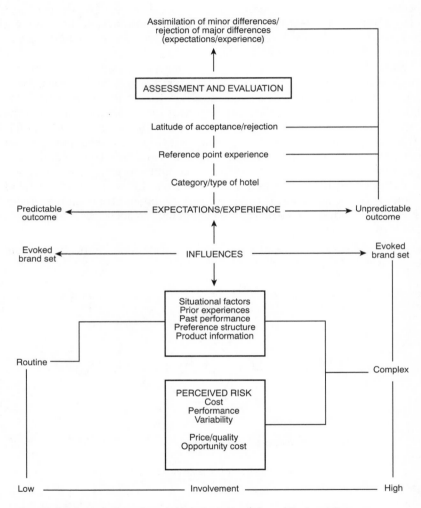

Figure 5.
The role of decision
rules

Source: Adapted from Teare, R. *et al., Marketing in Hospitality and Tourism: A Consumer Focus,* Cassell, London, 1994, p. 52

feeling of satisfaction occurs when the two perspectives coincide or if perceived brand performance exceeds expectations. Disconfirmation occurs if perceived brand performance falls below expectations and a feeling of dissatisfaction is experienced.

Experience-based norms. An alternative view proposes that after using a brand the consumer will note how it performed. When there are many attributes to consider, overall brand performance is likely to be determined by a combination of beliefs about the most important dimensions of brand perfor- mance. In this way, beliefs are either strengthened or weakened according to how closely actual matches expected brand performance, thereby providing a meaningful frame of reference.

Summary. To identify different patterns of consumer decision making, it is necessary to establish a theoretical framework for comparative analysis (Teare, 1994c, pp. 44-67) and this is depicted in Figure 6.

The review has highlighted a number of promising variables and their potential explanatory value is summarized as follows.

The likelihood that consumers with:

- extensive prior experience (in a given product field) will engage in high involvement decision making is related to the perceived importance of the product;

- extensive prior experience will engage in low involvement decision making is related to product familiarity and personal confidence in product class decision-making ability;

- limited prior experience will engage in high involvement decision making is related to perceived risk and limited personal confidence in product class decision-making ability;

- limited prior experience will engage in low involvement decision making is related to pre-knowledge of product suitability and low perceptions of risk.

Additionally:

- The use of pre-purchase decision rules and their relative effectiveness during the assessment of choice criteria is related to the extent of prior product experience.

- The link between product expectations and experience is related to product familiarity.

- The consumer's ability to accurately predict and evaluate a consumption experience is related to the extent of prior experience.

- Satisfaction during consumption is a function of many differently weighted impressions and experiences.

- Satisfaction during post-consumption evaluation represents the sum total of individual assessments made during the consumption period.

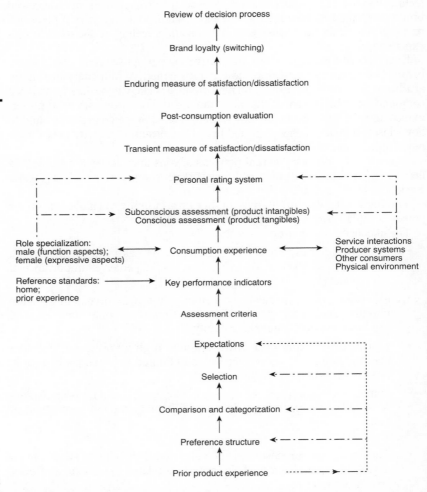

Figure 6.
A consumer framework
for assessing and
evaluating hotels

Source: Adapted from Teare, R. and Boer, A. (Eds), *Strategic Hospitality Management: Theory and Practice for the 1990s,* Cassell, London, 1991, p. 28

Designing and delivering services

Marketing is concerned with exchange relationships between the organization and its customers. The extent to which this is successfully achieved largely depends on the quality of the product/services and the effectiveness of the customer service before, during and after service delivery. In order to achieve total customer satisfaction and maintain long-term customer relationships, a closer alignment is needed between the three areas (customer service, quality and marketing) so that they are inter-linked rather than separate, unrelated functions. In essence, the nature of the relationship marketing challenge is to achieve a form of integration between customer service, quality and marketing. Christopher *et al.* (1991) summarize this as follows:

Marketing and quality relationship. Quality should be determined from the perspective of the customer, based on a programme of continuous research and monitoring.

Quality and customer service relationship. The total quality concept should influence both the process elements (e.g. designing out failure points) and people elements (e.g. managing "moments of truth" in the service encounter).

Customer service and marketing relationship. Customer service levels should be determined by a research-based approach to monitoring and measuring customer needs in different market segments and the activities of competitors.

The concept of internal marketing and the value chain
Internal marketing is the term used to describe the application of marketing internally within the organization. Two key concepts underpin the practice of internal marketing:

- The notion of an internal customer. In essence, every person working in an organization has both customers and suppliers.

- The notion of a customer-focused culture. Here, the entire organization works in a co-ordinated way to achieve its mission, goals and strategies by recognizing customer-supplier relationships and by maintaining close relationships with external customers.

The complex web of relationships between the internal and external markets share four key characteristics. Supplier-customer relationships:

(1) can be external or internal;

(2) are mutually dependent;

(3) require close co-operation;

(4) provide links in value chains.

Scheuing (1995) shows how the chain of value creation culminates in the experience that the hospitality organization provides to the external customer. It begins well before the service is delivered, with the supplier's supplier – a relationship that is entirely external to the organization. In this sense, the value chain is a chain of dependency. The quality of the external customer's experience with the hospitality organization depends on the quality of the equipment, supplies and services it receives from external suppliers. It is equally important to differentiate between core activities (a hospitality organization's unique strengths might include multilingual staff or a renowned chef (see for example Ferrone *et al.* 1995)) and support activities. Seen in relation to the value chain, support services are often better handled by specialist external suppliers with the resources to provide excellent service. Typically, support services could include kitchen equipment repair, industrial cleaning and business centre services.

Hospitality organizations and the internal customer. The external customer or guest is the organization's focal concern and delighting guests is more a matter of attitude and commitment on the part of employees than any other single factor. If it is to thrive and succeed, the notion of service excellence needs to be embedded in the organization's statement of purpose or mission and continually reinforced by its corporate behaviour. This is how Ritz-Carlton Hotels – a recipient of the Malcolm Baldrige Award for world class service quality – initiated its efforts to inspire employees with its goal of achieving service excellence. Although systems and procedures provide essential support, the real difference lies in the human touch at the "moment of truth" when a guest encounters an employee. Some hotel chains (e.g. American firms like Hampton Inns and Embassy Suites) use service guarantees while others (e.g. Fairfield Inns) provide guests with the opportunity to log comments at the check-out computer terminal. Most firms still use written guest survey forms and comment cards to obtain customer feedback and while they may help to track guest satisfaction, they are relatively meaningless unless the organization is committed to creating a service culture that recognizes and supports productive internal customer-supplier relationships.

Internal customers are colleagues or associates who depend on an internal service provider's outputs for their own ability to perform successfully. The nature of the dependency extends to quality of work, timeliness of delivery and the relative cost of the outputs provided which become inputs to the next link in the value chain. Any delays, defects or cost overruns directly affect the ability of the next link to render satisfactory service to its customers. A key corporate challenge is to foster a collective sense of responsibility so that all associates see themselves as part of a total process that generates customer satisfaction consistently and continually.

The naturally occurring contacts between employees and customers have been referred to as service encounters, service interactions or " moments of truth". In relation to the process of hotel service delivery and perceived customer benefits – key elements of the customer's total experience – there are four different types of interaction (Teare and Gummesson, 1991, pp. 148-9):

(1) Interactions between the customer and employees;

(2) Interpersonal interactions between customers;

(3) Interactions between the customer and service delivery systems;

(4) Customer interactions with the physical environment during the service experience.

All four types of interaction have contrasting characteristics and may combine in different ways, according to the type and duration of the service production/delivery process.

In order to fully understand and accurately interpret customer expectations, it is necessary to identify sources of guest satisfaction and dissatisfaction. It is rarely possible to identify specific, recurring causes of satisfaction and the concept of a "zone of tolerance" (Parasuraman *et al.*, 1991) reflects this. Experiences within a range from "acceptable" to "desired" make a relative contribution to a feeling of satisfaction, while experiences that are not "acceptable" promote feelings of dissatisfaction.

Designing a contemporary hotel service culture
Traditionally, hotel firms have considered themselves to be good at meeting the expressed wishes of their guests, but in the late 1990s and beyond, increased attention to their non-expressed needs is likely to provide a more fruitful source of competitive advantage (Teare and Senior, 1992; Teare *et al.*, 1989). The purpose here is to examine a number of design considerations for hotel companies wishing to improve the service climate or culture within their organization. These are developed with reference to "best practice" illustrations from Hilton International (Bould *et al.*, 1992a; 1992b), Holiday Inn Worldwide (Nibbelink and Teare, 1991; Parker and Teare; 1991) and Hyatt International Corporation (Chorengel and Teare, 1991). The examples show how each separate initiative provides an effective mechanism for contemporary, customer-led service development (Teare, 1993b).

Hilton International: a new service culture. Hilton International's core components of guest room, restaurant and bar provision are augmented by more than 200 ancillary services spanning laundry and dry cleaning, entertainment, healthcare, business services, telecommunications and many others. To determine the optimum service positioning, Hilton undertook customer and employee surveys to identify market needs and expectations and the views of employees on issues such as job content, work conditions, management and, crucially, what they believed customers wanted them to provide. This work was instrumental in shaping a programme designed to create a more contemporary service-led organization. A process of analysis had led to the identification of key areas of guest service concern and these offered several natural focal points for service enhancement. For example:

- the arrival...the entire process of preparing for welcoming and introducing the guest into the hotel. By completely meeting guest expectations in this area, 55 per cent of all key guest service concerns would be resolved.

- problem solution...a further 30 per cent of guest concerns could be met by equipping employees with the skills to play a more positive and active part in resolving problems on behalf of guests.

This line of enquiry led to the creation of The Hilton Promise – essentially a commitment from the company, delivered by its employees to superior and distinctive service which guests would remember and come back for again.

In attempting to reinvigorate its service culture on a global basis, Hilton had to examine the nature of the global service challenge, how it communicated to customers and staff and research evidence in order to identify the implications for changes in the front-line cultures. Under the umbrella of the Hilton masterbrand, a number of service brands were developed.

Hilton International's service brand for the Japanese market. Hilton's service branding research highlighted the need for a product development approach which would enable customers to easily match their needs against a specially adapted style or area of hotel service. This led to attempts to define the concept of a service brand which might support the kind of innovations fundamental to Hilton's planned growth. The adopted approach was to consider different service clusters which combined would provide key benefits to customers. The number of Japanese visitors to Hilton International hotels worldwide had been growing rapidly, doubling since 1988 to reach a figure close to 21 per cent of the company's total visitor volume, equalling the number of American guests. The total Japanese outbound market was projected to double again by 1995 but the Japanese have very different cultural expectations from Americans and Europeans for instance, who are in themselves culturally distinctive groups, but with more similarities than differences. To identify the best approach, hotels that were already receiving significant numbers of Japanese guests were identified, as were hotels that were located close to Japanese commercial, industrial and residential areas. This activity was primarily focused on Hilton hotels in Europe, as the majority of Hilton hotels in the Far East had already incorporated service features and styles suited to the Japanese market.

Initially, efforts were concentrated on identifying "best practice" within the organization by finding out how Hilton hotels with an established Japanese clientele were responding to guest requirements. Hilton hotels which, because of their location, should have been receiving a higher proportion of Japanese guests were also examined, and a close correlation was identified between increasing Japanese business share and the successful implementation of customized service features that Japanese guests had requested. On completion of the audit-based comparison, an extensive consumer research programme began in Japan, using Hilton hotel database information in order to find out what Japanese customers who regularly travel internationally wanted Hilton hotels to provide. The culmination of the research was the development of the Hilton Japanese service brand "Wa No Kutsurogi" Service meaning "comfort and service, the Japanese way". It consists of distinctive service features and special amenities appealing to both Japanese business and leisure travellers. These include Japanese speaking staff at the participating hotels, the provision of safe deposit boxes, hotel information, menus, wine lists etc. and safety instructions in Japanese, the provision of an Oriental food selection, often with authentic Japanese cuisine, and the availability of Japanese green tea and items such as slippers, bathrobes and Japanese newspapers. In essence, the brand, symbolized by a Japanese crane, the Tsuru, which is the national emblem of Japan signifying "freedom, good luck, long life and happiness" aims to attract more Japanese business to more Hilton hotels. The underlying assumption is that if the majority of visitors feel comfortable with the hotel service environment they experience, the development will have been fully justified in terms of the additional guest satisfaction and new business it will generate. The Japanese Service Brand illustrates the first key design consideration, which is that wherever possible, hotel services should be customized by purpose of visit and/or origin of guest.

Holiday Inn Worldwide: universality, quality and consistency. The original Holiday Inn hotel concept or "core brand" gained international recognition for setting and achieving consistently high standards in product design and service. Early innovations pioneered by Holiday Inn were remote controlled television and direct dial telephones and in the 1990s, a uniquely sophisticated satellite communication network provides instantaneous information transfer between North America and Europe. Standard features include spacious guest rooms with large beds, private bathrooms and a minimum 16-hour room service. Every hotel has a variety of meeting and conference rooms and most offer a range of leisure facilities as well as the convenience of free car parking. The basic parameters of the Holiday Inn product provide a standardized framework and a universally marketable brand. To safeguard this, two procedures are used to scrutinize operating standards. First, standards are clearly and precisely defined in relation to specifications for hotel design and construction as well as for operations and service. The design specifications include detailed reference to every facet of the operation, ranging from the size of the guest room to the adequacy of life and fire safety systems.

As the network is franchised, it is policy to restrict contract and licence agreements to those who understand the precise requirements for constructing and operating hotels to Holiday Inn standards. This requires a comprehensive quality audit system and every hotel participates by undergoing an independent quality audit inspection twice a year as a minimum requirement. If problems are reported, the hotel fails the inspection and typically undergoes scrutiny three times over the next six months. At the same time, a programme to correct the deficiency is drawn up and a timetable for implementation agreed. The quality audit programme is continually refined so as to improve the effectiveness of the assessment process. Holiday Inn's strict policy on design and operating standards illustrates the second design consideration, which is that product consistency is essential to the retention of customer loyalty.

Hyatt International Corporation: a global service network. Hyatt hotel properties are renowned for the dramatic architectural atrium lobby designs featured at Hyatt Regency and Grand locations. Hyatt International Corporation (Hyatt) also operate the smaller "European style" Park Hyatt hotels, which are mainly situated in international business destinations. Each hotel type represents differences in size and design but they share the same corporate identity and de luxe standards of comfort and service. Hyatt defend their market position by concentrating on what the organization is best placed to deliver. This is reflected in Hyatt's experienced and professional inventory of managers, many of whom have spent most or all of their career with Hyatt delivering what customers perceive to be a stylish, contemporary, innovative brand of service. Hyatt aim to blend their product with the best cultural traditions of the country in which every hotel is situated. The richness and variety of this global service experience is portrayed by their corporate logo design which features a stylized version of the word Hyatt with a crescent that represents a sunrise, crossing through the letter "A". The crescent, depicted in red, aims to symbolize the sunrise to sunset experience of the Hyatt guest.

Given Hyatt's market positioning, it is of fundamental importance that the organizational network is responsive to customer requirements. The aim is to develop and maintain a service culture which closely mirrors certain Hyatt standards and customer expectations but at the same time draws on aspects of local culture so that the service is as natural and authentic as possible. In this way it is possible to promote localization and preserve the charm of individual customs and traditions. These should be reflected in every Hyatt hotel so that the guest is aware of the unique features of the host country. To achieve this Hyatt deliberately seeks to avoid replicating design and service concepts in a standardized way by ensuring that all services and amenities assume national characteristics. In Japan for example, Japanese slippers are provided for the guest to use in their bedroom and there are variations in the layout of the bathroom to reflect a Japanese style. This helps to ensure that guests find interesting variations in food, décor, layout and many other features and that Hyatt is recognized in every other country in which it operates as a company that uses a familiar cultural framework as the basis for planning and providing a high quality product.

Hyatt's ability to sustain this approach to customization is helped by the multinational composition of the corporate management team. Senior staff at the corporate office in Chicago represent eight different nationalities from Europe, Asia Pacific and the Americas. A similar degree of diversity can be found throughout the organization, both in specialist support functions as well as within the individual hotel operations. Hyatt managers are constantly exposed to a variety of cultural perspectives in discussions spanning a wide range of issues. Consequently new policies and procedures are tested against multinational views to identify the possible implications arising from implementation in different places. As the corporate staff number around 40 people, which in comparison with other multinational hotels firms is a relatively small team, it is possible to devise policy which is flexible enough to fit with different cultures. This means that hotel staff around the world can relate more easily to the instructions which are given. Each Hyatt hotel is then required to interpret the policy framework in an appropriate style which is sympathetic to customs, traditions and values. The general managers understand the key quality points and if any of them are not consistently achieved, the situation is soon revealed. Information is transferred quickly because the decentralized approach prevents management organization and reporting structures from becoming too bureaucratic. This has enabled Hyatt to develop a responsive organization that reacts quickly to customer and employee needs and priorities. In this sense, Hyatt policies and procedures encourage individualism and flair in planning, implementing and controlling guest services and they believe that by investing in managers who are encouraged to interpret quality standards in a cultural context that they are also helping to sustain a distinctive type of service culture in Hyatt hotels around the world. In so doing, Hyatt epitomize a third design consideration, which is that organizational flexibility and responsiveness to guest needs is essential to service development, especially in meeting guest expectations of "localization" at the destination hotel.

Summary. Service branding initiatives have already uncovered a degree of tolerance among international travellers to subtle forms of customization based on cultural and or country characteristics. This would suggest that there are numerous possibilities for extending, refining and formulating new service brand variations by concentrating on the origin of the guest to develop services which meet culturally different needs. Increased service flexibility will almost certainly require improved team work, which in part at least, could be accomplished by encouraging all employees to fully participate in the process of analysing and improving the hotel environment and the guest experience. In turn, greater participation will require a deliberate shift in emphasis on the part of hotel firms from the centre to the regions so that the organization as a whole can respond more quickly to regional changes and maintain employee commitment to quality improvement. In these and other ways, hotel firms are re-focusing and revitalizing their organizational culture so that service comes first.

Assuring total quality services

The effective management of service quality in an organizational context is a multidisciplinary paradigm. It is anchored in the relationship between the customer and the service provider and as such constitutes a dynamic service process (Olsen *et al.*, 1995). Managing the process to try to provide quality service requires a thorough understanding of concepts in organizational behaviour, human resources, operations, marketing and information management among others. The literature reflects this and provides evidence in the main of discipline-bounded views of service rather than indisciplinary action lines for embedding an ethos of providing quality services internally as well as externally.

This section introduces the concept of customer perceived quality as judged by the relative match between what customers expect and what they experience. If a mismatch occurs between the two, the difference can be described as a "quality gap". The difficulty this raises as a basis for marketing action is as follows:

- Expectations need to be fully researched and understood as they help the customer to predict what should happen rather than what will happen.

- Quality is a multi-perspective variable as it is a function of both customer perceptions and the organization's resources and activities. For this reason, it is difficult to achieve and maintain alignment of thinking among all the stakeholder groupings (customers and people with different roles throughout the organization).

Although service quality issues are generally held to fall within the domain of operations management, quality gaps are equally important to marketing managers. Quality gaps, which are potential breakpoints in the relationship linkages, have been categorized as follows (Parasuraman *et al.*, 1985):

- Type 1 – occurs when managers do not know what customers expect;
- Type 2 – occurs when managers fail to take corrective action so as to ensure that customer expectations are met;
- Type 3 – represents variability in the delivery of what customers expect;
- Type 4 – occurs when external communications about the offering increase customer expectations and in consequence, decrease perceived quality.

The four types of quality gap can combine to produce a fifth type – a gap between quality expected and perceptions of quality received and this is presented as a five-dimension set (Parasuraman *et al.*, 1988):

- *Reliability* – ability to perform the promised service dependably, accurately and consistently. This means doing it right, over a period of time.
- *Responsiveness* – prompt service and willingness to help customers, involving speed and flexibility.
- *Assurance* – knowledge and courtesy of staff and their ability to inspire trust and confidence.
- *Empathy* – caring, individualized attention to customers.
- *Tangibles* – physical facilities, equipment, staff appearance – the physical evidence of the service which conveys functional and symbolic meaning.

As noted earlier, the real difficulty in managing quality arises from the traditional division of specialist functions in organizations. If relationship marketing is taken seriously, how can customer-supplier relationships be sustained and improved unless everyone takes personal responsibility for quality improvement? This is especially the case in service industries, where production, delivery and consumption can occur at the same time. To make the connections between customer perceived quality, activities, departments and functions at all levels, an organization-wide quality management system is needed.

Measuring service quality performance
Managing service quality essentially involves:

(1) defining how service quality performance can be quantified and measured; and

(2) identifying how the responses of customers to the level of performance will be monitored.

The main challenge is to find a way of measuring perceived performance, as it is the customers' perceptions of performance that counts rather than the reality of performance. Additionally, it is helpful to benchmark performance so as to obtain a relative measure against "best practice" systems, procedures or competitors in the marketplace.

Ideally, service quality benchmarking should measure performance against:

(1) competitors (to seek out opportunities for achieving competitive advantage) and

(2) non-competitors (to identify opportunities for adopting "leading-edge" strategies from outside the market or industry in which the organization is competing).

Christopher *et al.* (1991) set out a practical approach to service benchmarking, accomplished by adopting a five-stage process:

- *Step 1: Define the competitive arena.*
  To be seen as an excellent organization, it is important to recognize that the real assessment takes place in the customer's mind. With whom is the organization compared by customers and with whom does it want to be compared? Use focus groups or individual "depth" interviews to obtain customer perspectives on the competitive arena. Ask customers to begin by talking in general terms about service quality and then ask them to nominate good and bad examples of service from their recent experience.

- *Step 2: Determine customer-based definitions of service.*
  Which aspects of service are rated most highly by the customer? The answers can be obtained by linking customer research efforts for steps 1 and 2. It is important to understand the factors that influence purchase behaviour and in the context of customer service, which particular elements are seen by the customer to be the most important. If for example, a supplier places emphasis on stock availability, but the customer regards delivery reliability more highly, it may not be allocating its resources in an appropriate way.

- *Step 3: Establish the relative importance of those service components to customers.*
  Suppliers often fail to explore the differences in the service preferences of different customer types and the opportunity it provides for developing specific, service or "benefit" segments. To discover the importance that customers attach to each element of customer service, the data generated by step 1 can be used. Ask a representative sample of customers to rank order the elements from the "most important" to the "least important". A rating scale can also be used in conjunction with this exercise and to ensure that the elements are separated, ask respondents to allocate a total of 100 points (according to perceived importance) among all the listed elements. Alternatively, respondents might be asked to complete a

more realistic "trade-off" exercise. This works by presenting the respondent with feasible combinations of customer service elements and asking for a rank order of preference for the combinations.

- *Step 4: Benchmark performance against key competitors.*
  Now that the key elements (and combinations) of customer service and their relative importance are known, the next question is how do customers rate the organization on these elements and combinations compared with competitors? Steps 1-3 draw on relatively small samples and to identify comparative service performance, a larger scale response is needed. This can be achieved by devising a postal questionnaire and selecting a sample which reflects a particular customer type. The main purpose is to present the elements of service (drawn from step 1) and to ask respondents to rate the perceived performance of the organization and its competitors on each element.

- *Step 5: Develop a service profile and service performance matrix.*
  Using data from the survey (step 4) it is possible to contrast the findings. The key questions are:

  (1) what are the important dimensions of service?; and

  (2) how well is the organization performing in relation to the key dimensions?

One way of displaying the data is to construct a service performance matrix. One axis portrays the importance rating and the second shows the actual perceived performance rating. The two ratings normally use a scale of 1 to 5.

The concept and application of total quality service
During the early 1990s, total quality management (TQM) became the most widely publicized philosophy of quality management. "Total" emphasizes that everyone is involved and that its influence extends across all areas of organizational life. Key principles include:

- Conforming to specifications – or working to agreed standards and procedures, but the inherent problem here is that it promotes a rather rigid approach that equates with "static" quality.

- Do it right – or "fitness for use" emphasizes that quality is about finding solutions through continuous improvement ("dynamic" quality). This is helpful, but will all improvements bring benefits to customers and how should this focus be maintained?

- Do the right thing – means listening and responding to customers in an appropriate way. This requires flexibility and responsiveness and implies that employees are empowered to initiate customized solutions and responses to customer queries.

- Delight the customer – a goal for customer-focused organizations is to consistently exceed the expectations of its customers by giving better service and support.

Quality management provides an infrastructure for maintaining standards and making improvements but to make it work, an array of techniques is needed. Some of these are especially well suited to the work of the marketing function and include:

- customer value chain analysis;
- cross-functional work flow charts;
- internal customer-supplier audits; and
- supplier partnership audits.

To align the change process with market forces and to foster a "dynamic" quality, a continuous improvement approach is needed.

Scott's Hotels, now part of the Whitbread Hotel Group, was until Autumn 1995 a wholly owned subsidiary of Scott's Hospitality Incorporated. It runs hotels in the UK under the Marriott brand name. Its implementation of TQM is underpinned by evolving structures and processes which, above all, emphasize quality improvement through teamworking at every level in the organization (Hubrecht and Teare, 1993; Simmons and Teare, 1993; Teare, 1993a; 1994d).

Its earliest TQM initiatives were in 1989 and the aim was to capture the energy and enthusiasm of employees throughout the company via a quality circles programme. Employees rapidly saw the benefits of a shift towards collective responsibility for day-to-day problem solving. To support quality circle team development and enable members to use problem-solving techniques, a training programme was implemented. This also included sessions on communication skills, relationship building and team dynamics. In 1991, the company launched its own internal video communications and training package. Shortly after this, Scott's began to collaborate on quality management training initiatives with Marriott in the USA, using the catch-phrase "Whatever it Takes" to describe its continuous improvement programme. Some years on, the principal driving force for continuous improvement comes from the company's hotel unit team structures. Quality circles which mainly comprise staff who work together and meet regularly on a long-term basis, provide a sense of continuity, stability and direction. As a counterbalance, specialist and cross-departmental groups (task force, process improvement teams and working parties) are used to take on specific improvement projects. The potential for rapid and effective improvement, engineered by project groups with a problem-solving remit, means that they provide a natural focal point for ongoing TQM training and personal development.

To monitor the effectiveness of its action teams, the majority of Scott's hotels use a cost of non-quality (CNQ) account, against which the cost of corrective action taken to resolve guest complaints is charged. In fact, employee empowerment requires this form of support as staff are encouraged to use their initiative and skill in deciding on the best way to resolve complaints the moment they arise. These and other initiatives mean that Scott's actively sell "service" in its advertising, knowing that it has a supportive infrastructure and a service culture that is dynamic and responsive to customers and to market forces. Scott's feedback from staff and customers confirms that its efforts to achieve a cultural shift had succeeded. It become an organization that encouraged its people to ask questions, to promote change and to challenge outdated thinking and ineffective methods.

This was achieved through staff by:

- Employees providing a service that exceeds customer expectations
- Employee involvement and decision making at all levels in the organizations
- Improved retention rates for employees (linked to more effective communication and feedback, training and empowerment).

Key measures were:

- Quarterly improvement on a rolling annual basis of controllable employee turnover (monitored quarterly, internal)
- Achievement of employee attitude survey target ratings (monitored annually, external)
- Success of quality initiatives (quality circles, improvement and action teams) following external guidelines for effective quality management.

It was also achieved through customers by:

- Retention of customers (tracking/feedback and responding to guest issues)
- Increasing overall market share.

Key measures were:

- Attainment of service audit target scores (monitored annually, external)
- Attainment of customer response ratings (from a given percentage minimum of customer base) (monthly, internal)
- Achievement of market share and penetration targets (monitored monthly, internal)
- Attainment of performance targets in the marketplace (monitored by market audit comparisons, annually, external)
- Long-term retention of key accounts (monitored quarterly, internal).

Summary

This article has sought to review the implications of consumer decision making for hospitality services, especially in relation to the delivery and total quality assurance of customer service. This gives rise to a number of questions for workplace learning initiatives relating to customers:

Understanding customers

(1) Which services might be standardized and which should be customized (or personalized)? What are the design and delivery implications of these approaches for hospitality services?

(2) In what circumstances are consumers likely to attribute more credibility to internal information than external information sources (and vice versa)?

(3) How do prior experience and familiarity with the product category affect the consumer's "preference structure" and the formation of expectations, assessment criteria and reference point experiences (key performance indicators)?

(4) To what extent does role specialization in family purchase situations influence choice? What are the implications for the marketing of hospitality services?

(5) When are customers likely to use a "decision rule"? How does this approach help to confirm the appropriateness of the decision?

(6) How does the "personal rating system" operate and vary between different consumer groups and across different hospitality/tourism settings?

(7) In what circumstances might consumers be willing to "compensate" for a feeling of dissatisfaction with hospitality/tourism services? How might a feeling of dissatisfaction affect the approach to a re-buy situation?

(8) What practical steps might the organization take to minimize the potential impact of dissonance?

(9) How might the experiences of consumers and employees be used to monitor and improve customer satisfaction levels?

Designing and delivering services

(10) How should the organization integrate or at least co-ordinate its customer service, quality assurance and marketing effort throughout the "value chain"?

(11) How might the organization re-focus its internal service culture so that it is customer-led? What practical steps does this involve and how should they be reinforced?

(12) To what extent could the organization benefit from service branding?

(13) How might the organization interrelate its efforts to maintain customer loyalty and product consistency?

(14) How might the organization "localize" its operations so as to adapt and respond to culturally and geographically different customer needs and expectations?

Assuring total quality services

(15) How might customer perceived quality measures be used to identify and rectify "quality gaps" in the organization?

(16) What practical steps does the organization need to take in order to design and implement its own programme for service quality benchmarking? To what extent might this activity drive organizational learning both internally and in partnership with other service providers?

(17) How might the organization ensure that its quality and performance improvement efforts are customer-focused?

References

Arndt, J. (1976), "Reflections on research in consumer behavior", in Advances in Consumer Research, Vol. 3, *Association for Consumer Research*, Ann Arbor, MI, pp. 213-21.

Belk, R.W. (1975), "Situational variables and consumer behavior", *Journal of Consumer Research*, Vol. 2, December, pp. 157-64.

Bloch, P.H. (1981), "Involvement beyond the purchase process: conceptual issues and empirical investigation", in Mitchell, A. (Ed.), *Advances in Consumer Research*, Vol. 9, Association for Consumer Research, Ann Arbor, MI, pp. 413-17.

Bould, A., Breeze, G. and Teare, R. (1992a), "Culture, customization and innovation: a Hilton International service brand for the Japanese market", in Teare, R. and Olsen, M.D. (Eds), *International Hospitality Management: Corporate Strategy in Practice*, Pitman, London and John Wiley, New York, NY, pp. 221-7.

Bould, A., Breeze, G. and Teare, R. (1992b), "Promoting service excellence through service branding", *International Journal of Contemporary Hospitality Management*, Vol. 4 No. 1, pp. iii-vi.

Chisnall, P.M. (1994), *Consumer Behaviour*, 3rd ed., McGraw-Hill, Maidenhead, pp. 59-78.

Chorengel, B. and Teare, R. (1991), "Hyatt style and personality: an investment in quality", *International Journal of Contemporary Hospitality Management*, Vol. 3 No. 1, pp. i-ii.

Christopher, M., Payne, A. and Ballantyne, D. (1991), *Relationship Marketing*, Butterworth-Heinemann, Oxford.

Ferrone, L., Teare, R. and Jones, P.A. (1995), "Social roles and the chef: a total quality perspective", in Teare, R. and Armistead, C. (Eds), *Services Management: New Directions and Perspectives*, Cassell, London and New York, NY, pp. 100-3.

Foxall, G.R. (1986), "Consumer theory: some contributions of a behavioural analysis of choice", *Management Bibliographies & Reviews*, Vol. 12 No. 2, pp. 27-51.

Hubrecht, J. and Teare, R. (1993), "A strategy for partnership in total quality service", *International Journal of Contemporary Hospitality Management*, Vol. 5 No. 3, pp. i-v.

Jacoby, J. (1978), "Consumer research: a state-of-the-art review", *Journal of Marketing*, Vol. 2, January, pp. 87-96.

Karmarck, A.M. (1983), *Economics and the Real World*, Basil Blackwell, Oxford.

Kassarjian, H.H. and Sheffet, M.J. (1981), "Personality and consumer behavior: an update", in Kassarjian, H.H. and Robertson, T.S. (Eds), *Perspectives in Consumer Behavior*, Scott Foreseman, Glenview, IL.

Kelly, G.A. (1963), *A Theory of Personality: The Psychology of Personal Constructs*, Norton, New York, NY.

Newman, J.W. (1977), "Consumer external search: amount and determinants", in Woodside A.G., Sheth J.N., Olshavsky, R.W. and Granbois, D.H. (1979), "Consumer decision making – fact or fiction?", *Journal of Consumer Research*, Vol. 6, September, pp. 93-100.

Nibbelink, A. and Teare, R. (1991), "Hotel services for the international business traveller", *International Journal of Contemporary Hospitality Management*, Vol. 3 No. 2, pp. iv-vi.

Olsen, M.D., Teare, R. and Gummesson, E. (1995), "Exploring the service quality paradigm: an overview", in Olsen, M.D., Teare, R. and Gummesson, E. (Eds), *Service Quality in Hospitality Organizations*, Cassell, London and New York, NY, pp. 1-5.

Olshavsky, R.W. and Granbois, D.H. (1979), "Consumer decision making – fact or fiction?", *Journal of Consumer Research,* Vol. 6, September, pp. 93-100.

Parasuraman A., Berry, L.L. and Zeithaml, V.A. (1991), "Understanding customer expectations of service", *Sloan Management Review,* Vol. 39, pp. 39-48.

Parasuraman, A., Zeithaml, V.A. and Berry, L.L. (1985), "A conceptual model of service quality and its implications for future research", *Journal of Marketing,* Vol. 49, Fall.

Parasuraman, A., Zeithaml, V. A. and Berry, L.L. (1988), "SERVQUAL: a multiple scale item for measuring consumer perceptions of service quality", *Journal of Retailing,* Vol. 64 No. 1, Spring, pp. 12-40.

Parker, A.C. and Teare, R. (1991), "A brand extension strategy for European expansion", *International Journal of Contemporary Hospitality Management,* Vol. 3 No. 2, pp. i-ii.

Pizam, A., Neumann, Y. and Reichel, A. (1978), "Dimensions of tourist satisfaction with a destination area", *Annals of Tourism Research,* July/September, pp. 314-22.

Scheuing, E. (1995), "Delighting the customer", in Olsen, M.D., Teare, R. and Gummesson, E. (Eds), *Service Quality in Hospitality Organizations,* Cassell, London and New York, NY, pp. 41-2.

Simmons, P. and Teare, R. (1993), "Evolving a total quality culture", *International Journal of Contemporary Hospitality Management,* Vol. 5 No. 3, pp. v-viii.

Teare, R. (1988), "Generating consumer theory for the hospitality industry: an integrated approach to the treatment of practical and theoretical issues", in Johnston, R. (Ed.), *The Management of Service Operations,* IFS Publications Ltd, Bedford, pp. 269-79.

Teare, R. (1990), "An exploration of the consumer decision process for hospitality services", in Teare, R. *et al.* (Eds), *Managing and Marketing Services in the 1990s,* Cassell, London, pp. 233-48.

Teare, R. (1991), "Consumer strategies for assessing and evaluating hotels", in Teare, R. and Boer, A. (Eds), *Strategic Hospitality Management: Theory and Practice for the 1990s,* Cassell, London, pp. 120-43.

Teare, R. (1993a), "Quality is…never having to say that the laundry is shut!", *Strategic Insights into Quality,* Vol. 1 No. 3, pp. 4-6.

Teare, R. (1993b), "Designing a contemporary hotel service culture", *International Journal of Service Industry Management, Special Issue: Advances in Research on Service Quality,* Vol. 4 No. 2, pp. 63-73.

Teare, R. (1994a), "An overview of consumer and producer perspectives on hospitality services", in Teare, R., Mazanec, J., Crawford-Welch, S. and Calver, S. (Eds), *Marketing in Hospitality and Tourism: A Consumer Focus,* Cassell, London and New York, NY, pp. 5-13.

Teare, R. (1994b), "The consumer decision process: a paradigm in transition", in Teare, R., Mazanec, J., Crawford-Welch, S. and Calver, S. (Eds), *Marketing in Hospitality and Tourism: A Consumer Focus,* Cassell, London and New York, NY, pp. 14-36.

Teare, R. (1994c), "Generating consumer theory", in Teare, R., Mazanec, J., Crawford-Welch, S. and Calver, S. (Eds), *Marketing in Hospitality and Tourism: A Consumer Focus,* Cassell, London and New York, NY, pp. 37-70.

Teare, R. (1994d), "Closing the gap between consumer and services", in Teare, R., Mazanec, J., Crawford-Welch, S. and Calver, S. (Eds), *Marketing in Hospitality and Tourism: A Consumer Focus,* Cassell, London and New York, NY, pp. 71-96.

Teare, R. and Gummesson, E. (1991), "Integrated marketing organisation for hospitality firms", in Teare, R. and Boer, A (Eds), *Strategic Hospitality Management: Theory and Practice for the 1990s,* Cassell, London, pp. 144-57.

Teare, R. and Senior, M. (1992), "Guest services", in Olsen, M. *et al.* (Eds), *Encyclopedia of Hospitality and Tourism,* Van Nostrand Reinhold, New York, NY, pp. 487-94.

Teare, R. and Williams, A. (1989), "Destination marketing", *Tourism Management,* Vol. 10 No. 2, June, pp. 95-6.

Teare, R., Davies, M. and McGeary, B. (1989), "The operational challenge of hotel short breaks", *Journal of Contemporary Hospitality Management,* Vol. 1 No. 1, pp. 22-4.

Chapter 11

Developing a curriculum for organizational learning

Richard Teare

Granada Professor, Oxford Brookes University and Academic Chair,
International Management Centres

Introduction

This article sets out a prospectus for facilitating learning, development and research by means of an organizationally integrated framework of action learning, supported by internet-based resources and tutored sessions in the workplace. The themed approach, developed in response to corporate needs and aspirations, provides a uniquely crafted learning framework which is derived from a generic curriculum and augmented to address industry and corporate specialisms and themes. The theming is derived from: an internet Forum; an experiential knowledge base (distributed by Internet and intranet); the assessment approach and the concept of a long-term learning partnership between a corporate client and International Management Centres (IMC). The article is underpinned by the work of Gordon Wills and especially his book *Your Enterprise School of Management* which contends that managers "learn best at work":

> My proposition is that each and every enterprise must institutionalize its workplace learning systems and opportunities in such a way that it radiates what it has already achieved, and from such a well-understood platform moves on to realize its full potential. There can be no self-doubts. The enterprise itself is the key. There is no other cost-effective way to motivate managers to learn, or to provide the opportunities to learn, that are the inescapable requirements for today's and tomorrow's successful enterprise (Wills, 1993, p. 9).

International Management Centres (IMC) in conjunction with Universities in Australia and the UK (for example, the alliance between the University of Surrey and IMC is known as Surrey IMC) provide an integrated resource dedicated to supporting the aspirations of industry, commerce, the professions and adult learners in the wider field of continuing education. The learning resource encompasses action learning, applied and basic research and learner support provided by MCB University Press, Anbar Electronic Intelligence and the British Library. IMC is dedicated to supporting life-long learning and corporate aspirations to become a "learning organization". To support these goals, IMC aims to establish long-term learning partnerships with organizations and to work with them in building and maintaining in-company learning networks.

This article first appeared in *The Journal of Workplace Learning*, Vol. 10 No. 2, 1998, pp. 95-121.

The article considers the concept and vision of a learning organization and reviews the role of teamworking in enacting change and sustaining innovation. The value and potential of workplace action learning is assessed in relation to the hospitality industry and the Hospitality and Tourism Global Forum on the Internet provides a means of distributing interactive learning resources worldwide. The concept of industry and corporate theming is also illustrated in this section with reference to the Airport Business Forum and BAA Plc, the airport owner and operator. Industry applications in the form of project-based assignments and assessment and a broader interface for learning, development and research are used to explain and illustrate the dynamics of partnerships between IMC and its clients.

A vision of the learning organization

An organization's rate of learning must be equal to or greater than the rate of change in its external environment" (or: L > = C) (Reg Revans)

A recent report from the Henley Centre commissioned by The Joint Hospitality Industry Congress (JHIC) reflects the scale of the change agenda and the challenges facing industry:

The challenge:
… to be flexible, convenient, good value, custom made, accessible, safe and in touch with the consumer…
… to be unified, professional, informed, innovative and inspired…
(*Vision for the Future*, JHIC Report, June 1996).

In responding to change, a growing number of organizations are seeking to embed a culture of continuous learning and development, characterized by:

Continuous improvement (teams, recognizing achievements)
Human resource development
(recognizing that learning is an investment not a cost)
Encouraging a commitment to learn
Prototyping radical ideas (thinking and acting differently)

The characteristics of learning organizations and some of the array of evidence that organizations "improve and learn by doing" provide a basis for interpreting the role of action learning in learning organization "partnerships" (see Figure 1).

Organizational sources of learning
Enablers

(1) *Policy and strategy:*

- Management have made a visible and clear commitment of their desire to consciously manage learning in the organization;
- this commitment is backed by policy and values statements;
- systems and processes reinforce the policy;

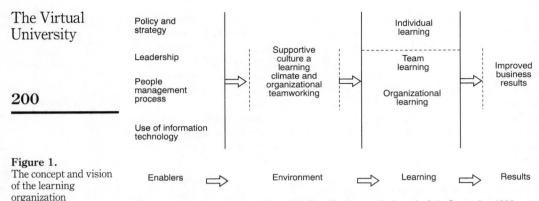

Figure 1.
The concept and vision
of the learning
organization

Source: Adapted from: Andrew Mayo, BAA Plc., "Conference for Learning", 24 September 1996

- it is consistently referred to in company communications;
- resources are dedicated to making the policy effective.

(2) *Leadership:* Leadership behaviours that support learning are defined and used in appraisal, selection and promotion – they might include:
- coaching/mentoring of others;
- defining and articulating a vision;
- courageous, risk taking, empowering;
- open-minded, experimenting, admitting mistakes;
- encouraging views/dissent;
- visibly a learner personally;
- collaborator/sharer, listener, seeker and giver of feedback;
- conscious/generous provider of learning opportunities.

(3) *People management processes:*
- Feedback on performance is rigorous and complete – not reliant on just one input;
- both monetary and non-monetary rewards encourage continual learning;
- internal selection takes account of learning needs – recognizes the special value of learning from experience;
- where possible, roles are described in ways which give people scope to grow and experiment.

(4) *Use of information technology:*
- People are connected electronically and can both communicate and work together;

- people have access to information easily and simply, both internal and relevant external;
- experience and knowledge gained from the past is captured and made available to all;
- people are able to use electronic interactive learning opportunities.

Environment

(1) *A supportive culture:*
- People talk about learning naturally (not just training) and build it into their daily way of working;
- people take personal responsibility for their learning and development and freely help others;
- knowledge is not regarded as power but freely shared;
- people are open-minded, free to question assumptions and to make mistakes without recrimination;
- time and money are committed and regarded as a priority.

Learning

(1) *Individual learning:*
- Individuals take responsibility for their own learning and development and can do so competently;
- they have personal learning plans, derived from an understanding of their own needs and those of the business;
- they understand their own learning style and how to both choose and utilize different learning options;
- they are skilled at both giving and receiving feedback;
- they know how to use others, and help others, in the learning process.

(2) *Team learning:*
- Teams and working groups utilize the capability of each member for the benefit of all;
- they frequently learn and unlearn together, in order to share a common approach;
- they support each other in individual learning objectives;
- the organization encourages cross-boundary groups, communities of common interest, and internal and external networks in order to maximize sharing of learning;
- teams help other teams and learn from each other.

(3) *Organizational learning:*
- The organization consciously adapts its strategies to the changing environment – planning processes are flexible and iterative;

- there are mechanisms for listening to all the stakeholders, for benchmarking against best practice, and for adapting objectives as a result;
- there is a systematic and disciplined approach to the flow of knowledge across the organization;
- mergers, acquisitions and alliances are seen as opportunities for learning as much as financial gain;
- structures are designed to consider learning and knowledge flow.

Results
Improved business results:
- Formal learning activities are derived from a business goal;
- costs due to ineffectiveness as a "learning organization" are identified and tracked;
- revenue losses are equally identified and tracked;
- "human intellectual asset value" increases steadily;
- improvements can be measured for each stakeholder.

Enacting change and sustaining innovation
This section draws from case study research conducted in 14 UK and US-based manufacturing and service firms, most with mature teamworking structures. The aim is to examine practitioner perspectives and current practices in teamworking and to assess the strategic contribution that work-based teams are making to quality improvement.

Processes or functions? The role of teamworking in workplace learning
In recent years a growing number of organizations have adopted a process paradigm and approach and among those that have, most are currently exploring ways of attaining higher levels of service and responsiveness. Here, emphasis is placed on processes (such as the activities of supporting customers or supporting those that do) that transcend traditional functional boundaries. In the early stages of change this may mean little more than the creation of a matrix structure wherever a readily identifiable service chain exists. Evidence suggests that process-based organizations can derive a number of benefits and especially where "process owners" "process champions" and "process teams" are encouraged (Garvin, 1995). A team concept is central to the development of process-based management and it is one of the few means by which large business processes can be integrated. Further, teamworking holds especial significance for the management structure as those who move to a process-based approach take a team-based approach as a paradigm for managing the business (Ingram *et al.*, 1997a; 1997b)

The aim here is to explore the contemporary role of teamworking in a selection of award-winning UK and US firms (Teare et. al., 1996a; 1997a; 1997b).

The examples draw on: single problem-solving team projects; self-directed team projects and organization-wide quality improvement based on a team philosophy and approach. The section concludes by drawing together some of the notable benefits derived from team-based initiatives in these different contexts.

Total teamworking
Twelve of the case study organizations were 1995 finalists in UK national competitions run by the National Society for Quality through Teamwork (NSQT), a registered charity dedicated to enabling member organizations in all sectors of British Industry to achieve their goals in continuous improvement, people involvement and customer service. Its "recipe" for total teamworking is based on the premiss that a climate of continuous change is needed to stimulate a never-ending programme of improvement and this is sustained by drawing on a mix of six "ingredients" (see Figure 2).

These are: management commitment (visible at all levels, but led from the "top"); education (ensuring that everyone knows the language and uses the improvement tools and techniques); measurement (visible in all workplaces and self-set goals, benchmarked against the best); recognition (appreciation of members' and teams' improvement achievements) and regeneration (ensuring that the programme continuously evolves).

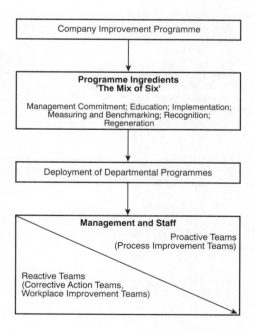

Figure 2.
Ingredients of change:
the NSQT's view

The NSQT/Michelin Excellence Awards introduced in 1990 and sponsored by the Michelin Tyre Company, are given each year to up to three teams who have demonstrated excellence in the way they have identified a problem, solved it and then implemented an effective solution. The six examples here, reflect two categories – single problem, management promoted projects (Table I) and continuous improvements made by self-directed teams (Table II).

Single problem/management promoted projects
The three illustrations typify the ways in which teams can provide a means of dealing with:

(1) a "crisis" situation (Albright & Wilson);

(2) design improvement (BSF Garringtons); and

(3) unwanted process outcomes (Severn Trent).

In each case, solutions were found and in so doing, team members reported other benefits (see Table I). These included: increased commitment and motivation; improved communications; a sense of learning from each other and of satisfaction derived from drawing upon a blend of team member skills and abilities. In essence, the "unexpected" benefits were personal and interpersonal as well as organizational (see Figure 3).

Team	Main features of the action taken	Principal outcomes
The Potassium Phosphates Improvement Team[1] (Albright & Wilson Plc)	Formation of a "process change cross functional team; use of work shift overlaps for team meetings; introduction of a process log book to record problems, comments and decisions and to identify project trial options"	Excellent teamwork (visible commitment to the project and each other); increased levels of motivation (driven by the desire to succeed and not by personal reward); free-flowing information, trust and a willingness to learn from each other
The Hub-Run-Out Team[2] (British Steel Forgings, Garringtons)	A supplier-based core team forming two multi-functional teams. Each used databased problem-solving techniques. One team used cause and effect charts to improve machining capability, the other worked with the customer on design and process modifications	The team achieved process improvement and a product design change which resulted in a permanent solution to a recurring problem. This is attributed to the use of a logical problem-solving approach and the effective blend of core team skills and qualities
The Goscote Team[3] Severn Trent Plc.	The team, with the support of a Quality Facilitator and laboratory analyses, studied data collected over a 24 month period. The team also used cause and effect analysis and "problem-solving discipline wall-charts" to identify action "delivery dates"	Solutions were mainly implemented on a day to day basis as improvements were trailed and left in place. Refinements arose from brainstorming, testing ideas against up-to-date information and by drawing on process experts who provided technical advice

Table I.
Single problem/
management promoted
projects

Team	Main features of the action taken	Principal outcomes
Quality Street[4] (Britannia Airways)	The team used a standard problem-solving model to identify the servicing problems associated with providing ashtrays to all passengers. Action included: brainstorming; information gathering/fact finding; and a "solutions effect" diagram to test ideas for reducing cabin servicing time and costs	The project led to the introduction of an innovative "blanking plate" solution to the misuse of ashtrays. By removing ashtrays (except in "smoking" sections reductions in cleaning time, the turnover of ashtrays and stock holding of ashtrays were achieved
New Star Trekkers[5] (Land Rover)	A range of assembly-related problems were identified using brainstorming and cause and effect diagrams. After this, the team used its analysis to construct a solutions effect diagram. Line trials were used to test several possible solutions and data from the trials were used to refine the specification for "scrap mats" used to prevent paint damage	By refining the means of preventing paint damage during vehicle assembly, the cost in time and materials needed to re-work on average 14 vehicles per week has been eliminated. This improvement has been achieved by switching from wooden boards to rubber mats. Further, a time and motion study has confirmed operational benefits from using the mats
Dyane Team[6] (The Varity Perkins Group)	The team used brainstorming, process mapping and action planning techniques to identify the scope of the problem. This prompted a review of the volume of paper work transactions needed to process the work. A long and variable turnaround time for reconditioned parts was also investigated and a radical solution adopted after a series of carefully planned project trials	An "in-house" total quality cycle provided the investigative and planning framework for identifying and testing a new process and, procedure. Prior to total quality (TQ) innovative solutions were rarely possible, as "solutions" were handed down rather than devolved to the people facing the problem to solve. The TQ infrastructure meant that all objectives – cost, lead-time, improvement and end user satisfaction were attainable

Table II.
Continuous
improvements/self-
directed team projects

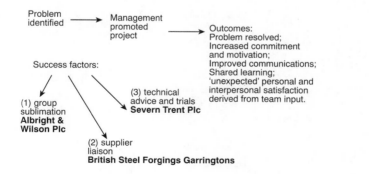

Figure 3.
Single team project
outcomes

Continuous improvement/self-directed team projects
In many respects, the lifeblood of continuous improvement emanates from self-directed teams seeking to identify problems and improvement opportunities and then apply solutions themselves. In the following cases, teams sought to make process improvements with multi-disciplinary inputs and, while this approach is well established in manufacturing, it is much less widespread in services (see Table II). The key point here is the potential to refine, innovate or re-invent processes so that they serve their purpose more effectively (see Figure 4).

The Britannia Airways example demonstrates inventive thinking in dealing with the problems associated with servicing and replacing passenger seat ashtrays. A relatively simple, cost-saving solution meant that the work of cleaning staff was also easier and cleaner to perform – a nice illustration of internal customer-centred improvement, greatly appreciated by cabin servicing staff. An example from Land Rover is indicative of the way its business has been literally transformed during the past few years by adopting a total teamwork approach. In this instance, a discussion group found a "perfect" solution to an imperfect provision for preventing scratching and paint damage during vehicle assembly. Here a simple solution was found and the cheapest possible way of implementing it accomplished by the assembly line team members themselves because they felt committed to getting things right.

The opportunity to "re-invent" the familiar yet ineffective is clearly shown in the Varity Perkins case. In this, a cross-functional team solved an array of problems (administrative, financial, technical, supplier and production-related) by setting-up a new process and procedure for procuring a vital piece of production line equipment (see also Teare *et al.*, 1997c). All three examples demonstrate an overriding commitment to make things better and to try the "unthinkable" if need be to achieve the desired result. At the unit or site level it is clear that single problem and self-directed team structures offer different yet interrelated vehicles for addressing problems and improvement opportunities. If they are to function effectively, an organizational framework for teamworking is needed and the basis for this is reflected in the NSQT/Perkins Award criteria.

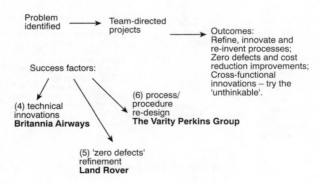

Figure 4.
Continuous
improvement/self-directed team project outcomes

Frameworks for organizational teamworking
The NSQT/Varity Perkins Quality Improvement Award, sponsored by Varity
Perkins was launched in 1987 (see Table III). The Award is presented to the
management team which best demonstrates its continuing commitment to a
programme of total people involvement, with quality and employee activities as
key elements. The judging criteria are designed to measure the management
team's progress during the immediate past year in relation to: the quality
journey; the deployment of quality improvement throughout the organization;
quality education and training; the systems of measurement applied;
achievements as recorded by the measurement system; management
commitment and the recognition process and future continuous improvement
plans. The featured organizations are:

Each organization uses a framework for organizational teamworking and in
this instance, sought to achieve specific improvement goals in the course of a
one year period. To illustrate the generic potential for organizationally-based
teamworking, the short profiles below relate the nature of the organization and
its main business to its teamworking focus and outcomes.

Co-operation and integration. The Benefit Enquiry Line[7] (BEL) Preston UK
is part of the Benefits Agency and it provides a national, free telephone advice
and information service for people with disabilities, their carers and
representatives. BEL's team structure of discussion groups and focus groups
are intentionally cross-grade and cross-team so as to encourage teamworking
and inter-departmental support. Each department operates an "open-door"

Company	Organizational vision, objectives and teamworking	Focus
Benefit Enquiry Line[7]	To foster an organizational culture that is enabling, empowering, co-operative and team-driven; and with "teams" that involve staff, customers and suppliers	Co-operation and integration
Britannia Topsides[8]	To create a learning organization to bring about cultural change and by this means achieve cost reduction goals	Learning and cost reduction
RHP Bearings Ltd[9]	To achieve business excellence by means of a team-based approach	Business performance improvement
Royal Insurance Life & Pensions[10]	To improve the company's competitive position by improving the teamworking culture, its business processes, customer satisfaction levels, retention rates and reputation and the ost effectiveness of its operations	Competitive positioning
Slag Reduction Company[11]	To improve workforce flexibility, human and physical resource utilization and improvements in working practices.	Improving resource utilization
Wellman International Ltd[12]	To involve every employee in meeting customer expectations, reducing process imperfections and quality costs and providing opportunities to improve work methods by real participation	Maximizing employee participation

Table III.
Varity Perkins quality
improvement award

policy and staff routinely work in other departments so that an atmosphere of co-operation and mutual understanding is sustained.

Learning and cost reduction. Britannia Topsides Project, London[8], part of the wider Britannia Field development project, creates facilities to produce gas and condensate from a UK North Sea field. Three companies, contractor AMEC and oil companies CONOCO and CHEVRON, form an "alliance" to jointly develop the offshore facilities. Topsides has established an effective cost control system, based on the principles of empowerment. A feature of this work is the data bank of more than 600 cost-saving ideas, all of which reflect open thinking and teamworking. A cost saving of around £10 million has been achieved since the inception of the "ideas" programme.

Business performance improvement. RHP Bearings Ltd, Ferrybridge[9] part of NSK, the world's second largest bearings manufacturer, employs 18,000 people worldwide. Ferrybridge is one of seven RHP manufacturing sites, with a workforce of 620 people. Team-based business performance improvement was achieved by undertaking a radical change programme. Its key features were:

(1) the introduction of a transparent structure to cascade the mission, plans, strategies and targets of the company throughout the factory and a concerted effort to encourage people involvement in deciding how targets could be met;

(2) the use of regular reviews to identify where things were going to plan and what corrective action was needed;

(3) the development of several key cross-departmental projects to address known problems;

(4) recognition that an open culture of mutual trust and support must be built gradually and that it must promote fairness and equality of status, irrespective of job role;

(5) the adoption and development of an annual quality process-based review incorporating objective and subjective, self-assessment measures.

Competitive positioning. Royal Insurance Life & Pensions, Liverpool[10] identified a need to incorporate new measures into its reporting system. A feature of the new measurement system is that it is "owned" by the continuous improvement group members, rather than by senior management. A key element is the balanced scorecard approach which consists of a range of measures designed to report on performance indicators relevant to the interests of customers, staff and shareholders. Employees see this as a wholly positive development, providing useful information which contributes to achieving quality targets.

Improving resource utilization. The Slag Reduction Company Limited, Redcar[11] is the industrial service division of Faber Prest plc on Teeside. Its quality improvement initiative achieved some specific breakthroughs including: the elimination of restrictive practices and the re-design of working methods to achieve improved efficiency levels and an improvement in employee utilization from 50 per cent to 88 per cent (verified by British Steel's work study and operational research department).

Maximizing employee participation. Wellman International Ltd, Kells[12], based in Ireland, is a premier supplier of polyester and polyamide fibres to customers in Europe and beyond. Its effort to maximize employee involvement has led to a more open style of management and a much greater emphasis on "softer" performance indicators like employee attitudes and morale, customer focus and the effectiveness of training, communications and teamworking activity. Evidence suggests that a greater sense of openness and freedom has fostered a much greater commitment to quality improvement among the workforce as a whole.

It is interesting to reflect on the universal potential of teamworking as a means of unlocking organizational capability, especially in the context of business process re-engineering which is generally viewed as a counter-teamworking step. While their journeys have necessarily been quite different, Corning Incorporated and the GTE Corporation both have corporate quality offices that are deliberately kept small to emphasize their facilitating role. Responsibility for quality performance rests with the operating units which all receive quality education in a cascading approach, starting with senior management. Further, both companies are global players with presences on several continents, making quality their basic business principle, regardless of where they operate. They do so because they define quality as meeting customer requirements. It is from this perspective of being customer-driven and customer-focused that they keep on re-inventing their organizations to remain customer-responsive and enhance competitive advantage (see Table IV).

Process re-engineering. A *Fortune 500* company, Corning[13] concentrates on the three key global markets that account for 60 per cent of its revenues: optical communications, life sciences and the environment. To achieve its re-engineering goals, Corning's President "championed" the initiative after which key processes were re-structured (rather than eliminating jobs) and the firm's employees were invited to participate. To achieve this, a strict timetable for each phase was needed – priority setting and team launch; opportunity detailing (focused on innovation effectiveness, the roles of the corporate and line organizations, manufacturing effectiveness, purchasing and inventory effectiveness and information technology) and action planning during which 17 teams totalling around 100 employees worked full-time to re-design processes and reduce complexities.

Decentralized planning. GTE[14] is the largest single provider of local telephone services in the United States and it sought to align itself more closely with its customers and re-engineer its business processes in order to keep pace with the rate of change. An over-arching consideration was its quality programme and GTE successfully encouraged its operating units to focus on business processes (via customer satisfaction) as a means of improving quality but without insisting on a standard approach. In essence, it encouraged teamworking and provided incentives to adopt quality processes that would deliver customer satisfaction but it gave each business unit the freedom to craft its own quality programme. This decentralized approach has enabled GTE to transform its organization and deliver its products and services much more efficiently and cost effectively.

Learning from teams
Figure 5 summarizes the array of evidence drawn from the 14 case illustrations relating to the role of teamworking in tackling single problem and team-directed projects; the development and refining of "tools and techniques" for total quality and its contribution to organizational change and development.

Workplace action learning and the curriculum
The "new vision" theme of partnership in workplace learning offers a timely opportunity to review the evolving nature of hospitality operations management and to discuss some of the likely challenges ahead. In the field of training, development and learning these include: assessing human resource needs and priorities (Linney and Teare, 1991; Teare and Brotherton, 1990) the implications for training and management development (Close and Teare, 1990) and the role of open and problem-based learning (Teare and Akehurst, 1988a;

Company	Recent organizational teamworking imperatives	Focus
Corning Incorporated[13]	"Corning competes" involved a re-engineering exercise to reduce costs and improve shareholder value	Process re-engineering
GTE Corporation[14]	Re-engineering to achieve excellence in process focus, quality/customer satisfaction levels and cost reduction	Decentralized planning

Table IV.
Teamworking organizational frameworks in North America: Corning and GTE

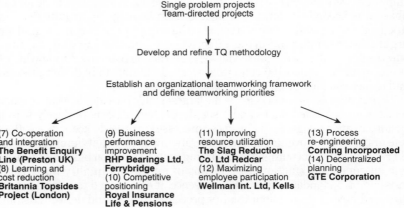

Figure 5.
Organizational teamworking frameworks and focused outcomes

1988b) among other non-standard forms of learning support. To assess the scope for workplace learning, it seems appropriate to speculate on the outcomes of gradual change brought about by technological advancement and other forms of innovation (Teare *et al.*, 1996b) as well as the pervasive influence of more dramatic, often uncontrollable forces like economic recession. The aim here is to review the way in which structural changes in the industry are influencing the nature and scope of managerial work at unit level (Teare, 1990). This in turn, has implications for the way in which the curriculum model is conceptualized and hospitality operations management teaching and learning is supported so that it aligns with the new realities of industry (Johns and Teare, 1995, Teare and Owen, 1996) and the needs of aspiring graduate managers (Teare *et al.*, 1996c).

Structural change and the implications for operations management
During the 1980s the European hospitality industry gradually began to shift away from its highly fragmented state as firms became bigger, better organized and more efficient. The main goal was to out-perform competitors, mainly by achieving higher profitability through geographical expansion and increased distribution. In their analysis of the macro-economic trends affecting the main European hotel markets in 1990, Litteljohn and Slattery (1991) conclude that competition will continue to be driven by the nature of demand, the opportunities for further expansion, and the threat to profitability posed by prevailing levels of industry competition. During the same year, Olsen (1991) profiled the events that were starting to shape industry structure, with the help of a dozen or so European hospitality industry executives representing hotel and restaurant firms, suppliers and industry associations. He begins by tracing the origins of the industry investment boom to the involvement of the capital-market community during the early 1970s. The prospects of sustained growth and above average levels of return on investment, coupled with the emergence of bigger firms who knew how to harness the benefits of buying power and advanced technology, fuelled the expansion which took place. In recent times, firms geared for expansion were forced to consolidate their market positions in response to recession in Europe. A potent cocktail of volatile and unpredictable events forced many European hospitality firms to "de-layer" or "downsize" their corporate organizations so as to address demand instability, high interest rates and other events. Consequently, most of the bigger hospitality firms are now "flatter and leaner" than at any point in their recent histories.

Olsen concludes his analysis by reflecting on the nature of the challenge facing firms who are trying to come to terms with internal re-structuring and with fewer senior managers working in specialist roles:

> It is clear from discussions with European hospitality executives that the most significant issue facing hospitality firms during this decade (the 1990s) will be how to accomplish the change in thinking necessary to develop operations-oriented unit-level managers into strategic thinking managers. While the increasing competitiveness of the industry in Europe is well recognised and the downsizing of corporate headquarters is nearly accomplished, in

most firms the managers in the field are not yet ready to accept the decentralisation challenge. What are required are unique and innovative ways to try to educate, and in many cases socialise, these managers about the need for and value of thinking strategically (p. 24).

In an empirical study of food and beverage management career paths in American luxury hotels, Nebel *et al.* (1994) confirm that corporate downsizing is still continuing.

It appears to be targeted in a similar way to European efforts to reduce middle levels of management and the numbers of staff specialists who are not directly responsible for operational activities. They conclude that in the current circumstances, a balanced educational curriculum of professional and technical skills is needed to prepare graduates for operations career paths. Further, that business and management subjects should be shaped to equip people for careers in hospitality operations so that they can "add value" by adopting a broader strategic view of operations management. In summing-up, they conclude that unit managers will be selected much more carefully in the future as they will be expected to adopt a wider managerial role.

It would seem that re-structuring has, and will continue to affect the nature of managerial work at unit level. The traditional view of operations managers as food and beverage or accommodation specialists with a comparatively narrow scope of responsibility is changing as they assume responsibility for managing other aspects of the business. It is reasonable therefore, to assume that graduate managers need a broader, strategic vision of operations management based on an updated view of the hospitality operations curriculum (Eccles and Teare, 1995; 1996). To achieve this, closer integration of technical and professional development is needed so that graduates can readily apply the principles of marketing, managing people and other specialist subject areas to the operations environment. The more limited opportunities for career enhancement in the immediate future will almost certainly depend on the extent to which young managers can demonstrate their ability to manage teams effectively, improve standards, control costs and meet profit targets.

If unit managers are having to work differently now and in the future, they must also learn to think differently and to facilitate this, the scope of hospitality operations management needs some re-definition. First, it is necessary to consider in more detail some of the key activities that unit managers are engaged in so that a conceptual view of the hospitality operations curriculum can be established. After this, it is possible to consider some of the implications for supporting appropriate teaching and learning activities.

Hospitality operations and managerial effectiveness
The content of hospitality management courses is the subject of much debate and it is interesting to observe that established ideas about managerial work are now being challenged by educators as well as by industrialists. The industry view reflects a pattern of continuous change requiring a more business-oriented hospitality manager who can deploy financial skills to analyse the business and "think outwards rather than inwards" about customer needs. Further, the

traditional autocratic style of doing business is steadily giving way to modern team-building and facilitation, partly so that "total quality" aspirations can be realised through greater people involvement which harnesses more of the talents, creativity and energy within the organization as a whole. The tasks that hospitality managers need to be able to perform effectively can be depicted in relation to four broad curriculum themes as shown in Figure 6.

Workplace learning and the curriculum:

(1) *Managing operations:*
- day to day operations;
- specialist technical areas;
- managing a crisis.

(2) *Managing people:*
- managing individuals;
- managing teams;
- managing external contacts;
- managing personnel administration.

(3) *Personal skills:*
- making presentations/training;
- interpersonal skills;
- using computers in management;
- self-development.

(4) *Managing the business:*
- managing business performance;
- managing projects;
- managing strategic decisions;
- managing legal complexity.

In order to facilitate managerial effectiveness, an appropriate blend of educational inputs (technical, professional, personal development) is needed so

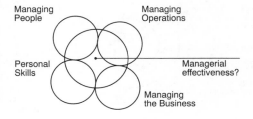

Figure 6.
Workplace learning and the curriculum

that hospitality managers are equipped with the basic tools needed to perform well in the workplace. Further, the educational goal should be seen as nurturing individuals who have "a sense of commitment, vision and the ability not only to do things right but also with the wider understanding of doing the right thing". A closer partnership with industry seems to be the logical way of achieving a better fit between the student experience of the curriculum and the realities of operations management. It does, however, prompt a question as to how this can this be achieved without stifling an exploration of the more theoretical, often abstract ideas which can in themselves be so enriching. A conceptual model of curriculum development which links managerial effectiveness to prevailing industry conditions offers a relatively flexible way of keeping in touch. The logical focal point is the creation and continual enhancement of a realistic work environment so that managers can begin to build a holistic understanding of the intellectual challenge of managing operations effectively. Further, that all other subject areas can be linked to and shaped by the operational focus. These relationships are depicted by using an outer wheel to portray the wider economic environment and inner segments representing all the activities which directly influence operational effectiveness (see Figure 7). These are:

- business performance, monitoring and control;
- manpower organization and structure;
- scientific support activities such as safety, hygiene and health;
- technology and product development;
- the consumer of hospitality services;
- operational support and infrastructure; and
- the hospitality business environment.

In some respects, it is easier to conceptualize than to deliver a curriculum that parallels the contemporary developments in hospitality operations management. Summarizing so far, the aim has been to support an industry-driven view that operations management should be positioned at the centre of

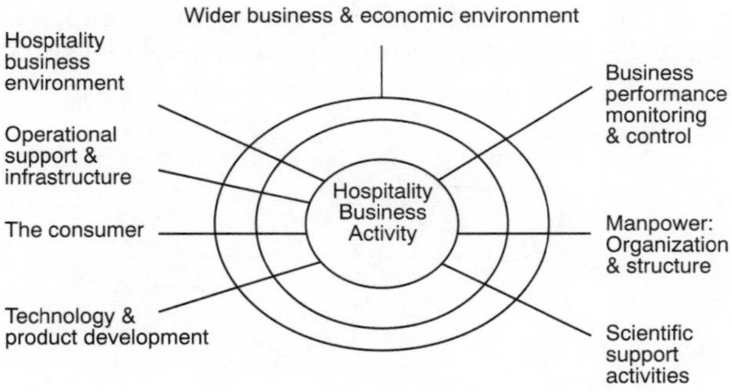

Figure 7.
A conceptual model for hospitality operations curriculum development

the curriculum. If it is intended to serve industry, it must mirror the changes that have been occurring during the last few years. Further, if it is to serve young managers who aspire to become accomplished managers, it must provide a balance of technical and professional skills that will equip them with a detailed understanding of day-to-day operations and a broader, strategic vision of how to manage and analyse every facet of unit and multi-unit business activity. To achieve this, a new, more radical vision for operations management is needed to support the teaching and learning needed to make this happen.

Operations management: an integrated, resource-based approach
The changing nature of managerial work at unit level suggests that educationalists should monitor the implications for up-dating or even re-shaping their curriculum to ensure that it reflects industry needs and developments. In these circumstances, a logical step is to develop teaching and learning courseware which is sufficiently flexible to use in different situations and with different types of managers (see Figure 8).

The concept of a resource-based approach to hospitality operations management is founded on many of the observations made above and in particular, the need for a modern curriculum using student-centred learning methods. Each title in the series follows a standard, 60 page format and draws from a core of text book and journal reading to provide an integrated study guide consisting of concise explanations, commentary and extension material. The three hospitality operations management titles are designed to facilitate a logical and progressive study of Operational Techniques (foundation level) Operations Management (intermediate level) and Strategic Management (advanced level).

The overall aim of the three interlinking titles is to equip students with the conceptual understanding of how to manage hospitality operations effectively. An important distinction from prior work is that the advanced level studies in strategic management seek to equip the graduate manager with the broader

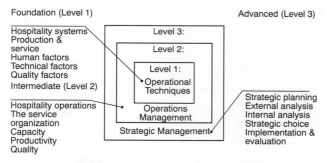

Source: *Hospitality & Tourism*, Resource-Based Series, Cassell, London

Figure 8.
A conceptual model for
hospitality operations
curriculum development

perspective of unit management that industrialists are pressing for. Further, a key objective is to try to break-down the somewhat artificial divide that exists between accommodation and food and beverage management, by focusing on shared operational themes at foundation and intermediate levels.

Operational Techniques (Johns *et al.*, 1994) introduces systems theory as a basis for understanding and analysing the function and management of operations. A review of "hard" and "soft" systems techniques provides a broad methodological framework. In line with a general systems view, hospitality operations are treated in an integrated way by drawing parallels between food, beverage and accommodation operations wherever possible. It is hoped that this will enable the techniques to be learned in a way that makes them completely transferable. Foundation level study also seeks to address issues which distinguish hospitality operations from the broader body of operations management knowledge. Personnel, marketing and other "functional" issues are therefore included wherever appropriate, since they are a normal part of the hospitality manager's work.

Foundation (Level 1) Operational Techniques:

(1) *Hospitality systems*
   - Systems theory;
   - Hospitality systems;
   - Hospitality environments.

(2) *Production and service*
   - The hospitality cycle;
   - Menus and tariffs;
   - Product styles and concepts.

(3) *Human factors*
   - Jobs, roles, functions and structure;
   - Employee specification and selection;
   - Employee evaluation.

(4) *Technical factors*
   - Work co-ordination and control;
   - Facilities layout and design;
   - Equipment specification and selection.

(5) *Quality factors*
   - Product quality;
   - Service quality;
   - Legal standards.

Operations Management (Johns and Edwards, 1994) builds on the coverage of systems theory at the foundation level and on the integrated approach to the treatment of food, beverage and accommodation operations management. The five Parts deal with the scope of hospitality operations, the organizational context and the key issues of capacity, productivity and quality.

Intermediate (Level 2) Operations Management:

(1) *Hospitality operations*
  - Operating systems;
  - Production and service;
  - Operations management.

(2) *The service organization*
  - Organization structure;
  - Organizational culture and climate;
  - Motivation and change.

(3) *Capacity*
  - Work study and capacity;
  - Forecasting and managing demand;
  - Scheduling.

(4) *Productivity*
  - What is productivity?;
  - Productivity and performance;
  - Productivity management.

(5) *Quality*
  - What is quality?;
  - Solving quality problems;
  - Quality management systems.

Strategic Management (Teare and Ingram, 1994) seeks to explore the wider issues associated with the hospitality operations environment. All organizations, large and small must make decisions about the nature of the activity in which they wish to engage, the goals they seek to achieve and the overall direction they want to pursue. After this, they must consider how to plan and co-ordinate their activities and make best use of resources, meet customer needs, compete effectively, monitor performance and review their achievements. In order to do all this, managers must devise structures that define task-related boundaries, processes for making decisions and procedures to carry them out. As the decisions are made, implemented, monitored and controlled, the

decision-makers need to think strategically so as to assess the wider
implications of their actions for the organization as a whole.

Advanced (Level 3) Strategic Management:

(1) *Strategic planning*
- Structures;
- Processes;
- Procedures.

(2) *External analysis*
- Business and economic analysis;
- Structural (industry) analysis;
- Competitor analysis.

(3) *Internal analysis*
- Portfolio analysis;
- Operations analysis;
- Resource analysis.

(4) Strategic choice
- Generating and evaluating options;
- Strategies for change;
- Planning for change.

(5) Strategic implementation and evaluation
- Monitoring business strategy;
- Achieving structure and strategy co-alignment;
- Sustaining strategic focus.

Implications for workplace learning

Hospitality operations management has once again become the focal point for
curriculum development and the structural changes occurring in the industry
suggest that scope exists for re-shaping specialist subject areas so that students
are fully equipped and prepared for the opportunities that change creates.

According to Olsen's analysis this means that unit managers need to know
more about the interrelationships between technical and business issues:

> ...unit managers are now being asked to perform differently. They are being asked to compete
> effectively on the local level, where conditions are becoming extremely competitive, to scan the
> environment for threats and opportunities, and to build a strategic plan for their units based
> on this type of analysis. This leaves the unit manager with the need to become a much more
> independent decision-maker and one who is much more aware of the forces in the environment
> and how they affect the future of the unit (Olsen, 1991, p. 23).

It seems likely therefore, that unit managers will assume a greater degree of influence as their operational role expands to fill the gaps created by restructuring and consolidation. In this scenario, a fresh strategic vision of operations management will be needed.

The concept of industry and corporate theming

The concept of an Internet forum: a global meeting point for industry and education

The challenge of managing a comparatively rapid transition from print to electronic publishing prompted MCB University Press (MCB-UP) to explore both academic and practitioner uses of the internet so that its portfolio of journals and other products and services might be combined to provide a meaningful cluster of resources for subscribers, authors and students (or Associates) undertaking programmes delivered by its affiliate company IMC. The concept of a Forum – a global meeting point for people with shared interests in a topic or subject area or more broadly in relation to a given industry, has emerged during the past 18 to 24 months. The concept is already capable of sustaining a broad-ranging industry theme via print and electronic journal publishing, related internet conferencing, World Wide Web (WWW) hyper-text linking and homepage areas dedicated to "state of the art" exchanges between academics and practitioners around the globe. Further innovations in electronically distributed materials will reinforce this powerful distribution and networking medium in the near future. The Hospitality and Tourism Global Forum has been operational since Autumn 1995 during which time it has hosted four Internet conferences with papers delivered by conference "speakers" and participants drawn principally (though not exclusively) from Europe, North America and the Asia Pacific region.

The Hospitality and Tourism Global Forum on the Internet

The aim of the Hospitality and Tourism Global Forum (see Figure 9) is to provide a definitive global meeting point for hospitality and tourism practitioners and academics. The Forum currently hosts a variety of Web pages and sites and for user convenience, they are arranged in categories. By hyper-text linking to existing Web sites it is possible to travel the world from the Forum (without spending hours "surfing the net").

In addition to the institutional categories, the Forum provides access to a variety of on-line resources and hosts a Virtual Academy (VA) series. The aim of the VA series is to enable students, researchers, writers and practitioners interested in specialist areas and their application to hospitality and tourism settings to meet, share news and ideas and to network globally via the Internet. The vision is to enable a worldwide community of people to share openly and constructively, shape new concepts and disseminate the latest thinking and managerial practice as reflected by:

- A quarterly newsletter with contributions from around the globe.

NEW The National Hospitality Archive

*Hospitality
& Tourism*

Welcome to the Hospitality and Tourism Global Forum on the Internet

The Internet presages major changes in the way information and intelligence is communicated over the coming decade. Whilst it is still in its infancy both in respect of product/service development and customer connectivity, much of what can be offered can now be discerned and action learning can begin.

Under the Chairmanship of Richard Teare, Editor of the *International Journal of Contemporary Hospitality Management*, MCB University Press has established the *Hospitality and Tourism Forum* as a co-operative learning vehicle for leading professional and academic organizations globally.

So far, the Hospitality and Tourism Forum has 'Open House' Partners in the following areas:

[Virtual Academy] [Associations] [Industry] [Government]
[Education] [Journals] [Conferences] [Resources]

Home   Introduction   Partners

The *Hospitality & Tourism Global Forum* can be found at: http://www.mcb.co.uk/htgf/

Figure 9.
The Hospitality and
Tourism Global Forum
welcome pages

- Regular updates, reviews and comments on the latest developments in (VA subject area) from a hospitality and tourism perspective.
- E-mail contact groups and news groups to facilitate an exchange of views and information.
- A "What's New" page.
- Continuous Internet conferences on topical themes in (VA subject area).
- Links with specialists in other service fields.

There are currently 12 VAs:

(1) Accounting and finance;
(2) Economics and industry trends;
(3) Gaming and enterprise;
(4) Human resource management;
(5) Information management;
(6) Marketing;
(7) Operations management;
(8) Science and technology;
(9) Service quality;
(10) Small business management;
(11) Strategy and organizational behaviour;
(12) Yield management.

Each VA is managed by four academics, currently representing Europe, North America and the Asia Pacific region.

Although the Hospitality and Tourism Global Forum has attracted a good deal of interest among academics, it has yet to establish the volume of visitors necessary to make it an invaluable reference point. In part, this is due to the comparatively slow uptake among practitioners, the limited range of services currently available and a degree of uncertainty about the best ways of designing and implementing new features and encouraging wider participation.

It seemed timely to initiate a wide-ranging review and discussion about these and other issues together with MCB-UP Forum conveners, designers, users and system support staff and a good deal of shared experience has and continues to influence our thinking about the characteristics of the "ideal" Forum, aspects of which are summarized in the following sub-section.

Designing internet Forums: shared learning on structure, content and participation
In September 1996 a Forum Conveners' discussion group involving 30 IMC and MCB University Press Internet Forum conveners, designers and development team members, began to share experiences and debate the issues relating to the design of Forums and how to encourage wider participation and involvement in their development. The team are currently involved in building and maintaining more than 20 Forums.

The aim of the ongoing discussion group is to exchange information between Forum convenors managing sites on the MCB-UP server in order to learn from each other and keep up to-date with ideas for future developments. These include:

- ideas from conveners;
- announcing new pages across the range of Forum sites;
- design issues, advice and feedback;
- sourcing material and Forum participation (referred to as the volume of "hits");
- Forum promotion;
- tips on Web resources for site developers;
- postings from MCB-UP Internet design staff on general Web activity as it affects conveners (including sites they may wish to create hyper-text links with);
- guidance and advice from system operations staff as well as questions (and answers) to systems operations;
- Internet design advice on other resources from MCB-UP that might assist Forum conveners (e.g. other discussion list(s), top ten updates, new to the server updates, system upgrades, system downtimes among others).

The strands of discussion are broadly divisible into issues relating to Forum design and innovation; the characteristic features of "good" internet sites and achieving wider participation in Forum development. While it is possible to initiate a Forum with a small team of people, to create interest and a sense of community it is essential to build a wider network of contributors. For academics, this offers opportunities to help build a virtual global community related to the Forum theme. In part, this is illustrated by the Virtual Academy concept which provides a means of inter-linking academics with practitioners in any field of industry and commerce or in special interest areas in the wider field of continuing education. To ensure team commitment at the inception of a Forum it has been necessary to seek out the enthusiasts – people with a particular interest in internet communications – John Peters, an experienced Forum convener calls this the "shoulder tap":

> My methodology has been the shoulder-tap (which was the specific joining instruction individually tailored to the recipient); the dual reminder that we are open and a circular to expose some of the comments and debate to-date in the Forum area. At the heart of the whole thing is the question – how do we incentivize (participation)…if we are working to a premiss that a lively discussion will attract others to it and centrifugally maintain the interest and attention of those already in it – how do we get discussion and how do we get lively discussion? It is an action learning Q question and until we generate some P captured experience we can't codify what are appropriate group modelling/influencing behaviours.
> John Peters (October, 1996)

Assuming that the convener succeeds in establishing a core team of enthusiasts who share his or her vision, the key development challenge is to create a Forum structure that is capable of providing fast, user-friendly access and maintaining the interest of site visitors. It is vital that visitors feel encouraged to participate and to come back regularly, thereby joining the network themselves as regular contributors. A few of the key issues that Forum conveners need to consider at inception and during the ongoing development of a Forum site are outlined in Table V.

The Forum concept will evolve as Internet communications improve and in order to explore the scope for innovation, most MCB-UP Forum conveners had been fully engaged in site development during the past two years. This has typically involved trialling new features, experimenting with the mix of graphics and text, listening to users and designers as well as evaluating other sites. While the early development phase had been a rapid one, it is already clear that Forums are both popular and appealing (all conveners are able to point to early successes and growing visitor volumes) as they offer a cluster of themed resources and services in a convenient format. They also provide a means of extending the wider concept of electronic publishing and MCB-UP are expanding the range of subscriber services and other resources that support many of the current and foreseeable needs and aspirations of Forum users. The main challenge for most conveners during the next 12 to 18 months is to achieve a level of mass participation that will enable them to become definitive meeting

Comments	Implications
"…write…so that you cannot be misunderstood"	Forum sites need effective signposting
"…most participate in Forum activities for no payment (because they want to) there is no command structure"	The site should be structured so as to facilitate open-ended participation within a carefully designed framework
"…how do you create value for money strategies – such as reduced connect time and lower "phone charges?"	In the short term – home pages should provide rapid and easy access (and in so doing, lower-cost user time). In the medium/long term – explore distribution by cable and satellite TV
"…the Internet is not yet sufficiently time efficient to make it attractive"	Use hyper-text linking to create "one stop" industry Forums encompassing, trade, professional, industry, government and educational links
(Forum participants) "…Forum users that come to you (the enthusiasts) are better prospects and (potentially) worth far more effort"	Find roles for the enthusiasts who want to participate and can encourage others to do so by facilitating and inviting others to join a growing, sharing community
"…the bottom line…the best/most effective but very imperfect measure is site hits – without this we have no (clear directions) for future R&D"	Aim to ensure that hyper-text linking is two-way so that potential users can easily find their way to the site – the more pathways (via hyper-text links) the greater the prospect of creating a definitive global meeting point for an industry, discipline or topic area
"…far too many commercial sites seem far too keen to get a credit card number before they have demonstrated that they will deliver value for money"	Maintain the principles of free access, though a joining fee (like club membership) may help to foster a sense of belonging – the benefits of membership should include an opportunity to participate fully – perhaps non-members can observe and try before joining

Table V.
Managing Internet
Forums: some
challenges for
conveners

points for academics and practitioners in emerging fields like Airport Management.

The transition from special interest group Forums (mainly populated by enthusiasts) to mass participation is therefore a focal issue for ongoing discussion and debate. John Peters observes that wider involvement, encompassing new generation Internet users might be achieved by adopting a "centrifugal participation" approach and he suggests a number of practical steps for encouraging wider involvement.

"Centrifugal participation" some observations from John Peters (7 October 1996):

- extrovert propensity task – find and recruit activists/extroverts and while their attention is held, they will contribute (at the risk of dominating the discussion).

- self-esteem reinforcement task – convener looks for "self-conscious" postings and offers reinforcement and encouragement.

- provocation task – convener seeks controversy in order to stimulate lively contributions (note: may only work with a well-established and trusting community of lively individuals – not a typical cross-section).

- lower-order need reinforcement task – site owners/conveners make financial and other incentives available either randomly or in return for some form of prescribed, desirable response (such as a Literati Award for Excellence re: best/most consistent contribution to a conference.)

- command culture establishment task – populate every conference with "paid" conveners and/or contributors who participate daily to "seed" the conference and help create a centrifuge effect.

- value for money effect – charge a "joining fee" so that "value for money" is related to the level of active participation in the event or conference.

A broader strand of discussion aims to specify the characteristics of an "ideal" Internet site and in order to accomplish this, the Forum Conveners' group is considering the design and development implications of user "satisfiers" and "dissatisfiers" derived from the many hundreds of Internet sites reviewed by members of the discussion group. (For a summary of findings and observations, please see Appendix) Preliminary findings (compiled by Gordon Wills) reveal a number of key themes:

Forum ideals…

- Good Internet sites engender a sense of community where participants feel that they are sharing in and belonging to a community with a shared focus (such as industry and academia shaping and sharing insights on theory and practice) that we cannot see or touch but with whom we have a lot in common. Furthermore, the overwhelming feeling was that this community of interest was one where the state of the art in the topic was being discussed – not trivia but things we really either had no idea about or are uncertain about as we explore.

- The second strand was that the site was a place because it was as described at (1) above, that enabled each one of us to promote and explore our own ideas with the other members – the reciprocal of course of finding out from others. The use of Question and Answer routines was an illustration of this.

- The third key element relates to the logistical issues – we all liked one-site hits – not stringing along too long; good links that guided; logical layouts and the whole site kept up-to-date.

Internet site dissatisfiers…

- The most frequently mentioned source of dissatisfaction is graphics/images that don't work and/or take forever to download. Several pondered how long this will last and whether it will still be a complaint in the longer term. A close runner-up is "too many gimmicks" – surely a plea for simple communications at the site.

- Other criticisms include: too much advertising or requests to visit the sponsoring organization's pages and invitations to pay beyond the free taster pages. The logistical complaints were led by "under construction" messages; out of date details, missing e-mail response provision and pages that are too long or too short (with too many links onwards).

These observations and the ongoing Forum Conveners' discussion group provide a valuable source of shared learning and guidance for conveners and designers. The discussion is also helping to shape a variety of new initiatives such as the criteria for an annual MCB-UP Best Forum Award – an extension of its successful series of Literati Awards for Excellence held each year to celebrate author and editor achievements in journal publishing. In establishing a formal mechanism for recognizing excellence in Forum design, implementation and management, it will be necessary to ensure that objective assessments can be obtained and in so doing, a team of Forum assessors will be needed. In order to guide the next phase of development, a Forum advisory role is also being considered so that the convener and his or her team can seek "next step" guidance from an independent expert in the subject area or industry field.

As Forums establish Virtual Academy communities of academics in hospitality and tourism, airport management and other fields of interest, they will be able to support electronic peer reviews of articles submitted for print and electronic journal publication. This offers all the advantages of conventional "double blind" reviews but with the added benefit of wider international involvement and "real time" transmission of manuscripts and reviewer reports.

The role of the Forum in delivering themed programmes: Airport Management and BAA Plc
A natural extension of the themed approach to Forum development is to hyper-text link programme courseware resources to a Forum site and seek to build on the range of complementary and themed resources provided at the site. In courseware design and updating terms, there are several important advantages – updating is not tied to re-printing schedules and journal reading updates can be automated by using Anbar on-line Management Intelligence as the access point to a world library of management literature, complete with on-line ordering and a document supply service provided by the British Library.

The user perspective is equally attractive as the learner (or Associate) has access to learning resources at their place of work (the study environment) and via a dedicated "set meeting place" he or she can keep in constant touch with other members of the learning Set and the tutorial team. As the sole access point to the MCB-UP and Surrey IMC sites as well as day-to-day course materials, assignment schedules, and many hundreds of Internet pages of material relating to course regulations and management (the learning environment, tutor support, the role of external examiners, course regulations and procedures, quality assurance among many others) the learner can read and print any information they need with the single exception of confidential personal information and marks which are not held on the Internet.

The following examples presented in Figures 10, 11 and 12 show the main elements of the Airport Business Forum infrastructure that are in place to support the delivery of a themed AP(E)L to MBA in-company programme for BAA Plc, a core element of a learning partnership commitment to Surrey IMC

Airport Business Forum
in association with BAA Plc

SET HOMEPAGE	ANBAR ABSTRACTS
The Set Homepage is essentially a hub of communications and interaction for the associate. From here he or she can access their courseware, 'talk' to other members of the set via the Set Meeting Place, order Anbar Abstracts on-line and access the Surrey IMC Site in general. View your sample Set Homepage here.	Anbar Management Intelligence abstracts articles from 400 accredited international management journals and produces them quarterly on CD-ROM. This is now also searchable via the Internet. A search using the keywords 'Airport Management' produced 60 abstracts a sample of which are available for you to view here.

MANAGEMENT JOURNALS	WWW SITES
MCB University Press is a multinational publishing house specializing in management and academic journals and periodicals. Their Internet site contains a wealth of management information and complementary resources. Detailed below is a selection of titles from the site that fall within the 'Airport Management' interest area.	Other interesting WWW sites. An intensive search of the Internet using the Metacrawler Parallel Search Engine produced the links below:

- Aircraft Engineering and Aerospace Technology
- Managing Service Quality
- Facilities Journal
- International Journal of Retail & Distribution Management
- International Journal of Operations & Production Management
- Police Studies - The International Review of Police Development

- Flight Path to the future - Hong Kong's new airport
- Airport Analyst - Asia Pacific
- BAA Homepage - Heathrow
- BAA - Air Cargo Homepage
- British Airways Global Homepage
- Airportnet Homepage - AAAE/IAAE

RESOURCES	CONFERENCES

- Hospitality & Tourism Forum
- Coolsites
- Qualnet
- Human Resources Network

- Aerospace Corrosion Control Conference
- Disaster Prevention Conference

Figure 10.
An overview of the Airport Business Forum resources

(workplace learning programmes) and the University of Surrey (research and development). The main features of the Coolsites Directory – an element of the Airport Business Forum resources – are presented in Figure 13.

The knowledge base: formalizing the learning agenda for the future
While the generic learning framework necessarily reflects the cornerstones of management education that are traditionally associated with Certificate, Diploma and Master of Business Administration courses, it is wholly in keeping with the philosophy of action learning to relate "programmed knowledge" (P) to the workplace environment. All organizations, whether large or small, provide opportunities for people to think, observe, solve problems and learn from action-oriented outcomes. This corpus of knowledge and expertise, derived from workplace learning, is reflected in the relative strengths and weaknesses of the enterprise as a whole. Yet "questioning insight" (Q) is rarely formalized in a way that is easily disseminated to future generations of

Airport Business Forum
Action Learning Set Communications

Surrey IMC
MBA - BAA 1
Set Communications

Set Meeting Place

Your Set Meeting Place is available for communication and discussion about your programme, assignments and to gain feedback from other set members. It is an Internet Newsgroup and help for using Newsgroups is available if you have not used Newsgroups before.

The Meeting Place is only available to members of this Set.

| Enter Meeting Place |

International Meeting Place

The International Meeting Place is available to all Surrey IMC Internet users worldwide. It can be used for general discussion and research updates. Again, help for using Newsgroups is available.

| Enter Meeting Place |

imc.test Meeting Place

Use the imc.test Meeting Place to practice and experiment with the Newsgroup functions - attaching files, posting and replying. Read the help for using Newsgroups for guidance on Newsgroup features.

| Enter Meeting Place |

Return to the Set Home Page

Developing a curriculum

227

Figure 11.
BAA plc Set meeting places

Surrey IMC
MBA - BAA 1
Set Information

Email Directory...

This is a listing of all your Set members, with email addresses. To send an individual an email, click their name and enter your message into the box, clicking 'Send' when done.

If you have an email address and it is not entered here, please email imc@mcb.co.uk and it will be added.

Set Adviser & Programme Manager:

- Information to be confirmed

Set Associates:

- Information to be confirmed

Set Tutors:

- Information to be confirmed

Set Meeting Timetable

This is a timetable of your scheduled Set meetings, from start date to finish date, with tutor and meeting details.

- Information to be confirmed

Set Assignment Submission Dates

- Set Assignment Submission Dates - *a timetable of your assignment submission dates, with core course, tutor and date for final submission* (information to be confirmed)

Courseware...

Access your Programme Courseware. *Please note that Netscape 2.1 (2.0+ recommended) is required to read your programme courseware, although some browsers and versions may work. Also, a copy of Adobe Acrobat is needed if you wish to view articles accompanying certain resources* (Adobe Acrobat is freely available from the Courseware Homepage).

Anbar Abstract Ordering...

Use Anbar Management Intelligence *to access resources in support of your assignment research and course reading. Anbar now has an On-Line Order Form so you can order your articles across the World Wide Web.*

Figure 12.
Learning set
information, resources
and Anbar library
support

managers who "learn on the job" and, if they are fortunate enough to be mentored in an appropriate way, receive the benefit of insight and wisdom from those who themselves gained expertise from doing, applying, making mistakes and taking corrective action. In balancing these very different yet equally important dimensions of learning, it is appropriate to envisage outcomes in the form of an equation: $L = P + Q$ (where L = Learning). To achieve a balance between "P" and "Q" (learning from doing) an industry specific "knowledge base" is being created (as appropriate to client organization needs) by pairing Surrey IMC tutors and other academics with managers so as to produce publishable outputs and electronic media resources. The process of "capturing" and formalizing "Q" based knowledge will both theme and augment the generic curriculum framework.

COOLSITES
Welcome to the Coolsites Directory,
a resource of quality rated internet sites in your area of interest

Please select an area of interest...

[Economics]	[Education]
[Finance]	[General Management]
[Health & Environment]	[Human Resources]
[Information Management]	[Library & Information Services]
[Materials Science & Technology]	[Marketing]
[Production Management & Engineering]	[Police Management & Policies]
[Property Management]	[Quality Management]

HOME	SEARCH	HELP	FEEDBACK
[Home]	[Search]	[Help]	[Feedback]

Coolsites is Netscape 2.0 Enhanced

Figure 13.
Coolsites – Anbar
quality-related Web
directory

The concept of a practitioner knowledge base
The development of an industry specific knowledge base provides an opportunity to disseminate expertise in the form of published works (articles, cases, textbooks, work books, workshop proceedings, Internet resources) wherever public domain outputs are applicable. This will encourage shared learning in rapidly changing fields such as the international Airport Business. Commercially sensitive, company-specific resource outputs will be distributed (as appropriate) by intranet. It also contextualizes learning by augmenting generic core course materials with an array of industry and company specific resources (see Figure 14).

A framework for learning, participation and personal development
The qualifications framework for BAA Plc is based on an incremental route to MBA with multiple entry points appropriate to prior experience, qualifications and the needs and aspirations of the individual (see Figure 15). Each cohort consists of a learning Set of between 12-18 Associates (with its own tutorial team and external examiner) with sub-Sets of three or four Associates for some discussion group activities and self-help support. A range of learning support is provided, beginning with start-up residential sessions on learning styles, and "learning to learn" (among others); how to access and use the Internet site and briefings for in-company mentors, project clients, steering group members (as appropriate). The in-company support (mentors, clients, steering group) coupled with inputs from functional specialists provides the formative infrastructure for an "Enterprise School of Management" (ESM) which in time, should grow organically as MBA graduates themselves contribute to the learning partnership by mentoring or tutoring as faculty members.

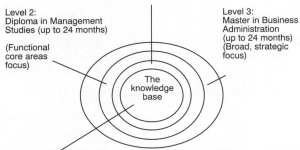

A framework for organizational learning
Themed support for incremental action learning routes to MBA

Level 1: Certificate in Management Studies (12 months)
(skills development focus)

Level 2:
Diploma in Management
Studies (up to 24 months)

(Functional
core areas
focus)

The
knowledge
base

Level 3:
Master in Business
Administration
(up to 24 months)
(Broad, strategic
focus)

Figure 14.
The concept of a
knowledge base as a
corporate

The knowledge base represents a corpus of expertise and 'best practice'
experience. Wherever possible knowledge will be 'captured' so as to provide
a meaningful reference point for personal and organizational development.
Outputs will include: Internet and intranet resources; E-Journal articles and
Internet conferencing; print publishing.

Corporate theming and workplace learning
The incremental pattern of action learning draws on a multiplicity of inputs
which are applied and interpreted in both an industry and a corporate context
(see Figure 16). The theming elements are integral to the learning process as
they provide a means of augmenting and sustaining a dynamic curriculum and
a framework for interpreting the much broader field of management as reflected
by the core courses, textbook principles and access to the world's management
literature on-line via the Anbar service to Associates.

Applying the learning framework
Incremental action learning and project-based assessment
If managers are to become more effective in the workplace they must be able to
use and apply the body of programmed knowledge (P) and learn from doing (Q)

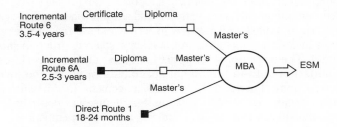

Surrey IMC
Incremental Action Learning Routes to MBA

Incremental
Route 6
3.5-4 years

Certificate   Diploma

Master's

Incremental
Route 6A
2.5-3 years

Diploma   Master's

MBA ⇨ ESM

Master's

Figure 15.
Incremental action
learning pathways

Direct Route 1
18-24 months

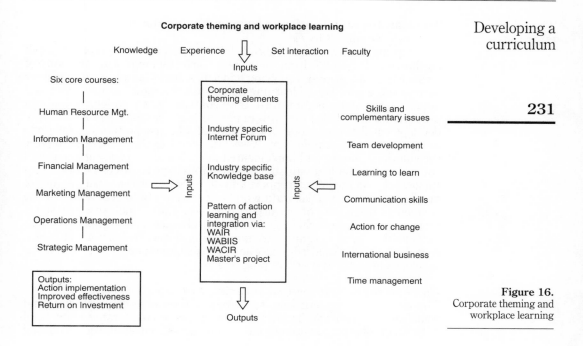

Corporate theming and workplace learning

Figure 16.
Corporate theming and
workplace learning

by undertaking meaningful project assignments that require careful specification, in-company client support and the attainment of specific outcomes that demonstrate that learning has occurred. In this sense, questions and questioning insight – the ability to find and apply optimal solutions – constitute an important dimension of the curriculum. The courseware resources and in particular the core courses, provide a minimal framework that tutors and Associates will invariably build on as they seek the best fit between (P) and (Q). Access to the latest management thinking via Anbar provides a fast, intuitive way of searching an on-line database of abstracts from more than 400 academic and professional journals (the journals list is accredited by a panel of internationally respected academics). Anbar on CD-ROM is issued quarterly and more recently, Internet delivery facilitates daily updating by the Anbar product team. Further, on-line electronic ordering with full-text document supply by the British Library direct to the workplace, ensures that Associates have a uniquely flexible form of resource support as they seek to apply the literature to the challenges provided by the learning environment – encapsulated by the assignments they undertake. A progressive series of assignments relate to the pattern of study, starting from a personal perspective and building to a broader, company-wide strategic focus.

The learning organization: a partnership approach

Corporate theming: BAA Plc

The learning framework and embedded theming, provide three types of output as shown in Figure 17. First, managers learn from exploring the body of management literature and applying it in a meaningful way. Second, managers become more effective by learning how to ask the right questions and find appropriate solutions and third, they contribute to a collective body of practitioner knowledge that will in part at least, set the agenda for future development. The knowledge base concept affords an opportunity to integrate assignment work completed by Associates and together with other inputs, the solutions sought and implemented in each and every assignment will collectively, provide a valuable interdisciplinary resource. The learning framework also provides an opportunity to build an international network of people interested in collaborating and/or contributing to debates about the component disciplines of the airport business. The Virtual Academy series provides the means of achieving the wider involvement of academics and other universities in managing and facilitating Internet Forum activities, contributing to the knowledge base and publishable outputs and partnering the development and delivery of the programme.

UK Plc (hospitality and tourism): a learning partnership approach

The benefits of a long-term learning partnership between a corporate client and a university are two-way; it provides opportunities for collaborative writing and other forms of scholarly activity (like secondments, industrial placements and

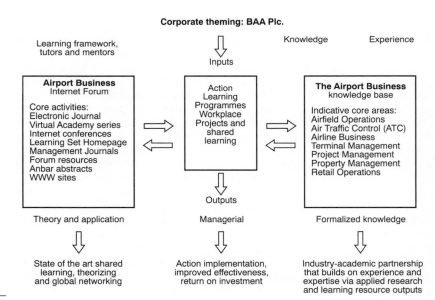

Figure 17.
An overview of the corporate and industry theming approach

the development of undergraduate and postgraduate study options) and opportunities to conduct basic and applied research. By ensuring that the partnership is as broad as possible with academic and practitioner contacts across the range of discipline areas it is possible to collaborate on multidisciplinary projects while at the same time, maintaining an appropriate industry and company specific focus. The scope that a learning partnership offers includes the opportunity to work with an array of other institutions – other universities and academic teams, professional and trade associations, customers, suppliers and contractors. Further, the ongoing programmes of study provide a natural point of connection for related scholarly activity and research and a channel of communication for discussing project ideas, problems and opportunities. Together, mutually supportive programmes of study and research will provide a significant means of sustaining innovation and responding to change through teamworking and an organizational commitment to learning (see Figure 18).

UK Plc (hospitality & tourism): programmes for learning, development and research
To provide a "point of presence" for "virtual" in-company learning, development and research (the beginnings of an Enterprise School of Management) a Corporate Development Centre aims to:

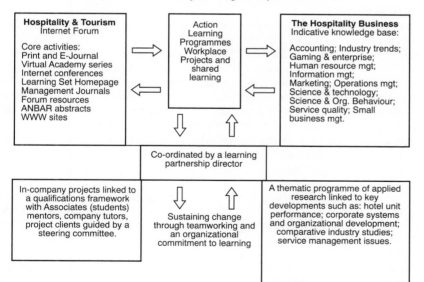

Figure 18.
UK Plc (hospitality and tourism): a learning partnership approach

(1) develop and manage a framework for organizational learning;
(2) co-ordinate and monitor a wide-ranging programme of collaborative research in keeping with organizational needs and aspirations;
(3) promote and support innovation in keeping with quality and profit improvement goals;
(4) build relationships with customers, suppliers and organizations with mutual interests in shared learning.

This brief is linked to a programme of at least five years' duration and a commitment to sponsor a Chair or Fellowship with the post-holder acting as the Learning Partnership Director (LPD).

The next steps?
All that remains for the ESM to become reality is for brave souls in organizations to stand up and ask whether the Emperor really does have any clothes, and if not, what are we all doing in this parade. For there are many senior people in industry who also believe that the system we all created as a cartel supplier of management education and development has failed us. Management learning, and its consequent actions on the real issues which affect organizations, is the lifeblood which keeps enterprise vital. It is the business of businesses, not of academies, and in devolving that responsibility and in becoming dependent upon outside suppliers, enterprises risk the flow of this lifeblood, this vitality (Wills, 1993, p. 87).

Media partnering
The IMC network of partners provides a "total learning" support resource for organizations seeking to nurture their own Enterprise School of Management (ESM). Yet as the internet has shown us, the technology is constantly improving and Surrey IMC aims to recruit a "media" partner such as Granada Media Group (GMG) to help jointly design and deliver the "next generation" of workplace learning materials. The likelihood that dedicated Internet channels will be provided by cable and by satellite to interactive TV receivers in the foreseeable future, offers the prospect of stable, fast and inexpensive access to internet-based resources. Coupled with IMC's worldwide partner network and the creative resources that an organization like GMG can provide, the market opportunities for action learning-based educational programmes are virtually limitless.

Further, the corporate appeal of action learning and its role in sustaining ESMs should ensure that there is sufficient advertising revenue to make a joint venture with GMG (or similar) a viable commercial proposition.

Industry partnering
The concept of a medium- to long-term learning partnership encompassing programmes for learning, development and research offers an attractive way of

building industry-education partnerships, especially as the role of a sponsored Chair/Fellow can be linked to the role of learning partnership director (LPD). The LPD should be an academic with appropriate research experience but he or she must also be able to organize, encourage, envisage, build networks of people with mutual interests and shared problems and interface with trade and professional associations, university and industry specialists wherever they happen to be so as to harness the collective talents of a global community via the industry Internet Forums that provide the industry and corporate theming for client organizations.

Global partnering
IMC's multinational character is also one of its key strengths – providing culturally sensitive workplace learning with regional and local tutor support. A key challenge for IMC and its partner universities, is to harmonize (but not standardize) its delivery so as to adhere to the dynamic quality assurance procedures now in place and to achieve improvements in courseware design and updating, faculty extension and enrichment and responsiveness to the "life-long" organizational agendas of firms like BAA Plc.

References
Close, A. and Teare, R. (1990), "Effective management development", *International Journal of Contemporary Hospitality Management,* Vol. 2 No. 4, pp. i-ii.
Eccles, G. and Teare, R. (1995), "Strategic thinking: a new vision for hotel managers?", in Teare, R. and Armistead, C. (Eds), *Services Management: New Directions and Perspectives,* Cassell, London and New York, NY, pp. 94-7.
Eccles, G. and Teare, R. (1996), "Integrating strategy and structure: perspectives and challenges for hospitality managers", in Kotas, R., Teare, R., Logie, J., Jayawardena, C. and Bowen, J.T. (Eds), *The International Hospitality Business,* Cassell, London and New York, NY, pp. 42-51.
Garvin, D.A. (1995), "Leveraging processes for strategic advantage", *Harvard Business Review,* September-October, pp. 77-90.
Ingram, H., Teare, R., Ridley, S. and Ferrone, L. (1997b), "Strategic competitive advantage through structure, quality and teamwork", in Teare, R., Farber Canziani, B. and Brown, G. (Eds), *Global Directions: New Strategies for Hospitality and Tourism,* Cassell, London and Herndon, VA, pp. 133-64.
Ingram, H., Teare, R., Scheuing, E. and Armistead, C. (1997a), "A systems model of effective teamwork", *The TQM Magazine,* Vol. 9 No. 2, pp. 118-27.
Johns, N. and Edwards, J. (1994), *Operations Management: A Resource-Based Approach for the Hospitality Industry,* Cassell, London and New York, NY, pp. ii-iv.
Johns, N. and Teare, R. (1995), "Change, opportunity and the new operations management curriculum", *International Journal of Contemporary Hospitality Management,* Vol. 7 No. 5, pp. 4-8.
Johns, N., Ingram, H. and Lee-Ross, D. (1994), *Operational Techniques: A Resource-Based Approach for the Hospitality Industry,* Cassell, London and New York, NY, pp. ii-iv.
Linney, C. and Teare, R. (1991), "Addressing the human resource challenges of the 1990s", *International Journal of Contemporary Hospitality Management,* Vol. 3 No. 2, pp. iii-iv.
Litteljohn, D. and Slattery, P. (1991), "Macro analysis techniques: an appraisal of Europe's main hotel markets", *International Journal of Contemporary Hospitality Management,* Vol. 3 No. 4, pp. 6-13.

Nebel, E.C., Braunlich, C.G. and Zhang, Y. (1994), "Hotel food and beverage directors' career paths in American luxury hotels", *International Journal of Contemporary Hospitality Management*, Vol. 6 No. 6, pp. 3-10.

Olsen, M.D. (1991), "Structural changes: the international hospitality industry and firm", *International Journal of Contemporary Hospitality Management*, Vol. 3 No. 4, pp. 21-4.

Teare, R. (1990), "Structural and organisational change: theories for hospitality managers", *Marketing Intelligence & Planning – In Action*, Vol. 8 No. 5, pp. 12-14.

Teare, R. and Akehurst, G. (1988a), "Exploring the potential for problem-based learning in syndicates", *Business Education*, Vol. 9 No. 1, pp. 13-18.

Teare, R. and Akehurst, G. (1988b), "Developments in open learning for the hospitality industry", *International Journal of Hospitality Management,* Vol. 7 No. 2, pp. 99-103.

Teare, R. and Brotherton, R. (1990), "Assessing human resource needs and priorities", *Journal of European Industrial Training*, Vol. 14 No. 3, pp. 5-6.

Teare, R. and Ingram, H. (1994), *Strategic Management: A Resource-Based Approach for the Hospitality and Tourism Industries,* Cassell, London and New York, NY, pp. ii-iv.

Teare, R. and Owen, D. (1996), "Driving top line profitability through the management of human resources", in Kotas, R., Teare, R., Logie, J., Jayawardena, C. and Bowen, J.T. (Eds), *The International Hospitality Business,* Cassell, London and New York, NY, pp. 185-90.

Teare, R., Anderson, A. and Gray R. (1997c), "TQ Dyane: a new technical process and procedure at Perkins Engines, Peterborough", in Teare, R., Scheuing, E., Atkinson, C. and Westwood, C. (Eds), *Teamworking and Quality Improvement: Lessons from British and North American Organizations*, Cassell, London and New York, NY, pp. 67-83.

Teare, R., Armistead, C. and Eccles, G. (1996b), "Services management: emerging patterns in industry and education", *International Journal of Contemporary Hospitality Management,* Vol. 8 No. 4, pp. 33-4.

Teare, R., Scheuing, E. and Armistead, C. (1996a), "Teamworking and quality performance improvement: lessons from UK and US-based firms", in Edvardsson, B., Brown, S.W., Johnston, R. and Scheuing, E.E. (Eds), *Advancing Service Quality: A Global Perspective,* International Service Quality Association Inc. New York, NY, pp. 57-66.

Teare, R., Bosselman, R.H., Chon, K.S. and Costa, J. (1996c), "A review of graduate education and research in hospitality and tourism management", *International Journal of Contemporary Hospitality Management,* Vol. 8 No. 4, pp. 37-40.

Teare, R., Ingram, H., Scheuing, E. and Armistead, C. (1997b), "Organizational teamworking frameworks: evidence from UK and US-based firms", *International Journal of Service Industry Management,* Vol. 8 No. 3, pp. 250-63.

Teare R., Scheuing E., Atkinson, C. and Westwood, C. (Eds) (1997a), *Teamworking and Quality Improvement: Lessons from British and North American Organizations,* Cassell, London and Washington, DC.

Wills, G. (1993), *Your Enterprise School of Management,* MCB University Press, Bradford.

Appendix
Sources of satisfaction and dissatisfaction with Internet sites
Satisfiers
(1) super-fast;
(2) predictable;
(3) interesting content – "I don't care how interesting the content is, if the site is slow, I'm gone".
(1) easily navigable pages with plenty of page breaks so I don't have to scroll;
(2) interesting, relevant articles;
(3) ASCII text (rather than PDFs on my machine).
(1) short pages;
(2) excellent graphic design;

(3)   easy to find, relevant content;
(4)   sites that know what they are doing.
(1)   references to books or articles I haven't heard of;
(2)   people posing pointed questions – reminds me that "received wisdom" isn't the only source;
(3)   humour – it makes the people behind the forum real;
(4)   a sense of community – evidence that the forum is put together by several people working as a team;
(5)   literacy – it's heartening to read well written text and communications;
(6)   questions and answers;
(7)   other people's e-mail addresses – people I wouldn't necessarily know or come into contact with;
(8)   the opportunity to promote own ideas and services.
(1)   a global village feel – having neighbours worldwide and being able to talk to them (on a given subject) and find out what's going on elsewhere;
(2)   finding obscure information quickly – without leaving my desk;
(3)   a new marketing medium – a forum is the place to promote relevant services to a community of users.
(1)   links to a world community of practitioners and academics in an industry-specific area;
(2)   hyper-text linking of "associations", "education", "government", and "industry", WWW sites relating to an industry-specific area (in support of industry-academia links);
(3)   database and archive access, including "grey literature", supplied by industry.

Dissatisfiers

(1)   cluttered pages with too much activity;
(2)   images and graphics that add no value at all;
(3)   registration pages (unless there is an incentive to "enter here");
(4)   downloadable software – something always seems to go wrong whilst I'm trying to obtain it;
(5)   arrows that point up when I've spent ten minutes coming down.
(1)   long lists of ill thought-out links;
(2)   pages that grow and grow;
(3)   registration pages;
(4)   sites where you get lost;
(5)   bored;
(6)   irritated;
(7)   sites that include cryptic comments.
(1)   having to follow too many links (probably more than one) to get the information – I'd gladly trade this off against a slightly longer download time as my browser occasionally crashes mid-link and I have to start all over again;
(2)   computer security and computer hackers.
(1)   under construction signs (if the site or page isn't ready, why link it?);
(2)   image maps (ages to download, present badly on 16 colour monitors);
(3)   no/missing e-mail references;
(4)   restricted access and registration pages on free sites;
(5)   browsers that don't recognize HTML in a consistent way.
(1)   sites that are high on design, low on content;
(2)   sporadic updating;
(3)   compuspeak and Internet jargon – assumes that everyone knows what you mean.
(1)   pages that are too busy – including overuse of animated graphics;
(2)   "Please visit our sponsor", signs;
(3)   poorly executed HTML (all work should meet the specification for HTML 2.0);
(4)   poor creative design and unnavigable Web pages.

Chapter 12

Implementing virtual support for workplace learning

Richard Teare

Granada Professor, Oxford Brookes University and Academic Chair,
International Management Centres

Introduction

> There is an urgent need for a concerted effort to boost the capabilities of the UK workforce...
> IPPR argues that the University for Industry should not be a new institution that competes
> with other providers of education and training. For maximum impact, it should serve to
> extend existing and emerging provision to people, where, when and how it is most convenient.
> Everyone, in the workplace, the home, or in local centres in the community, should have
> lifelong access to a galaxy of supported learning activities at the levels they need. This
> requires the University for Industry to act as the hub on a national learning network, to broker
> high-quality materials and service, and to motivate people to exploit burgeoning
> opportunities. ("University for Industry: Creating a national learning network", Institute for
> Public Policy Research (IPPR), Report overview, 1996)

The aim of this article is to review the prospects and potential for meeting
industry-specific learning and development needs with particular reference to a
"University for Industry" initiative for hospitality and tourism. Its design and
implementation draws on a global industry forum and its infrastructure
provides: an access point for workplace learning programmes; a resource for
addressing project and personal updating needs; a reference point for training
and internal corporate communications (via intranet) and a means of
interacting with "communities of interest" (e.g. industry-education linkages) via
virtual conferencing on key issues and trends and future scenarios. To realize
their potential, global industry forums will need to provide an array of real time
"current awareness" material coupled with "archive" resources and it is thought
that on-going development might be financed by member subscriptions,
advertising and sponsorships. Beyond this, the wider role of knowledge
generators and distributors (publishers, media and telecommunications
owners) is considered in relation to the future of on-line business learning with
interactive services such as "pay as you go" printing of database articles,
textbooks and other learning resources. The next logical step will be to
integrate internet-based resources and video-based media and so the concept of
an interactive television channel for business learning is outlined. It is argued
that fast, low cost access to on-line business knowledge using broadcast and
telecommunications technologies offers unlimited scope and commercial
potential for joint venture partners in workplace learning.

This article first appeared in *The Journal of Workplace Learning,* Vol. 10 No. 2, 1998, pp. 122-137.

Developments in Internet-based resource support for workplace learning

It is generally accepted that the dawning of an "information age" coincides with the phenomenal growth of personal computer access and ownership during the 1990s. Recent advances in information technology and its relatively low cost application to computing in the workplace and the home has reinforced the ownership trend. The means of distributing information has changed too – first came CD-ROM-based material, now established as the most cost-effective means of distributing software and archiving data and then, the Internet. It seems likely that electronic communications will revolutionize organizational behaviour during the late 1990s and Table I profiles the range of Internet-based developments currently occurring in support of workplace learning.

Authors	Focus	Sub-theme
Sandelands and Wills (1996)	Presents a "virtual university" model as a means of supporting lifelong learning. Discusses the creation, maintenance and distribution of courseware, accessing current and archival literature, programme supervision and the role of a community of learning	Creating electronic courseware resources
Wills (1995)	Sees a future where interactive multimedia products and services are the norm and describes how MCB University Press has managed a transition from print to electronic publishing. Sees authors as a constant point of reference with the growth on networked PCs	The future of electronic publishing
Wills and Wiles (1995/96)	Describes the leading-learning strategy adopted by MCB University Press since 1991 when it established the Literati Club for its authors and editors. Five years later, it has positioned the company as a world-class publisher on the Internet.	Electronic publishing implications for authors and editors
Davies (1996)	Outlines the procedures used and the benefits derived from an Internet conference on telecommuting. Notes that organizations that manage by results are better able to manage telecommuters as they will concentrate on outputs rather than on how people do their job	Telecommuting in the electronic age
Peters (1995/96)	Discusses electronic peer review of academic papers on the Internet and concludes that electronic review is likely to influence the review process, making it more open and developmental and less judgemental	Electronic peer review
Sandelands (1997)	Observes the increasing influence of new communications technologies on information transfer and business practices, and highlights features of the Internet which could prove essential for marketing managers and academic researchers	Utilizing the Internet for marketing success
Ainslie and Wills (1997)	Action learning (AL) requires a "deconstructed" curriculum so that the customer can drive its re-creation. Provides a case analysis of International Management Centres' (IMC) journey of dynamic continuous quality improvement in support of its AL programmes	Internet-based quality assurance of action learning programmes

Table I.
Electronic learning resource support for workplace learning

Sandelands (1997) points out that the Internet population has diversified in various ways during the past ten years or so: "What was once the preserve of the scientists and engineers is now being embraced by a plethora of providers and users". This in part, is due to the key characteristics of internet communications: it enables genuine, two-way communication and it enables information resources to be acquired or projected relatively easily. Sandelands lists the growing range of communication services available to Internet users and these include:

- E-mail to transfer text and multimedia messages.
- Listserves to communicate with groups of Internet users and update them on latest information on specific topics.
- Newsgroups that support electronic conferencing and open information exchange.
- The World Wide Web that provides menu-driven access to an endless array of Web sites and on-line resources.

Commenting on the changes that are occurring in the use of electronic media, Sandelands (1997) observes that CD-ROM-based electronic information is comparatively straightforward to deliver and easy to access and use. At best, archived material will have been reviewed, edited and classified to enable the user to optimize information retrieval using intuitive, menu driven options and reasonably precise search keywords. The information source is tangible and finite until superseded by the latest update. Further, there is no on-line time, so the cost of access is known beforehand and can be accurately predicted for budgeting purposes. A CD-ROM can also be networked within or even beyond a single organization and so the cost per user is low. However, CD-ROM-based technology has its limitations and like the paper-based materials it replaces, it is out of date even before it is installed on the user's system. Nor is it interactive in the sense that users can add their own contributions to the knowledge archive that it contains or access on-line services such as full text document ordering of archived literature abstracts. This lack of flexibility means that Internet access to "real time" information such as current awareness material (as well as archive material) and related hyper-links to supplier sites offers user options that were until quite recently, difficult or even impossible to provide. These and other considerations led MCB University Press (MCB-UP), the world's largest publisher of management journals, to invest in a major electronic publishing initiative. Wills (1995) lists the three broad-ranging questions that MCB-UP set out to explore:

- What might be the formulation of mainstream knowledge and information electronic products and services in the future? Will it be articles *per se*, collections/issues or keyworded abstracts leading to full publication and interactive contact?

- What will be the channels of capture, transformation and dissemination through which the products and services will flow, that is, the future of publishing logistics?

- What will be the transformed framework and ownership of the incoming supply chain of knowledge and information from, and in interaction with, authors?

In pursuit of answers to these questions, Wills defines electronic publishing as: "Conceiving, creating, capturing, transforming, disseminating, archiving, searching and retrieving academic and professional knowledge and information". He foresees a number of scenarios and likely outcomes as the transition from paper-based to electronic publishing gathers pace. In market terms, the networking of offices and homes will extend market reach to the point whereby a dearth of knowledge and information products and services will occur. He sees parallels here with the advent of digital broadcasting and the consequent "problem" of sourcing sufficient TV programme content to attract a viewing audience, now accustomed to a multiplicity of choice, throughout the day and night. The authors who generate materials for publication will inevitably want to make use of whatever medium or media mix optimizes their goals of publication to their chosen market. This will include options to access literature by searching and retrieval and to refine their own work through peer group processes, either by conferring or by review. Of prime importance to academic authors is that their work receives high level accreditation after it has been published and so on-line abstracting services such as Anbar Management Intelligence, owned by MCB-UP has responded by building accredited lists of the journals it abstracts.

Sandelands (1997) lists the benefits of MCB-UP's Internet access for authors and users of the on-line materials they produce and these are shown in Table II.

The reality of Internet capabilities and electronic publishing mean that the concept of a "virtual university" as a means of supporting life-long learning can be readily implemented. Sandelands and Wills (1996) and Sandelands (1997) list the main features of IMC's Internet-based, action learning programmes as they relate to the procedures used by students (or Associates) and their tutors:

- All faculty and course participants (Associates) are required to have access to the Internet at home and/or at work.

- Courseware is created, delivered, maintained and updated as an Internet resource. The "open architecture" courseware design means that all topic areas use searchable keywords. All reading lists are updated at six monthly intervals (or sooner with automated updates) using the keywords from the Anbar thesaurus to pinpoint the latest relevant additions to the Anbar Management Intelligence database.

- All Associates and tutors have access to an on-line library of current and archive published material. The Anbar Management Intelligence database provides categorized and star-rated abstracts of articles reviewed by subject specialists from a defined coverage list of more than 400 accredited academic and professional journals. Computer desk-top access to Anbar is provided by Internet and full-text articles can be ordered electronically and supplied by fax or post from the British Library. Additionally, tutors and Associates can access full text on-line, provided by MCB-UP (its full text product is called Emerald) and similar services provided by other publishers.

- Associates and tutors communicate with each other via dedicated newsgroups (known as Set meeting places) and the meeting place enables tutors to brief the learning Set prior to a meeting, provide feedback, receive and answer questions and for the course participants to share ideas and engage in structured group discussion. Further, associates in any given learning Set can visit many other meeting places, each supporting a learning set in different parts of the world.

- Journal sponsored electronic conferences at MCB's virtual conference centre enable Associates and tutors to join debates with academics and managers who themselves are participating in the virtual university network that exists at the periphery of the participants' course.

Authors
- Immediate access to a world library using customer-designed search criteria
- The advice of fellow authors can be sought prior to publication via MCB-UP's Literati Club
- Author support services are provided to help ensure that ideas and research findings are presented as effectively as possible
- Electronic peer review procedures speed up the publication process allowing "blind refereeing" at twice the normal speed
- The continuous Internet publishing initiative means immediate publication once the article has been accepted by the editor
- The published work reaches a mass audience and can be purchased as a single article as well as within a journal collection
- Information is networked across organizations, so that wider reach and "opportunities to see" the article occurs
- Assistance is available for academics to launch their own electronic journals

Readers:
- Immediate access to the latest literature is possible
- Search criteria defined by the user enable precise targeting of individual articles and other information
- Listserve updates are available to readers so that they are automatically informed of newly published articles in subscriber areas of interest
- Readers can "talk" directly to academics and professionals worldwide via MCB journal sponsored electronic conferences
- Knowledge forums in functional and industry-specific areas provide an array of services and links to professional associations
- The body of knowledge is related to workplace learning so that readers can follow up areas of interest and enrol on practitioner qualification programmes (with IMC)

Table II.
Benefits of author and reader Internet access to on-line articles

Source: adapted from Sandelands (1997, p. 9)

- The Internet provides an ideal forum for keeping in touch with IMC's Alumni and for past associates to keep in touch with each other, wherever they happen to work.

This combination of features provides a well structured and supportive learning environment for Associates undertaking a formal programme of learning. In building on the notion of learner support, MCB University Press has sought to support the on-line needs of its customers by crafting a themed series of meeting points for specific interest groups. The next section profiles this development and considers the wider implications for workplace learners.

Resourcing global forums

The concept of a forum as a meeting place for Associates undertaking workplace learning is outlined in Chapter 8, with specific reference to the author's involvement with BAA Plc. The purpose here is to outline the developments in thinking and practice that have led to the definition of a standard set of design inputs and the routinization of procedures for implementing and maintaining forums at MCB University Press. Forum structure draws on publishing resources, principally journals, abstracts and articles to support interactive services such as virtual conferencing and on-line workshops run by subject specialists.

MCB University Press (at http://www.mcb.co.uk/mcbhome.htm) provide a one-stop destination for on-line information services and an access point to a world library of management literature and applications. The site includes on-line searchable databases (abstracts and articles) in management and other specialist areas (Anbar Electronic Intelligence); a detailed portfolio of 150 + journals in management, applied science and technology and 98 on-line journals (Emerald). The site includes tailored services and resources for MCB's subscribers and authors and for librarians, practitioners, academics and researchers and an array of global forums that draw on the full range of electronic resources to support categories (or communities of interest) in:

- publishing;
- geographical regions;
- functional disciplines; and
- industry sector and professional areas.

The MCB homepage invites visitors to use its open access interactive services (virtual conference centre, global forums):

> …where you can participate in, and influence, discussion on key issues and innovative ideas. These international meeting places are sponsored by the world's leading management journals and provide a unique environment for academics and practitioners to come together for debate, current awareness and research. Share your experiences and views – learn from others (and share with)…management communities worldwide.

The general approach is to provide a cluster of category-related resources that combine print and electronic publishing materials, searchable database services (abstracts and articles) and interactive services and other activities via a newsgroup infrastructure inside each forum. While the sources differ, the services and means of resourcing them have been routinized with the aim of providing:

- Latest news and views from experts...
- Access to specific information on practices and procedures in the field of interest...
- Access to research data, analysis and interpretation (where practicable)...
- Views on latest publications in the field (including book reviews)...
- Access to journal publications in the field...
- Advice, guidance, support and practical solutions (via facilitated question/answer workshop sessions)...
- Worldwide advertising and recruitment services...
- Worldwide virtual conferencing...
- Advice and instant access (via hyper-text links) to other useful Internet sites...

(1) Publishing forums
MCB is the world's largest publisher of management journals for practitioners and academics and has sought over many years to build and maintain close links with the stakeholders in journals publishing. Its Literati Club offers a meeting point for authors and a means of focusing debates about writing and "getting published". The Club's author services are founded upon MCB's extensive database of authors and this can be searched and segmented in numerous ways. For example, the database can be used to identify development opportunities (such as new journal launches) and ways of implementing services for subscribers, librarians, authors and editorial teams – all of whom are customers with distinctive interests and needs. Similar forums have been established for librarians (the Library Link Forum and a regional Asian Libraries Forum). As customers use and subscribe to electronic publishing services, they become more interested in the range of possibilities for using the Internet to publish and to communicate with others interested in a given subject or vocational area. MCB has responded by establishing two forums to enable interested parties to learn more about the internet and the opportunities it affords (Internet Free Press; Internet Research Forum). In part, the aim is to enable those who are sufficiently interested to publish and even establish their own electronic journals in association with MCB University Press:

- *Internet Free Press.* Supported by MCB University Press, the forum aims to facilitate wider access to electronic publishing.

- *Internet Research Forum.* A one-stop forum for information about the Internet, World Wide Web, newsgroups, html and other useful information about accessing and using Internet services worldwide.

- *The Library Link Forum.* Open to librarians worldwide, the forum provides priority access to information that can assist library users in their research and librarians in their day to day work.

- *Literati Club.* The meeting place for all those who write for MCB University Press with a database of around 15,000 authors worldwide.

(2) Regional forums

As a multinational business with a substantial proportion of its journal subscriptions outside the UK, the evolving typology of forums includes an aspiration to reflect the distinctive needs and developments in geographical regions. The concept of a regional forum has been successfully prototyped in South East Asia and the Asia Pacific Management Forum (APMF) is a mature, critically acclaimed site. Regional forums not only provide a focal point for people living and working in a given region but a place where practitioners and academics from other parts of the world can learn more about a country (Japanese Management Today) or region (APMF). Further, a regional forum offers the prospect of enabling those engaged in workplace learning programmes in a given region to interact and network with people working in similar or different organizations in their own geographical area:

- *Asian Libraries Forum.* A meeting place for librarians in the Asia Pacific region and for those with an interest in library resources and Internet sites in the region.

- *Asia Pacific Management Forum.* An award-winning site that provides resources and networking services for those interested in Asia Pacific business and management issues, contacts and current events.

- *Japanese Management Today.* Aims to reflect debate and discussion and to examine the evolving patterns and practices of Japanese management styles and techniques.

(3) Functional forums

A key development in support of workplace learning and journal subscribers, authors and readers is the launch of a series of functional, discipline-based forums. This is a logical extension of MCB's journals portfolio as each forum draws upon a cluster of existing journals. In so doing, it draws in authors and readers who bring with them a corpus of expertise that can be harnessed so as to drive the interactive services and in particular, the virtual conferencing. Extracts from the Convenors' introduction to the Global Forum for Marketing & Logistics reinforce this:

Who we are and Why we are here…in Cyberspace

The Marketing and Logistics (M & L) Forum is established by MCB University Press to provide an excellent "first stop" for marketing and logistics professionals, academics and learners in these fields.

There are two key dimensions to what can be found here:

(1) Dynamic current awareness "buzz" including "latest" issues and "newest" ideas

(2) A resource and archive section featuring a body of professional and academic knowledge

In offering these services, MCB University Press will be making full use of the resources it has in these areas – nearly a score of world class journals, available on-line in our Emerald service with full text and abstract search engines....to encompass other resources, you will find that M&L's Convenors have looked far and wide. We have pinpointed and graded "Coolsites" about marketing and logistics; we have via the Anbar Management Intelligence service with the support of the British Library, abstracted many other top class marketing and logistics journals – and full text is available worldwide by fax/airmail via our unique alliance with the British Library.

The dynamics are added weekly – so it well worth bookmarking the M&L Forum for a weekly visit. But more than that…we want you to visit the M&L Virtual Conferencing workshops and add comments to them as they proceed – better still, volunteer to host one yourself and get the proceedings edited for subsequent publication in one of the several journals we have. And if that is not enough, or you think all journals should be e-journals, GO to our Internet Free Press and start your own. We will give you all the guidance we can and your can join the growing list there already.

…we (also) have a couple of "satirical" columns from Mungo Park and Burke & Wills at which the more bizarre aspects of marketing and logistics will be chronicled from time to time. Have a browse, drop a line. The more bizarre the better..The first you will see is M&L explorations at large; the second will seek to cover the M&L of using the Internet – for selling or database marketing or whatever M&L usages we can discern…

So please look, enjoy and join in as often as you can. This site is for all with a genuine professional and academic interest in Marketing and Logistics. Where we fall short, tell us and preferably volunteer to join in and put it right…

Gordon Wills
Convener in Chief

The current suite of functional forums also includes: financial management; human resources; information management; operations and production; property management; quality management and strategic management (TopMan Global Forum):

- *Financial Management & Services Global Forum.* Aims to provide coverage of developments in the broad-ranging field of financial services and service industries more generally.

- *Human Resources (HR) Global Forum.* A meeting place for human resources and training professionals.

- *Information Management Global Forum.* Aims to examine the role of information in assisting businesses to stay competitive and the many issues related to using and managing information personally, professionally and in organizational settings.

- *The Global Forum for Marketing & Logistics.* Current awareness, interactive services and a comprehensive resource archive of material for practitioners, academics, authors and others interested in marketing and logistics.

- *Operations & Production Global Forum.* Provides an international meeting place for senior managers, decision makers and academics interested in all aspects of operations and production.

- *Property Management Global Forum.* An international forum for those with a personal or professional interest in property management issues and commercial considerations.

- *Global QualNet Forum.* An international forum for those with a personal or professional interest in quality management issues and applications.

- *TopMan Global Forum.* An international meeting place for senior management interested in exploring aspects of strategy and business development via articles and facilitated discussion and tailored study programmes.

(4) Industry and professional forums
While industry-specific forums do relate to MCB's journals portfolio they also reflect the programmes run in conjunction with IMC. Here, the concept of a "themed" access point to generic workplace learning materials has been pioneered in partnership with BAA Plc (Airport Business Forum) and Fina Plc (Petrochemicals Forum). In anticipation of further learning partnerships with organizations operating in different industry sectors, other forums have been established in hospitality and tourism, education and health care and environmental studies. A further logical step is to extend forum coverage to professional and vocational areas (such as police studies and Christian ministry) provided that overlaps with industry sector initiatives can be avoided and distinctive and appropriate resources can be identified and embedded. This category of forums may well help to "capture" aspects of "new" practitioner knowledge and expertise that has yet to be formalized and disseminated in literature form. For instance, over the next 18 months the aim is to establish an electronic journal in Airport Business Management founded in part, on the assignment and project work undertaken by Associates employed by BAA Plc:

- *Airport Business Forum.* Developed in association with airport owners and operators, BAA Plc, the ABF supports a range of action learning programmes and aspires to become a hub of knowledge, expertise and current thinking in airport management and related areas.

- *Hospitality & Tourism Global Forum.* Provides on-line access to the worldwide hospitality and tourism trends databases and annual review and a virtual academy series related to functional discipline areas in hospitality and tourism facilitated by an international team of academics.

- *Global Education Forum*. A first stop for educationists and others interested in all aspects of education.
- *Global Health Care & Environment Forum*. Aims to provide a first stop for practitioners, academics and professionals interested in the health care industry and the field of environmental studies.
- *Petrochemicals Forum*. Developed in association with the petrochemicals company, Fina Plc., the PCF supports a range of action learning programmes and aspires to become a hub of industry knowledge, expertise and current management thinking.
- *Global Forum for Police Studies*. Provides an international meeting place for professionals and academics interested in law enforcement and the administration and management of police services.

The interrelationships between functional and industry forums are depicted in Figure 1.

Relating forums to workplace learning: from courseware to learnerware

Electronic publishing resources fit naturally with on-line business learning and updating and so a progressive extension of the forum concept is to integrate their design with IMC's Internet-based courseware resources. The current IMC courseware model uses abstracts and readings from the Anbar Electronic

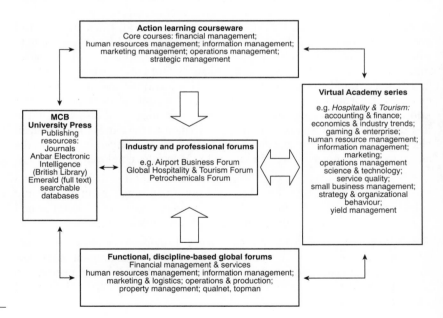

Figure 1.
Relating industry forums to workplace learning

Intelligence databases and recent technological advances mean that embedded abstracts and readings can be automatically updated – re-vitalizing programmed knowledge on a weekly basis if need be, so that it is never outdated. This is a revolutionary breakthrough in resource-based learning materials. It utilizes the power of technology to ensure that "classic" works and "latest" theory and application can be selected, filtered and retained or replaced at any time, such that courseware becomes a dynamic resource, drawing on the best possible range of subject-specific readings and applications.

In this development context, courseware units are no longer viewed as free-standing resources but as a basis or platform for exploring internet connectivities with hyper-linked resources such as subject or industry-related "cool sites" (Anbar quality-rated and classified Web sites) and other forums. In essence, hyper-linked courseware enables the user to print material on demand, read and absorb subject overviews, pose questions and/or respond to them by visiting cross-referenced Web sites that offer virtual case study illustrations and applications. For example, links to the Market Research Society (MRS) Web site from marketing courseware might enable users to view and participate in MRS activities on-line. Similarly, generic courseware units can be "themed" by adding links to industry-specific applications. Aspects of marketing promotion might be applied to a hospitality industry setting by embedding links to one or more hotel chain Web sites so that the learner is able to explore familiar, Web-based applications. In this way, courseware takes on an added dimension and becomes a starting point for wider exploration by following the embedded hyper-links.

Assuming that the learner adopts a proactive (rather than a reactive) approach it is possible to glean an array of "added value" information and enrich the learning process by drawing on World Wide Web "signposting" (see Figure 2).

At best, this approach enables workplace learners to travel from "Q" (questioning) to "P" (programmed knowledge) and back again via a cycle that involves capturing and disseminating real time knowledge from the forums. The cycle termed here a "learnerware" process is depicted as an unbroken circle of information shared dynamically via Set meetings, on-line conferences and virtual academy workshops which in turn feed into print and electronic journals, Anbar, new cool site entries and from here, into courseware updates. These elements should not be seen in isolation neither in virtual space or printed space, but as a whole, feeding mutually on each other. The learnerware process is especially helpful in capturing and formalizing practitioner knowledge. The airport business is a good example of a comparatively new, fast-paced, rapidly expanding and sophisticated industry. Managing an airport is rather similar to managing a town or in the case of Heathrow, a city and there are many communities of interest – some that overlap, some that converge and some that conflict. BAA Plc is the UK's largest owner and operator of airports – the equivalent of the UK population (in passenger numbers) passes through Heathrow alone, every year. Yet, there are few textbook or journal sources that

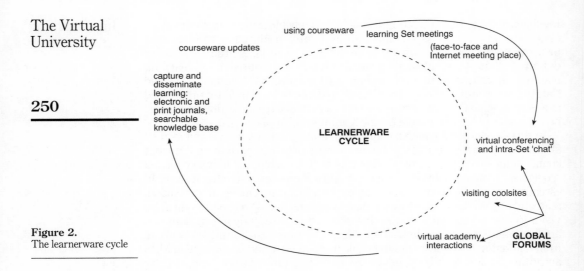

Figure 2.
The learnerware cycle

deal with the complexities of managing airports in the late 1990s and beyond. The programmes with BAA therefore offer a significant opportunity to facilitate managerial and organizational learning and to capture and disseminate the considerable body of knowledge and expertise that exists inside the organization. The dynamics of capturing knowledge in the form of assignments written by BAA managers and making them available via a searchable on-line database is currently under investigation. Termed "project harvest" the aim is to construct and build-up a practitioner knowledge base that will augment the learnerware cycle. As it is implemented, some of the material will be published and an electronic journal (the Airport Business) will be set-up at the Airport Business Forum.

The contextualization of learning and the means of extending generic areas of study by implementing the learnerware process, may well provide a tangible way of developing the action learning paradigm and optimizing return on investment for the learner and his or her sponsoring organization (see Figure 3). In so doing, it is important that the learner is able to utilize the whole of the learnerware cycle to its fullest extent so that objectives for personal learning and future development, career aspirations and enhanced visibility (via actionable project assignments) are achieved. While the formula for action learning remains unchanged (L = P + Q) there is little doubt that the inputs and outputs associated with programmed knowledge will be greatly enhanced by the added dimensions of searchable and hyper-linked on-line knowledge available from the global forums that are currently under development.

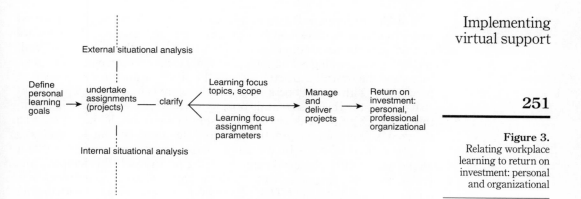

External situational analysis

| Define personal learning goals | undertake assignments (projects) | clarify | Learning focus topics, scope / Learning focus assignment parameters | Manage and deliver projects | Return on investment: personal, professional organizational |

Internal situational analysis

Figure 3.
Relating workplace
learning to return on
investment: personal
and organizational

Resourcing the Hospitality and Tourism Global Forum

> I am encouraged to hear of the progress you are making on this and other initiatives for tourism and hospitality. It is vital that we ensure that graduates are equipped with the skills this growing industry needs.
>
> (Chris Smith, Secretary of State, Department for Culture, Media and Sport, personal letter to the author, July 1997)

The final sections of this article focus on the application of virtual support for workplace learning in the hospitality and tourism industries. Taken together, they are reputed to be the world's fastest growing industries, encompassing the commercial provision of accommodation and catering and related travel, transport and leisure infrastructures, services, facilities and products. The principles of programme design outlined in the prior piece "Developing a curriculum for organizational learning", as does the routinized approach to forum design and resourcing outlined above. But to ensure the relevance and value of the resources provided, and to maximize the Forum's potential as a "first stop" Web site, a series of challenges need to be addressed. These are presented here in the form of several action plans and key steps that constitute the author's agenda for implementing a "University for Industry" initiative.

Forum overview: goals and actions

The Hospitality and Tourism Global Forum (HTGF) aims to become the international hub for workplace learning programmes offered by IMC and its joint venture partners. A key challenge for Forum Conveners is to attract and retain an "active" core of visitors who will help to generate "buzz" and momentum and in so doing, attract others. The Appendix lists and describes the current suite of resources, which coupled with the virtual academy series described in the "Developing a curriculum..." piece, provide the basic infrastructure needed to support electronic conferencing on key issues and questions, viewpoints, global networking and debate.

The Airport Business Forum provides a good example of "buzz" as it is used weekly and in some cases daily by a group of nearly 50 managers. The presence and active participation of managers who routinely use the site to "chat" with each other via learning Set meeting places and to access courseware resources, increases the overall attractiveness of the site to academics interested in networking with practitioners. The goal therefore is to engineer a feeling of "balance" at the HTGF so that theorizing is tempered by pragmatism and in this way, each grouping draws out the best from each other. In the longer term, the goal is to encourage practitioners to pose questions and academics to suggest or find solutions by way of re-focusing academic research so that it aligns with industry's agenda and emerging priorities. If this happens, the prospect of a meaningful industry-education partnership in applied research is a realistic one, with the HTGF playing out the key roles of "networking facilitator" "broker" and "deal-maker". At this point, practitioners will readily see the "value added" from participating in forum discussions and academics will "learn" from industry and adjust their own research agendas so that they are acceptable and in time, wholly welcomed by industry. This scenario is far removed at the present moment as UK colleges and universities stand accused of "academic drift". Industry is flexing its collective muscle in criticising the structure, content and outcomes of "static" curricula largely designed and delivered by academics who the industry claim are "out of touch" (British Hospitality Association, 1997).

To accomplish these two mutually dependent goals – to become the international hub for workplace learning programmes and the arbiter and "broker" of an industry-education partnership worldwide, several action plans have been identified and developed. In overview, the aims are as follows:

- To contexualize the body of knowledge accessible from the HTGF. This is to be achieved in partnership with the Hotel and Catering International Management Association (HCIMA) and its Worldwide Hospitality and Tourism Trends (WHATT) project.

  Worldwide Hospitality & Tourism Trends is an HCIMA project with research centres in Europe, North America and Australia. The Annual Review is published by MCB University Press and Cassell plc (London & Herndon, VA) with sponsor support. Participation is encouraged via the Worldwide Hospitality and Tourism Trends Forum at http://www.mcb.co.uk/htgfwhatt/ (for subscription details, the full text article service and contributions in the form of abstracts and contact details from analysts and researchers) and the Hospitality and Tourism Global Forum at http://www.mcb.co.uk/htg/

- To stimulate widescale interaction between senior practitioners and academics. The task is to link the HTGF to an annual, industry sponsored Investment Conference in Europe and thereafter to similar, well established events held in New York and Los Angeles.

A service to the European Investment Conference organized by Hotel Partners International in association with BDO Hospitality Consulting and Hotel and Motel Management magazine, with active participation in discerning and capturing industry themes (concerns, opportunities, industry issues and market trends) as they happen via the Hospitality and Tourism Global Forum (see URL: http://www.mcb.co.uk/htgf/).

Assuming that the forum resources are in place, that they have been augmented and contextualized to support industry programmes of workplace learning and that the forum is attracting practitioners and academics interested in crafting future scenarios and an industry-led research agenda – what next? Beyond this lies a significant challenge – that of creating and maintaining a network of joint venture partnerships with industry and professional associations, media and telecommunications owners and other educational providers – in effect, a University for Industry initiative for hospitality and tourism – worldwide.

Implementing a university for industry initiative for hospitality and tourism

I was particularly interested to hear of your project to develop a workplace learning initiative for tourism and hospitality, using the Internet. This Government gives the highest priority to encouraging participation in learning through life and I welcome initiatives to widen access to education and training.

(Chris Smith, Secretary of State, Department for Culture, Media and Sport, personal letter to the author, July 1997)

The UK Government has been exploring the possibilities of establishing a "University for Industry (UfI) for some time. A recent report by the Institute for Public Policy Research (Hillman, 1996) presents the case for a "radical initiative" which would:

- be the hub of a national learning network extending to workplaces, homes and local learning centres
- act as a cataloguer and broker of information, materials, courses and services
- provide access to user-friendly services on the internet and create links with tutors, experts and other learners
- commission new learning programmes in strategic areas
- sustain an accessible system of support and guidance services
- stimulate mass-marketing of learning opportunities.

While ambitious, these goals are achievable but the sheer scale and complexity of responding to the opportunities for learning in "workplaces, homes and local learning centres" would suggest that the learning network infrastructure will be difficult to assemble, co-ordinate and direct – most certainly in the short term. It is however, viable and desirable to launch such an initiative by building on what has been achieved by MCB University, IMC and their joint venture

partners in the form of a UfI for hospitality and tourism. Writing for
Parliamentary Review magazine, Tom Clarke, Minister for Tourism, sets out his
priorities for education:

> I want to discuss with colleagues in the Department for Education and Employment and the
> industry how the courses on offer may be better geared to produce people with the business
> skills and abilities which the industry so desperately needs...there is anecdotal evidence that
> most of the students who study tourism and leisure at university eventually find their way
> into another career. If that is true, I want to know the reasons why and how we can ensure that
> the courses are made more relevant to the industry's requirements.
>
> (*Source:* cited in "Colleges face mounting criticism of 'academic drift'", British Hospitality
> Association, August, 1997)

While the debate rages about the nature and delivery of college and university-
based curricula, the vast majority of managers, supervisors and operatives
working in hospitality and tourism jobs are excluded from the "just in time"
development they so evidently need and deserve. The contention of this report
has been that a prospectus for organizational learning in the workplace is long
overdue and that the time is right and the delivery technology is available to
implement such an initiative. In so doing, there are principally two challenges:

- To enlist the active participation of the major industry and professional
  associations. Key roles are to accredit, endorse, promote and assist in
  administering the learning network for hospitality and tourism –
  worldwide.
- To harness "state of the art" broadcast and communications technology.
  The aim being to ensure low cost, fast, reliable and stable access to
  interactive on-line learning resources in the workplace and the home.

*Action plan: enlisting the active participation of industry and professional
associations*

> A University for Industry hospitality and tourism learning partnership – worldwide.
> Validated by the International Management Centres in association with its partner
> universities, accredited by the Hotel and Catering International Management Association
> (HCIMA) and endorsed by the British Hospitality Association (BHA). Workplace learning
> programmes will offer direct entry to Master's level programmes for HCIMA Members and to
> Doctoral level study for HCIMA Fellows.

While graduates can apply for full Membership status of the HCIMA (the
world's largest professional association for hospitality managers, with 23,000
members) as soon as they have acquired two years of managerial experience,
the current reality is that many experienced and successful hospitality
managers are not able to gain entry to full Member status because they lack
academic qualifications.

The initiative involves a number of related action lines which include the
adoption of a "credit mapping" methodology (Davies, 1997) so that clear and
actionable guidelines are provided for credit rating the outcomes of training
courseware. The purpose of this is to provide industry with the necessary tools
and techniques to inter-link their existing training materials and programmes

to the action learning awards at undergraduate, graduate and postgraduate levels. In so doing, it becomes possible to "connect" training and management development and create a framework for career-long learning in the workplace. This offers the prospect of "just in time" development for all employees (prior to career moves and promotions) and the likelihood of greatly enhanced employee retention rates. The rationale is simply that by developing people in an appropriate and timely way, they will acquire a career-long learning habit and actively seek to improve their portfolio of skills and competences, sponsored by their employer. The employer sees results in the form of actionable outcomes from project work and improved managerial effectiveness, while the employee improves his or her prospects of promotion or enhanced responsibility, gains a qualification and in many cases, the elusive professional status they are seeking.

Action plan: harnessing "state of the art" broadcast and communications technology
In his recent book *Engendering Democratic Action* Gordon Wills offers a vision of virtual learning in the information society (Wills, 1997). He does this by telling a fictional story about the experiences of an academic and a consultant on study leave in Internetica. Extracts from the electronic postcards they send back to their colleagues at home ("E-postcards from the other side"). The key point he is making is that workplace learning is no longer "bounded" by the constraints of printed materials and that the Internet offers unlimited potential for "democratizing" knowledge and providing access to a world of learning opportunity and resources. Whilst the full potential of the Internet has yet to be exploited, its "newness" means that it is less than ideal as a vehicle for disseminating information. It is chaotic, unstructured and "clogged" with traffic and Wills likens its current state of development to the "silent movie" era. The next step is to add sound, colour and much improved all round resolution. It would help too if access was cheap, fast, stable and as convenient as possible – in fact, television is the ideal medium for most people who own or rent and use their TVs everyday, in every country and on every continent.
   In summary, the aim is to:

- Harness the full potential of the UfI hospitality and tourism network (scope, global reach, participation) and explore the wider possibilities of on-line business learning by drawing on the full range of global forums and electronic publishing resources;

- Achieve this by integrating internet-based resources and video-based media in a joint venture broadcast and telecommunications partnership;

- Establish an interactive television channel for business learning (as soon as the technology to do so is more widely available) and fund its development by personal subscription, commercial advertising, sponsorship and "pay as you go" instant printing of database articles, textbooks and other non-subscription resources (see Figure 4).

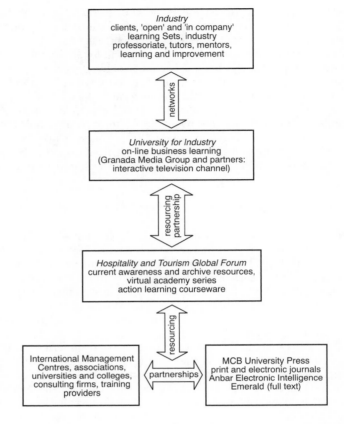

Figure 4.
A university for
industry (hospitality
and tourism) learning
network

The concept of such a service is founded upon the considerable actual and latent demand for convenient, easily accessible and searchable forms of on-line business learning. In essence, the service would enable subscribers to search and print materials from Anbar Electronic Intelligence, Emerald full text service and interact via the Global Forums. The added benefits of being able to search, select and play video material and other broadcast resources in the same way means that a mass market potential for supporting "real time" business updating and learning can be realized. Services might include: stock market and financial market news; project briefing guidelines using "latest" thinking and readings from the Forums and personal skills and knowledge updating using the on-line searchable databases. The collective resource also provides enhanced "state of the art" programmed knowledge for workplace learning including the interactive facilities needed to pose, explore and find answers to business challenges and options.

Summary: a vision for workplace learning in hospitality and tourism

Progress so far and the real prospect of implementing a UfI partnership framework founded on the principles of workplace learning, will bring with it a number of tangible benefits for employers, their employees and industry-education relations:

A universal access point for workplace learning programmes…
A partnership framework for industry and the associations with the active participation of many of the educational, training and consulting providers, will help to ensure that a corpus of knowledge and an industry-based curriculum becomes established and firmly embedded. Beyond this, the main challenge will be to refine and apply it so that the future challenges facing managers and their organizations in the world's fastest growing industry can be addressed.

A resource for addressing project and personal updating needs…
The concept of a Global Industry Forum though new, has numerous possibilities for interacting with others and accessing on-line resources for personal updating and re-skilling. Corporate responses to the "information age" and the growing importance of managerial and organizational "intellectual capital" suggests that career-long patterns of learning will assume greater importance. In this scenario, a personal commitment to lifelong learning is essential.

A reference point for training and internal corporate communications (via intranet)…
The artificial and unhelpful divide between training and management development will diminish as organizations establish their own frameworks for learning and "just in time" pathways for developing their human assets. The UfI initiative will seek to facilitate this by taking a holistic and inclusive view of prior qualifications, experience and expertise and by deploying tools and techniques for credit mapping and credit rating training courses. While the Global Forum offers a gateway to a wealth of external information and knowledge, the internal knowledge base will assume equal if not greater importance. Workplace learning can be used to leverage and optimize organizational "know how" capture it in assignment form and make it available by intranet inside the organization as a searchable knowledge resource. In this way, the return on investment in training and learning can be made tangible and shared as an internally networked resource.

A means of interacting with "communities of interest" via virtual conferencing on key issues and trends and future scenarios…
A drawback of organizationally-focused learning is that by its very nature, it tends to be inward-looking and bounded by cultural and behavioural norms. As a counter-balance to this, the external "one stop" gateway – the Global Hospitality and Tourism Forum – will encourage the widest possible form of

interchange – nationally, internationally and between the numerous communities of interest.

Self-financing development...
A UfI initiative founded on a network (rather than buildings, traditions and high running costs) means that it can and should be responsive, entrepreneurial and above all, innovative in nature. Its success depends on commitment, co-operation and the main outcome of action learning – improved managerial effectiveness. As these distinctive features of learning are adopted and understood, then industry will fund its development by sponsoring employees to undertake programmes, applied researchers to tackle more complex issues and use the network to promote their own successes.

These and other action lines, together with the commitment of industry, the associations, IMC and its partners will make a difference in realizing the prospectus for workplace learning in hospitality and tourism.

References
Ainslie, M. and Wills, G. (1997), "Designing a quality action learning process for managers", *Journal of Workplace Learning,* Vol. 9 No. 3.
Anbar Management Intelligence (1997), "Evaluation of Anbar Cool-Sites: criteria" at URL: http://www.anbar.co.uk/coolsite/rating.htm
British Hospitality Association (1997), "Colleges face mounting criticism of 'academic drift'", Education Matters, special supplement of *Hospitality Matters,* Vol. 9, August, pp. i-iv.
Davies, D.W. (1997), "Re-conceptualising lifelong learning: from closed to open systems of knowledge", DPhil explication report, International Management Centres, Buckingham, UK.
Davies, R. (1996), "Internet conference on telecommuting", *International Journal of Career Management,* Vol. 8, pp. 1-9.
Hillman, J. (1996), *University for Industry: Creating a National Learning Network,* Institute for Public Policy Research, London.
Peters, J. (1995/96), "The hundred years war started today: an exploration of electronic peer review", *Literati Club*, MCB University Press, pp. 1-6.
Sandelands, E. (1997), "Utilizing the Internet for marketing success", *Pricing Strategy & Practice,* Vol. 5 No. 1, pp. 7-12.
Sandelands, E. and Wills, M. (1996), "Creating virtual support for lifelong learning", *The Learning Organization*, Vol. 3 No. 5, pp. 26-31.
Smith, C. (1997), Secretary of State, Department for Culture, Media and Sport, personal correspondence, 22 July.
Wills, G. (1995), "Embracing electronic publishing", *The Learning Organization*, Vol. 2 No. 4, pp. 14-26.
Wills, G. (1997), "E-postcards from the other side", in Wills, G. (Ed.), *Engendering Democratic Action*, MCB University Press and Cassell, London and Washington.
Wills, G. and Wiles, C. (1995/96), "Author authority in the ascendant", *Literati Club,* MCB University Press, pp. 1-9.

Appendix
Contextualizing action learning programmes for hospitality & tourism – worldwide
Hospitality and Tourism Global Forum
Welcome to the Hospitality and Global Forum
(http://www.mcb.co.uk/htgf/main.htm)

An initiative by MCB University Press to provide a common English language Internet Forum for those providing professional and academic services to the global hospitality industry.

The Forum is divided into two main areas, these are Current Awareness and the Resources and Archives section. The Current Awareness link will enable you to access a list of constantly updated areas that provide the latest thinking and discussion within the hospitality and tourism field. By accessing the Resources and Archive section, a body of professional and academic knowledge can be found by linking to the selected locations.

First time visitors to the Forum may like to go to the Introduction to find out more about the aims of the Hospitality and Tourism Global Forum.

Current awareness

The Current Awareness menu below alphabetically lists direct links to the continuously updated areas of the Hospitality and Tourism Global Forum. For a more detailed description of the link, click on the specific question mark button to the right of the menu.

Anbar Weekly Express	?
Annual Review and Trends	?
Cyber Highlights	?
Cyber Selection	?
Internet Conferences	?
Meeting Place	?
The Social Room	?
The Virtual Academy	?

Every week the *Anbar Management Express* team of reviewers brings you the most significant new ideas and practice from over 400 of the world's top management journals and from an array of areas of interest. Our aim is to bring you the latest reviews of articles. Use our reviewers' judgements to determine whether or not you need to know more, then order the full-text articles which are of interest to you.

Annual Review and Trends – last year's trends and hospitality and tourism features.

Cyber Highlights – home of the quarterly e-news flyer that goes to many links from here and provides information on the latest Internet developments in the fields of hospitality and tourism.

The *Cyber Selection* is the Forum Convener's personal selection from all the hospitality and tourism articles published in the last quarter.

Internet Conferences – offers the opportunity to participate in interactive discussions on key issues in hospitality and tourism. It is a forum for innovative ideas and an international meeting place for academics and practitioners which transcends the barriers of culture and geography.

The *Meeting Place* – is an on-line discussion which allows Associates and visitors alike to discuss the latest developments, ask questions and suggest new ideas for the Hospitality and Tourism Global Forum.

The *Social Room* hosts the editorial and chronicles the more bizarre aspects of life in the hospitality and tourism industries.

The *Virtual Academy* is the place to go for all the latest activity in your field. There are 12 academies covering an array of hospitality and tourism subjects – from accounting and finance to science and technology. Each has its own discussion area with research papers and news items posted on a regular basis.

Resources and Archives

The Resources and Archives menu below provides an alphabetical listing of direct links to services for hospitality and tourism practitioners and academics. For a more detailed description of the link, click on the specific question mark button to the right of the menu.

Anbar	?
Anbar Coolsites	?
Associates	?

Emerald	?
Internet Free-Press	?
Internet Research	?
Join the Forum	?
Literati Club	?
Partners	?
Practitioner qualification programmes	?
Related Sites	?
Search the site	?

Anbar Coolsites provide access to quality rated Internet sites in 16 areas of management interest. This initiative will provide managers and researchers with the intelligent access to Internet resources that Anbar has been providing to more traditionally published material since 1961. Specialist reviewers evaluate every site on five key criteria, then award a quality rating between one and five. Coolsites are for managers and researchers who don't have the time to surf the Net...

Anbar Electronic Intelligence gives practitioners and academics immediate access throughout the world, to both the latest and the most significant management, computing and civil engineering thinking, practice and solutions. Articles are abstracted from over 400 accredited international management journals and are searchable via the Internet. From this link you can access the Anbar Management Library and register for a 30 day free trial of Anbar.

The *Associates* page contains information on all the members of the Hospitality and Tourism Global Forum with a short profile and e-mail contact details for each member.

Emerald Intelligence + Full Text Emerald is a collection of more than 100 full text, top rated academic and professional journals, published by MCB University Press. From this page, users at registered sites can access the library. Librarians responsible for subscriptions can register to obtain access and non-subscribers can apply for a 30 day free trial.

Internet Free-Press – with the support of MCB University Press, IFP is dedicated to pushing electronic publishing ever onwards...By creating a site which brings together the people involved in electronic publishing and information surrounding a given subject, IFP aims to facilitate a new era of publishing. The Internet offers the prospect of publishing globally on any topic – come and try it!

The *Internet Research Forum* provides you with information about the Internet, World Wide Web, e-mail, newsgroups, html – in fact, everything you need to know about how to access and use information on the Internet...

If you'd like to become an Associate (individual member) or Partner (hyper-link your organization's Web site to the Forum), go to the Join section and complete the appropriate application form.

The *Literati Club* is the world's largest author's club with more than 15,000 members and lots of tips and guidance on writing for publication. This link will take you to the heart of publishing action, where you can network with others, learn how to improve your writing skills and access MCB's articles of the year.

The *Partners* page is a list of hyper-links to premier Web sites associated with the Hospitality and Tourism Global Forum. From here, you can visit a world of hospitality and find out what is happening on the front line...

Practitioner qualification programmes takes you to International Management Centres and its partner universities who specialize in providing workplace learning programmes at all levels, with learning resources delivered by Internet, direct to your desktop.

Related sites contains links to other Internet sites of interest.

You can *Search* for a particular site, article, Associate, partner or search the entire site by subject by visiting the Forum database.

SECTION 3
Where the architects meet the building contractors...

Eric Sandelands

Chapter 13

Re-engineering knowledge logistics

Gordon Wills

*Professor of Customer Policy, International Management Centres and
Chairman of Electronic Publishing Division, MCB University Press, and*

Mathew Wills

Vice President, ANBAR Electronic Intelligence

The search for understanding what electronic academic and professional publishing using the Internet can deliver in terms of cost benefit is well illuminated by the discipline known as logistics. Logistics is the science of the movement or flow of people, materials and information. It had its origins in the military which was until recent times the most concerned with the need to accomplish such major movements in a relatively short space of time. Southworth (1993) and Worsford (1995) exemplify this focus in the context of the Gulf War and the British Army Logistics Corps respectively.

In most human activities, the need for rapid and effective response is not so critically significant and as such merited only limited scientific attention until the last quarter of this century (Kearney, 1991). With the aid of mathematical and statistical approaches linked to computing capability, organizations which expended up to 30 per cent of total cost on achieving effective distribution of their products in the marketplace then began to take the field most seriously.

As a science, it seeks to identify the least cost way of achieving a given level of availability or service to customers. Five key elements have been identified as determining the efficacy of such movements or flows: facilities, unitization, communications, inventory and transportation.

It is the analysis of the trade-offs between each in achieving the requisite availability or service that shows the way to the least cost solution within each cycle (Pohlen and LaLonde, 1994).

This straightforward framework can be well illustrated in commerce:

- Many ladies' fashions in footwear or clothing last for only a short season. Preparations for launch normally have a sufficiently long lead time to enable suppliers to source the items from across the world at the lowest cost. Least cost transportation can be accomplished by sea container. Inventory can be set conservatively in case the fashion does not take off. However, if the fashion catches hold, the supplier needs to know as rapidly as possible both to procure and to deliver more items to retail stores. The additional inventory required can seldom come by least

This article first appeared in *Logistics Information Management,* Vol. 10 No. 2, 1997, pp. 304-314.

cost transportation or it will arrive too late, nor can it be made far away by a least cost source unless a higher cost transportation mode is used – such as air freight. The speed with which the supplier gets feedback from the information system on sales uptake, enabling him to forecast his need for additional inventory, determines his ability to meet demand. This has seen rocketing growth in marketing/point-of-sale intelligence systems which is apparent any time we shop today with barcode scanners capturing intelligence the moment we buy linked to our customer loyalty card demographics and replenishment cycles (Hagon, 1994).

- Industrial components, whether at manufacture/assembly stage or in the replacement after market, are required in the right place at the right time. However, to achieve that without massive inventory holdings across the marketplace would be impossible without instant access to the information on where a component might be and a willingness to use high cost transportation methods to deliver it. With straightforward statistical analysis of inventory demand, it is normally suitable to hold far less inventory, thereby reducing the risks of obsolescence, loss and damage into the bargain.

The managerial challenge in commerce has been to ensure the consideration of the "total" logistics concept, i.e. view the output of a logistics system as being the result of the trade-off between all five significant elements over an appropriate cycle time (Wenkels, 1995). Their discrete management normally leads to net loss to the enterprise. Simply to minimize transport costs or communications expense will normally give rise to much higher inventory expenditures to achieve a given level of service.

What level of logistics service is requisite?
The notion of a scientific approach seeking to achieve a least cost solution to deliver a requisite level of service or availability begs the question: what level of service is requisite? Not surprisingly, much analysis has addressed this question (Lambert, 1992) – which has an exact equivalent in the currently popular query as to what "quality" a product ought to embody.

The paramount response is, in almost every circumstance, that "reliability/ consistency of the level of service offered is more important than speed". If a promise is made, it needs to be 100 per cent certain that it will be kept. The customer for the service can plan accordingly. The precise pattern can be tailored to the customers' needs (Fuller et al., 1993).

The second response, not unnaturally, is that the speed required depends on the context in which the need has arisen. The item designations of A, B and C have been used in inventory control for many years. An A item must be there at all times – oxygen in a hospital or an aeroplane, or engines at the right assembly point in the manufacture of a car. Other items, such as a light bulb in the home, can be regarded as a B or C item. You can borrow one from another room.

Third, the potential substitutability of a given item with an identical/satisfactory competitive alternative will give saliency to the need for a high level of service, indeed preferably 100 per cent availability. It is unlikely that most customers will change their choice of a car, or aeroplane manufacturers their choice of engine because availability is not immediate. However, a chocolate bar or beverage will often be substituted, as will a passenger seat from one airline brand to another.

The traditional logistics model for academic and professional knowledge

In Figure 1, the total logistics flow cycle in traditional publishing is modelled across 12 months.

Academic and professional knowledge first arises in the minds of scholars and practitioners. It is mainly distributed in print or by word of mouth as at conferences, professional workshops or discussions with colleagues. These methods of distribution allow for greater or lesser levels of interaction/proactivity. In a discussion, one can readily proact and evolve a line of analysis and thought; with a book, TV programme or an article, the knowledge is not so readily negotiable. It takes much longer to take up a question and get a response from an author or TV programme contributor than it does to raise a point at a conference or discussion.

Facilities
The retail facilities used to store knowledge are most typically a library or bookstore – although journals will often go directly through the post to readers most particularly in the professions. Publishers use warehouses extensively in the distribution channel and library agents frequently offer consolidation services.

Conference workshop and discussion facilities typically are provided either by hoteliers or by enterprises themselves in countless seminar/meeting rooms around the globe.

Many individuals also create their own libraries, often more an archival stack of previously read or browsed material, in their own homes or offices.

Each of these facilities has its own aura, its own charisma. A library and a bookstore share a quietude not always to be found or even sought at a conference or a workshop, because they are not offering an interactive knowledge consumption process.

Unitization
The unit of knowledge ranges from the well maligned "sound byte" to the impressive tome. In other words, we may seek to acquire access either by simply hearing or seeing a few short sentences, or by necessarily acquiring a book. To gain access via a library, there may be a membership fee and even a fine for taking too long to read/return a particular book.

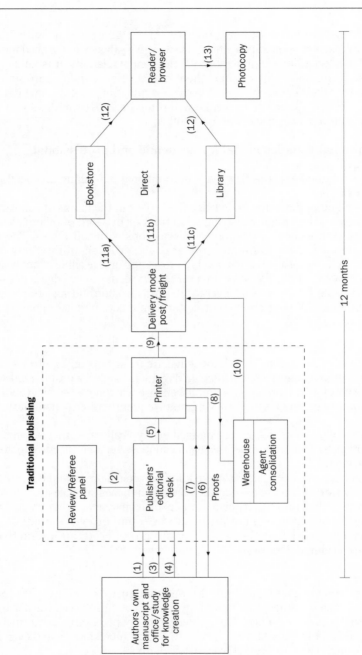

Figure 1.
The logistics of
knowledge flows in
traditional publishing

Exhibit 1: The logistics of knowledge flows in traditional publishing

Journals and professional magazines are frequently sold by annual subscription or at least by the issue. Most conferences expect you to attend the whole at a comprehensive fee or to purchase the printed proceedings afterwards for a far lower fee.

So, while the unit of knowledge is the "byte", its sale and availability are normally in multiple bytes, as a printed volume, an annual subscription to several instalments or an entire conference. A scholarly meeting, to be truly effective, normally requires all its main contributors to be in one place at the same time.

Communications

In logistics this word is used essentially to describe the awareness available to all potential users of what units of knowledge exist and are available in what facilities or, if they are *en route*, precisely where they are at any given moment. To do this in commerce, large and extremely costly intelligence systems have been developed. Each one of us can ascertain from a bank's autoteller machine what our balances are, and a manufacturer can similarly pinpoint stock locations and levels and where they have reached in transit (Sheombar, 1992).

For knowledge today, we can ascertain the existence of a book-in-print if we know its title/author, of a journal if we know its title, and of an article if we know who wrote it and in what journal. But as to the precise location where we will find it once it has left its publisher, whether it is out on loan or out of stock, and if so how long before we can gain access – such intelligence is not normally readily available.

Inventory

The great majority of libraries will be able to identify whether a book or journal has been acquired and whether it is currently out on loan. So too will many bookshops, albeit on a more reactive basis. Some will know the rate of usage of the knowledge and the average waiting period experienced by customers for availability when it is temporarily out of stock. Knowledge of inventory held elsewhere other than in the particular location will be scant unless a regional information exchange has been established.

The inventory of conferences and workshops on offer is far less well documented. There is no global equivalent of books or journals in print with allocated ISBNs and ISSNs. The inventory is almost totally fragmented and most academics and professionals rely on personal networks and mailed information to access them. They are, however, frequently translated into book/journal format later and then become more accessible.

Finally, the inventory of authors unfinished and/or unsubmitted articles is virtually inaccessible except by word of mouth.

Transportation

The physical transportation of knowledge is usually accomplished ultimately by the reader going to the library or bookshop to collect or by delivery via the post or fax. In the case of conferences and workshops, the transportation is by participants transferring themselves to a faraway, albeit sometimes exotic place. The considerably higher expense involved in the latter mode is regularly justified by the trade-off with access to:

- the most recent knowledge not yet available in books or journals;

- the opportunity to interact and proact and thereby heighten the value of the knowledge transfer; and

- the opportunity to build networks that can of themselves become very efficient media for future learning and knowledge flows.

Requisite service at least cost
The literature of librarianship has frequently reported the application of service levels to the availability of books and journal articles, e.g. by carrying multiple copies or by offering fax or postal delivery services at differential prices. No studies have been located that attempt the total logistics systems analysis with trade-offs costed, mainly because the cost/benefit of academic and professional information and knowledge is grossly underdeveloped. Whereas a commercial product not available can normally lead to substitution of another, this will not usually be the case for knowledge. It is likely to be possible for textbooks but most unlikely for state-of-the-art articles. And the potential value of the missing knowledge must be assessed before any conclusion can be reached as to whether it should in future be provided because it justifies the cost involved.

It is not infrequent to wait for a book from a publisher for a month or more; and to await an article by interlibrary lending for 14-48 days. In such circumstances, it is not surprising that much of the lag time in completing or even preparing a serious draft paper is occasioned by delays in gaining access to particular known items.

This of itself begs the question as to how the potential beneficiary is made aware of its existence, or has a cost-effective way of searching to find all that might be deemed cost beneficial (cp. Vinze, 1991).

It must generally be concluded that users of knowledge are conditioned to accepting that it takes a long time to find something, that the lag time will be inconsistent and that, if it cannot be substituted, the overall output will have to be delayed.

Supply side logistics
I have left until last discussion of the ways in which articles or manuscripts are traditionally procured – whether for books or journals or as conference papers. First, it must be observed that it is an especially lengthy process, rationalized as ensuring high quality but more often than not mainly reflecting inefficiencies. An article or book is normally expected to take 12 months but can take as long as 18 to appear in print. During that time, the actual working time is perhaps four weeks; the remainder is delay or misconnections in the channel of supply.

The author's work in early draft format will be circulated for comments. When finalized, it will go to a reviewer/refereeing panel whose comments will be fed back for incorporation in the manuscript – or, if a rejection, to re-commence the sequence again. Once accepted for publication, the article or book will go through a production process often requiring consolidation into an issue with eight/ten other articles, or await a seasonal catalogue or launch event. These stages, together with repeated proof checking and graphic design contributions, are what take up the 12 months.

The supply side, least cost approach delivering these service levels is, of course, not consistent, not speedy and alas not readily open to substitution of another medium of production. But there is much good news to be heard...

The purpose of this paper is to share just how great the opportunity is to re-engineer both the supply and the demand side of knowledge flows, of knowledge logistics (Ayers, 1995; Badarecco, 1991). In particular, "time to market" as a key contemporary logistics issue is addressed.

Re-engineering supply side knowledge logistics
As has been suggested, supply side flows begin when an author seeks to present research or philosophical outcomes to appropriate academics or professionals. To achieve that task to the necessary quality level inevitably will be an iterative process of formulation, feedback commentary and refinement. It will normally also include a vitally important prior necessity which is to be aware of and in command of what other knowledge exists on the issue concerned – of which more later when we discuss demand side knowledge logistics.

If, however, we commence with the draft article, or preprint, we can explore (see Figure 2) the transformations available from emerging electronic publishing approaches:

Step 1: The author's preprint is created on a PC which can connect to the Internet.

Step 2: The author submits to a "virtual academy" of like-minded academics/ professionals for constructive critique and feedback.

Step 3: Comments are digested and the final version prepared.

Step 4: The author re-submits for final review and acceptance in a housestyle/ template that conforms to the publisher's specification for Internet publication.

Step 5: The editor alerts the refereeing panel by e-mail to the article's presence on the journal-protected database and asks for "credit scores" plus comments.

Step 6: The scores and final comments are fed back to the author for incorporation.

Step 7: The refereed finalized article or book is published on the Internet.

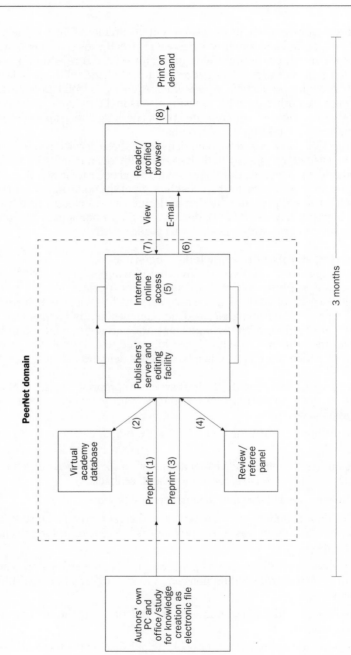

Print on
demand

(8)

Reader/
profiled
browser

View

E-mail

(7)

(6)

PeerNet domain

Internet
online
access
(5)

Publishers'
server and
editing
facility

Virtual
academy
database

(2)

Review/
referee
panel

(4)

Preprint (1)

Preprint (3)

Authors' own
PC and
office/study
for knowledge
creation as
electronic file

3 months

Figure 2.
The logistics of
knowledge flows in
electronic publishing

Exhibit 2: The logistics of knowledge flows in electronic publishing

Step 8: All interested parties are notified by e-mail of the event and invited to view and/or download.

Clearly links to the earlier critique of traditional knowledge logistics. Accordingly it is not surprising to find such a sequence, known as Project PeerNet, currently under development with MCB University Press for all its journals. It goes further, however, than reducing up to 75 per cent of the lag time in getting articles or books into print. These are some of the major improvements to the very publishing process itself:

- The virtual academy allows a much wider audience to see and comment on a preprint. MCB University Press' Literati Club of 15,000+ authors across the world is keyworded to achieve this broader canvass.

- The preprints in process are assembled in an electronically available "citation/list/register" – thereby enabling others to be aware sooner of what is on the way and at the same time to protect the author against plagiarism.

- The online credit scoring in the refereeing process can be expected to produce more consistent and reliable results.

- There is no need to wait for a full issue or a seasonal catalogue to be assembled. Each article can be published as it is accepted.

- The article's abstract can be added immediately to the global abstracting and citation sources rather than awaiting consolidation.

- The author and publisher can proact with interested readers rather than await a visit to a library, a bookshop, a conference or the post to arrive – by e-mail notification to all concerned about publication.

- The interested reader can proact with the author to follow up on a line of argument or analysis.

- The references to the works of others cited in any article or book can be traced and accessed speedily using the newly arriving PII references which are unique indicators for each article.

Verdict

This process will be more consistent in the service levels and the quality judgements experienced. It will be faster. It will be very much cheaper to accomplish once all parties have access to the required technologies. It will, however, almost certainly increase the substitutability of one journal or publisher for another. It will be easier for an author to "shop around" and less time-consuming and expensive for that process too.

The prize accordingly goes to the publisher with the most helpful and supportive supply side process, the best virtual academy resource and the best accreditation of the publication by branding of the collection or list within which it appears. Finally, the best publisher will have the maximum outreach to the author's intended listeners (cp. Brown and Watts, 1992). This gives a whole new meaning to the concept of database marketing and marketing intelligence/loyalty systems. In electronic terms, the more intended listeners one can alert by e-mail to the publication of the article, the stronger the desire of authors to commit their knowledge to that particular publisher.

Re-engineering demand side knowledge logistics

The author is, of course, just one example of a user of knowledge. The great majority of users are not involved with knowledge in order to benchmark their own nascent contribution. They are there either:

- to take it on board for an educational or professional purpose – a course to follow with an examination to pass or a known professional need to learn or implement a strategy; or

- to browse to stay abreast with no specific goal or expectation, which can be satisfied both by finding nothing exceptional and by serendipitously learning, e.g. database mining approaches (Computing, 1992 and Grupe and Owrang, 1995).

The ultimate requirements of the author, of the tasked student or professional and of the serendipitous learner will be the full text of the article or book concerned, but all will find it more than helpful to be able to scan/search all the literature available in a designated field speedily and appropriately. The premium here accordingly is on the design of user-friendly, user-conscious search engines of the burgeoning archive of knowledge.

With the benefit of standard general mark-up language (SGML) tagging of electronic text, searching by keywords can readily be accomplished, together with textual mentions. This requires sympathetic thesaurus development within subject fields. Further search criteria can differentiate the recent from the less so, take one to all the contributions of a given author, select by country of origin or reference to industry or corporation, theoretical vs. practical case study as opposed to literature review, and most recently and boldly to the allocation of quality criteria within several key categories.

One can readily see the advantage to being able to select the most recent literature review in a chosen field from a total of 2,000 or more articles on offer. However, even more so, one can readily see the advantage for any professional or educator presenting to an audience to be absolutely up to date with the field concerned so speedily. Before electronic publishing, such a realization was simply impracticable.

The revolution dawning is even greater for the process of updating course materials as in distance learning institutions. On average, the materials they despatch were last updated two-and-a-half years ago. Using automated electronic searching links they can be supplemented with the latest literature as it appears. All that is required is to allocate keywords to each course module and make hyperlinks to the database concerned. This approach is now in operation on a prototype basis. It is no dream; it is a reality and its contribution is awesome.

Similar keyworded or behaviour derived/ modelled (Tafti and Nikbatht, 1993) profiling of individual managers can be automated wholly to deliver current awareness. By linking agreed personal key areas of interest to the knowledge database, e-mail alert routines with full text retrieval on demand are being delivered. Complaints that this is tomorrow's junk mail are as well founded, but no more so, than the complaint against postal messages in the mailbox today. We are always at liberty to ignore such messages or to have a separate file structure/ pending tray for them that does not interfere with the routine of important messaging – just as we may have an ex-directory phone line or a PA/secretary to intercept calls and messages on our behalf.

Knowledge logistics is clearly poised on the threshold of artificial intelligence/expert systems/neural networks for academics and professionals. The leveraging of the contribution of knowledge workers (Lewis, 1992; Li, 1994; Mockler 1990; Mykstyn *et al.*, 1994; Osyk and Vijayaraman, 1995; Quinn, 1992, 1993; Ryman-Tubb, 1993; Venugopal and Boets, 1995) has been examined extensively elsewhere in services, manufacturing industry and the professions but not directly for the field of electronic publishing.

Verdict
This process will be both more comprehensive in its ability to trace and retrieve knowledge and will do so almost instantaneously. The data overload which will inevitably arise can be attended to by use of search engines for keywords and abstracts which do not militate against serendipitous browsing or searching but do not necessarily require it.

The benefits of the outreach in distribution first by alerting interested parties in profiled areas but also by immediate availability in the global databases will be of great value to authors both to publicize their work and to elicit interaction.

How key elements in knowledge logistics flows are changing
In Figures 1 and 2, the two logistics flows are modelled. Thirteen discrete phases have been replaced by eight. That presages a major cycle time transformation, but it becomes clear just how wide the re-engineering required truly is when we examine the five key elements of logistics (Persson, 1995).

Facilities
At a minimum, the printing house, the warehouse and the library/bookstore (Schneider, 1994) are either substantially or totally eliminated or metamorphosed as the move grows apace for electronic publishing. However, no progress can be accomplished until:

- publishers establish the host server for the incoming preprints and their proactive discussion with the virtual academy and referee panel; and

- authors and readers have PC and printer facilities at their disposal for the beginning and end of the process.

It is a classic chicken and egg argument of course. Who moves first? The expense for a publishing house in creating a host server that most of the readers currently do not know how/are not inclined/are unable to use is daunting. But the prizes are paradigmatic if the patient investment can be made. The threatened facilities are slow to respond because they are largely sunk costs and accordingly seem to have only a marginal incremental cost in comparison with a total investment/payback model for the incoming publishing investments. Furthermore, extant budgetary procedures in libraries, for instance, give the funding to the facility and inventory manager not to the reader/browser – to whom knowledge often seems to be a free good – if only you can find it and wait until it arrives. The electronic publishing paradigm requires the reader/browser to have the discretion to buy (within a budget) as appropriate. Institutional inertia and power structures will certainly delay not alleviate change in such circumstances (Smith and Saint-Onge, 1996; Woodside, 1996).

Unitization
The unit of knowledge for the commencement of searching and retrieval in electronic publishing is the keyword not the journal issue or book title. Keywords lead to abstracts and abstracts to full text, with paper wastage eliminated at each stage (Wu and Dunn, 1995). Ultimately, only the articles that cannot be digested on screen will be printed, and only the areas profiled will be drawn to anyone's attention in the first instance if the service offered is proactive.

The need to publish batches of articles for effective traditional publishing and distribution is gone. So is the constraint on how many articles can be published or acquired in any given time period. The remaining challenge which is to quality assure the knowledge offered is not accomplished by a journal per se but the quality procedures its editors employ.

Communications
Perhaps the most significant change in the communications element of logistics is the immediate, categorized access to the total body of knowledge for searching and retrieval. This does, of course, include quality guarantees of the knowledge offered. These latter aspects will surely see a transformation from one being driven solely by the editorial review/refereeing procedures to one driven also by the keyword/abstracting services. Many readers or browsers will be unaware of the status of many suppliers of knowledge. The strength of the "retailer branding" via the abstract providers will readily overcome that dilemma (cp. ANBAR Management Intelligence).

The major challenge still to be overcome, albeit with PIIs emerging as the equivalent of barcodes, is how to have a universal referencing system for all units of knowledge for retrieval and within the search engine a uniform thesaurus. These are not unfamiliar problems in the world of knowledge and have been resolved for books (ISBN) and journals/ serials (ISSN). As the appropriate unitization changes, however, the new order has to be addressed.

There are, in a range of disciplines such as management/human studies, referencing systems that have been pioneered by the major abstracting services for paper-driven retrieval systems. But these will need to give way to a universally accepted article referencing system and keywording thesaurus.

Once these are in place, the residual role for document supply services, such as are to be found in the British Library and other major archival centres, will surely disappear. Only the archival role will continue to provide for historical research and to act as a backup for lost electronic knowledge. Some electronic publishers are now simply depositing a "golden copy" with these national archives to this end.

This new scenario compares with a helpful librarian who assists a reader/browser to undertake a search beginning with the knowledge in stock in the library concerned, or the bookstore, and then moving to bibliographies and abstracting services one by one – either paper or CD-ROM-based... and then awaiting paper delivery from afar after a time lapse of greater or lesser proportions.

Inventory

The only physical inventory remaining in the electronic publishing paradigm is the printout on demand created by the professed interested party; and the "golden copy" in the national archive and backup for electronic memory.

The startling conclusion for all concerned is that all the warehousing and retailing inventory necessitated by the printed form will eventually be eliminated.

In this context, CD-ROM clearly can be seen as a transitory form of distributed electronic storage/supply because the transportation and connectivities of the total system are not yet in balance. In comparison with only calling on what you need as opposed to the whole inventory on a CD-ROM and a price to match it, it is clear that the future belongs to online access provided that the reader/browser facilities are well able to access it which is closely intertwined with the fifth and final key element in logistics.

Transportation

The use of air and surface postal services to deliver knowledge, increasingly supplemented in the past 30 years first by photocopiers and then by faxes, is destined to be transformed further by server to PC interchange either using the telephone providers or cable networks. Cable provision, linked with television programming, is gaining rapidly on telephone services most especially where telephoning is an expensive access mode. Those centres such as Singapore and Hong Kong with no or almost no charges for local phone calls have shown just how the absence of the cost hurdle can accelerate adoption.

In every scenario presented, the expenseof interconnection between PCs and publishers' services using data compression techniques will be well below that of current post or fax services. In many circumstances, dedicated telephone lines and fixed annual access fees are already sufficient to stabilize the transformation cost of knowledge to make it manageable.

The "total" systems challenge

The rapidity with which the re-engineering of the total logistics system of knowledge takes place will be determined by push and pull factors.

Authors will push for more rapid publication with guaranteed quality assurance. Readers and browsers will pull because of the efficiencies and effectiveness of the new approaches, although requiring involvement on their part and competence with the various connectivities.

However, there will be a combination, as has been shown of socio-economic and psycho-technological blockages to the re-engineering process. Where a single unifying entity is able to redesign a substantial part of the total system, using a balanced approach across all fields, progress will be greatest (Kaplan and Norton, 1992; 1996). Any new age logistics system that can build critical mass for the PeerNet construct identified in Figure 2 is in a very strong position to exploit the trade-offs (Wills, 1995; Wills and Wiles, 1996; Wills and Wills, 1996). A number of extant publishers with very strong links both with supply side authors and demand side library and reader markets are now attempting this.

Their six key strategies are to:

(1) put in place the interactive server routines for author preprint manuscript review that attract the best quality knowledge in the first instance;

(2) develop Internet sites that have a critical mass to attract readers and browsers;

(3) build virtual academies-cum-professions as well-classified, benefit-oriented databases – that have their own life in Conferencing, ListServers and NewsGroups;

(4) drive hard for E-mail/Internet connectivities with their end-users via awareness and assistance – Cybercafés online and on-site;

(5) create search engines of the highest quality with customer-user-focused search criteria backed by full text delivery online;

(6) empower customers/users to exploit the benefits of the knowledge at their disposal via educational and self-development guidance and support.

A total systems perspective such as this, encompassing strategy (6) above, questions the dividing line between knowledge logistics for publishing and knowledge for education and learning. The new age total knowledge logistics model must expect to see the backward integration of the librarian into knowledge distillation and capture rather than warehousing and stock control – a higher order, higher value-added cognitive task in any event. And it must expect to see the publisher reaching forwards into alliances and joint ventures with educational institutions offering the constant updating of knowledge against given curricula. This can be most clearly achieved in the realm of distance learning where the infrastructure inertia will be least. The high value-added role of the tutor of the future will be to design the curriculum and to facilitate the learning processes in an interpersonal, interactive way. The delivery of mass lectures to students, along with vain attempts to provide adequate levels of tutorial support, will be replaced with tutoring as a caring profession. Staff will be freed up from a myriad domestic tasks by the electronic publishing phenomenon.

Those educational enquiries taking place around the globe to see how education and learning can be cost-effectively achieved for the future, as more and more people have higher and higher expectations and needs, have an agenda item they can now address and can take the bold leap forward. They can disaggregate the budget for acquiring information from its central focus and share it among the customers and users at their PCs. They can follow that through by transforming library buildings into tutorial centres. And, finally, they can agree on limited hard copy national archiving strategies, i.e. get rid of the obsolete stockholdings or inventory in educational institutions in favour of downloading on demand. To make progress, however, requires high level managerial skills (Barclay *et al.*, 1994).

The other breakthrough opportunity can be expected among those who have not yet invested in the massive infrastructure of the traditional logistics systems who can go directly to the new paradigms. This will certainly include all major new universities being developed in the Asian region over the next two decades as well as in Latin America and India – which together encompass nearly half the world's population. And it will equally apply to Russia and its own Commonwealth partners as they begin to access the full gamut of Western knowledge.

References

ANBAR Management Intelligence, @ http://www.anbar. co.uk/home.htm – which abstracts the world's top 400 management journals monthly and ascribes quality ratings to them on diverse dimensions.

Ayers, J.B. (1995), "What smokestack industries can tell us about re-engineering", *Information Strategy*, Vol. 11 No. 2, Winter.

Badarecco, J.L. (1991), "Alliances speed knowledge transfer", *Planning Review*, Vol. 19 No. 2, March/April.

Barclay, I., Holroyd, P. and Potton, J. (1994), "A sphenomorphic model for the management of innovation in a complex environment", *Leadership & Organization Development Journal*, Vol. 15 No. 7.

Birkett, W. (1995), "Knowledge management", *Chartered Accountants Journal of New Zealand*, Vol. 74 No. 1, February.

Brown, J.H. and Watts, J. (1992), "Enterprise engineering: building 21st century organisations", *Journal of Strategic Information Systems*, Vol. 1 No. 5, December.

Computing (1992), "Nuggets of information: data mining", 22 October.

Fuller, J.B., O'Connor, J. and Rawlinson, R. (1993), "Tailored logistics: the next advantage", *Harvard Business Review,* Vol. 71 No. 3, May/June.

Grupe, F.H. and Owrang, M.M. (1995), "Database mining: discovering new knowledge and competitive advantage", *Information Systems Management,* Vol. 12 No. 4, Autumn.

Hagon, A. (1994), "Electronic trading: the logistics manager's strategic tool", *Logistics Focus,* Vol. 2 No. 5, June.

Kaplan, R.S. and Norton, D.P. (1992), "The balanced scorecard – measures that drive performance", *Harvard Business Review,* Vol. 70 No. 1, January/February.

Kaplan, R.S. and Norton, D.P. (1996), "Using the balanced scorecard as a strategic management system", *Harvard Business Review,* Vol. 74 No. 1, January/February.

Kearney Lecture, (1991), "Reflections on a lifetime in logistics", *Focus on Physical Distribution and Logistics Management,* Vol. 10 No. 7, August/September.

Lambert, D. (1992), "Developing a customer focused logistics strategy", *International Journal of Physical Distribution & Logistics Management*, Vol. 22 No. 6.

Lewis, J. (1992), "Brain gain – artificial intelligence", *Computing,* 18 June.

Li, E.Y. (1994), "Artificial neural networks and their business applications", *Information Management,* Vol. 27 No. 5, November.

Mockler, R.J. (1990), " Non-technical manager's modelling of management decision situations", *Journal of Systems Management,* Vol. 41 No. 5, May.

Mykstyn, P.B., Mykstyn, K. and Raja, M.K. (1994), "Knowledge acquisition skills and traits", *Information Management*, Vol. 26 No. 2, February.

Osyk, B.A. and Vijayaraman, B.S. (1995), "Integrating expert systems and neural networks", *Information Systems Management,* Vol. 12 No. 2, Spring.

Persson, G. (1995), "Logistics process redesign: some useful insights", *International Journal of Logistics Management,* Vol. 6 No. 1.

Pohlen, T.L. and LaLonde, B.J. (1994), " Implementing activity based costing in logistics", *Journal of Business Logistics*, Vol. 15 No. 2.

Quinn, J.B. (1992), "The intelligent enterprise: a new paradigm", *Academy of Management Executive,* Vol. 6 No. 4, November.

Quinn, J.B. (1993), "Managing the intelligent enterprise: knowledge and service based strategies", *Planning Review,* Vol. 21 No. 5, September/October.

Ryman-Tubb, N. (1993), "How Thomas Cook uses neural networks", *Direct Response,* Vol. 12 No. 9, September.

Schneider, F. (1994), "Virtual retailing", *International Trends in Retailing,* Vol. 11 No. 1, July.

Sheombar, H.S. (1992), "EDI-induced redesign of co-ordination in logistics", *International Journal of Physical Distribution & Logistics Management,* Vol. 22 No. 8.

Smith, P.A.C. and Saint-Onge, H. (1996), "The evolutionary organization: avoiding a Titanic fate", *The Learning Organization*, Vol. 3 No. 4.

Southworth, M.S. (1993), "When war wouldn't wait", *Focus on Logistics and Distribution,* Vol. 12 No. 3, April.

Tafti, M.H.A. and Nikbakht, E. (1993), "Neural networks and expert systems", *Information Management and Computer Security*, Vol. 1 No. 1.

Venugopal, V. and Boets, W. (1995), "Intelligent systems for organizational learning", *The Learning Organization*, Vol. 2 No. 3.

Vinze, A.S. (1991), "Performance of a knowledge based system", *Information and Management*, Vol. 21 No. 4, November.

Wenkels, H.-M. (1995), "Re-engineering logistics processes", *European Supply Chain Decisions*, Spring.

Wills, G. (1995), "Embracing electronic publishing", *The Learning Organization*, Vol. 2 No. 4.

Wills, G. and Wiles, C. (1996), "Author authority in the ascendant", *Innovation and Learning in Education*, Vol. 2 No. 1.

Wills, M. and Wills, G. (1996), "The ins and outs of electronic publishing", *Journal of Business and Industrial Marketing,* Vol. 11 No. 1.

Woodside, A.G. (1996), "Theory of rejecting superior, new technologies", *Journal of Business and Industrial Marketing,* Vol. 11 No. 3/4.

Worsford, R. (1995), "Royal Logistics Corps in a changing world", *Logistics Focus*, Vol. 3 No. 4, May.

Wu, H.J. and Dunn, S.C. (1995), "Environmentally responsible logistics systems", *International Journal of Physical Distribution & Logistics Management*, Vol. 52 No. 2.

Chapter 14
Creating virtual support for lifelong learning

Eric Sandelands
Director, Internet Research and Development Centre, and
Mathew Wills
Vice President, Anbar, Bradford, UK

Few would doubt that the concept of lifelong learning, or at least periods of learning activity at stages within working lives, is one with "legs" – it will be seen by many as the route to ongoing managerial effectiveness. Drucker[1], for one, has identified it as one of the true growth industries of the next century. Those currently involved in enabling others to learn and who can adapt to the possibilities brought about by technological change, are ideally placed to see their activities grow on a worldwide basis. But the threat is there too for the complacent. New entrants to the learning market will not carry the baggage of the existing players. They will develop architectures that work in delivering world-class services at low cost, uninhibited by national boundaries.

In this article, the concept of the "virtual university" as the method of delivering lifelong learning is proposed. It is a concept that can be adopted by the traditional learning institutions seeking new markets whose brand names will travel. It is also an approach that can be utilized by new, innovative institutions which can structure themselves to deliver academic programmes anywhere in the world.

The medieval notion of the university had many similarities with monastic life. The offspring of the wealthy would retreat from the outside world to study books, learn from the wise and mix with others engaged in study and contemplation[2]. The socio-economic situation changed in the centuries which followed, but the central concept of universities as places to go to learn did not change fundamentally until the rise of the distance learning model in the latter decades of this century.

Distance learning opened up opportunities for ongoing learning for students without the need for a career break. At the same time it changed the concept of university capacity which was no longer limited by the size of the campuses. Corporations could utilize distance learning principles in developing staff. The BBC, for example, could train engineers in remote Ascension Island without removing them from their posts[3]. Among the drawbacks, however, have been

This article first appeared in *The Learning Organization,* Vol. 3 No. 5, 1996, pp. 26-31.

the lack of student/student and student/supervisor interaction and the expense in keeping learning packages up to date.

The emerging virtual university model uses technology to build in to learning programmes the type of interaction found in the original university concept. The model uses advances in electronic communications to provide fully participative programmes. Use of the Internet offers great opportunities to provide education which is available to many and which is adaptable and flexible[4]. This is being realized by learning institutions, but also by corporate organizations seeking effective and cost-effective management development.

The future appears to be very bright for distance learning which constructively draws on communications technology[5]. This is not to underestimate the short-term challenges that frustrate Internet use, but as Wills[6] put it: "The obvious fact that the impacts of electronic publishing will not happen on a particular day of the week or month of the year, but will arrive piece by piece as a jigsaw comes together, does nothing to lessen its metamorphosing role or allow us time to wait and see".

Constructing a wish list
Let us take a blank sheet of paper and define the learning institution of the twenty-first century by constructing a wish list.

We want to recruit students from all over the world. We do not want to provide them with living accommodation, recreational facilities or lecture theatres. They all cost money and our budgets are always being squeezed. To make it really attractive to the students we want to allow them to carry on working, should they choose to, without a lengthy career break.

We want to deliver courseware that is based on the best available published knowledge, up to date, needs little maintenance and can be delivered to the student instantaneously. What we do not want is to be spending all of our time revising it and all of our money storing and despatching it.

We want our students to have access to the best possible library of published information. We want the collection to be better than the budget-constrained one we currently make do with and we want it instantly available on the desk of every student.

We want to run seminars that focus on key issues and give everyone their say. Participation and community spirit is vital to our learning processes. We also want to participate as faculty and students in conferences, challenging the assumptions of leading figures in our field.

We want to supervise our programmes effectively. Students need deadlines and coaches and mentors. Also we want to appoint the most appropriate supervisors to projects no matter where they are in the world.

Electronics advancing the scholarly process
This seems quite extensive, but is actually very modest in its scope. The parameters used here have been fairly tightly defined around the delivery of course material. While it will not be a comprehensive list of benefits available

from advances in electronic publishing, it is worth considering briefly how the virtual university model can extend beyond course delivery and supervision. Having said this it is recognized that some of the glitches are still being overcome, and we remain constrained by the limits of our imagination.

Butler[7], for example, noted the benefits of electronic journals making articles available to readers within 48 hours of approval of the manuscript by peer review, contrasting it with the lengthy wait that is the custom for inclusion in a hard copy journal before moving on to comment on academic discussion lists. "Electronic discussion groups give immediate access to hundreds (perhaps thousands) of people to whom you can listen or address questions, opinions and concerns."

Great things are becoming eminently feasible, but achieved only spasmodically. In A Survey of STM On-line Journals, Hitchcock *et al.*[8] bemoan the fact that, "A random glance at an on-line journal in this survey is likely to reveal few innovations. One feature is that electronic journals can be searchable, and some are. Papers can include hypertext links to other resources. Many biology journals make particular use of this facility to link to relevant databases, but few other journals offer links to other resources beyond the journal".

While a progress report card would state "could do better", it would also point to the significant progress being made. The benefits to authors and readers of electronic publishing outlined by Wills and Wills[9] are manifold and significant, including precision access to the knowledge archive, updates on current material involvement in conferences and forums and effectively disseminated published material. They point also to the rise of a community of practice and memory, building on the work of Marshall *et al.*[10] who wrote of this entity: "To make this wealth of on-line resources truly useful to emerging electronic communities, we must forge a link between the distributed repositories and practices of information workers who will use them. Community memories will form this vital link between the large-scale collections and information-intensive work".

Researchers and readers also will have access to the best possible university bookshop. As Batty and Lee[11] propose: "The idea of shopping over computerized networks certainly suggests many potential advantages. These networks can span geographical space and create markets where literally thousands of businesses offer millions of products to billions of consumers. The technology available can provide not only text but also video, sound, and even perhaps the virtual reality experience of using a product".

The list could easily continue to cover further examples. The point being made is that a virtual university can be about much, much more than a more efficient distribution channel for distance-learning courseware.

Who is doing it?
Pioneering institutions are designing architectures that exist only in the virtual world. Business School Nederland is the leading MBA provider in Holland. All

of its programmes are delivered using the World Wide Web. All of the items on our wish list are present in their learning programmes. Action learning sets are supported in an open learning environment, yet there is no distribution centre or mail contract, and the reading lists are never more than six months out of date.

Commenting on the development of electronic publishing, Gotze[12] reached the conclusion: "If we look back only two or five years, and read today what was said and feared at the time, I think we have come down a long and stony path in a surprisingly short time".

The same is likely to be said about the virtual universities that are building on the outcomes of this electronic publishing revolution in two to five years' time.

The path is often stony, but rapid progress can still be made by those journeying along it. Having used a bulletin board system to supplement printed courseware, International Management Centres (IMC) were an early adopter of electronic support services. With activities in Europe, the Pacific Rim, Australasia and Central and South America, IMC has had a greater urgency than most in seeking to utilize the Internet to support those supervising and participating in learning programmes.

According to Oliver and Wynder[13]: "Internet, with the World Wide Web (WWW), quite obviously is less cumbersome for accessing pages and news items. EDI routines are eliminated. Its linked e-mail service makes for speedy exchanges of ideas. Its low cost, immediate, global reach removes a key constraint on communications. The WWW formatting makes the appearance of learning resources and all other elements far more attractive in comparison with the printed word – and maintains the major benefit of low-cost revision to be kept up-to-date. List servers provide the opportunity for proactive rather than reactive usage of the system. The linkage with MCB University Press gives access through its Open House site (hypertext links to partner Internet sites) to a greater breadth of resources, and thereby enhances the probability of logging on by members and Associates alike.

"All this is being offered in a global context where Internet is being heralded as the major future for education and where more individuals are seeking access to it every day."

Business School Nederland and IMC make no secret of the virtual university models they have adopted. The majority of their course structures are freely available to all who care to search for them on the WWW. Outlined below are the main features of the models being used:

(1) All faculty and course participants must have access to the Internet at home and/or in the workplace. This is a precondition of joining the programmes; however, it is diminishing rapidly in significance as a barrier to entry given the rapid growth in Internet access.

(2) Courseware is delivered using the Internet as the delivery mechanism (Figure 1). There are no packs to be despatched from warehouses. The

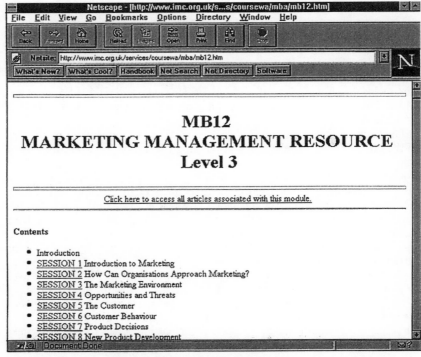

Figure 1.
Courseware using the
Internet as the delivery
mechanism

Source: Anbar Electronic Intelligence (www.anbar.co.uk/anbar.htm)

faculty designing course materials concentrate on the structure and course content. Each module is defined in terms of the keywords of the material being covered. The reading lists are updated every six months using the keywords to pinpoint recent material from the Anbar Management Intelligence database. This ensures access to the most significant recent thinking in the field[14].

(3) All faculty and students have access to an on-line library for current or archival published material. The Anbar Management Intelligence database provides abstracts of articles reviewed by subject specialists from a defined coverage list of journal material (Figure 2). It is delivered to the desk top of users over the Internet. The full-text article can be ordered by E-mail if required, to be delivered by fax or mail from the British Library, or users can link to publishers providing on-line full-text.

(4) Participation in seminars and conferences is encouraged. Newsgroups, an established feature of the Internet enabling group discussion, are used as forums to share feedback ideas and to explore concepts and ideas.

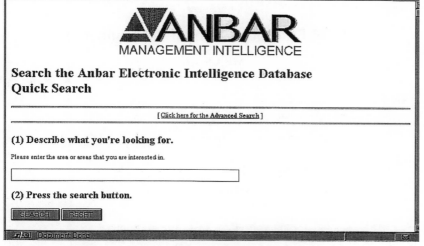

Search the Anbar Electronic Intelligence Database
Quick Search

[Click here for the Advanced Search]

(1) Describe what you're looking for.

Please enter the area or areas that you are interested in.

(2) Press the search button.

SEARCH   RESET

Source: Anbar Electronic Intelligence (www.anbar.co.uk/anbar.htm)

Figure 2.
An on-line library

These can provide a set meeting place for course participants, an international meeting place for students around the world to "meet" regardless of their level or area of study (Figure 3). Journal-sponsored or other facilitated conferences enable students to lock horns and debate with academic researchers from beyond the confines of the virtual university.

(5) Effective course supervision is a key factor in ensuring a successfully completed programme. Business School Nederland and IMC tutors use E-mail to set deadlines, provide feedback and encourage and cajole. They are also able, on a worldwide basis, to match the student with the most appropriate faculty member to act as supervisor.

(6) Another feature of these institutions is the establishment of active alumni. These encourage ongoing learning beyond graduation. The alumni are encouraged to feedback advice and experience via the Internet seminars. They form a powerful networking club with reach into many parts of the globe.

This is not to say that people never meet. Residential start-ups, summer schools and shorter workshop sessions form a key part of course structures. Electronics have not yet brought us the chat over a beer or similar aspects of the human bonding process. The mutual support that characterizes group learning experiences that work as easier to foster if such sessions are built in to programmes. The distance learning model that emerges in the medium term seems certain to include a blend of face-to-face teaching and discussion groups,

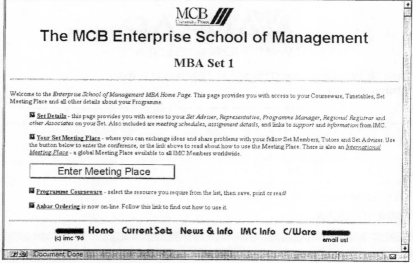

Figure 3.
Global programme
supervision

Source: Anbar Electronic Intelligence (www.anbar.co.uk/anbar.htm)

packaged materials in print and other media, complemented by electronic access. The emphasis placed on each of these elements looks set to shift as the virtual university concept matures.

When we allow ourselves space for reflection in two to five years' time we will surely see a multiplicity of virtual universities offering sophisticated educational experiences. The need of governments and corporations to train and develop people points to this low cost/ high quality approach to learning being of major significance in the provision of lifelong learning.

References

1. Drucker, P., "Drucker predicts the future", *Strategic Direction*, No. 106, September 1994, pp. 27-28.
2. Peters, J., "Quality assuring the virtual business school – the IMC experience", the David Sutton Fellowship paper, 1995, available at http://www.imc.org.uk/imc/home.htm.
3. Boulding, T., "Long-distance learning", *Personnel Management,* Vol. 21 No. 1, January 1989, p. 31.
4. Puesey, S., "An evaluation of distance learning via the Internet and market opportunities for AEI", BPub dissertation, 1996.
5. Massey, J., "Long-distance information", *Computing,* 28 September 1995, p. 52.
6. Wills, G., "Embracing electronic publishing", *The Learning Organization,* Vol. 2 No. 4, 1995, pp. 14-26.
7. Butler, J., "Scholarly resources on the Internet", *Campus-wide Information Systems*, Vol. 12 No. 3, 1995, pp. 12-14.

8. Hitchcock, S., Carr, L. and Hall, W., *A Survey of STM On-line Journals 1990-1995: The Calm before the Storm, 1996*, accessible at http://journas.ecs.soton.ac.uk/survey/survey.html

9. Wills, M. and Wills, G., "The ins and the outs of electronic publishing", *Journal of Business & Industrial Marketing,* Vol. 11 No. 1, 1996, pp. 90-104.

10. Marshall, C.C., Shipman, F.M. and McCall, R.J., "Making large-scale information resources serve communities of practice", *Journal of Management Information Systems,* Vol. 11 No. 4, Spring 1995, pp. 65-86.

11. Batty, J.B. and Lee, R.M., "InterShop: enhancing the vendor/customer dialectic in electronic shopping", *Journal of Management Information Systems*, Vol. 11 No. 4, Spring 1995, pp. 9-31.

12. Gotze, D., "Commercial electronic STM publishing: a survey of market development, copyright issues, enabling technologies and actual status", report to the International Association of Scientific, Technical and Medical Publishers, 1995.

13. Oliver, C. and Wynder, N., *IMC's Internet Action Learning,* 1995, accessible at http://www.imc.org.uk/imc/home.htm

14. Sandelands, E., "Which journal? The politics of where to publish", *Collection Building*, Vol. 15 No. 1, 1996, pp. 27-37.

Chapter 15

A learning organization's syllabus

John Peters

Editor of The Learning Organization

What does a learning organization learn about?

Over the past several years I have had the opportunity to confront this question
in a number of guises. As Editor of this journal, I have been privy to some of the
brightest and best thinkers in the field. As a sometime consultant, I have been
able to work with a number of organizations which aspire to the principles of
the learning organization. Furthermore, as a researcher and teacher with an
independent, action learning-based business school, International Management
Centres, I have been able to explore principles, concepts and practices with an
increasing number of my practitioner-students.

As such I have taken this opportunity to draw some of those thoughts and
experiences together into an editorial statement and discussion paper.

The purpose of this paper is to explore a syllabus-driven approach to a
learning organization. It identifies six important learning syllabuses for the
organization, and seeks to address them by suggesting interventions for
individuals, groups and organizational systems. It concludes by suggesting
action learning as a development methodology of value to those interested in
the learning organization. My aim is to be simple and prescriptive. All the
interventions described have been tested in organizations. Some of them are
named, some not. Some suggested further reading is listed at the end of the
article, much of which can be found in back issues of *The Learning
Organization*.

The six syllabus areas

Details of the six learning syllabuses are as follows:

(1) Learning about your job in the organization, and how to do it better. To
borrow from Senge, "personal mastery"[1].

(2) Learning how to create alignment in the organization – what Collins and
Porras[2] call "ideological indoctrination"; to create shared "mental
models" (Senge[1] again), which creates an alignment of culture and
strategy in your organization. That means, when people do their own
thing, they do the right thing, and you do not have to stand over them
and watch them all the time.

This article first appeared in *The Learning Organization,* Vol. 3 No. 1, 1996, pp. 4-10.

(3) Learning about the future – using scenario planning, and anticipatory competence development.

(4) Learning about the operating environment – understanding supply chains – which near-enough corresponds to the good old "fifth discipline"[1] of systems thinking.

(5) Learning how to challenge the existing paradigms – avoiding myopia, considering present and future possibilities, not getting locked into paradigm protection and groupthink.

(6) Developing an organizational memory – the ability to capture, store and retrieve knowledge and expertise.

I would not expect everyone in an organization to do all those things. Well, put it this way – if they did, I certainly would not buy any shares in it, because they would all be so busy learning that they would not be doing any work; their customers would be off to a less introspective supplier, and their staff would all be looking for new jobs.

Learning about your job in the organization
My publishers at MCB University Press publish a journal called the *International Journal of Clothing Science and Technology*. I love it, because it is so tangible compared with some of the esoteric stuff of management and social science. It publishes vastly learned articles on how not to get your seams puckered when they get sewn, what the tearing strain is in nylon as opposed to cotton, and so on.

Furthermore, it is a great reminder about relativities. If you are a machinist, quality is about sewing a straight seam. Does it help to understand the great universality of how your firm fits into the chain from cotton growers to shippers to manufacturers to retailers to customers, and all the pressures and variables around them? Should you be aware of the changing dynamics in the industry and its customer base? Well, no, actually. It helps if you can sew a straight, unpuckered seam.

What about if you are the CEO of an international textile manufacturer and trader? Well, you definitely need to know all that stuff, and it really does not help much if you can sew a straight seam.

For most people, in most organizations, learning how to do your job better is the heart of the matter. Learning in an organization is about learning, deeply and profoundly, how to do a great job within that organization. Something like this used to be called "training" before it went out of fashion.

You cannot miss this one. Learning about the organization in a meaningful way is the bedrock on which all else rests. You have to be able to do the business – otherwise you are out of business. This area is addressed in some more detail in the section on "action learning", below. Learning how to do your job better within the organization means two things:

(1) an understanding of the technical aspects of your job;

(2) an understanding of the dynamic interplays of people around you.

The first does not work without the second, which is why many brilliant technicians make lousy managers, and why many successful managers spend more time networking and playing politics than they do managing *per se*.

Here is a way of addressing both. Pretend everyone in your organization is a doctor or a lawyer, and obliged by dint of his or her profession to demonstrate professional updating. How would that apply for each individual? What is, or should be, each person's demonstrated continuing professional development? People can create CPU/CPD plans themselves, with a little encouragement; their presentation can be rolled into the annual appraisal process.

At the same time, ask everyone to think of their job as being at the centre of a spider's web of people within and outside the organization. What are their most important and regular interfaces? What is good and bad about each of those? How could they be improved? Spontaneous self-help groups will start to appear as people put together their analyses and try to address problems.

If you do nothing more than ask for regular analyses of interface relationships, and demonstrated continuing professional updating/ development – you will be ahead of most of your competitors in creating a professionalized organization seeking to improve its technical competence and improve the dynamics of their interplays.

Learning about alignment
The most sensible thing I ever read about organizational strategy was coined by Henry Mintzberg of McGill University in Canada. He called it emergent strategy.

The concept was this. We put a plan together, but over time it does not quite work out the way we intended it to. In fact, it is quite often way off. That is because the interpretations of our intended strategy change it. People charged with implementation say, helpfully, "I'm not sure what this means, but I think it means this" or "Well, we tried that a couple of years back, and it didn't work, but this might" or "Well I know that won't work, so I'll try this instead". They might also say, unhelpfully, "That would be bad for me, so I'm not going to do it" or "That's all very well, but I'm too busy, so I'll ignore it and they'll forget about it" or "They don't know what our problems are serving real customers – there's no way I'm doing this".

Intended strategy falls away, and what takes place to create the realized or delivered strategy is emergent strategy. Emergent strategy is a function of two horrible intangibles – organizational culture and personal or group interpretation.

In the seminal *Fifth Discipline,* Senge[1] points to "shared values" as being crucial to the effective organization, and follows in the footsteps of many profound thinkers on management such as Peters[3] and Collins and Porras[2]. Why? Because of emergent strategy.

You cannot make emergent strategy go away. You can try incentives, tricks, motivational seminars, videos, posters, memos – but it still emerges. It is just one of those things.

So roll with it. If it emerges in a beneficial way, as a dynamic response to the changing dynamics of deliverers, customers and environments, then that is good news. Because if we stick to a plan and disregard the dynamics of the marketplace, then we are likely to be in real trouble. If everyone understands what we are about – what our business is, what we think is really important, what we think is less important, what you get fired for doing – you have more chance of the emergent strategy being of immense benefit.

Syllabus area two is learning about alignment in an organization. That requires determination and effort. The values have to be articulated and believed, then inculcated by whatever means possible. In an organization serious about its values, those who do not buy them should be rehabilitated, and if that will not work, asked to leave.

One of the best CEOs I ever worked with was Brian Wilson of Allied Irish (now AIB) Bank Britain in the mid-1980s. Brian has engineered the bank in the UK through a great change to be one of the first banks to embrace customer service. A little while later we were talking about what went well, and what did not. "The real mistake I made was being too patient with those who would not come on board. They were senior, they had been around a long time, but trying to accommodate them took up too much time and energy, and held us up. I should have given them one more chance, then removed them". Don't like it? Then go and get a job with a bank that does not say that the customer is the be-all and end-all.

In *Build to Last*[2], successful companies are compared to cults. They indoctrinate their staff. They brainwash them. "McDonald's make hamburgers. What does Disney make?" they ask at the Disney University. (Answer: we make people happy[2]). Learning about and then reinforcing the values is a long process, and not for the faint-hearted. But unless you want to have a managerial secret police force constantly checking that behaviours and actions are aligned to culture and values, you will be at the mercy of your emergent strategy.

What you could do is this. Get all your power holders together, and all your brightest and best next in line. Take them away for a couple of days. Their agenda is to put their beliefs and motivations on the table about the organization and construct, if at all possible, the shared bits. That is – why are we in business? What will the organization still believe in 20 years? Disney say, "We use our imagination to bring happiness to millions". Boeing say, "We live at the leading edge of avionics". Note that they do not say, "We make cartoons" or "We build theme parks" or "We make jumbo jets". Those are just how the values are made manifest.

Then, if you can get a coherent and believed coda together, try doing what AT&T did. Write down one of the values ("Respect for individuals"). Next to it, write down what it means. ("We treat each other with respect and dignity... we communicate frequently and with candour... we give individuals the authority to use their capabilities... our environment supports personal growth"... and so on). Next to that, write down what that means for individuals ("We expect you to recognize and respect the value of differences between individuals, participate actively in the performance and review process", and so on). Then, next to that, write down what that means in a managerial role ("We expect you to create and sustain an environment that recognizes and values differences between individuals", and so on).

Then put that all on to a single sheet of paper, and deliver it to everyone. Finally, incorporate all the articulated behaviours into your performance review system. That is to say, give people rewards such as pay rises and promotions for conforming to the values, and discourage people from not conforming to them by not giving them rises, not promoting them, or getting rid of them.

This learning organization business is not easy. However, much of it is quite simple. Furthermore, being a learning organization certainly is not about being nice to all your staff. It is about treasuring the ones who are on side and doing their best, but about weeding out and showing the door to those who are, deliberately or otherwise, sabotaging the effort. If you want to be nice to everyone, however they behave, go and get a job in a church or something.

If alignment cannot be delivered, because there are no shared beliefs, then I am afraid that either you are going to cross your fingers about emergent strategy, or you are going to search out some other ways of aiming for organizational alignment.

Learning about the future
On the side of Mount Etna in Sicily are a number of small towns, plus innumerable hotels, gift shops, restaurants, and even a small ski area complete with chair lifts for the winter. They gather there because the soil is good, the tourist trade is good, and maybe because there is great air and a great view. Every time Etna erupts they do not run around in amazement wondering what is happening. The local economy does not get ruined. They just incorporate the possibility into their lives and carry on, planting vines, building garages, serving tourists. It is a great place to visit for any existential Angst-ridden executives unsure of what the future in their industry might hold.

Learning about the future would be on my syllabus for an organization, but not for all the individuals in it. Everyone in an organization plays a role, but not everyone is the same, or needs to be good at the same things. I am fooling myself if I ask my cleaning staff to contribute meaningfully to debates about future strategy. I would like them to be really great at cleaning my office, and maybe present really smart improvement ideas about how they can do it better, and be really nice to people if ever they have to answer the phone. That is what I pay them to learn about.

I met once with the training and development people at NEC in Telford who told me how NEC approach learning about the future at the operational level. NEC Telford assemble a few NEC products – telephones, video monitors and so on. As a small part of a global organization, it may be called on at short notice to assemble other products, such as printers. There are a fairly limited range of possible products, but there is no local production plan beyond the short term. That is because, as a global player, NEC choose to alter their production capability and redeploy activities as they see best, and want to do so at short notice.

The training challenge is then, as they used to tell me in the Boy Scouts, to "be prepared". We will give you a couple of weeks' notice about changes in assembly, and we will ask for something from the menu of possibilities (monitors, phones, printers and so on), but we expect you to do it seamlessly. To "be prepared" at NEC Telford meant multiskilling all the operational people to be able to work on any of the possible products. This meant familiarity with and practice on all the possible products, plus job definitions which embraced flexibility within the bounds of the product and process menus. Also it meant designing and installing movable and reconfigurable assembly lines. In addition to this, it means working on a zero defects programme at every workstation where the assembly process is constantly re-examined by the workers on the line, and improvements made when they are found.

Learning about the future is not the same as trying to predict the future. Unless you are Merlin the Magician, you cannot do it. Forecasts about the world, or your industry, or your sales figures, in five years' time, or a year, or three months, are just guesses. The future is dynamic – it unrolls with too much complexity for us to understand beyond informed guesses about ranges of possibilities. Unless something really bizarre happens, we can forecast a range for bank interest rates in a year's time with reasonable confidence. However, tell me what the actual percentage point interest rate actually will be in one year, and you are just guessing.

Learning about the future involves two important steps. One is understanding the range of likely possibilities, and the other is getting ready to operate effectively within that range. To use some jargon, we are talking about scenario planning and anticipatory competence development.

The Internet is something which will impact heavily on many organizations, although most are not sure how. Here is how you can have a shot at learning about the future fairly painlessly. Get a mixed group of staff together, including some of your high-potentials. Think of as many ways as you can as to how the Internet might affect your business over the next ten years, both opportunities and adverse consequences. Having done so, prepare two or three likely-looking scenarios. Now think of some ways in which some key people within the organization can start to gain experience and knowledge now, to allow them to deal with the scenarios if and when they arrive, and put them to work on it. Repeat frequently, with other scenarios.

Learning about the operating environment
One of the greatest follies we have is that what we produce, whether product or service, has some intrinsic value just because we have made it and put a price on it, or spent money on producing it. It does not. It only has value when it is valued, i.e. when someone wants it. And someone only wants it when they see some benefit from it.

It was Sam Walton of Wal-Mart who said "If you're not serving a customer, you should be serving someone who is serving a customer. Any further away and you aren't any use". Most of us would not be quite that bold about our organizational configurations, but Walton had a point. It you are not serving a customer, or serving a server, just who are you serving? What value are you adding?

To help people address this kind of question, take a randomly selected bunch and put them on an "on-the-road" project for the next three months to suppliers and customers, and suppliers' suppliers, and customers' customers. Have each one hold an hour's workshop back in the organization on what he or she has learned. Then take a look at how you are organized, how people spend their time, how you communicate with customers and how you reward people's efforts – and involve your on-the-road team in your thoughts.

If you can understand big pictures, you have much more chance of getting decisions right.

Learning to challenge existing paradigms
Jurassic Park[4] is an interesting story. Briefly, for those of you who have been on the Moon for the past few years, it concerns a billionaire entrepreneur who manages to clone dinosaurs and builds a theme park around them. The fences of course are failure-proof and and fail-safe. And, of course, *Tyrannosaurus rex* manages to escape.

But the billionaire (Richard Attenborough in the movie) cannot accept that his systems have crashed. With rampaging dinosaurs all over the place, he is insisting that everything is OK. It has to be OK. The systems were designed to be perfect. And he simply will not accept it until *T. rex* sticks his head through the window and tries to eat him.

It is a marvellous paradigm protection illustration. We can get very sure about ourselves, and choose to ignore evidence which does not fit that world view. It is something which is particularly manifest in a strong culture, which given the notion of shared vision and indoctrination into the chosen ideology (see syllabus two) is a worry.

That means we have to engineer paradigm challenge. This should not be for everyone – in fact, it should be for a few selected people only. However, here is how you can do it. Take a small, mixed group away for a day or two, and get them to pull apart some sacred cows. What is our business? Why do we set prices the way we do? Why do we have a separate head office building? For each challenge, the group should come up with a well-argued alternative and present it on paper or in person (depending on how brave they feel) to the board. See what happens. Repeat every six months with a new group.

Develop an organizational memory
Individuals can learn. At a simple level I can put my finger in a fire, note the pain, generalize the experience to include every fire and all of my fingers, and

try not to do it in the future. That is an ability made possible by my memory. If I could not remember, I might keep repeating the experience. I would not learn.

Organizationally, if we do not have a memory, a means of storing and recovering information and experience, we will not be able to learn. Memory development is something for everyone in the organization to address.

In an organization I worked for several years ago we used to debrief projects by preparing a "Lessons wot we learned" report. As a young smug MBA graduate I was dismayed by having to sit in the boardroom for half a day and read these rather folksy reminiscences before I was let loose on my first project – but 20 years of snapshot wisdom resided there, and in due course I too produced my "Lessons wot we learned" summary and added it to the archive for some other trainee. I wonder if they are still there.

Here is how you can develop a corporate memory. First, map all your processes. Every individual, alone and in teams, is engaged in processes and procedures. Everyone can note down what the steps are and what the interactions and flows are. Some interesting suggestions might emerge. Furthermore, if you are not already registered to ISO 9000, mapping your processes is a useful step towards so doing.

Second, introduce the "Lessons..." project debriefing system. Keep them in binders in the boardroom. Make new recruits read them.

Action learning: a methodology for organizational learning

Action learning can be used to address any or all of these issues. For those unfamiliar with action learning (why are you unfamiliar? Get with it!) here is a brief summary of what it is and does.

Action learning puts forward a simple proposition – that we learn best about work, at work and through work, within a structure which encourages learning. So if we want really to learn how to improve the assembly of a monitor, we really have to get the soldering iron out, on a real line. If we want to learn how to create and implement a marketing plan, we have really to create one. In so doing, our knowledge gaps become apparent, so we learn how to access and draw from the body of knowledge on a particular subject (whatever it is).

The reason we really have to do it is that theory alone will not tell us the real difficulties – that the person three places before us on the line is setting a component in such a way that the solder will not go in properly, or that the finance director resists the idea of marketing planning, and blocks initiatives at the board. Improvement of the line therefore becomes the *technical* knowledge of soldering in the right place, plus the *dynamic* skill of helping the person three steps up to do it differently. Marketing planning becomes the *technical* knowledge of information assimilation, portfolio analysis and industry demographics plus the *dynamic* skills of convincing the finance director.

This is done in a framework of action (try it and feel how it feels) plus reflection (why is it working? why is it not? who can help? who can hinder?), plus concept construction (if these variables are in place in this way we can reasonably assume it will work the same way next time; if one of them changes, how will it affect the whole?), plus planning for the future (next time we should make sure we do this, this and this). Normally action learning groups are helped or facilitated by someone who is guiding the process, and aiming to make the participants themselves able to identify issues and search, find and use information to bring to bear on the issues.

Because it works within the constraints and realities of organizations which cannot be captured in textbooks (political games, stupidities, private agendas, differing world views and so on) and assimilates them cheerfully and necessarily into the learning process. It is the best methodology we have for learning for real about organizations.

To organize an action learning intervention, take a problem which is annoying you, take a cross-functional group of people who can touch the problem in some way, and charge them to deliver a solution in three months' time. Put them together for a half-day every two weeks, and work with them by guiding the process only. Stay out of the content. Keep asking questions like "Why?" "So what?" "Who can help?" "Who can block?" "How can we do it better next time?" Arm them with some research design skills; ask for a written report and a presentation to the board at the end of the project, and see what happens. Keep notes – you will be learning about how to do it too.

Such an approach directly impacts on four of the six syllabus areas. It directly addresses "learning about your job/the organization". It should, properly facilitated, address "learning about the future" and "learning about the environment". In addressing and tackling real problems for real, learners can and should be encouraged to think about future scenarios, and about impacts on the supply chain.

A key part of properly executed action learning programmes is the maintenance of a learning log, and an intellectual project write-up at termination, as a reinforcement of the learning. This serves to add to the organization's memory banks.

An action learning initiative can address paradigm challenge, with appropriate facilitation and encouragement, although normally it is rooted in a more concrete project. It could, also, as an investigative area, be a methodology by which alignment, shared values and emergent strategy were addressed, although the process of action learning *per se* does not specifically address this.

Summary
This paper has set out to provide, in a simple and prescriptive format, a syllabus approach to learning organization development. It has done so by suggesting six areas which an organization and its people should learn about, and simple steps to starting work in all of the areas. It has also recommended action learning as an effective methodology for organizational learning.

Implications for those charged with learning organization development are:

- Address first and foremost the area of learning about jobs in the organization. This is a bedrock on which organizational success rests.

- Ensure that a level of debate is taking place in the organization which addresses future scenarios and challenges existing paradigms, and that such debate is institutionalized as part of the organization's development and policy-making activities, rather than left to fester as rumour and discontent.
- Ensure that future competences are being anticipated and developed.
- Prevent organizational learning from being overly introspective by bringing organizational learning out into the supply chains, both backwards and forwards.
- Tackle the dangers of emergent strategy in a non-aligned organization by learning about and aiming for organizational alignment.
- Oversee the creation of organizational memory banks.

The path towards a learning organization would appear to be long and arduous, requiring discipline and persistence. The effectiveness of the learning organization concept will be properly tested when all the steps have been put in place by a number of firms – then we can see if the reality truly matches the expectations.

References
1. Senge, P., *The Fifth Discipline,* Doubleday, New York, NY, 1990.
2. Collins, J. and Porras, J., *Built to Last,* Century, London, 1994.
3. Peters, T.J. and Waterman, R.H., *In Search of Excellence,* Harper & Row, London, 1982.
4. Crichton, M., *Jurassic Park,* Century, London, 1992.

Further reading
Drew, S. and Smith, P. (1995), "The learning organization: 'change proofing' and strategy", *The Learning Organization*, Vol. 2 No. 1.

Hamel, G. and Prahalad, C.K. (1994), *Competing for the Future*, HBS Press, New York, NY.

Kock, N., McQueen, R. and Baker, M. (1996), "Learning and process improvement in knowledge organizations", *The Learning Organization*, Vol. 3 No. 1.

Kransdorf, A. (1996), "Using the benefits of hindsight – the role of post-project analysis", *The Learning Organization*, Vol. 3 No. 1.

Limerick, D., Passfield, R. and Cunnington, B. (1994), "Transformational change: towards an action learning organization", *The Learning Organization*, Vol. 1 No. 2.

Mintzberg, H. (1994), "The fall and rise of strategic planning", *Harvard Business Review*, Vol. 72 No. 1.

Mumford, M. (1994), "Four approaches to learning from experience", *The Learning Organization*, Vol. 1 No. 1.

Wills, G. (1993), *Your Enterprise School of Management*, MCB University Press, Bradford.

Wills, G. (1995), "Embracing electronic publishing", *The Learning Organization*, Vol. 2 No. 4.

Chapter 16

Creating an online library to support a virtual learning community

Eric Sandelands

Director, Internet Research and Development Centre

Is the educational promise of the Internet real? I believe it is.

So begins Neil L. Rudenstine (1997), President of Harvard University, in a short paper outlining his observations on just how the Internet can enrich the educational experience. For Rudenstine the excitement of the media is as follows:

- the Internet can provide access to essentially unlimited sources of information not conveniently obtainable through other means;
- the Internet allows for the creation of unusually rich course materials;
- the Internet enhances the vital process of "conversational" learning;
- the Internet reinforces the conception of students as active agents in the process of learning, not passive recipients of knowledge from teachers and authoritative texts.

International Management Centres (IMC) was formed in 1982 by a group of academics and corporate executives disillusioned with the failings of the "mainstream" business education being offered. Rather than view managers as empty vessels to be filled up with theoretical concepts in the cloistered surroundings of a business school campus, IMC adopted an approach which begins by recognising that the workplace is where the action is, and managers learn by tackling real problems. The action learning philosophy, pioneered by Dr Reg Revans since 1944, is central to all IMC learning programs.

IMC is a networked organization active in 29 countries, including: Australia, Canada, the Caribbean, China (including Hong Kong), Malaysia, The Netherlands, Papua New Guinea and the UK. The move toward using the Internet was a natural one to make. It enhanced dramatically the communications between academic and administrative staff internationally. As our understanding of the potential of the media developed, we were also able to develop richer educational experiences capable of being delivered to ISO 9002 standards on a global basis.

Ives and Jarvenpaa (1996) considered the opportunities and threats facing the business school community, concluding, "The inflexibility of traditional universities, however, suggests that nontraditional educational suppliers may

This article first appeared in *Internet Research: Electronic Networking Applications and Policy*, Vol. 8 No. 1, 1998, pp. 75-80.

be best positioned to exploit the lucrative market for business education in an electronic world."

IMC's flexibility as a nontraditional provider allowed them to both address and become an early adopter of the virtual university concept. In this paper, the development of the online library needed to support this virtual learning community is discussed. The library must be able to sustain learners and faculty globally with access to a broad base of knowledge required to complete programs successfully.

IMC's approach has been to work with joint venture partners in ensuring high quality library coverage, and to focus efforts on specialist areas of expertise, as custodians and developers of action learning, thinking and practice.

What is action learning?

Action learning involves working on real problems, focussing on learning and actually implementing solutions. It is a form of learning by doing. It provides a well-tried method of accelerating learning which enables people to handle difficult situations more effectively.

Action learning is a process of inquiry, beginning with the experience of not knowing "what to do next," and finding that answers are not available through current expertise. When expertise fails to provide an answer, collaborative inquiry with fellow learners who are undergoing the same questioning experience is always available. To be effective, this partnership in learning needs to be both supportive and at the same time challenging, deeply caring yet questioning. Such partnerships actually create themselves when different people with different ideas engage whole-heartedly with each other to resolve each other's problems (IFAL, 1997).

To be successful, action learning takes place in groups, or "sets" of managers who are comrades in adversity. In the IMC experience, this has created a powerful set of learning dynamics which is effective in developing "mixed sets" of managers from a number of organizations and "in-company sets" of managers from the same firm.

Bunning (1997) raised some fundamental questions affecting corporate competitiveness:

> Why do some organizations which employ so many intelligent people continue with strategies which are obviously not working, or fail to take actions which are clearly called for, or repeat their mistakes, over and over? Why do some organizations put so much time and energy into not changing – into defending the past and avoiding the future? Why is it that large organizations, particularly, have a tendency to bring out the worst in human nature, so that instead of behaving with the collective wisdom of a thousand, management, at various levels, can display a profound commitment to defensiveness and short-term self-interest?

The action learning methodology applied in an in-company learning environment has been used to confront these challenges.

IMC's virtual business school

A pioneering spirit, combined with real needs to control the cost base and service learners internationally, drove the strategy to develop IMC as a virtual business school. A number of benefits were identified at an early stage. However, the picture has become richer as our understanding of both the technology and learning processes have deepened. Back in 1995 it was observed (Wills *et al.*, 1995):

> the World Wide Web… is less cumbersome for accessing pages and news items. EDI routines are eliminated. Its linked e-mail service makes for speedy exchanges of ideas. Its low cost, immediate global reach removes a key constraint on communications. The WWW formatting makes the appearance of learning resources and all other elements far more attractive in comparison with the printed word – and maintains the major benefit of low cost revision to be kept up to date. List servers provide the opportunity for proactive rather than reactive usage of the system.

All this is being offered in a global context where Internet is being heralded as the major future for education and where more individuals are seeking access to it every day.

Partnership with Anbar Electronic Intelligence

The partnership with Anbar Electronic Intelligence has been the cornerstone alliance which has driven both courseware development and IMC's ability to provide a virtual library. Anbar invest around US$1.5 million per annum in creating the Anbar Management Intelligence service. The processes involved include accrediting and reviewing journals, creating consistency in the database and publishing each month.

For IMC a partnership is a natural way to proceed. The organization does not have the in-house expertise to develop and maintain the world-leading virtual library. The competences of IMC are based on a deep understanding of the action learning process, and the ability to develop, promote and deliver action learning-based management development programs internationally.

The essential elements of the relationship are:

(1) that Anbar is paid a commercial rate for the service provided. IMC is a key customer, but a relatively small proportion of Anbar's sales turnover. Anbar continues to service the needs of academic and corporate accounts, and a growing number of distance learning institutions;

(2) that IMC provides a living prototype for Anbar, hastening understanding of the emerging virtual universities and their application in a corporate setting;

(3) Anbar gains corporate accounts where IMC facilitated virtual corporate universities are developed, and has the opportunity to reach participating managers and their organizations once their studies have been completed.

The Anbar Management Intelligence service is designed to target the world's most influential journals printed in English, then provide a comprehensive reviewing service, user-oriented search routines and the provision of the full-text article (Sandelands, 1996). The system of accreditation and reviewing used draws heavily on the findings of a journal quality benchmarking study undertaken by Day and Peters (1994). Here is how the system works:

(1) Journal coverage is signed off by an international accreditation board (Professor Philip Kotler, Northwestern University signs off the marketing coverage, Alfred Lynch, CEO of J.C.Penney International the strategy coverage). They base their decisions on a composite list of the library holdings of more than 40 centers of excellence in management. They ensure that coverage has enough depth within their subject area, that superficial or superfluous journals have not been included, and that new journals are given an opportunity to be included.

(2) Full bibliographic details are provided, including author affiliations. These are essential if research work is to be properly referenced.

(3) Abstracts and reviews are written by specialist reviewers to ensure that they accurately describe the article, book or resource. A user should be confident that appropriate material has not been missed, and that any full-text articles retrieved will meet their needs.

(4) The system utilises comprehensive electronic indexing, classifying and keywording to facilitate retrieval.

(5) Reviewers assess each article against set quality criteria and allocate an article type. The quality criteria used are: importance to the researcher; importance for practising managers; originality; and readability. These are designed to assist the user in pinpointing suitable material (AMM, 1997).

(6) The full-text article is available for all material included. This can be downloaded instantly or ordered for express document supply depending on copyright permissions. Where book reviews are used, all books can be ordered online from partner bookshops.

This provides a wide-ranging base of literature online to IMC faculty, learners and alumni. In addition to what could be termed "traditional virtual library use" – going to the search screen and defining a search routine – the Anbar Management Intelligence service is now integrated within courseware.

Knowing that the library is in place to support generic learning programs, IMC is able to concentrate resources on the one area of core expertise central to its activities, developing access to research, practice and expertise within the field of action learning.

The virtual university model

The elements of the virtual university model currently being utilised are outlined below:

(1) All faculty members and course participants must have access to e-mail and the World Wide Web at home or at work. Ideally their managers and mentors will have similar access.

(2) Course materials (courseware) are accessed over the World Wide Web. They are updated semi-automatically. The recommended readings from the literature base are automatically updated every month. Recommended books are reviewed and amended every six months. A fundamental review of courseware is undertaken every three years (Dealtry, 1997).

(3) All faculty, course participants and alumni have access to an online management library, including access to more than 400 of the world's leading journals, using Anbar Management Intelligence (Sandelands, 1996). Full-text articles can either be downloaded online, or forwarded by fax or express mail from partner organization, The British Library.

(4) All recommended books are available for purchase online from book shops Amazon.com and the Internet Book Shop.

(5) Dissertation abstracts for all IMC final projects are available as a searchable database online.

(6) The *Global Accumulative Bibliography of Action Learning* provides the world's most complete bibliography of the discipline. It combines review articles and courseware structures with pre-ordained, defined access to the Anbar Management Intelligence database, and hyper-text links to library holdings with action learning collections.

(7) The *Global Anthological Journal of Action Learning* is an e-journal, launched with publisher Internet Free Press, to facilitate the communication of new concepts and action learning best practice.

(8) Faculty biographies are captured to a pre-determined format and fully searchable. These are utilised for everything from appointing project supervisors to seeking online conference speakers and participants.

(9) Faculty and learners from all over the world meet for seminars and online conferences using Webforum software.

(10) Course supervision requires faculty to use the Webforums and e-mail to set deadlines, provide feedback, encourage and cajole. Assignments are sent as E-mail attached files.

(11) Alumni are encouraged to remain active, participating in conferences and discussions, writing papers for publication, and for some, being inducted into faculty.

The basic framework set out for the IMC virtual business school model was:

- that it should provide the "learning sets" with a communications infrastructure;
- that it should be the publishing media for courseware;
- that it should be a research tool for current and archival information; and
- that it should facilitate communications with academic and business networks.

The model has been refined, even in recent weeks, and the process is rapid and ongoing. However, the benefits are being realised in terms of our ability to reach new areas, well beyond those countries where we have a physical presence. In fact, our ability to bring together in one "learning set" managers from a number of countries is yielding distinct benefits for learners seeking an international perspective on management. The very low drop out rate among learners is both an advantage, and a measurement of the effectiveness of these new learning processes.

Designing virtual library resources
The creation and evolution of the Action Learning International Internet forum marked a distinct stage in the progression of IMC's reflective research on its own andragogical delivery mechanism and ethos, action learning. It provides a public face to what was once considered to be the internal mechanics of learning program delivery. The Action Learning International forum provides an opportunity to share ideas and experiences with the wider action learning community.

The Action Learning International forum provides access to current and archival research and practice material pertinent to this field, and provides access to a network of action learning researchers, learning program providers, and practitioners from industry. A significant proportion of the research materials provided are from IMC's emerging virtual library resources.

The specialist resources now available are: the electronic journal (*Global Anthological Journal of Action Learning*), the online bibliography (*Global Accumulative Bibliography of Action Learning*), dissertation abstracts, action learning courseware, and the online faculty biographies. This concentration of effort into this one field of learning has expanded our concept of what a library can do. We have the access to the books and journal articles we initially sought. But we have gone beyond this in terms of literature provision with searchable dissertation abstracts, literature review papers, and courseware structures leading directly to the virtual library by keywords and other criteria.

We have also rethought what we wanted from the virtual library, providing faculty biographies, indexed against a number of criteria online. The networking and program effectiveness implications of this are only beginning to be realised. The library we envisaged has ceased to be just about literature access, although it provides this exceptionally well, and developed as a route to information networks as well as information archives.

In creating the new dissertation abstracts and faculty biography databases, lessons learned earlier by our partner, Anbar Electronic Intelligence, were used in reaching database specifications:

(1) Users must be involved, identifying the questions they will ultimately ask the database. Different groups of users will have different questions. All identifiable groups must be involved in generating the questions.

(2) Some users will need to browse through the retrieved information, possibly for the very latest material. Others users will need specific

search routines designed to pinpoint material from within a relatively large mass of material. The specification must enable appropriate browsing and searching to meet user requirements.

(3) Certain questions require very specific answers. This is particularly important when there is a wealth of information available which needs to be managed. On an Anbar Management Intelligence search, someone seeking real life examples of change management initiatives can save themselves an awful lot of time by accessing only the case studies on the subject. Similarly, a director of studies seeking experienced faculty in Malaysia must be able to retrieve pertinent details.

(4) All assumptions must be tested with users at all design stages. This includes post-implementation feedback, review and improvement.

(5) The technical solution chosen must be on the basis of its fit with the user-driven specification and the flexibility of the technology in accommodating subsequent improvement.

(6) Keyword allocation, classification and data entry must be consistent. Systems must be designed to capture historical data consistently, and ensure consistency as data are updated.

These six points guided the methodology adopted; the "right" specification being crucial. The other major challenge of the project has been to gather and manage the data fed into the databases. This required the collation of comprehensive biographical material from more than 360 faculty members located around the world. It also required the inputting, classifying and editing abstracts from archival and newly published dissertations, together with a template for new dissertation abstracts to be undertaken in an orderly manner.

Benefits of the online action learning library
The benefits of the online library are beginning to filter through and be noticed at the service delivery level. We did have a problem with obsolete courseware. This has been dramatically improved through the development of the online library.

Other benefits will take a little longer to be realised. Worthwhile success will be recognised once faculty and external examiners highlight that final dissertations have improved as a result of:

• a more appropriate supervisor being located than otherwise would have been had we not been able to select internationally;

• the student's ability to refer to the most recent books and papers as well as the most significant historically in their literature review;

• the student's ability to draw on the lessons of earlier dissertations in crafting their own.

The next phase of activity is to develop, in partnership again with Anbar Management Intelligence, knowledge management infrastructures for corporate clients sponsoring in-company MBA programs, "Project Harvest."

Project Harvest will work with the client in developing infrastructure for the storage, retrieval and dissemination of knowledge. An in-company programme can generate anything up to 300 projects examining critical issues for the firm. If the program runs for a number of years, the knowledge accumulated can be substantial.

The models outlined have been developed on an action research basis as one might anticipate from an action research/action learning institution like IMC. Early feedback from interested parties has been complimentary. However, ultimately, it is the feedback from our customers, the students themselves and their organizational sponsors, which is the measure of success of any of our activities. This is sought and analyzed as a routine activity in any learning program. The results of this analysis will guide our review of online learning resources.

References and further reading

Anbar Management Magazine (1997), No. 2, pp. 7-10.

Bunning, C. (1997), *Action Learning Resource*, available at http://www.imc.org.uk/imc/coursewa/alr/alrhome.htm

Day, A. and Peters, J. (1994), "Quality indicators in academic publishing," *Library Review*, Vol. 43 No. 7, pp. 4-72.

Dealtry, R. (1997), "Anbar Electronic Intelligence courseware review 1997," available at http://www.imc.org.uk/imc/ coursewa/ais/ais-paper-001.htm

International Foundation for Action Learning (1997), available at http://www.tlainc.com/index2.htm

Ives, B. and Jarvenpaa, S.L. (1996), "Will the Internet revolutionize business education and research?", *Sloan Management Review*, Spring, pp. 33-41.

Rudenstine, N.L. (1997), "The Internet and education: a close fit," *The Chronicle of Higher Education*, February 21, pp. 28-9.

Sandelands, E. (1996a), "The future of brands in academic publishing," *Online & CD-ROM Review*, Vol. 20 No. 4, pp. 181-4.

Sandelands, E. (1996b), "Which journal? The politics of where to publish," *Collection Building*, Vol. 15 No. 1, pp. 27-37.

Wills, G., Oliver, C. and Wynder, N. (1995), "IMC's Internet action learning," accessible at http://www.imc.org.uk/ imc/home.htm

Wills, M. and Wills, G. (1996), "The ins and the outs of electronic publishing," *Journal of Business & Industrial Marketing*, Vol. 11 No. 1, pp. 90-104.

Notes

Many of the resources featured in this article are available on the World Wide Web. Some Web sites which readers may choose to investigate are:

Action Learning International http://www.imc.org.uk/imc/al-inter/

Anbar Electronic Intelligence http://www.anbar.co.uk/anbar.htm

Global Accumulative Bibliography of Action Learning http://www.free-press .com/journals/gabal/

Global Anthological Journal of Action Learning http://www.free-press.com/journals/gajal/

International Management Centres http://www.imc.org.uk/imc/welcome.htm

Chapter 17

ISO 9000 as a global educational accreditation structure

John Peters

Professor of Strategy and Quality Management, and

Gordon Wills

Professor of Customer Policy and CEO, International Management Centres

Introduction

This paper will set out to argue the merits of ISO 9000 as a global quality assurance (QA) and accreditation structure for educational institutions, and furthermore argue its merits as being a superior methodology to existing local accreditation structures in terms of customer orientation.

In so doing, we draw primarily on our experiences over the past 16 years in working within an independent business school, International Management Centres (IMC), and in a number of traditional universities around the world. Some of the flavour of IMC's history and activities is given to illustrate this as a case study.

Designing a QA system to suit IMC posed unusual challenges, in that IMC is both a network organisation, operating through semi-autonomous distributors, and an international organisation, with active regional offices in the UK, Western and Northern Europe, North America, Australia and South East Asia. However, the approach described and the solution reached was, we believe, applicable to more traditionally constituted higher education institutions, and we will be making that point in the article.

Market-driven roots of quality assurance

Formal systems of quality assurance such as ISO 9000 are sometimes criticised on the counts of being overly bureaucratic, not really suited to service businesses, and being focused on production rather than end product. To address these criticisms, and to explain why we at IMC took a decision to seek a formally accredited QA system (and become one of the few higher educational institutions in the world to do so) we will consider QA from a marketing perspective.

The discipline of QA arose from two desires of owners and managers of businesses; a marketing need, as well as the well-cited operational needs. From

This article first appeared in *Quality Assurance in Education*, Vol. 6 No. 2, 1998, pp. 83-89.

a marketing point of view, a disciplined approach to QA arose in response to a market desire for reliability and replicability of goods and services.

A marketer's ears will always prick up when the words "replicability" and "reliability" are used, for they enable customer and consumer trust in products and services, which thereby create the possibility of the branded good. The clearest antecedent of both the modern QA and control movements, and the modern notion of branded goods, is Eli Whitney, the US armaments manufacturer, who, in the nineteenth century, made his weapons the product of choice for the US army by being both cheaper and more reliable than any other manufacturer. The brand was born as a direct result of the harnessing of the principles of QA.

The significance of the branded good can hardly be understated to businesses. Brands make an immeasurably powerful statement to consumers. They say, simply stated: "What you expect is what you get, and until we tell you differently, that's what you will get every time". Brands deliver trust in a product or service, and customers pay handsomely for products and services they can trust, for trust takes away the inherent risk of the purchase decision.

We can take a wide view of the brand to encompass the service brand as being reliable and replicable, even if it is not exactly the same all the time. The reliability customers may crave is to be reliably surprised, pleasantly, by a service encounter. While a more complex challenge than delivering a reliable manufactured product, the creation and delivery of a service brand has not proved beyond the wit of the world's best service organisations.

But without QA, brands become an impossible proposition. A brand is not a brand if it does not posses a reliable, trustworthy "personality".

Thus the earliest lessons of the quality movement, still current today, are those of:

- understanding consumer and customer product usage and desires, and delivering a product which matches those needs ("fitness for purpose");

- drawing detailed specifications and producing products and services carefully to them ("conformance to specification");

- understanding and managing the variables in the production process which can lead to deviation from specification ("process control");

- keeping detailed records of the process, allowing deviations to be traced and rectified ("quality audit/document control").

These tenets can be clearly traced directly to the much later notion of codifying and independently setting third-party issued quality standards, best exemplified by the ISO 9000 quality standards series.

The failure of the educational brand
As service businesses, universities have by and large failed to build a brand strategy in the eyes of their customers. While the university is often the embodiment of what we have come to recognise as the empowered organisation,

the benefits have been felt more keenly by staff (in the form of teaching and research faculty members) than by customers (students) and the wider publics of universities, being employers and the community at large.

To state the issue in another way, there is a tension between the quite appropriate professional autonomy of the professor and the researcher, and the equally appropriate calls for accountability among state and institutional funders of the academic community. If we wince sometimes at Draconian and heavy-handed moves on budget restrictions and governmental interference in our seats of learning, one might say that we only have ourselves to blame for not demonstrably reassuring our financiers and policy makers that our houses are in order.

From a customer's point of view, we would argue that the market is crying out for the kind of branded goods and service reliability offered by the best of the product and service organisations. When buying a can of Coca-Cola or staying the night at a Marriott hotel; when buying a Honda or a British Airways flight – we expect to get, uncompromisingly, what we think we paid for.

In relationship marketing terminology we talk of the promise, and the delivery of the promise, as paramount. If we do not deliver on the promise, we do not have a trust relationship with our customers and we do not get referrals to other customers.

Why prescribing educational content must fail

However, the promise as a whole cannot be specified or assured by a centralised body in anything resembling a market economy. Our experiences have led us to believe, though, that this is precisely what our educational policy-makers will often seek to do. And it is bound to fail, as a way of delivering an appropriate product to a free-choice consumer.

Several years ago within IMC, we were advised by the then UK Secretary of State for Education that we must seek shelter within the umbrella accreditation institution for non-university higher educational institutions, the Council for National Academic Awards (CNAA), to continue to trade, following the 1987 Education Reform act in the UK. The debate went on for four futile years, with the crux of the argument being this.

Them: We will tell you what you should be teaching your students worldwide, and tell you how many contact hours that involves, what books they should read, and how they should be examined.

Us: No, our students and their sponsoring organisations will drive our syllabus based on their localised challenges, within broadly agreed limits, and you should be auditing us on whether we are really delivering what we say we are delivering.

Them: No, you cannot leave syllabus design to the consumers of the syllabus. We will tell you what should be in your syllabus...

And so on.

Were we wrong? We cannot accept that we were, for to do so goes against every principle of both customer sovereignty and successful international business. Our students' outputs were and continue to be judged academically by our peers in the best traditions of reputable academia. But to propose to a manager-student in a hotel in Finland, a brewery in South Africa, a bank in Malaysia or an insurance firm in England that they had to conduct themselves regardless of the personal and organisational challenges facing them flies in the face of common sense. Our contention is always that, to take the best known business education product in the world, the MBA; a student must demonstrate mastery in the administration of his or her business as evidenced by requisite action in his or her sponsoring organisation supported by a theoretical understanding. Show you can do it, and show you understand why it is going to be successful. Managerial economics, the establishment of international franchise arrangements, managerial psychology, or one of 50 other business disciplines clearly may play a greater or lesser role in a syllabus – but that is not one we can sit and prescribe precisely from a central campus somewhere where the action is not.

Our own plea to policy-makers has hardly changed in 14 years. Do not tell Coca-Cola how the Coke should taste – but make sure, by all means, that 330ml goes into a 330ml can, and make sure it will not poison its consumers. Do not tell Marriott's where to put the beds, or what sort of salad to serve in the restaurant – but for everyone's sake, make sure that people can get out in a fire, or that the kitchens are clean. In other words, let us all gladly embrace QA standards, but understand where to let go and let customers decide. Higher education should be no different.

Assuring the process
Some years ago we worked with a student from a major consultancy group. Her particular challenge was to introduce a QA system into the firm. She came to IMC for a developmental approach to so doing, by studying for our diploma in quality management, for previous efforts had failed miserably. This was why.

Quite reasonably, one might think, previous analysis had revealed that the key to the consultancy's business lay in the client's office – at the encounter where consultant met client and offered advice and guidance. That, therefore, had to be the place to start. All possible best practice and wisdom was distilled into guidelines for how the consultant should "work" the client, and programmed into a handbook.

The consultants ignored it wholesale, of course, and quite rightly so. The consultant-client encounter is effectively a dynamic one, where "success" is measured by the dynamic responses to unfolding situations. But surrounding that dynamic encounter are a whole host of "static" processes which can be effectively assured, to third-party auditable standards; access to advance information about the client's situation, recruitment and training of consultants, debriefing of consultants and the documentation of their experiences, billing systems, expense reimbursement systems and so on.

Our proposition is that the unfolding and contextualisation of a normative syllabus is effectively dynamic, but that the trappings surrounding this –

student registration, faculty recruitment and training, billing, certification, arranging viva voce assessments – are static systems which can and should be accountably assured.

Thus we say, to ourselves, and to other academic institutions – let us embrace a QA system which gives branded reliability of service by assuring what we can reasonably assure. Let us allow our customers to vote with their feet and their referrals on the content and approach to our educational product offering. Let us isolate our static assurance variables and assure them to the best existing standards, congruent with those similarly embraced by the organisations our customers work for and hope to work for.

The particular challenges of a global educational provider
As one of an increasing number of global education providers, we have been faced with a keen QA challenge, for which this time we must draw on the theory and practice of international business. The problem which every multinational operator wrestles with is that of balancing the advantages of global homogeneity with those of localised, acculturated heterogeneity. How do we "think global, but act local" while providing a brand integrity?

Again we have found the notion of the global assurance of our static variables to ISO 9002 standards, while leaving the dynamic challenges of macro- and micro-cultural variations to our local providers, and indeed customers, to be a neat solution, and again it is a solution we would recommend to others.

We are comfortable insisting on global standards of service in registry, feedback, scheduling, etc. – and such standards can readily be adhered to regardless of local conditions. Our recent uses of the Internet to circulate both materials and as a centrally-run records-keeping database, able to be accessed easily at any point in the world with an Internet connection, have also greatly eased the logistical problems of operating a multinational educational institution. Internet-based services can and must be, of course, subject to the same stringent QA management as any more traditional media.

We are similarly comfortable in isolating local tutor-student interaction as being essentially dynamic in nature, and therefore not assurable in the same manner. The assurance of dynamic interactions, as cited in the example above, is more about information provision, recruitment, induction and training than work-instruction policing.

Addressing ISO 9002
In brief, listed below is an outline description of how we conceptually addressed the disciplines of ISO 9002, bearing in mind that IMC operates as a central co-ordinating hub with its programmes operationally delivered worldwide by largely self-funding partner agencies. IMC was assessed by the British Standards Institution in late 1996 and certification to ISO 9002 recieved at the first time of asking.

The principal clauses of ISO 9002, with (highly simplified) comments as they apply to IMC and its network member operations are:

(1) *Management responsibility.* Management shall define its policies and objectives for quality, specify responsibilities and authorities for personnel, appoint a person with responsibility for the quality system, ensure the quality system is effective, and demonstrate its commitment to quality.

We have prepared statements of service commitment to network members and thereby to consumers; requiring a person nominated with responsibility for, specifically, central registry services, and statements of intent towards customers out in our distributed networks, with nominations for QA system responsibility.

(2) *Quality system.* System for ensuring that customer requirements are met by products and services shall be established, documented and maintained.

We have prepared service level statements on registration, access to research materials, external examination and graduation/certification, tuition, marking, supervision, etc.

(3) *Contract review.* Contracts with customers shall be reviewed to ensure that their needs are adequately defined and that the deliverer is capable of meeting them.

We have prepared delivery plans based on the service level agreements, with reviews at times of major systems or resource changes.

(4) *Design control.* Product and service design shall be planned and organised so that products and services emerge which meet designed user needs and requirements.

User needs are as specified above. Regular surveys will be conducted annually and amendments within existing structures accommodated if possible. Programmes offered are ratified by our academic board which conform to "design control". Self-direction of learning should always be made explicit.

(5) *Document and data control.* Controls should be employed which ensure the use of valid documents and data.

Documents such as registration forms need not be completed to a uniform standard, provided that necessary information is present. Documents such as pro-forma marking sheets need not be completed uniformly, provided that valid feedback is given across necessary areas conforming to marking criteria.

(6) *Purchasing.* Controls shall be employed which ensure that purchased products and services affecting the quality of services provided to customers conform to specified requirements.

Addressed largely as purchase of tutorial services.

(7) *Customer supplied product.* The condition of any product provided by the customer shall be controlled and the customer notified should its condition deteriorate or should it be lost.

Registration data and completed academic submissions must be stored carefully.

(8) *Product identification and traceability.* Products, processes and services shall be identified by suitable means.

Records of registration forms, assignments, marks, tutors used on programmes, payment and certification, etc., should be kept securely.

(9) *Process control.* The result-producing processes shall be planned, executed and controlled such that equipment, personnel, etc., deployed delivers a product or service which meets requirements consistently.

Processes which deliver service levels should be planned and executed, and the execution recorded. The Internet system providing IMC materials should be maintained, with contingency plans prepared to rectify any problem in supply (e.g. machine downtime).

(10) *Inspection and testing.* Products and services received and produced by the organisation shall be verified as meeting requirements prior to use, processing and despatch.

All materials and the media for delivering materials, whether by books, journals, paper-based readings, disks, CDs, or the Internet, should be inspected and their condition verified that they are both suitably operational and fit for the purpose intended as specified in our programme syllabuses.

(11) *Inspection, measuring and test equipment.* Devices, etc., used to verify that products or services meet specified requirements shall be controlled, calibrated and maintained.

Largely not applicable.

(12) *Inspection and test status.* Products shall be identified such that uninspected product is distinguishable from inspected product.

Largely not applicable – addressed at (10) above and (13) below.

(13) *Control of nonconforming product.* Product which fails to meet the customer requirements shall be prevented from inadvertent use and measures employed to control remedial action taken to make such products acceptable for use.

Media and materials which do not function to specification must be corrected and the correction recorded. Tutors and supervisors deemed to be unacceptable by students should be counselled and trained where appropriate, over and above regular faculty training/updating.

(14) *Corrective and preventive action.* Action shall be taken to prevent the occurrence and recurrence of nonconformities and ensure these actions are effective.

Logging of and action where possible on service level breakdown. Also see above.

(15) *Handling, storage, packaging, preservation and delivery.* Measures shall be taken to detect and prevent damage or deterioration to product while under the organisation's control.

Largely not applicable, although see (8).

(16) *Control of quality records.* Records shall be established, documented and maintained which demonstrate achievement of the customer requirements and the effectiveness of the quality system.

Develop and keep records of services provided to agreed levels, plus complaints and action taken.

(17) *Internal quality audits.* Audits shall be planned and executed to verify that the quality system is effective in ensuring that products and services conform to customer requirements.

All documentation is audited and a report detailing any amendments or improvements prepared by the persons responsible for QA at regular intervals – normally half-yearly.

(18) *Training.* The training needs of personnel whose work affects quality shall be identified and such personnel qualified to carry out the work assigned to them.

Records of training and induction for all staff members should be kept.

(19) *Servicing.* Controls shall be employed which ensure that servicing operations meet the customers' requirements.

Largely not applicable.

(20) *Statistical techniques.* Measures shall be taken to control the selection and application of statistical techniques used in accepting product and determining process capability.

Largely not applicable.

Conclusion – market-driven quality assurance

The QA movement was, in its original conception, intuitively customer-oriented, in looking for brandable replicability. Customers crave brands. Brands mean reliability of service, even if the reliability customers crave is to be reliably surprised by pleasing variation. QA exists to deliver reliability coupled with operational efficiency – the ultimate double prize.

The first question for market-driven practitioners in both education and indeed in wider industry must be – how does what I do support brandable replicability of service?

Our conceptual answer lies in the separation of the essentially static, and therefore subject to the disciplines of traditional QA, from the essentially dynamic. While this is a problem more keenly felt in an international business, it holds true also in a localised service business.

Static variables can be isolated and made subject to documented QA disciplines. We are addressing the ISO 9000 standard as our own way of assuring a branded replicability of service.

Dynamic variables, which we classify as the more essential element of our business, must also be assured, but in a different way – addressed at the interaction between student and tutor, and managed in the dynamically unfolding environment therein by the service deliverer. All we can do is to do our best to ensure that our service delivery professionals have the information, training and reward structures which enable them to operate most effectively.

In bringing some rigour to this process, we are auditing and documenting our "moments of truth", as defined by Jan Carlzon, former CEO of Scandinavian Air Services (SAS). Moments of truth analysis takes a view of quality which says that direct experience carries more weight than anything else. If an organisation's brand proposition says "service with a smile", moments of truth analysis would ask – when a customer meets the organisation or one of its representatives (or manifestations) – do they physically get smiled at? Do they metaphorically get smiled at? When the customer receives an invoice, is there anything "smiling" about that invoice? When the customer is being serviced by a subcontractor, do they still get smiled at? If service with a smile leads to repeat business at a premium price, moments of truth analysis would in effect conduct a smile "audit".

Carlzon had to try to carry the SAS service promise not only on his own flights but also through the whole flight experience – from booking, ticketing, through airport ingress, check-in and egress, to baggage reclaim. How do you assure all that? Well, that is a quality challenge. No one said it was easy. Several years of detailed, disciplined data gathering and personal experience played a large part.

Viewed from a customer-orientation point of view, QA has to take the whole range of moments of truth into account, and work to assure them. It can do so by the creation and management of work instructions, recorded and documented, for certain static systems, and the proper recruitment, training and management of operational people for more dynamic systems.

Our recommendation is therefore for a QA system to also encompass a detailed analysis of our educational institutions' moments of truth, and a clear QA system to be drawn up, which includes both skill development and personnel systems adaptation (reward, recognition, appraisal, etc.) to support it. While some of the variables are inherently dynamic, contextual and situational, they too must be addressed. In an educational institution, static systems, which include registration and scheduling, can and should be assured to externally-assessable standards. Dynamic systems, such as tutor-student encounters and, in our own case, syllabus tailoring to address students' own work and personal contexts, should likewise be assured, but through carefully-managed training and development.

The former can and should be externally accountable to external policy makers who might insist that any educational institution is managing its static systems to the levels that commercial industry would find acceptable. The latter is externally accountable to its customers – and, realistically, them alone. In the end, one can make one's personal choice between Coke and Pepsi.

A challenge for educational policy makers and practitioners alike

Our challenge to educational policy makers is – focus on the keeping of promises, not the content of the promises. Our customers can decide for themselves whether they like our promises, just as they can choose between brands in a supermarket. The keeping of promises can most easily be delivered through an encouragement, or even, eventually, an insistence, that practising educational institutions have their houses in order through the establishment and maintenance of a recognised QA system – preferably one which has general currency and familiarity among our wider publics.

And to practitioners we would say – if you want true autonomy, demonstrate that you can behave accountably in a way which your publics and financiers understand. Our great educational institutions should be years ahead of the game, not trailing our heels and following dolefully and reluctantly behind.